"Drawing upon his authoritative grasp of the big picture, Griffin cuts through the lies, deceptions and propaganda that have paralyzed the minds of so many. From 9/11 and the ensuing regime-change wars, to the terrifying dangers now posed by climate change, this work is an essential wake-up call."
—Piers Robinson, Chair in Politics, Society and Political Journalism, University of Sheffield

"Griffin has cogently explained the events and agendas that shaped the Bush-Cheney years. These events are as relevant today as ever, partly because they derailed the Obama era. Just as Bush-Cheney influence over domestic and foreign policy frustrated Obama supporters, today this influence frustrates Trump supporters who voted for an outsider to 'take back Washington' and give us a respite from perpetual warfare. A timely and necessary read."
—Karen Kwiatkowski, PhD, Lt Col USAF (ret), Office of Secretary of Defense 2000-2003

"The United States and the world have changed in fundamental ways—entirely for the worse —since the events of September 11, 2001. In his new book, Griffin clarifies why this has happened, as well as why the official explanation of 9/11 could not possibly be true. If one is to read only one book to understand the world in which we now live, it should be this immensely important book."
—John V. Whitbeck, International Lawyer; author of *The World According to Whitbeck*

"Sadly, this book is necessary, because US press won't cover the facts. From the first, Griffin contributed his scholarship (and his career!) to unmasking the Bush-Cheney administration for what it was. His latest account nails down a full indictment."
—Josh Mitteldorf, National Institute of Biological Science (Beijing), Senior Editor of OpEdNews, and author of *Cracking the Aging Code*

"A clear and non-sensationalist presentation of the historical and scientific facts, by one of our generation's most cogent thinkers. This book should convince any honest and objective person—with a political and scientific I.Q. above room temperature—that we have been systematically lied to about the events of 9/11 and the American invasions in the Middle East."
—Daniel Sheehan, Visiting Professor of Constitutional Law, UC Santa Cruz, and Chief Counsel to the U.S. Jesuit Headquarters' National Office of Social Ministry

"*Bush and Cheney* is a study of the successful efforts of 'Neoconservative' forces to take over US foreign policy in order to create a global empire, using the 9/11 attacks as a key lever. Griffin demonstrates that this Neocon agenda has shredded the US constitution and produced a foreign policy that is immoral, criminal, and quite literally insane. Griffin also shows how some of its worst policies were continued under Obama. As a result, the United States has become the most serious threat to life on our planet."
—E. Martin Schotz, author of *History Will Not Absolve Us: Orwellian Control, Public Denial, & the Murder of President Kennedy*

"In his latest book, Griffin meticulously documents how 9/11 may have provided a pretext to carry out pre-existing plans for the invasion of Afghanistan and Iraq. Griffin takes us back to Bernard Lewis' framing of 'Muslim rage' as the perfect rationale to characterize its hatred of the West as irrational. Griffin discusses Cheneyism as anti-constitutional authoritarianism, a state of permanent war, and aggressiveness toward adversaries, especially Russia. Griffin also documents how Bush-Cheney created the conditions for ISIS. A must read."
—Pepe Escobar, Editor-at-Large, Asia Times, author of *Empire of Chaos*

BUSH AND CHENEY:
HOW THEY RUINED
AMERICA AND THE WORLD

BY DAVID RAY GRIFFIN

OLIVE
BRANCH
PRESS

An imprint of Interlink Publishing Group, Inc.
www.interlinkbooks.com

First published in 2017 by

Olive Branch Press
An imprint of
Interlink Publishing Group, Inc.
46 Crosby Street, Northampton, MA 01060
www.interlinkbooks.com

Library of Congress Cataloging-in-Publication Data

Names: Griffin, David Ray, 1939- author.
Title: Bush and Cheney : how they ruined America and the world / by David Ray
    Griffin.
Description: Northampton, Massachusetts : Olive Branch Press, an imprint of
    Interlink Publishing Group, Inc., 2016.
Identifiers: LCCN 2016038376| ISBN 9781566560610 (hbk.) | ISBN 9781566560719
    pbk.)
Subjects: LCSH: United States--Politics and government--2001-2009. | Bush,
    George W. (George Walker), 1946---Influence. | Cheney, Richard B.--
    Influence. | United States--Foreign relations--2001-2009. | September 11
    Terrorist Attacks, 2001.
Classification: LCC E902 .G749 2016 | DDC 973.931092--dc23
LC record available at https://lccn.loc.gov/2016038376

Cover design by Ideologija Creative Team

Printed and bound in the United States of America

CONTENTS

PREFACE

This book was written to try to reduce the influence of the neoconservative movement, headed by Dick Cheney, which has been the major source of the violence, illegal regime change, killing, and dislocation of millions of people since the attacks of September 11, 2001. In spite of the disastrous consequences of the neocon policies, now acknowledged to have been based on lies about Afghanistan, Iraq, Libya, and Syria, these policies continued to dominate Washington insiders and the mainstream press.

The assumption prevailing in my mind during the writing of this book was that it would be published considerably before the 2016 presidential elections, and that the next president would be Hillary Clinton (unless Bernie Sanders were miraculously able to overcome the 500-vote lead given to her in advance by the Democratic National Committee). In light of her explicit alignment with leading neocons, her victory would have meant that the Democratic Party as well as the Republican Party would be following the neocon playbook even more fully than it had during the administration of Barack Obama—who had given less whole-hearted support to neocon wishes.

However, the publication of this book became delayed, so that it did not appear until after the transition from the Obama to the Trump White House. Given the enormous hostilities and fears created by the prospect of a Donald Trump presidency, Washington and the mainstream media began focusing almost entirely on this issue, seemingly turning the disastrous results of the Bush Cheney administration into concerns of the past, less important than the dangers of the future. I believe that this would be a serious mistake.

After Hillary Clinton's loss, I modified this book slightly, given reasons to believe that the US attempt to remove Assad from power—so that Syria could no longer stall America's imperialistic drive—would be lessened, with Trump rather than Clinton in the White House. A Trump presidency also promised to lessen the related and even greater danger that US behavior would lead to a war with Russia, one that could become nuclear. Indeed, the primary reason for the development of Washington and media hostility to Trump was his expressed desire to establish better relations with Russia.[1]

But this possible benefit of a Trump presidency might bring about no lessening of the danger of nuclear holocaust, given Trump's hostility to Iran, with which Russia is aligned, and his unpredictability.

But these changes in America and the world since this book was first conceived provide no reason to have less concern with the neocon movement, because there is little sign that it will lessen its drive, after the disappearance of the Soviet Union, to create an all-inclusive empire under US hegemony.

This book was designed to explore some of the most disastrous effects to both America and the larger world of this imperial drive—one of which became the election of Donald Trump, which resulted significantly from the fact that Washington and the Democratic Party were so concerned to have US foreign policy in the hands of Hillary Clinton, and hence in line with the neocon drive, that they ignored the overwhelming evidence that Bernie Sanders would have been much more likely to defeat Trump.

Besides focusing attention on the disasters caused by this drive, this book also seeks to undermine the power of the neocons to determine policy by emphasizing the fact that this power came from lies, which were told even before the well-known lies used to attack Iraq.

INTRODUCTION

In the past few years, there has been a growing consensus that the 9/11 attacks started a series of processes that led to destructive transformations of America and the world as a whole. According to this consensus, the Bush-Cheney administration, besides failing to prevent the 9/11 attacks, responded to them by adopting extreme, unwarranted policies, many of which had been advocated by neoconservatives, often called "neocons."

These policies included launching a "war on terror," increasing the already enormous military budget, adopting a policy of preemptive war and regime change, attacking Afghanistan and Iraq as first steps in taking control of the Greater Middle East, encouraging Islamophobia, starting an assassination-by-drone program, passing the USA PATRIOT Act, initiating a drive to bring about regime change in Russia, and stopping all progress in slowing global warming.

STATEMENTS REFLECTING THE CONSENSUS

For example, with regard to changes in America, the Center for Constitutional Rights published an essay entitled "The 9/11 Decade and the Decline of US Democracy," which said:

> In response to the terrorist attacks on September 11, 2001, George W. Bush shredded the US Constitution, trampled on the Bill of Rights, discarded the Geneva Conventions, and heaped scorn on the domestic torture statute. . . . [I]n response to the attacks, the Bush administration engineered and presided over the most sustained period of constitutional decay in our history.[1]

With regard to the larger world, former State Department employee Peter Van Buren wrote a 2015 essay entitled "How the US Wrecked the Middle East." It began by asking "What if the US had not invaded Iraq in 2003?" Prior to the invasion, he pointed out that

> Libya was stable, ruled by the same strongman for 42 years; in Egypt, Hosni Mubarak had been in power since 1983; Syria had been run by the Assad family since 1971; Saddam Hussein had essentially been in charge of Iraq since 1969, formally becoming president in 1979; the Turks and Kurds had an uneasy but functional ceasefire; and Yemen was quiet enough, other than the terror attack on the USS *Cole* in 2000.

But today, in addition to the fact that Iraq has been virtually destroyed and Syria has become so violent that millions of people have emigrated,

Libya is a failed state, bleeding mayhem into northern Africa; Egypt failed its Arab Spring test and relies on the United States to support its anti-democratic (as well as anti-Islamic fundamentalist) militarized government; and Yemen is a disastrously failed state.[2]

On the 14th anniversary of the 9/11 attacks, Tom Engelhardt, discussing both America and the larger world, wrote:

> Fourteen years of wars, interventions, assassinations, torture, kidnappings, black sites, the growth of the American national security state to monumental proportions, and the spread of Islamic extremism across much of the Greater Middle East and Africa. Fourteen years of astronomical expense, bombing campaigns galore, and a military-first foreign policy of repeated defeats, disappointments, and disasters. Fourteen years of a culture of fear in America, of endless alarms and warnings, as well as dire predictions of terrorist attacks. Fourteen years of the burial of American democracy. . . . Fourteen years of the spread of secrecy, the classification of every document in sight, [and] the fierce prosecution of whistleblowers. . . . Fourteen years of our wars coming home in the form of PTSD, the militarization of the police, and the spread of war-zone technology like drones and stingrays to the "homeland." . . . Fourteen years of the expansion of surveillance of every kind and of the development of a global surveillance system whose reach . . . would have stunned those running the totalitarian states of the twentieth century.[3]

The perceived destructiveness of the US government's response to 9/11, for both America and the larger world, can be illustrated more broadly by the headlines of articles, such as

- "9/11 Used to Demonize Muslim World, Justify NSA Spying of US Citizens."[4]

- "9/11 After Thirteen Years: Continuous Warfare, Police State, Endless Falsehoods."[5]

- "The Tyranny of 9/11: The Building Blocks of the American Police State from A-Z."[6]

- "Since 9/11, We've Had 4 Wars in the Middle East. They've All Been Disasters."[7]

- "9/11 Hurt America, But It Destroyed the Middle East."[8]

- "Yes, Bush Helped Create ISIS—and Set up the Middle East for a Generation of Chaos."[9]

- "Fifteen Years After 9/11, Neverending War."[10]

Although some of the stories discussed above speak about "Bush" or the "Bush administration," the present book refers to the "Bush-Cheney administration."

BUSH, CHENEY, AND THEIR ADMINISTRATION

This terminology is appropriate, because Dick Cheney, the most powerful vice president the country has ever had, was widely considered the real president, especially during the administration's first term. For example, John Nichols in 2004 published a book entitled *Dick: The Man Who Is President*. The Bush administration during its first term, he said, would more appropriately be called the "Bush-Cheney administration."[11]

To understand how Dick Cheney could have been the de facto president, and why the Bush-Cheney administration was so disastrous, it is necessary to have some understanding of these two men and their relationship.

George W. Bush

George W. Bush was the least capable, least articulate, least prepared person ever to become the American president. He had been a terrible student at college and perhaps an alcoholic.[12] After the Vietnam War started, Bush used connections to dodge the draft. Moreover,

> [Bush] struggled, often painfully, with the English language. . . He had no international experience. He had no Washington experience. He had no military experience. . . . His business experience was a tragic record of one failure after another. . . . [As governor, he] proceeded to create [an overwhelming] fiscal crisis.[13]

Bush became president only because of three factors. First, he was the oldest son of George H. W. (Herbert Walker) Bush, who was generally considered a passably good president. Second, Dick Cheney, who had been nominated to be Bush's running mate, helped interrupt the vote counting in Florida, which—if it had been continued—would have shown the Gore-Lieberman ticket to have received the most votes. Third, the Supreme Court, especially because of Cheney's friend Justice Antonin Scalia, stopped the vote-count and gave the election to Bush and Cheney.[14]

Dick Cheney

In college, Cheney was a heavy drinker and a bad student, even flunking out twice. Like Bush, he was a proficient draft dodger. After later earning a master's degree in political science (the woman he wanted to marry, Lynne Vincent, said this could happen only if he made something of himself), he used connections to become an aide of US Congressman Donald Rumsfeld. When President Richard Nixon brought Rumsfeld into the White House as a counselor, Cheney came with him. By chance, Rumsfeld and Cheney were out of the administration when the Watergate scandal forced Nixon to resign, so Rumsfeld and his aide were taken into the Gerald Ford administration, with Rumsfeld being the chief of staff and Cheney his deputy. When Ford made Rumsfeld the Secretary of Defense, Cheney was moved up to chief of staff. As the director of Ford's reelection campaign, Cheney did not do well, being significantly responsible for Ford's loss to Jimmy Carter in the 1976 presidential race.[15]

Nevertheless, after winning a seat in Congress as a representative from Wyoming, Cheney started moving up, becoming the Republican whip in 1988. Having become an ultra-conservative, his voting record showed him to be to the right of Newt Gingrich and Ronald Reagan. Besides opposing the Endangered Species and Clean Water acts, which Nixon had proposed, Cheney even voted against legislation calling for the release of Nelson Mandela from prison, calling his African National Congress a terrorist organization.[16]

Cheney's time in Congress revealed the most fateful feature of his attitude, his extreme commitment to the power of the executive branch of government. For example, after it was learned that the Reagan administration had violated a Congressional prohibition on giving financial aid to the Contras seeking to overthrow Nicaragua's Marxist government, most Republican as well as Democratic members of Congress criticized the administration. But Cheney, along with only seven other Republicans, signed a minority report, saying that the attempt to give Congress a major role in foreign affairs undermined the presidency.[17]

After George H.W. Bush became president in 1988, he surprisingly named Cheney secretary of defense, after the first nominee could not be confirmed. In this role, Cheney advocated the use of force "to protect our interests, to protect those of our friends and allies," even though the Cold War was over. In his first chance to use American force with a post-Cold War rationale, Cheney master-minded the invasion of Panama to remove dictator Manuel Noriega.

Cheney's next chance came when Iraq, under the dictatorship of Saddam Hussein, invaded Kuwait to protect his country's oil. Cheney argued that the United States should use this invasion as a basis for going to war with Iraq. Doing so required permission to put US soldiers in Saudi Arabia by the border with Kuwait to prepare for the invasion. Cheney obtained this permission by falsely claiming, with the help of doctored satellite photos, that Iraq was about to invade Saudi Arabia.[18]

Besides encouraging Bush to attack Iraq (on the basis of lies),[19] Cheney urged him to do so without getting Congressional approval. In his book *Takeover,* Charlie Savage commented:

> By urging Bush to ignore the War Powers Resolution on the eve of the first major overseas ground war since Congress enacted the law, Cheney was attempting to set a powerful precedent, establishing the right of presidents to start wars on their own.[20]

Also, after US forces had driven Iraqi fighters out of Kuwait, Cheney encouraged Bush to have his army continue on to Baghdad in order to bring about regime change, even though this would have meant going beyond the Congressional authorization.

Cheney's advocacy of the attacks on Panama and Iraq reflected his desire to have money possibly freed up by the end of the Cold War to remain in the military budget, rather than be used for domestic social programs that he despised.[21] By doing so, Cheney also provided money for the vision for global dominance laid out in his notorious "Defense Planning Guidance" of 1990 and in the Project for the New American Century, described in Chapter 2.[22]

After the George H.W. Bush administration was removed from office by the election of Bill Clinton in 1992, Cheney started touring the country to build support for his own presidential bid. But he was such an uninspiring candidate that he gave up.

Soon, however, his connections led the oil-and-gas corporation Halliburton, to which he as secretary of defense had tunneled billions of dollars, to appoint him as its CEO. During the five years in which Cheney had this position, the corporation's revenues increased by billions—not because he was particularly good at deal-making but because of his connections. These connections allowed Cheney, for example, to make deals with Saddam Hussein and other dictators—deals that Cheney justified by saying: "The good Lord didn't see fit to put oil and gas where there are democratic regimes friendly to the United States."[23]

However, Cheney still wanted to exercise presidential leadership. Having realized that voters would never elect him to that position, he hoped to become the power behind the throne. Accordingly, thinking that former President Bush would be able to put one of his sons in the White House, Cheney attached himself to one of them. Although Jeb Bush seemed to be the more capable one, a complication prevented him from running in 2000, so Papa Bush backed his other son, George W., who won the Republican nomination. Being aware of this son's deficiencies, the senior Bush concluded that "finding the right running mate was the essential task that lay before his son's campaign."[24]

Given the various criteria Bush Senior had, the choice seemed to narrow to Cheney and Rumsfeld. Because Cheney had proved himself helpful, the young George Bush talked to him about the process. When Cheney was asked if he wanted to be considered a candidate for the vice-presidency, he emphatically said "no." Cheney was then asked to guide the selection process.[25]

In that process, he, many people have said, selected himself. Actually, said Barton Gellman—the author of *Angler: The Cheney Vice Presidency*—"Bush selected him, but Cheney did maneuver the process."[26] During this maneuvering, Cheney did a lot to make it appear that he was vetting all the candidates, requiring them all to fill out a very long, extraordinarily detailed, questionnaire, providing evidence about their backgrounds. But then neither Cheney nor Bush interviewed any of these candidates. Moreover, Cheney did not fill out the form himself or provide the normal kinds of evidence (medical files, tax and corporate records).[27]

After Bush had made his choice, he said: "Gradually, I realized that the person who was best qualified to be my vice-presidential nominee was working by my side."[28] Bush surely saw Cheney as best choice because, having held so many important positions in the government—congressional whip, chief of staff, secretary of defense—he was strong in areas where Bush was especially weak. And there may have been another factor. According to a *Washington Post* story in October 2001: "When Bush surprised the nation by picking uncharismatic Cheney as his running mate, he confided to an aide that something unknown would happen that would vindicate the choice of Cheney."[29]

In any case, Bush was certainly right that Cheney would be helpful to him. In fact, Cheney proved his value even before he and Bush were elected, as without his manipulation of the vote-counting process in Florida and without his friendship with Supreme Court Justice Antonin Scalia, there probably would have been no Bush-Cheney administration.

The Bush-Cheney Administration: The First Years

In light of this history, it is not surprising that, in the first years of this administration, "Bush was president in name only. Dick Cheney was in charge." This became apparent in the administration's first major focus, its secret meetings with an energy task force. Besides being in charge of the meetings, Cheney had selected all 63 of the task-force members.[30] During the seven months prior to 9/11, moreover, Bush did not—after meeting briefly with the National Security Council to state that Condoleezza Rice would run the meetings—join the Council again until 9/11.[31]

Bush's secondary role became even more obvious in the White House's response to the 9/11 attacks. Cheney was in charge all day, partly because Bush was down in Florida at the time of the attacks. But also, when Bush wanted to come back to Washington, Cheney told him to stay away. According to writer James Mann, "Cheney was the dominant figure on September 11," and United Press International said that this dominance "reintroduced nagging questions about who was really in charge in the Bush White House."[32]

This dominant role of Cheney is important because his beliefs, purposes, and instincts were quite different from Bush's. If Bush had chosen a different person to be his vice president, the effects of his administration would likely have been much less destructive.

Part One of this book deals with various ways in which the Bush-Cheney administration's responses to 9/11 have seriously harmed America as well as the world in general, especially the Middle East and Europe. Part Two discusses the relationship of the Bush-Cheney administration to 9/11 itself. The book begins with a discussion of the obvious fact that the Bush-Cheney administration did not prevent the 9/11 attacks.

PART 1

HOW THE BUSH-CHENEY ADMINISTRATION RUINED AMERICA AND THE WORLD

1 • THE FAILURE TO PREVENT 9/11

As indicated by the titles of articles quoted in the Introduction, the harmful effects of the Bush-Cheney administration were significantly rooted in 9/11. It is usually said that these harmful effects resulted not from the 9/11 attacks themselves, but from how this administration responded to them. There is truth in this view. But it is also true that the attacks themselves resulted in negative effects, especially a huge increase in Islamophobia, and the rising fear and antipathy toward Islam and Muslims was a factor in most of the other destructive effects of 9/11. This increase in Islamophobia will be discussed in Chapter 5. The present chapter looks simply at the fact that the Bush-Cheney administration failed to prevent the attacks.

THE DONALD TRUMP/JEB BUSH CONTROVERSY

Although this fact is obvious, it actually became a point of contention in the contest to become the Republican nominee for the 2016 presidential race. During the debate on September 16, 2015, Donald Trump made a criticism of George W. Bush, after which Jeb Bush said, "There's one thing I know for sure: he kept us safe." Trump replied: "Say what you want, the World Trade Center came down during his time."[1]

As to why this fact could seem debatable, Jeb Bush and some commentators interpreted Trump's statement to mean that he was blaming George Bush for 9/11. However, Trump's basic statement was simply that the president had not prevented the attacks. "He was president, OK?" said Trump. "Blame him, or don't blame him, but he was president. The World Trade Center came down during his reign."[2] As several commentators pointed out, Trump was obviously right on this point.[3] In fact, this point had been made previously. In 2013, for example, the Daily Kos had an article entitled "Never Forget: The Bush Administration Failed to Prevent the September 11 Terrorist Attacks."[4]

However, although this point can be made without implying blame, many writers have gone on to say that the failure to prevent the attacks carries with it some blame. In 2003, there were stories with titles such as "9/11 Chair: Attack Was Preventable."[5] Numerous stories have pointed out that, in spite of having received warnings that al-Qaeda was planning to attack the United States, New York City in particular, the Bush-Cheney administration did nothing. The most famous of these warnings was the presidential daily brief of August 6, 2001, which was headed: "Bin Laden Determined to Strike in US."

Although learning the fact that Bush and Cheney had been given this brief was shocking, a 2012 *New York Times* article said that it was "not nearly as shocking as the briefs that came before it," which had started coming in the spring of 2001. When read in context of these earlier warnings, concluded the writer, the non-response to the August 6 brief "reflected significantly more negligence than has been disclosed."[6]

In 2015, in response to the argument between Trump and Jeb Bush, Peter Beinart of the *Atlantic* said:

> There's no way of knowing for sure if Bush could have stopped the September 11 attacks. But that's not the right question. The right question is: Did Bush do everything he could reasonably have to stop them, given what he knew at the time? And he didn't. It's not even close. When the Bush administration took office in January 2001, CIA Director George Tenet and National Security Council counterterrorism "czar" Richard Clarke both warned its incoming officials that al-Qaeda represented a grave threat.

Moreover, Beinart continued, Tenet and Clarke, joined by CIA counterterrorism head Cofer Black, continued to make appeals to the White House, but the Bush-Cheney administration took no action. "Bush was insufficiently vigilant," concluded Beinart. "The evidence is overwhelming."[7]

NEW EVIDENCE

Furthermore, about a month after Beinart's article was published, the evidence became even more overwhelming. In November 2015, *Showtime* presented a film, *The Spymasters: CIA in the Crosshairs,* which was written by Chris Whipple. Along with Jules and Gedeon Naudet, the film's directors, Whipple had over 100 hours of interviews with Tenet and the other living CIA directors. From these interviews, these filmmakers learned that the Presidential Daily Brief of August 6 was neither the first nor the most chilling of the warnings given to the Bush-Cheney administration.[8]

By May 2001, Cofer Black, who was chief of the CIA's counterterrorism center, told Whipple that "it was very evident that we were going to be struck, we were gonna be struck hard and lots of Americans were going to die." Black's boss, George Tenet, told Whipple:

> The world felt like it was on the edge of eruption. In this time period of June and July, the threat continues to rise. Terrorists were disappearing [as if in hiding, in preparation for an attack]. Camps were closing. Threat reportings on the rise.

On July 10, Richard Blee, the head of the agency's Al Qaeda unit, burst into Black's office and said: "Chief, this is it. Roof's fallen in." The information that his agency had compiled, he told Black, was absolutely compelling. It was multiple-sourced. Accordingly, Black and Blee rushed to Tenet's office, and the three men agreed that an urgent meeting at the White House was needed. Tenet called Bush's national security advisor, Condoleezza Rice, and said: "I have to come see you. We're comin' right now. We have to get there." At the meeting, Blee said:

> There will be significant terrorist attacks against the United States in the coming weeks or months. The attacks will be spectacular. They may be multiple.

When Rice asked what they should do, Black said that they should immediately go on a wartime footing. Accordingly, Black and Tenet worked up a plan, "the Blue Sky paper," which they proposed to Bush's national security team. The plan called for a covert CIA and military campaign to end the Al Qaeda threat—"getting into the Afghan sanctuary, launching a paramilitary operation, creating a bridge with Uzbekistan."[9]

But then nothing happened. Black told Whipple: "To me it remains incomprehensible still. I mean, how is it that you could warn senior people so many times and nothing actually happened?" It seems that this July 10 warning evoked amnesia: Rice said in her memoir, "My recollection of the meeting is not very crisp." And *The 9/11 Commission Report* did not even mention the meeting.[10]

CONCLUSION

Bush apologists say, to be sure, that the claim that George Bush "kept us safe" refers only to the time after the 9/11 attacks. However, as the heading of an article by Conor Friedersdorf of the *Atlantic* pointed out, "George W. Bush Didn't Keep Americans Safe Before or After 9/11."[11] The fact that Bush did not keep Americans, its allies, and other countries safe *after* 9/11 is discussed in the remaining chapters of Part One.

2 • THE WAR ON TERROR AND THE AFGHANISTAN WAR

On September 11, 2001, President George W. Bush and Vice President Dick Cheney each had an eventful day (some of which will be discussed in Chapter 11). The next day, Bush said:

> The deliberate and deadly attacks which were carried out yesterday against our country were more than acts of terror. They were acts of war. . . . This will be a monumental struggle of good versus evil.[1]

On September 14, there was a National Prayer Service in Washington, at which Bush said: "Our responsibility to history is already clear: to answer these attacks and rid the world of Evil."[2] On that same day, Congress passed an Authorization for Use of Military Force (AUMF), which authorized "the use of United States Armed Forces against those responsible for the recent attacks launched against the United States." In particular:

> The President is authorized to use all necessary and appropriate force against those nations, organizations, or persons he determines planned, authorized, committed, or aided the terrorist attacks that occurred on September 11, 2001, or harbored such organizations or persons, in order to prevent any future acts of international terrorism against the United States by such nations, organizations or persons.

On September 15, while talking to reporters, Bush said: "This crusade, this war on terrorism, is going to take awhile."[3] The term "crusade" evoked, of course, the suggestion that the war on terror was to be a continuation of the medieval crusades of Christians against Muslims. Bush was careful, therefore, never again to use the term "crusade." Whether the Bush-Cheney war on terror would be, nevertheless, a war on Muslims is discussed in Chapter 5.

In any case, although the AUMF authorized war only against "nations, organizations, or persons' responsible for the attacks," the Bush-Cheney administration expanded the target enormously. As Jonathan Schell wrote:

> By calling the campaign a "war," the administration summoned into action the immense, technically revolutionized, post-Cold War American military machine, which had lacked any clear enemy for over a decade. And by identifying the target as generic "terrorism," rather than as al-Qaeda or any other group or list of groups, the administration licensed military operations anywhere in the world.[4]

THE WAR ON TERROR BEGINS IN AFGHANISTAN

At that point, the Bush-Cheney administration had not decided where the war on terror would begin. Secretary of Defense Donald Rumsfeld, along with his assistant Paul Wolfowitz, were mainly interested in attacking Iraq, which they had been discussing since the administration's beginning. They wanted to attack Saddam right away.

Secretary of State Colin Powell, however, argued that the American people and other countries would at that time support an attack on Afghanistan, to do something about al-Qaeda, but not an attack on Iraq, as there was no evidence that it had anything to do with 9/11. Powell added, however, that after a successful campaign in Afghanistan, a war on Iraq would become more feasible. Accepting this argument,[5] Bush on September 17 signed a plan for going to war in Afghanistan while also directing the Pentagon to begin planning military options for an invasion of Iraq.[6]

On September 20, Bush gave an address to a joint session of Congress. Referring to the current government of Afghanistan, he said: "By aiding and abetting murder, the Taliban regime is committing murder." He then gave the Taliban an ultimatum: "Deliver to United States authorities all of the leaders of Al Qaeda who hide in your land."[7]

At this point, news stories commonly say that the Taliban refused. However, as CNN reported, "the Taliban refus[ed] to hand over bin Laden without proof or evidence that he was involved in last week's attacks on the United States."[8] Explaining the Taliban's position, CNN said:

> Bin Laden himself has already denied he had anything to do with the attacks, and Taliban officials repeatedly said he could not have been involved in the attacks.

However, Bush refused to supply evidence, saying "the demands were not open to negotiation or discussion."[9]

With this refusal, the Bush-Cheney administration made it impossible for the Taliban to turn bin Laden over. As Afghan experts quoted by the *Washington Post* pointed out, the Taliban, in order to turn over a fellow Muslim to an "infidel" Western nation, needed a "face-saving formula." Milton Bearden, who had been the CIA station chief in Afghanistan in the 1980s, put it this way: While the United States was demanding, "Give up bin Laden," the Taliban were saying, "Do something to help us give him up."[10] But the Bush-Cheney administration refused.

On September 23, Colin Powell said that he expected "in the near future" to put out "a document that will describe quite clearly the evidence that we have linking [bin Laden] to this attack." But at a joint press conference with President Bush the next morning, Powell withdrew this pledge, on the grounds that "most of [the evidence] is classified."[11] However, the real reason for withdrawing the pledge was a "lack of solid information," said investigative reporter Seymour Hersh, citing officials from both the CIA and the Department of Justice.[12]

The following week, British Prime Minister Tony Blair issued a document purportedly showing that "Osama Bin Laden and al-Qaeda, the terrorist network which he heads, planned and carried out the atrocities on 11 September 2001." Blair's report, however, began by saying: "This document does not purport to provide a prosecutable case against Osama Bin Laden in a court of law." The BBC then explained the reason for this caveat, saying: "There is no direct evidence in the public domain linking Osama Bin Laden to the 11 September attacks."[13]

But if the Bush administration did not have solid evidence, why did it claim, in giving the Taliban the ultimatum, to *know* that bin Laden was responsible? At this point, actually, it evidently did not explicitly make this claim. On September 16, a reporter asked, "Mr. President, do you believe Osama bin Laden's denial that he had anything to do with this?" Bush replied, "No question he is the prime suspect. No question about that." On that same day, Vice President Cheney, speaking on *Meet the Press*, said:

> The government of Afghanistan has to understand that we *believe* they have, indeed, been harboring a man who committed, and whose organization committed, this most egregious act.[14]

However, after indicating that they had no certain knowledge that bin Laden was guilty, Bush and Cheney spoke as if they did. Cheney said that he would like to receive bin Laden's "head on a platter," and Bush said that he wanted him "dead or alive."[15]

A month later, Bush was still refusing to provide evidence. After the US began bombing Afghanistan in October, the Taliban asked again for evidence, offering to turn bin Laden over if the United States would stop the bombing and provide evidence of his guilt. At this point, Bush claimed to know for sure that bin Laden was behind 9/11, saying: "There's no need to discuss innocence or guilt. We know he's guilty."[16] But he still did not provide the evidence on which this alleged knowledge was based.

The same dismissal of the request for evidence was expressed by other members of the Bush-Cheney administration. When White House press secretary Ari Fleischer was asked how he responded to the Taliban's complaint that they have been given no proof, he replied: "I don't respond to Taliban complaints." National Security Advisor Condoleezza Rice said: "[W]e did make very clear to the Taliban which kept asking—publicly . . .

about proof, that we didn't see this as a regime that was that concerned with western jurisprudence."[17]

EVALUATING THE BUSH-CHENEY DECISION
TO ATTACK AFGHANISTAN

Now that it is widely recognized that the Bush-Cheney administration's "war on terror" was disastrous for America and the world in general, it is necessary to evaluate its initial responses to the 9/11 attacks. There are four fundamental questions:

1. Was the Attack on Afghanistan Legal? No, said well-known professor of international law Marjorie Cohn. According to international law as codified in the UN Charter, disputes are to be brought to the UN Security Council, which alone may legally authorize the use of force. Without such authorization, military force can be legal as self-defense only in two circumstances:

- *A nation was attacked by another nation.* But the 9/11 attacks were not carried out, or even authorized, by Afghanistan.

- *A nation has certain knowledge that an armed attack by another nation is imminent—too imminent for the matter to be brought to the Security Council. The need for self-defense must be "instant, overwhelming, leaving no choice of means, and no moment for deliberation."* Although the US government claimed that its military operations in Afghanistan were needed to prevent a second attack, this need, even if real, was clearly not urgent: the United States waited almost a month to launch its attack.

So the US attack on Afghanistan was illegal.

The Bush-Cheney administration, to be sure, claimed that its war against Afghanistan was authorized by the UN Security Council resolution of September 20. President Obama repeated this claim in 2009, saying: "The United Nations Security Council endorsed the use of all necessary steps to respond to the 9/11 attacks," so US troops went to Afghanistan under the banner of "international legitimacy."[18] However, here is what the resolution in question said:

[The Security Council expresses] its readiness to take all necessary steps to respond to the terrorist attacks of 11 September 2001, and to combat all forms of terrorism, in accordance with its responsibilities under the Charter of the United Nations.[19]

So the Security Council did not authorize the United States to do anything. It merely expressed its readiness to carry out its own responsibilities.

2. Was it morally appropriate to attack Afghanistan? Some have argued that, legality aside, the Afghanistan war was morally justified. In 2009, President Obama, who had criticized the US invasion of Iraq as a war of choice, said of the US involvement in Afghanistan: "This is not a war of choice. This is a war of necessity."[20] However, the Afghan government was not involved in the attack. None of the men identified as hijackers were Afghans. And even Osama bin Laden was not an Afghan. (Having been brought to Pakistan from Saudi Arabia in 1979 by the CIA to battle against the Russian attempt to occupy Afghanistan, bin Laden moved back to Saudi Arabia and then moved [in 1992] to Sudan. Bin Laden returned to Afghanistan [in 1996] only because the United States had put pressure on Sudan to expel him.) Moreover, even if it were somehow relevant that bin Laden was living in Afghanistan in 2001, the United States, as we have seen, provided no evidence that he was responsible for the attacks, so there was no basis for the Taliban to hand him over to the Americans.

3. Was it appropriate to respond to the attacks with a war? Even if the war in Afghanistan was not justified, one might argue that it was appropriate to launch a war on terror. But a war could only have been appropriate if the attacks had been planned by another nation. In 2007, the UK government stopped speaking of the "war on terror," and a few years later, the former head of MI5 (the UK's counterpart to the CIA) gave a good reason why: The 9/11 attacks were "a crime, not an act of war."[21]

4. Was the attack on Afghanistan justified by later evidence of bin Laden's responsibility? One might argue that it was appropriate for Bush and Cheney to trust their intuition that bin Laden was guilty, because that was later proved to be true. However, the FBI's "Most Wanted Terrorist" webpage on "Usama bin Laden" said he was responsible for bombings of two US embassies in 1998, but it never listed 9/11 as one of the terrorist acts for which he was wanted.[22] When asked why not, the FBI's chief of investigative publicity replied that it was "because the FBI has no hard evidence connecting Bin Laden to 9/11."[23]

It has been claimed that proof was no longer necessary because bin Laden himself later confessed in a videotape. But America's leading academic expert on bin Laden, Professor Bruce Lawrence, called this tape "bogus," adding that he knew people in the Department of Homeland Security, assigned to work on bin Laden full time, who "also know it's bogus."[24] Although the Bush-Cheney administration came to tout this videotape as its prime evidence that bin Laden was responsible for the attacks, it evidently did not convince the FBI, because it never changed its Most Wanted Terrorist webpage about bin Laden.

Accordingly, there are many reasons why the US attack on Afghanistan was illegal and otherwise inappropriate. The Bush-Cheney attack on Afghanistan can be viewed as simply one more episode in the long US effort of—in the words of Ann Jones—"trying to remake Afghanistan to serve American aims."[25]

There is also the question of the behavior of US troops in Afghanistan. In 2016, the International Criminal Court announced that it plans an investigation of potential war crimes in Afghanistan.[26]

BACKGROUND TO THE BUSH-CHENEY WAR ON TERROR

Although the idea of a "war on terror" is now understood as the Bush-Cheney response to the 9/11 attacks, such a war had been declared in the 1980s by the Reagan administration, as Noam Chomsky has pointed out.[27] George Shultz, Reagan's secretary of state, warned of "a return to barbarism" by a plague spread by "depraved opponents of civilization itself." Such barbarism, Shultz argued, was a form of warfare, so it implied a military rather than a law-enforcement response.[28]

A war on terrorism was also suggested in the 1980s by Benjamin Netanyahu, while he was the Israeli ambassador to the United Nations. In 1984, Netanyahu organized a conference of Israeli and American policymakers held at the Jonathan Institute. This institute had been created by Netanyahu to convince Western governments that its "battle against terrorism"—meaning its battle against the Palestinian Liberation Organization—was part of a struggle "between the forces of civilization and the forces of barbarism." Although Netanyahu correctly defined terrorism as attacks on innocent civilians to inspire fear for political ends, he in practice—like Israel's prime minister, Menachem Begin—always applied the term only to Israel's enemies. In a 2014 essay entitled "Israel's Decades-Long Effort to Turn the Word 'Terrorism' into an Ideological Weapon," Rémi Brulin wrote: "Israeli elected officials used the term 'terrorist' incessantly, almost obsessively, to refer to members of the PLO."[29]

As one of the participants in this conference, Shultz argued for "preventive or pre-emptive actions against terrorist groups before they strike." Netanyahu then published a book out of the conference entitled *Terrorism: How the West Can Win*, which became one of Reagan's favorite books.[30] However, whereas Netanyahu identified terrorism with actions of Palestinians and Israel's other enemies in the Middle East, the Reagan administration identified terrorism primarily with activities of the Soviet Union, as discussed in the book that became the Reagan administration's "Bible"—Claire Sterling's *The Terror Network*. Sterling attributed responsibility for international terrorism to a Soviet-based "worldwide terror network aimed at the destabilization of Western democratic society."[31]

However, although the governments of Israel and the United States both tried mightily to get their people obsessed with terrorism, these efforts failed. There was, to be sure, concern about terrorism expressed in policy circles throughout the 1980s and 1990s. But it never became a central focus of the press and the public until September 11, 2001.

The Neoconservatives

The ideas informing the Bush-Cheney war on terror had been developed by a foreign policy group known as neoconservatives, or simply "neocons." Their foreign policy was originally oriented around opposition to Communism, so the end of the Cold War in 1989 created a crisis for some of the neocons. One leading member, Norman Podhoretz, even wrote a eulogy for neoconservatism.[32]

However, others saw it as a great opportunity—to create a global *Pax Americana*. At the close of 1989, *Washington Post* columnist Charles Krauthammer published a piece entitled "Universal Dominion," in which he argued that America should work for "a qualitatively new outcome—a unipolar world."[33] In 1990, he argued that unipolarity had already arrived, so the United States, being the "unchallenged superpower," should act unilaterally.[34]

The first effort to turn such thinking into official policy came in 1992, which was the final year of George H.W. Bush's presidency and thereby the end of Dick Cheney's tenure as secretary of defense. Before leaving office, Cheney had Paul Wolfowitz, the undersecretary of defense for policy, prepare—with the help of his assistant Lewis "Scooter" Libby—a draft of the Pentagon's "Defense Planning Guidance" (DPG).[35] Stating that America's "first objective is to prevent the re-emergence of a new rival," this DPG draft was, in Andrew Bacevich's appraisal, "in effect a blueprint for permanent American global hegemony."[36]

This draft was praised by neoconservative publications, such as the *Wall Street Journal*, which endorsed the draft's plan for a *Pax Americana*.[37] But most of the reaction was critical. For example, Senator Alan Cranston complained that the Bush administration was seeking to make the United States "the global Big Enchilada."[38] According to Senator Robert Byrd, the message of the draft was: "We love being the sole remaining superpower" so much that "we are willing to put at risk the basic health of our economy and well-being of our people."[39]

Although this draft came to be known as "the Wolfowitz plan," it was Cheney who, in Gary Dorrien's words, "hatched the original unipolarist blueprint in 1992."[40] According to the *New Yorker's* Nicholas Lemann, the DPG draft resulted from a secret team that Cheney had set up in the Pentagon "to think about American foreign policy after the Cold War."[41] It was appropriate, therefore, for David Armstrong in *Harper's* to call this draft "Dick Cheney's Song of America."[42] It was also appropriate that the neocon worldview later came to be called "Cheneyism."[43]

Seeking to calm the waters, George H. W. Bush distanced his administration from this draft, depicting it, in Andrew Bacevich's words, "as the musings of an insignificant lower-tier appointee acting without official sanction."[44] Wolfowitz and Cheney both claimed not to have seen it (even though Wolfowitz had essentially written it and one long section began by acknowledging "definitive guidance from the Secretary of Defense").[45] Cheney then had Scooter Libby rewrite the plan in language more acceptable at the time.[46]

This rewriting did not mean, however, that Cheney and other neoconservatives had dropped the ideas.[47] In fact, before leaving office, Cheney put out another revision of the DPG, in which some of the neo-imperial language was restored.[48] In 1996, Robert Kagan, "who emerged in the 1990s as the most influential neocon foreign policy analyst,"[49] argued that the United States should use its military strength "to maintain a world order which both supports and rests upon American hegemony."[50] Then in 1997, William Kristol—who in 1995 had started the *Weekly Standard*, which became the main organ of neocon thinking—founded, together with Kagan, the Project for the New American Century (PNAC), with a call to shape "a new century favorable to American principles and interests."[51]

In September 2000, just three months before the Bush-Cheney administration took office, PNAC published a document called *Rebuilding America's Defenses*. Saying, "At present the United States faces no global rival," this document declared that "America's grand strategy" should use its military supremacy to establish an empire that includes the whole world—a global *Pax Americana*. In fact, "the next president of the United States," declared this document, "must increase military spending to preserve American geopolitical leadership."[52]

Military Omnipotence

Actually, however, the US military had already developed in the 1990s policies to attain complete military superiority. One of these policies was "Full Spectrum Dominance," which is the attempt, said Bacevich, "to achieve something approaching omnipotence."[53] Bacevich was here referring to a document entitled "Joint Vision 2010," which was first published by the Joint Chiefs of Staff in 1996. Defining "Full Spectrum Dominance" as "the capability to dominate an opponent across the range of military operations," this document said that it "will be the key characteristic we seek for our Armed Forces in the 21st century."[54] Given the fact that the US military already had land, water, and air superiority, it needed to add dominance in space.

Space dominance was described in a 1997 document entitled "Vision for 2020," published by the US Space Command, a division of the Air Force. The unique mission of the Space Command, said this document, is to "dominat[e] the space dimension of military operations." With this addition, the US military will have Full Spectrum Dominance.[55]

This notion was further developed in the Pentagon's "Joint Vision 2020," which first appeared in 2000. It spoke of full spectrum dominance as involving not just four but five dimensions: "space, sea, land, air, and information." In addition,

> given the global nature of our interests and obligations, the United States must maintain its overseas presence forces and the ability to rapidly project power worldwide in order to achieve full spectrum dominance.[56]

PNAC's *Rebuilding America's Defenses* appeared in September of that same year. Besides arguing for increased spending across the board, this document argued in particular for increased funding for the US Space Command. Saying that "the ability to have access to, operate in, and dominate the aerospace environment has become the key to military success in modern, high-technology warfare," it advocated not only "missile defense" but also "placing . . . weapons in space." The weapons, moreover, were not intended only for defensive purposes, but also for "the ability to conduct strikes from space," which will give the US military a "global first-strike force."[57]

A New Pearl Harbor

To preserve "American geopolitical leadership," *Rebuilding America's Defenses* said, a "revolution in military affairs" will be needed. However, it warned, the needed transformation would not occur quickly, at least if the present climate continued. "[T]he process of transformation," said *Rebuilding America's Defenses*, "is likely to be a long one, absent some catastrophic and catalyzing event—like a new Pearl Harbor."[58]

PNAC's prayer was answered by 9/11: "The attacks of 11 September 2001," wrote Australian journalist John Pilger, provided "the 'new Pearl

Harbor.'"[59] According to the *Washington Post,* Bush wrote in his diary on the night of 9/11: "The Pearl Harbor of the 21st century took place today."[60]

This "new Pearl Harbor" was treated by leading members of Bush's administration as indeed an answer to prayer. Just as the attack on Pearl Harbor gave the United States the opportunity to enter World War II, the 21st-century Pearl Harbor gave, said Rumsfeld, "the kind of opportunities that World War II offered, to refashion the world."[61] "[I]f the collapse of the Soviet Union and 9/11 bookend a major shift in international politics," said Condoleezza Rice, "then this is a period not just of grave danger, but of enormous opportunity."[62] Nicholas Lemann reported that he was told by a senior official of the Bush administration (who insisted on anonymity):

> [T]he reason September 11th appears to have been "a transformative mo-
> ment" is not so much that it revealed the existence of a threat of which
> officials had previously been unaware as that it drastically reduced the
> American public's usual resistance to American military involvement
> overseas.[63]

The 9/11 attacks also emboldened various neoconservatives to become even more explicit about advocating the use of America's power for imperial ends. Mocking Clinton for being concerned to be "a good international citizen," Krauthammer praised Bush for understanding that "the US can reshape, indeed remake, reality on its own," because America "is the dominant power in the world, more dominant than any since Rome.[64] Fellow neocon Robert Kaplan argued that America should use its power unilaterally, leaving behind "the so-called international community," especially the United Nations, with its "antiquated power arrangement."[65]

It was 9/11 that allowed this imperial agenda to be implemented. In a volume entitled *Neoconned Again,* Claes Ryn said that the neoconservatives took "full advantage of the nation's outrage over 9/11 to advance their already fully formed drive for empire."[66] In their *America Alone,* Stefan Halper and Jonathan Clarke, two Reagan admirers, said that 9/11 allowed the "preexisting ideological agenda" of the neoconservatives to be "taken off the shelf and relabeled as *the* response to terror."[67] Writing from the left, Stephen Sniegoski said that "it was only the traumatic effects of the 9/11 terrorism that enabled the agenda of the neocons to become the policy of the United States of America."[68]

THE ATTACK ON AFGHANISTAN WAS ENABLED BY 9/11

The agenda of the neocons that was enabled by 9/11 included a pre-existing plan to attack Afghanistan. The background to this decision involved US support for a pipeline that would transport oil and gas from the Caspian Sea region through Afghanistan and Pakistan to the Indian Ocean.[69] This project had been on hold through the 1990s because of the civil war that had been going on in Afghanistan since the 1989 withdrawal of the Soviet Union.

In the mid-1990s, the US government had supported the Taliban with the hope that its military strength would enable it to unify the country, thereby providing a stable government. By the late 1990s, however, the Clinton administration had given up on the Taliban.[70]

When the Bush-Cheney administration came to power, it decided to give the Taliban one last chance. During a four-day meeting in Berlin in July 2001, representatives of the Bush administration insisted that the Taliban must create a government of "national unity" by sharing power with factions friendly to the United States. The US representatives reportedly said to the Taliban: "Either you accept our offer of a carpet of gold, or we bury you under a carpet of bombs."[71]

The Taliban, however, refused this offer, and in response the Americans said: "[M]ilitary action against Afghanistan would go ahead . . . before the snows started falling in Afghanistan, by the middle of October at the latest."[72] Thanks to the attacks that occurred on September 11, the Pentagon was able to be ready to begin its attack on Afghanistan by October 7.

This history suggests that 9/11, rather than being the reason for the invasion of Afghanistan, may have been a pretext to carry out a pre-existing plan. This hypothesis would certainly make sense of the refusal of Bush to give the Taliban a face-saving basis for handing over bin Laden.

In any case, there is no doubt that the attack on Afghanistan was made possible by 9/11. This fact was stated by both Donald Rumsfeld and Paul Wolfowitz. In 2004, Wolfowitz told the 9/11 Commission that if the Department of Defense had asked Congress for permission to invade Afghanistan prior to 9/11, this request would not have been taken seriously. Telling the Commission that "it can take a tragedy like September 11th to awaken the world to new threats and to the need for action," Rumsfeld said that prior to 9/11 the president could not have convinced Congress that the United States needed to "invade Afghanistan and overthrow the Taliban."[73]

British Prime Minister Tony Blair saw matters the same way, telling the House of Commons: "To be truthful about it, there was no way we could have got the public consent to have suddenly launched a campaign on Afghanistan but for what happened on September 11."[74]

To conclude: In light of this fact—that 9/11 merely enabled a US attack on Afghanistan that had been planned many months prior to the 9/11 attacks—it is clear that the Afghanistan war was neither legal nor morally appropriate.

DISASTROUS CONSEQUENCES

This illegal and immoral war has been harmful to both America and Afghanistan. But the harm has been much greater for Afghanistan. In his 2003 State of the Union address, George W. Bush said:

> In Afghanistan, we helped to liberate an oppressed people. And we will continue helping them secure their country, rebuild their society, and educate all their children, boys and girls.[75]

The Bush-Cheney "liberation" turned out to be disastrous for the people of Afghanistan in many ways.

Afghan Deaths

Probably most surprising to Americans in general is the sheer number of Afghans killed in the war—most surprising because the government and the media have not reported anything close to the truth.

- According to a widely quoted estimate from Brown University, a total of 450,000 Afghans were killed between 2001 and 2015, with 92,000 of the deaths (including fighters as well as civilians) from direct war violence, and the remainder coming from indirect causes (mainly deprivation).[76]

- Marc Herold, professor of economic development at the University of New Hampshire, has said that all of the figures reported by the mainstream press are very low, with even the reports of the United Nations Assistance Mission in Afghanistan (UNAMA) counting only 40 to 70 percent of the deaths.[77]

- Professor Gideon Polya, a retired biochemist in Melbourne, published a book in 2007 entitled *Body Count: Global Avoidable Mortality Since 1950*. In October 2011, on the 10th anniversary of the beginning of the Afghanistan War, Polya published an article estimating that there had been a total of 5.6 million war-related deaths—with "about 1.4 million violent deaths and 4.2 million non-violent avoidable deaths from Occupier-imposed deprivation," with about 2.9 million of those deaths occurring to under-5 infants.[78]

Moreover, the civilian death rate, after going down for several years, went back up in 2015. A report by UNAMA and the UN Human Rights Office said that the number of deaths that year was the greatest since the UN had started keeping track. The UN's special representative for Afghanistan said that the statistics do not "reflect the real horror." He wrote:

The real cost we are talking about in these figures is measured in the maimed bodies of children, the communities who have to live with loss, the grief of colleagues and relatives, the families who make do without a breadwinner, the parents who grieve for lost children, the children who grieve for lost parents.[79]

Continuing the Destruction of Afghanistan

Besides suffering perhaps over 5 million deaths from war-related causes, Afghanistan has been ruined by America, as stated in articles with headings such as "America's Destroying Mission in Afghanistan" and "We Destroyed Afghanistan."[80] Much of the damage was done in the decades before Bush and Cheney came to office—when America undermined the social, economic, and political progress that Afghanistan had attained by the 1970s. Most of this progress was undermined when the United States, wanting to drive out the Soviet Union, armed and paid fundamentalist, undemocratic, and women-hating Mujahideen forces in the 1980s. The Mujahideen were then replaced by the Taliban, the values and policies of which were not greatly different.

So, the Bush-Cheney administration can by no means be blamed for all of Afghanistan's problems. Nevertheless, it continued the destruction that had begun in previous decades. There are many dimensions of this destruction:

Women: A main reason for the attack was allegedly to liberate women. And in 2005, Bush repeatedly claimed to have liberated Afghan women.[81] However, any liberation was short-lived: By 2010, women's status had so deteriorated that the prevalence of self-immolation by discouraged women increased. Assassination of professional women also became prevalent and, said Ann Jones, "No Afghan has ever been brought to trial for any of these assassinations. . . . The government keeps no record of its women employees slain in the course of duty."[82]

Education: "Western leaders have taken particular pride in supposed advances in Afghan education since the defeat of the Taliban in 2001," wrote Ann Jones. However, she reported:

UNICEF reports that almost half the "schools" supposedly built or opened have no actual buildings. . . . Teachers are scarce and fewer than a quarter of those now teaching are considered "qualified.". . . No more than 10% of students, mostly boys, finish high school.[83]

Health Care: Western leaders have also claimed to have brought about great advances in health care. However, the claims turn out to be misleading. For example, The US Agency for International Development has reported that 85 percent of Afghans have access to healthcare. However, this means only that "85 percent of Afghanistan's districts have at least one basic health facility," and "a district can cover vast tracts of mountainous terrain, leaving district health facilities inaccessible to millions of Afghans."[84] The country has very high rates of infant mortality.[85]

Opium: The US invasion in Afghanistan has not been a total failure. When America started its proxy war against the Soviet Union, the country was producing only 250 metric tons of opium; in the early years of the post-9/11 occupation, it went up to 3,400 tons and, by 2007, the figure reached 8,200.[86] Tom Engelhardt, commenting on the research of Alfred McCoy, said that the only thing that has been "liberated" in Afghanistan is the opium poppy. "Washington's single and singular accomplishment," he added, "has been to oversee the country's transformation into the planet's number one narco-state."[87]

Employment: Whereas some of Afghanistan's problems do not impact other nations very much, that is not true of its problem with unemployment, which stands at about 40%. "Young Afghan men, mostly educated, full of energy and ambition, are leaving the country in droves every day," reported Ann Jones. "There is no work for them here. No future. The poorer ones don't find the makings of a single meal to feed their families." Previously, they headed for Pakistan or Iran, but now they head to Europe (including Turkey), where over 125,000 of them received asylum in 2015.[88]

Security: The United States has spent enormous amounts of money to get the Afghan government able to protect itself. After spending "over a trillion dollars on military operations, lavishing a record hundred billion more on "nation-building" and "reconstruction," [and] helping raise, fund, equip, and train an army of 350,000 Afghan allies," there has been little if any progress.[89] In an episode near the end of 2015, security forces numbering approximately 7,000 retreated in the face of a few hundred Taliban fighters.[90] Ann Jones wrote:

> [By 2015,] the growing strength of the Taliban, the intrusion of followers of the Islamic State of Iraq and Syria, the emergence of new splinter groups of Afghan ISIS supporters, and even the resurgence of 'remnants of Al Qaeda.' Yes, the very same bunch that President Obama assured us in 2013 could "never again establish a safe haven" in Afghanistan.[91]

In 2009, NPR suggested that Obama was in an "Afghan Box." On the one hand, the war appeared to be unwinnable. On the other hand, Obama in his 2008 presidential campaign had portrayed Iraq as a bad war, for which Hillary Clinton foolishly had voted, compared with Afghanistan as a "good war," which America needed to win—because it, unlike the Iraq War, was directly related to 9/11.[92]

Over the years, the war came to seem ever more unwinnable. Beginning in 2011, Obama repeatedly made plans to have military troops withdraw from Afghanistan. But every time, something happened to persuade him to continue the war. In 2015, he announced that the war would continue, even while stating: "I do not support the idea of endless war."[93] Shortly before the end of his presidency, Obama decided in June 2016 to expand the war in Afghanistan again.[94]

Obama did seem to be in a box: After having said that, because of 9/11, the Afghan war had to be won, how could he admit that he could not win it?

CONCLUSION

Although it is now widely said that the Iraq War was the greatest mistake, with the most disastrous consequences, made by any US administration, the Bush-Cheney administration's attack on Afghanistan was also deceitful, illegal, and disastrous. James Lucas observed:

> US officials talk about nation-building in Afghanistan. But what they neglect to say is that the US has actually done just the opposite: it has fostered the destruction of much of that nation.[95]

Besides ruining Afghanistan itself and killing millions of its people, the Bush-Cheney attack on this poor country resulted in chaos in the region, especially Pakistan, where at least 80,000 people have been killed, and about which Arif Rafic has written.

> Millions have fled violence in Pakistan's northwest, contributing to thousands of Pashtun migrants pouring into Karachi, settling in informal settlements in the crowded megacity, and putting its ethnic, economic, and political fault lines under great stress.[96]

The AfPak War, as it is sometimes called,[97] is responsible for part of the chaos in the greater Middle East, which is further discussed in Chapters 4 and 6.

3 • MILITARY SPENDING, PREEMPTIVE WAR, AND REGIME CHANGE

The ability to invade Afghanistan was only the first of the things that 9/11 allowed the Bush-Cheney administration to do. It allowed them to increase US military spending, to change their foreign policy to include preemptive war, and to use this policy to attack Iraq.

INCREASED MILITARY SPENDING

The main tool for fulfilling the drive for empire, neocons have always held, is military power. To a great extent, in fact, the neoconservative movement began in reaction to the widespread view, following the Vietnam war, that US military power should never again be used for imperialistic purposes. In the early 1980s, rejecting the left's conclusion that force had become "obsolete as an instrument of American political purposes," Norman Podhoretz argued that military power constitutes "the indispensable foundation of US foreign policy," adding that "without it, nothing else we do will be effective."[1]

The Cheney-Wolfowitz Defense Planning Guidance (DPG) of 1992, having said that America's "first objective is to prevent the re-emergence of a new rival," added that "we must maintain the mechanisms for deterring potential competitors from even aspiring to a regional or global role." These "mechanisms" referred, of course, to various kinds of military power.

The main point of PNAC's *Rebuilding America's Defenses*, which was published in 2000 to influence the next administration, was that "the next president of the United States . . . must increase military spending to preserve American geopolitical leadership."[2] This increased spending was necessary to finance a transformation of the military so as to exploit the "revolution in military affairs" (RMA), based on new information technologies.[3]

The emphasis on exploiting this revolution in order to transform the Pentagon's approach is no surprise, as one of the authors of *Rebuilding America's Defenses* was Paul Wolfowitz, who had long earlier fallen under the spell of Albert Wohlstetter (one of the models for "Dr. Strangelove").[4] Wohlstetter had been the main early proponent of the ideas that came to be dubbed the "revolution in military affairs" by Andrew Marshall, who later became the main advocate.[5] Marshall, who served as the Pentagon's RMA guru until his retirement in 2015, numbered Wolfowitz, Cheney, and Rumsfeld among his disciples.[6]

Besides allowing the Bush-Cheney administration to invade Afghanistan, 9/11 also allowed it to fulfill the neocon desire to increase the nation's military power, as the 9/11 attacks reduced Congressional resistance to providing increased funding for Pentagon programs. On the evening of 9/11 itself, Rumsfeld held a news briefing on the Pentagon attack, at which Senator Carl Levin, the chair of the Senate Armed Services Committee, was asked:

> Senator Levin, you and other Democrats in Congress have voiced fear that you simply don't have enough money for the large increase in defense that the Pentagon is seeking, especially for missile defense. . . . Does this sort of thing convince you that an emergency exists in this country to increase defense spending?[7]

Congress immediately appropriated an additional $40 billion for the Pentagon and much more later, with few questions asked.

The attacks of 9/11, moreover, aided those who favored a transformation of the military along RMA lines. In the weeks before September 11, reported Andrew Bacevich, "military transformation appeared to be dead in the water," because the military brass were "wedded to existing weapons systems, troop structure, and strategy."[8] However,

> President Bush's decision after September 11 to wage a global war against terror boosted the RMA's stock. After 9/11, the Pentagon shifted from the business of theorizing about war to the business of actually waging it. This created an opening for RMA advocates to make their case. War plans . . . became the means for demonstrating once for all the efficacy of the ideas advanced by Wohlstetter and Marshall and now supported by . . . Rumsfeld and his deputy Paul Wolfowitz.[9]

The neocon idea that the US should become the "unchallenged superpower" became official policy with the publication, one year after 9/11, of the Bush-Cheney administration's *National Security Strategy of the United States of America* (*NSS 2002*), which said: "We must build and maintain our defenses beyond challenge" so that we can "dissuade future military competition."[10]

Repeating one of the themes of the Bush-Cheney administration right after 9/11, *NSS 2002* said: "The events of September 11, 2001, . . . opened vast, new opportunities."[11] One of the main things for which it provided an opportunity was a doctrine of preemptive-preventive war.

PREEMPTIVE-PREVENTIVE WAR

This hyphenated term is used here for clarity. The doctrine in question, which involves attacking another country even though it poses no immediate threat, is technically called "preventive war." This doctrine, which violates international law as reflected in the charter of the United

Nations, is to be distinguished from what is technically called "preemptive war," which occurs when Country A attacks Country B after learning that an attack from Country B is imminent—*too* imminent to allow time for the United Nations to intervene. Preemptive war in this sense is legal. These technical terms, however, are problematic, because although preventive war, being illegal, is worse than preemptive war, to most ears "preemption" sounds worse than "prevention." As a result, many people speak of "preemptive war" when they mean preventive war. The term "preemptive-preventive war," while somewhat cumbersome, avoids this problem.[12]

THE IDEA OF PREEMPTIVE-PREVENTIVE WAR BEFORE 9/11

The idea of preemptive-preventive war had been advocated by neocons long before 9/11.

- The Cheney-Wolfowitz DPG of 1992 said that the United States should use force to "preempt" and "preclude threats."[13]

- In 1996, Richard Perle and two other neocons, who were working for pro-Israel think tanks, prepared a strategy paper entitled "A Clean Break" for Benjamin Netanyahu, who had recently been elected Israel's prime minister. This paper recommended that Israel, in making a clean break from previous strategies, establish "the principle of preemption"[14] (this is case when "preemption" is used when "prevention" is meant). This paper ended up providing a blueprint for the foreign policy of the Bush-Cheney administration.[15]

- In 1997, PNAC's "Statement of Principles" argued that to exert "global leadership," America needs to "challenge regimes hostile to our interests and values."[16]

- In 1998, a letter from PNAC, signed by 19 members—including Cheney, Perle, Rumsfeld, and Wolfowitz—urged President Clinton to "undertake military action" to eliminate "the possibility that Iraq will be able to use or threaten to use weapons of mass destruction."[17]

Although these neocons were anxious to have their doctrine of preemptive-preventive war accepted as national policy, this did not occur during the Clinton presidency or even during the first eight months of the Bush-Cheney administration.

THE POST-9/11 DOCTRINE
OF PREEMPTIVE-PREVENTIVE WAR

After 9/11, however, this doctrine became official policy. "The events of 9/11," observed Bacevich, "provided the tailor-made opportunity to break free of the fetters restricting the exercise of American power."[18]

The idea of preemptive-preventive war, which came to be known as the Bush Doctrine, was first clearly expressed in the president's address at West Point in June 2002 (when the administration started preparing the American people psychologically for the attack on Iraq). Having stated that, in relation to the "new threats," deterrence "means nothing" and containment is "not possible," Bush even took aim at the traditional understanding of preemption, saying: "If we wait for threats to fully materialize, we will have waited too long." Then, using the language of preemption while really meaning preemptive-prevention, he said that America's security "will require all Americans . . . to be ready for preemptive action."[19]

NSS 2002: However, although the West Point speech provided a first statement of this new doctrine, it was in the *National Security Strategy of the United States of America 2002* (*NSS 2002*), published that September, that the new doctrine was laid out at some length. The covering letter, signed by the president, says that with regard to "our enemies' efforts to acquire dangerous technologies," America will, in self-defense, "act against such emerging threats before they are fully formed."[20] The document itself, saying that "our best defense is a good offense," continues:

> Given the goals of rogue states and terrorists, the United States can no longer rely on a reactive posture as we have in the past. The inability to deter a potential attacker, the immediacy of today's threats, and the magnitude of potential harm that could be caused by our adversaries' choice of weapons, do not permit that option. We cannot let our enemies strike first.[21]

To justify this doctrine, *NSS 2002* argues that the United States must "adapt" the traditional doctrine of preemption, long recognized as a right, to the new situation, thereby turning it into a right of anticipatory (preventive) preemption:

> For centuries, international law recognized that nations need not suffer an attack before they can lawfully take action to defend themselves against forces that present an imminent danger of attack. . . . We must adapt the concept of imminent threat to the capabilities and objectives of today's adversaries. . . . The United States has long maintained the option

of preemptive actions to counter a sufficient threat to our national security. The greater the threat, . . . the more compelling the case for taking anticipatory action to defend ourselves, even if uncertainty remains as to the time and place of the enemy's attack. To forestall or prevent such hostile acts by our adversaries, the United States will, if necessary, act preemptively.[22]

With this argument, the authors of NSS 2002 tried to suggest that, since this doctrine of anticipatory preemption simply involves adapting a traditionally recognized right to a new situation, it involves no great change. But it does. According to the traditional doctrine, one needed certain evidence that the other country was going to launch an immediate attack. According to the Bush Doctrine, by contrast, the United States can attack another country "even if uncertainty remains" and even, more flagrantly, if the United States knows that the threat from the other country is not yet "fully formed."

The novelty here, to be sure, involves doctrine more than practice. The United States has in practice attacked several countries that presented no imminent military threat. But it always portrayed these attacks in such a way that they could appear to comport with international law, such as the attack on North Vietnam after the alleged incident in the Tonkin Gulf. "Never before," said Stefan Halper and Jonathan Clarke, "had any president set out a formal national strategy *doctrine* that included [preventive] preemption."[23] This is a step of great significance, because it involves an explicit statement by the United States that the basic principle of international law, as embodied in the United Nations, does not apply to it.

The Primary Drafter of NSS 2002: Max Boot, a neocon who became well known through his writing, has described NSS 2002 as a "quintessentially neo-conservative document."[24] Now that the basic ideas of this document have been laid out, one can see the accuracy of this description.

One can also see the importance of the fact that Philip Zelikow, who would later become the executive director of the 9/11 Commission, was chosen by Bush's national security advisor, Condoleezza Rice, to be the primary drafter of NSS 2002. According to James Mann in *The Rise of the Vulcans*, after Rice saw the first draft of this document (which had been prepared by Richard Haass, the director of policy planning in Colin Powell's State Department), she "ordered the document be completely rewritten. She thought the Bush administration needed something bolder. . . . Rice turned the writing over to her old colleague, . . . Philip Zelikow."[25] The statement that Zelikow and Rice were "old colleagues" refers to these facts:

- Rice and Zelikow worked together in the National Security Council in the administration of the first President Bush.

- When the Republicans were out of power during the Clinton presidency, they wrote a book together.

- When Rice was appointed National Security Advisor for the second President Bush, she brought on Zelikow to help with the transition to the new National Security Council.

In any case, given the content and tone of the document that Zelikow drafted, one might assume that Cheney, Rumsfeld, or Wolfowitz had been involved in the process of creating it. But according to Mann:

> [T]he hawks in the Pentagon and in Vice President Cheney's office hadn't been closely involved, even though the document incorporated many of their key ideas. They had left the details and the drafting in the hands of Rice and Zelikow, along with Rice's deputy, Stephen Hadley."[26]

Because *NSS 2002* was, as Max Boot said, a "quintessentially neo-conservative document," Mann's statement shows Zelikow and Rice to be full-fledged neocons. The full significance of this point will be shown later.

For now, it is sufficient to look at the main purpose of bigger military budgets and the preemptive-preventive war doctrine: regime change.

REGIME CHANGE

As pointed out above, PNAC's "Statement of Principles" argued that America needs to "challenge regimes hostile to our interests and values."[27] The term "challenge" in this context meant "replace"—to replace the governments of various countries with ones more in line with US interests. Without such "regime changes," a global empire would be impossible.

As indicated in the previous chapter, some members of the Bush-Cheney administration wanted to begin the war on terror by invading Iraq, but Bush followed Colin Powell's view that the United States would need to focus first on Afghanistan, because of al-Qaeda's presence there. At the same time, however, preparations should be made for an invasion of Iraq. That invasion will be discussed in the following chapter.

In any case, the Bush-Cheney administration planned to refashion the world still more fully, as indicated in a *Newsweek* article of August 2002, which reported that some of Bush's advisors wanted to attack not only Iraq but also Iran, Syria, Egypt, North Korea, Burma, and even Saudi Arabia.[28] This same intention was reported, in slightly different form, by General Wesley Clark, who had been the Supreme Allied Commander of NATO.

According to Clark, he was told by a three-star general in the Pentagon late in 2001 that the Pentagon was "going to take out seven countries in five years," starting with Iraq and ending with Iran—with the other countries being Syria, Lebanon, Libya, Somalia, and Sudan (the decision to attack Afghanistan had already been made).[29]

That the Pentagon was indeed thinking in those terms was confirmed in 2008 by neocon Douglas Feith, who had been under-secretary of defense for policy at the time. Feith revealed that on September 30, 2001, Secretary of Defense Donald Rumsfeld sent a letter to President Bush saying that the United States should seek to establish "new regimes" in those seven countries.[30]

The list mentioned by Clark and advocated by Rumsfeld did not, unlike the list in the *Newsweek* story, include Saudi Arabia. But this country was on the hit list of at least some of the neocons. In 2002, a speaker invited to address the Defense Policy Board by its chairman, arch-neocon Richard Perle, said that unless Saudi Arabia does as we wish, we should seize its oil fields and confiscate its other financial assets.[31] The following year, another neocon, Michael Ledeen, wrote that "we must bring down the terror regimes," after which he named Iran, Iraq, Syria, Lebanon, and "even Saudi Arabia."[32]

The Bush administration, led by Cheney, Rumsfeld, and other neocons, entered into its regime-change plan with great confidence that the *Pax Americana* would be achieved quite effortlessly. Trusting in America's military omnipotence, these people apparently did not worry that their efforts to bring about regime changes would result in disastrous unintended consequences.

4 • IRAQ WAR

As stated in Chapter 1, Secretary of Defense Donald Rumsfeld and his assistant Paul Wolfowitz together argued that Iraq, under the control of Saddam Hussein, should be attacked in the first round in the war on terrorism. There was quite a history behind that desire. This history shows, among other things, the truth of James Mann's statement: "The invasion of Iraq was in many ways Dick Cheney's war, just as the George W. Bush administration had been in some respects Cheney's administration."[1]

BACKGROUND

Several neocons, including some who became central members of the Bush-Cheney administration, had been wanting to bring about regime change in Iraq ever since Saddam Hussein's occupation of Kuwait in 1990. Leading voices for this policy included Cheney and Wolfowitz, who were then secretary and under-secretary of defense. But this idea was opposed by General Colin Powell, who was then chairman of the Joint Chiefs of Staff, and General Norman Schwarzkopf, the field commander. President George H.W. Bush agreed with them, saying that going to Baghdad would have gone beyond the UN authorization. This left many neocons with the determination to right what they considered a mistake.[2]

From 1991 to 2001

In the decade prior to 9/11, the neocons took many steps to try to get Saddam Hussein removed from office (and perhaps life):

- In 1992, Albert Wohlstetter, who had inspired Wolfowitz and other neocons, expressed exasperation that nothing had been done about "a dictatorship sitting on the world's second largest pool of low-cost oil and ambitious to dominate the Gulf."[3] (Wohlstetter's statement reflected his conviction, expressed back in 1981, that America needs to establish forces, bases, and infrastructure so as to enjoy unquestioned primacy in the region.[4])

- The 1996 paper "A Clean Break" proposed that Israel remove from power all of its enemies in the region, beginning with Saddam Hussein. This document, in the opinion of Arnaud de Borchgrave, president of United Press International, "provided the strategic underpinnings for Operation Iraqi Freedom seven years later."[5]

- In 1997, Wolfowitz and another neocon, Zalmay Khalilzad, published a statement arguing that "Saddam Must Go."[6]

- In 1998, William Kristol and Robert Kagan, in a *New York Times* op-ed headed "Bombing Iraq Isn't Enough," called for "finishing the job left undone in 1991." Wolfowitz told the House National Security Committee that it had been a mistake in 1991 to leave Saddam in power, and he wrote in the *New Republic*: "Toppling Saddam is the only outcome that can satisfy the vital US interest in a stable and secure Gulf region."[7]

- Also in 1998 came the PNAC letter to Clinton, urging him to "take the necessary steps, including military steps," to "remov[e] Saddam's regime from power." Then, getting no agreement from Clinton, PNAC wrote a similar letter to Newt Gingrich and Trent Lott, who were at that time the leaders of the House and the Senate, respectively.[8]

- In 2000, PNAC's *Rebuilding America's Defenses*—pointing out that "the United States has for decades sought to play a more permanent role in Gulf regional security"—added: "While the unresolved conflict with Iraq provides the immediate justification, the need for a substantial American force presence in the Gulf transcends the issue of the regime of Saddam Hussein."[9]

The Bush-Cheney Administration

In light of this background, combined with the fact that central positions in the Bush administration went to Cheney, Libby, Rumsfeld, Wolfowitz, and other neocons, it is not surprising to learn, from two former members of this administration, that it had come into office intent on attacking Iraq.

Paul O'Neill, who was secretary of the treasury and hence a member of the National Security Council, said that within days of the inauguration, the main topic was going after Saddam, with the question being not "Why Saddam?" or "Why Now?" but merely "finding a way to do it." Richard Clarke, who had been the National Coordinator for Security and Counterterrorism during the first Bush-Cheney term, confirmed O'Neill's charge, saying: "The administration of the second George Bush did begin with Iraq on its agenda."[10]

Until the attacks of 9/11, however, no one had found "a way to do it." Neocon Kenneth Adelman said: "At the beginning of the administration people were talking about Iraq but it wasn't doable. . . . That changed with September 11." Bob Woodward in *Bush at War* said: "The terrorist attacks of September 11 gave the US a new window to go after Hussein." And John Mearsheimer and Stephen Walt, in their important essay "The Israel Lobby," wrote:

The neo-conservatives had been determined to topple Saddam even before Bush became president. They caused a stir early in 1998 by publishing two open letters to Clinton, calling for Saddam's removal from power. . . . [They] had little trouble persuading the Clinton administration to adopt the general goal of ousting Saddam. But they were unable to sell a war to achieve that objective. They were no more able to generate enthusiasm for invading Iraq in the early months of the Bush administration. They needed help to achieve their aim. That help arrived with 9/11.[11]

However, even 9/11, by itself, was not a sufficient basis for getting the American people's support for an attack on Iraq. Rumsfeld and Wolfowitz began immediately, however, to turn 9/11 into a cause for such a war. On the afternoon of 9/11 itself, Rumsfeld said in a note to General Richard Myers—the acting head of the Joint Chiefs of Staff—that he wanted "best info fast. Judge whether good enough hit S.H. [Saddam Hussein] at same time. Not only UBL [Usama bin Laden]." In the following days, both Rumsfeld and Wolfowitz argued that Saddam's Iraq should be, in Woodward's paraphrase, "a principal target of the first round in the war on terrorism."[12]

But in spite of the desire of Rumsfeld and Wolfowitz for this attack to be launched immediately, the attack had to be delayed. "[A]lthough the 9/11 atrocities psychologically prepared the American people for the war on Iraq," explained Stephen Sniegoski, "those horrific events were not sufficient by themselves to thrust America immediately into an attack on Iraq." Rather, a "lengthy propaganda offensive" would also be needed.[13]

THE ADMINISTRATION'S PROPAGANDA OFFENSIVE

This propaganda offensive involved convincing a majority of the American people that Saddam Hussein was threatening to them—that Saddam Hussein was both able and willing to attack America.

Although this propaganda was necessary in order to get Americans to support an attack on Iraq, its success depended on 9/11. As Halper and Clarke said, "it was 9/11 that provided the political context in which the thinking of neo-conservatives could be turned into operational policy."[14] Spelling out the point more fully, Sniegoski said:

The 9/11 attacks made the American people angry and fearful. Ordinary Americans wanted to strike back at the terrorist enemy, even though they weren't exactly sure who that enemy was. . . . Moreover, they were fearful of more attacks and were susceptible to the administration's propaganda that the United States had to strike Iraq before Iraq somehow struck the

United States. . . . It wasn't that difficult to channel American fear and anger into war against Iraq.[15]

The essence of this propaganda offensive was stated in the minutes of a briefing on July 23, 2002, of British Prime Minister Tony Blair by Richard Dearlove, the head of MI6 (which is parallel to the CIA). Dearlove was reporting on meetings he had recently had with members of the Bush administration, especially CIA head George Tenet.

Dearlove's report confirmed the earlier-quoted statements by O'Neill and Clarke, who said that the Bush-Cheney administration began with a discussion of the need to remove Saddam. But these statements, which were published in books that appeared in 2004, said nothing about the pretext for removing him.

By contrast, Dearlove's report, besides saying that the administration planned to use military force to remove Saddam, said that the war was to be "justified by the conjunction of terrorism and weapons of mass destruction." Saddam's possession of such weapons was prohibited by the UN Security Council in the settlement of Iraq's defeat in the Gulf War of 1991.

The US plan, of course, presupposed that the intelligence agencies would report that Iraq did indeed have weapons of mass destruction (WMD). But that report, Dearlove explained, was guaranteed in advance: "The intelligence and facts are being fixed around the policy."[16]

The policy meant the plan to remove Saddam on the basis of terrorism and WMD. *Terrorism* was shorthand for saying that Saddam was capable of committing major acts of terrorism because he was affiliated with al-Qaeda. *WMD* (weapons of mass destruction) meant nuclear, biological, and chemical weapons.

Unfortunately, this memo was not made public until over three years later, when London's *Sunday Times*, to which the memo had been leaked, published it on May 1, 2005. Had it been published much earlier, it might have prevented the long debate on whether Iraq really had WMD. In addition, once it was published, it should have prevented the other long debate—whether the Bush-Cheney administration was misled by faulty intelligence, or whether it simply lied: The memo shows that the administration had made its decision to invade Iraq before there was any intelligence about Iraq's WMD and connection to al-Qaeda.

Also unfortunately, the mainstream press in the United States devoted very little attention to this memo. For example, no American newspaper gave the story front-page coverage until 17 days later. The *New York Times* and *Washington Post* did finally run stories about it, but buried them inside. The *Times* even ignored the most eye-popping fact—that the intelligence was to be "fixed."[17]

In any case, given the fear and anger that was evoked by the 9/11 attacks, it was not difficult, to repeat Sniegoski's observation, "to channel American fear and anger into war against Iraq." Some of this channeling was carried out by neoconservatives outside the government, who "linked their preexisting agenda (an attack on Iraq) to a separate event (9/11)." Through their propaganda—perhaps most widely spread in Lawrence Kaplan and William Kristol's *The War over Iraq: Saddam's Tyranny and America's Mission*—"Al-Qaeda and Saddam Hussein were morphed into the same enemy," said Halper and Clarke, and "the war on terror and war in Iraq were joined at the hip."[18]

But most of this channeling was carried out by people inside the Bush-Cheney administration, especially Bush and Cheney themselves, along with Donald Rumsfeld. The remainder of this chapter looks at their propaganda for the two major claims: (1) Saddam's Iraq had WMD of all three types: biological, chemical, and nuclear. (2) Saddam's Iraq was affiliated with al-Qaeda and was even involved in the 9/11 attacks.

The propaganda about these two points was incessant. In 2008, the Center for Public Integrity published a report on false statements about Saddam Hussein's Iraq made by leading members of the Bush administration during the two years following 9/11. The report enumerated 935 such statements.[19] Only a few examples will be quoted here.

CLAIMS ABOUT WEAPONS OF MASS DESTRUCTION (WMD)

With regard to weapons of mass destruction, there were charges of WMD in general, and also of biological, chemical, and nuclear WMD in particular.

WMD in General

"[T]here is no doubt," Cheney said in August 2002, "that Saddam Hussein now has weapons of mass destruction. There is no doubt he is amassing them to use against our friends, against our allies, and against us." The following month, Rumsfeld said: "There's no debate in the world as to whether they [the Iraqis] have those weapons. We all know that. A trained ape knows that."[20]

Biological WMD

The claim that Iraq had biological WMD originated from a low-level engineer who defected to Germany. Code-named "Curveball" by German intelligence, he said that Saddam had bioweapons in mobile weapons labs. There were many reasons why Curveball's claims should have been ignored:

British and German intelligence agents considered him "crazy" and "probably a fabricator"; Tyler Drumheller, CIA's European operations chief, was so skeptical that he told George Tenet that all references to Curveball's claims should be deleted.

In spite of these red flags, US agents never talked with Curveball or performed any background checks, and yet his claims were repeated by leading administration figures. In a presentation to the UN Security Council, shortly before the start of the war, Colin Powell said: "We have first-hand descriptions of biological weapons factories on wheels and on rails." Tyler Drumheller said, "My mouth hung open when I saw Colin Powell use information from Curveball." In any case, Bush the following day said: "Firsthand witnesses have informed us that Iraq has at least seven mobile factories for the production of biological agents, equipment mounted on trucks and rails to evade discovery."[21]

As Drumheller feared, the claim made by Powell turned out to be completely false. In fact, eight years after Powell's speech, Curveball—whose actual name was Rafid Ahmed Alwan al-Janabi—admitted that he had fabricated the story with the hope that it might help topple Saddam's regime.[22]

How could such an error have been made? The fact is that, with the exception of Powell, the leading figures in the Bush administration, especially Cheney and Rumsfeld, were not concerned with having a report that would prove to be accurate. They were concerned only with persuading the people to support an invasion of Iraq. This fact was shown not only by their use of Curveball's testimony, in spite of very good reasons not to trust it, but also by a report from the Joint Chiefs of Staff (JCS) entitled "Iraq: Status of WMD Programs." Part of the reason why Powell's speech was so terrible is that the JCS report was hidden from most people in the administration, including Powell.[23]

The JCS Report about WMD

This report had been prepared in response to Rumsfeld's question in August 2002 to the chairman of the Joint Chiefs of Staff's intelligence directorate, asking "what we don't know" about the Iraqi WMD program. On September 5, this report was given to Rumsfeld, as well as to Richard Myers, the chairman of the Joint Chiefs of Staff.

In response, Rumsfeld sent a note to Myers, saying: "Please take a look at this material as to what we don't know about WMD. It is big." In calling the report "big," Rumsfeld evidently meant that it contradicted the case that was being made to attack Iraq. Accordingly, Rumsfeld and Myers did not publicize this report. Although Rumsfeld almost certainly would have sent it to Cheney, he did not send it to Powell or other people in the administration.[24]

As a general statement, the report said: "Our assessments rely heavily on analytic assumptions and judgment rather than hard evidence." Had Powell seen the report before addressing the UN Security Council, he probably would not have said:

> My colleagues, every statement I make today is backed up by sources, solid sources. These are not assertions. What we are giving you are facts and conclusions based on solid intelligence.[25]

Likewise, whereas Powell spoke confidently in his speech about evidence that Iraq was hiding biological weapons in mobile labs, the JCS report said: "We cannot confirm the identity of any Iraqi facilities that produce, test, fill, or store biological weapons."[26]

Chemical WMD

In June 2002, Rumsfeld said: "They have weaponized chemical weapons, we know that." In February 2003, Bush said: "Sources that tell us that Saddam Hussein recently authorized Iraqi field commanders to use chemical weapons—the very weapons the dictator tells us he does not have."[27] And in his UN Security Council statement, Powell said: "Our conservative estimate is that Iraq today has a stockpile of between 100 and 500 tons of chemical weapons agent."[28]

However, the ignored JCS report said: "We do not know if all the processes required to produce a weapon are in place," and "we cannot confirm the identity of any Iraqi sites that produce final chemical agent."

Both Biological and Chemical WMD

There were also statements claiming that Iraq had both biological and chemical WMD. For example, on September 26, 2002, Bush said: "The Iraqi regime possesses biological and chemical weapons." Two days later, he made an even more frightening claim:

> The Iraqi regime possesses biological and chemical weapons, is rebuilding the facilities to make more, and, according to the British government, could launch a biological or chemical attack in as little as 45 minutes after the order is given.[29]

In crediting the British government with this information, Bush was referring to Tony Blair's foreword to the "September Dossier," which was the British government's assessment of Iraq's WMD. This foreword said that Saddam's "military planning allows for some of the WMD to be ready within 45 minutes of an order to use them."[30]

This statement resulted in panic-producing headlines, such as that of *The Sun*, Britain's biggest-selling newspaper: "Brits 45 Minutes from Doom." It also led to a heated controversy between the British government and the BBC, after its defense correspondent, Andrew Gilligan, reported that a senior British official told the BBC that the September Dossier had been "sexed up."[31]

(This official was later learned to be Dr. David Kelly, an authority on biological warfare who served as a weapons inspector in Iraq. In February 2003, Kelly said that if the US-UK attack went ahead, he would "probably be found dead in the woods." After it became known that he had been the official to whom Gilligan referred, Kelly was brought before a parliamentary committee on July 15, 2003, but Geoff Hoon, the defense secretary, sought to prevent him from speaking about WMD. Two days later, Kelly was found dead in the woods, with suicide-by-wrist-cutting being the official explanation.[32])

Nuclear WMD

Although the false reports about biological and chemical weapons played a role in creating fear of Saddam's Iraq, the greatest fear was created by claims about nuclear weapons. And these claims were abundant. For example:

- In March 2002, Cheney called Saddam "a man of great evil" who is "actively pursuing nuclear weapons."[33]

- In June of that year, Rumsfeld said that Saddam Hussein, besides having chemical weapons, had "an active program to develop nuclear weapons," adding that Saddam's denial of this fact shows him to be a "world-class liar."[34]

- In September, Bush said to the UN General Assembly: "The first time we may be completely certain he has a—nuclear weapons is when, God forbid, he uses one."[35]

- Having "experienced the horror of September the 11th," said Bush in October 2002, "America must not ignore the threat gathering against us. Facing clear evidence of peril, we cannot wait for the final proof—the smoking gun—that could come in the form of a mushroom cloud."[36]

- In March 2003, four days before the attack on Iraq, Cheney said: "We know he [Saddam Hussein] has been absolutely devoted to trying to acquire nuclear weapons. And we believe he has, in fact, reconstituted nuclear weapons." (Cheney surely meant, "reconstituted his nuclear weapons program.")[37]

Such claims to knowledge were not at all supported by the JCS report about Iraqi WMD, which said:

> The evidentiary base [for our assessments] is particularly sparse for Iraqi nuclear programs. . . . Our knowledge of the Iraqi (nuclear) weapons program is based largely—perhaps 90%—on analysis of imprecise intelligence.

However, because Rumsfeld suppressed this report, the Bush-Cheney administration was able to fabricate reports saying that Iraq was seeking to develop nuclear weapons. These reports consisted of claims about Iraq's acquisition of (1) aluminum tubes and (2) yellowcake (uranium ore) from Niger.

Aluminum Tubes: In September 8, 2002, Michael R. Gordon and Judith Miller published a front-page story in the *New York Times* entitled "US Says Hussein Intensifies Quest for A-Bomb Parts." It began:

> More than a decade after Saddam Hussein agreed to give up weapons of mass destruction, Iraq has stepped up its quest for nuclear weapons and has embarked on a worldwide hunt for materials to make an atomic bomb, Bush administration officials said today. In the last 14 months, Iraq has sought to buy thousands of specially designed aluminum tubes, which American officials believe were intended as components of centrifuges to enrich uranium.[38]

"The first sign of a 'smoking gun,'" concluded Gordon and Miller, "may be a mushroom cloud."

The "administration officials" to whom the authors refer were Cheney's people, especially Scooter Libby. Planning to use this story to begin their media blitz on the need to remove Saddam, several members of the administration were set to be interviewed on Sunday morning talk shows the day the Gordon-Miller story appeared. As James Bamford observed: "It was a perfect scheme—leak the secrets the night before so you can talk about them the next morning."[39] This scheme allowed these officials to make their claims by attributing them to the authoritative *New York Times:*

- "[I]t's now public," said Cheney on *Meet the Press*, that Saddam "has been seeking to acquire . . . through this particular channel the kinds of tubes that are necessary to build a centrifuge."

- On *Fox News*, Powell spoke of the "specialized aluminum tubing" that "we saw in reporting just this morning."

- Saying that the tubes "are only really suited for nuclear weapons programs," Rice told Wolf Blitzer's audience: "We don't want the smoking gun to be a mushroom cloud."

However, Rice's claim was untrue. State Department experts concluded that the tubes were *not* intended for use in Iraq's nuclear weapons program. Both the Department of Energy and Mohamed ElBaradei—the head of the International Atomic Energy Agency—said that the aluminum tubes were likely for artillery rockets, not centrifuges. Jonathan Landay of Knight Ridder Newspapers reported:

> Several senior administration officials and intelligence officers, all of whom spoke only on the condition of anonymity, charged that the decision to publicize one analysis of the aluminum tubes and ignore the contrary one is typical of the way the administration has been handling intelligence about Iraq.

In addition, Landay reported:

> [David] Albright, the director of the Institute for Science and International Security, a non-partisan think tank, said he has been told that scientists at the Lawrence Livermore National Laboratory in California and other US nuclear weapons facilities disagreed with that assessment but have been ordered not to say anything.[40]

With this dissent suppressed, Bush was able to say in his 2003 State of the Union address: "Our intelligence sources tell us that he has attempted to purchase high-strength aluminum tubes suitable for nuclear weapons production."[41]

Yellowcake from Niger: The Bush administration also claimed that Iraq had obtained hundreds of tons of yellowcake, an unprocessed uranium-rich ore. The claim was rooted in documents purportedly showing that Niger in 2000 had sold 500 tons of yellowcake. Upon learning of this story, Cheney asked the CIA to check out the story. The task was given to former ambassador Joseph Wilson, who had served in that region of Africa.

When Wilson arrived in Niger, he learned that the Niger story had been discredited by a four-star general, the ambassador to Niger, the CIA, the State Department, and the French, who said: "We told the Americans, 'Bullshit. It doesn't make any sense.'" Wilson also learned from experts that such a sale would have been improbable, likely impossible.[42]

When he returned to Washington, Wilson filed a report, which was circulated in the normal way, so he assumed that the president had seen it.

He was shocked, therefore, to hear Bush utter these 16 words in his State of the Union address: "The British government has learned that Saddam Hussein recently sought significant quantities of uranium from Africa."[43]

Wilson spent some time trying to correct the story, but finally gave up, saying to Seymour Hersh: "I gave them months to correct the record, . . . but they kept on lying." So he wrote a *New York Times* op-ed, "What I Didn't Find in Africa." As a result, there was much discussion about how those now-notorious "16 words" got into Bush's talk. "Had there been even a peep that the agency did not want that sentence," Rice said on *Face the Nation*, "it would have been gone." But there had been far more than a peep: Rice's National Security Council assistant Stephen Hadley had received two CIA memos calling the intelligence dubious, one of which had gone directly to Rice.

A little later, but prior to the attack on Iraq, the International Atomic Energy Agency showed that the documents about the sale of many tons of yellowcake were obvious forgeries. For example, they referred to an organization that had gone out of existence in 1989, and they were signed by an official who had been out of office for a decade. The documents were so error-filled, said an IAEA official, that "they could be spotted by someone using Google on the Internet."[44]

Nevertheless, although Wilson was only one of many people who discredited the yellowcake story, Cheney set out to discredit *him* by having Libby and Karl Rove inform journalists that Wilson was married to an undercover CIA agent, Valerie Plame Wilson. The idea was evidently to discredit Joseph Wilson by falsely suggesting that his trip to Niger was a junket arranged by his wife. Because revealing the identity of an undercover agent is a federal crime, a special investigation resulted. The White House for many months categorically denied that Libby and Rove were responsible for the leak, but that was later shown to be untrue.[45] Libby was convicted of lying to the grand jury. Joe and Valerie Wilson concluded that he had lied to protect Cheney.[46]

In Sum: Every claim made by the Bush Cheney administration about WMD proved to be false.

CLAIMS ABOUT AL-QAEDA AND 9/11

In addition to the Bush-Cheney administration's claims about illegal WMD, its propaganda equally argued that Saddam was linked with al-Qaeda terrorists. Indeed, there was a strong desire to link Saddam with the 9/11 attack, as shown by the quote above from Donald Rumsfeld shortly after the attack on the Pentagon. He wanted, he said, to know whether the information was "good enough hit S.H. [Saddam Hussein] at same time. Not only UBL [Usama bin Laden]."[47]

Without claiming that Saddam was involved in 9/11, the Bush-Cheney administration falsely said that he was connected to al-Qaeda. Rep. Henry Waxman showed that the Bush-Cheney administration made "237 misleading statements about the threat posed by Iraq," 61 of which "misrepresented Iraq's ties to al-Qaeda."[48]

Here are three examples:

- Bush said: "We have learned that Iraq has trained al-Qaeda members in bomb-making and poisons and deadly gases."

- Bush also said that we "know that Iraq is harboring a terrorist network headed by a senior al Qaeda terrorist planner."

- Cheney said: "If we're successful in Iraq. . . , we will have struck a major blow right at the heart of the base, if you will, the geographic base of the terrorists who have had us under assault now for many years, but most especially on 9/11."[49]

The claims about Iraq's WMD and Iraq's relation to al-Qaeda were equally important: Without fear that Saddam had WMD, the idea that he had connections with al-Qaeda would have created no great concern among Americans. But equally, the claim that Iraq had WMD would not have been very frightening to Americans apart from the idea that they would be employed by al-Qaeda—the organization able to outwit the world's most sophisticated defense system, attack the Pentagon, and destroy the World Trade Center.

As Bush put it, "Imagine those 19 hijackers with other weapons and other plans—this time armed by Saddam Hussein."[50] The equal importance of WMD and al-Qaeda was also expressed by Rumsfeld when he said:

> Iraq's weapons of mass terror and the terror networks to which the Iraqi regime are linked are not two separate themes—not two separate threats. They are part of the same threat.[51]

Connecting Iraq and al-Qaeda took some effort. Ten days after 9/11 Bush and Cheney were given a CIA briefing that said:

> [T]he US intelligence community had no evidence linking the Iraqi regime of Saddam Hussein to the attacks and there was scant credible evidence that Iraq had any significant collaborative ties with Al Qaeda.[52]

To deal with this problem, the Bush-Cheney administration tried to create the needed evidence. There were three major attempts:

Mohamed Atta in Prague

One claim of a link between Iraq and al-Qaeda involved Mohamed Atta. Two months after 9/11, Cheney was asked on *Meet the Press* whether Iraq was involved in 9/11. In response, Cheney referred to a story floating around about Atta meeting an Iraqi in Prague and said that had "been pretty well confirmed"—"[Mohamed Atta] did go to Prague and he did meet with a senior official of the Iraqi intelligence service in Czechoslovakia last April, several months before the attack."[53]

Cheney's dismissal of intelligence that contradicted his policy was illustrated by his assertion that this report had been "pretty well confirmed": Actually, the day just before Cheney's *Meet the Press* interview, the White House Situation Room had received this information from the CIA: "Terrorism Discovery That 11 September 2001 Hijacker Mohammed [sic] Atta Did Not Travel to the Czech Republic on 31 May 2000."[54] But Cheney refused to give up the story.

This refusal resulted in a controversy while Secretary of State Powell was preparing his speech for the Security Council. Cheney's staff pressed Powell repeatedly to include the story about Atta in Prague. Powell would take it out of his speech but Libby and others kept putting it back in. Powell finally "threw the paper down on the table and said, 'I'm not saying that.'"[55]

Ibn al-Sheikh al-Libi

In 2001, a low-level Al-Qaeda operative named Ibn al-Sheikh al-Libi was captured in Pakistan and sent to the US detention facility in Kandahar. A combination of torture and threats elicited from al-Libi the information that Iraq had provided training in chemical and biological weapons. Noting that his "information" contained no specific details, the DIA called it "likely" that "this individual is intentionally misleading the debriefers."

For the White House's purposes, however, the information was adequate. In a major speech just before Congress was to vote on the Iraq War resolution, Bush declared: "We've learned that Iraq has trained al-Qaeda members in bomb making and poisons and deadly gases." And although Colin Powell rejected the Atta story, he accepted this one. Speaking of a "sinister nexus between Iraq and the al-Qaeda terrorist network," he related the "story of a senior terrorist operative telling how Iraq provided training in [chemical and biological] weapons to al-Qaeda."[56]

Thanks to al-Libi's claims, he became, said Ray McGovern, "the poster boy for the success of the Cheney/Bush torture regime; that is, until he publicly recanted and explained that he only told his interrogators what he thought would stop the torture." To the Bush administration, however, this recantation was unimportant, because it did not come until after the invasion of Iraq was well underway.[57]

Cheney, of course, had long argued that torture, such as waterboarding, works. Most experts, however, accept the view of General John Kimmons, former head of Army intelligence, who said: "No good intelligence is going to come from abusive practices." However, added McGovern, "if it's bad intelligence you're after, torture works like a charm." That is, torture "induces those being tortured to fabricate answers that they think the torturers want to hear."[58]

Indeed, there is considerable evidence that the primary reason for torture after 9/11 was to produce false confessions. For example, Lawrence Wilkerson, Powell's chief of staff, said that the Bush-Cheney's administration's "principal priority for intelligence was not aimed at pre-empting another terrorist attack on the US but discovering a smoking gun linking Iraq and al-Qa'ida."[59]

Major Paul Burney, a US Army psychiatrist sent to Guantanamo in 2002, indicated that torture was used at that facility to get the desired statements:

> A large part of the time we were focused on trying to establish a link between al-Qaeda and Iraq and we were not successful. The more frustrated people got in not being able to establish that link there was more and more pressure to resort to measures that might produce more immediate results.[60]

Tahir Jalil Habbush

Early in 2003, prior to the start of the war, Tahir Jalil Habbush, the head of Iraqi intelligence, had secret weekly meetings in Jordan with an official of British intelligence. Habbush told this official that Iraq had no WMD programs or stockpiles. Rob Richer, the head of the CIA's Near East division, said that the White House wanted to go to war. So the White House simply ignored the report by Habbush, gave him $5 million to keep quiet, and had him resettled in Jordan. And then, wrote Pulitzer Prize-winning journalist Ron Suskind in *The Way of the World*:

> The White House had concocted a fake letter from Habbush to Saddam, backdated to July 1, 2001. It said that 9/11 ringleader Mohammed [sic] Atta had actually trained for his mission in Iraq—thus showing, finally, that there was an operation link between Saddam and al-Qaeda. . . . A handwritten letter, with Habbush's name on it, would be fashioned by CIA and then hand-carried by a CIA agent to Baghdad for dissemination.[61]

This fake letter appeared too late to help promote the drive to go to war, but being published on the day in December 2003 that Saddam was captured, it helped justify the war. On NBC, for example, journalist Con Coughlin called the letter "concrete proof that al-Qaeda was working with Saddam."[62]

CORRUPTION OF THE CIA

Any discussion about how Cheney and Rumsfeld were able to sell their war against Iraq would be incomplete without a treatment of how Cheney, with the acquiescence of CIA director George Tenet,[63] corrupted the CIA's assessments. This corruption was a big factor in why Powell gave such an inaccurate presentation.

Powell had wanted to make a trustworthy presentation, one that would not ruin his reputation for truthfulness. After he was persuaded to address the UN Security Council, he refused to base it on a dossier that had been prepared by Libby and other members of Cheney's team.[64] Assuming that CIA analysis was carried out in a professional way, free from distortion by political goals (as it had been prior to 9/11),[65] he went to the CIA to get reliable information. But he ended up giving the United Nations a lecture that was, in James Bamford's words, "[m]ade up almost entirely of false charges."[66] The basic problem was that Powell did not realize how thoroughly Cheney had corrupted CIA analyses with regard to Iraq.

Given his plan to justify war on the basis of WMD and terrorism, Cheney started traveling to CIA headquarters to talk to analysts. Some of them, reported the *Washington Post*, "felt they were being pressured to make their assessments fit with the Bush administration's policy objectives."[67] Some of the descriptions of the pressure were even stronger. One CIA official said:

> [T]here was a great deal of pressure to find a reason to go to war with Iraq. And the pressure was not just subtle; it was blatant. At one point in January 2003, the person's boss called a meeting and gave them their marching orders. And he said, "You know what—if Bush wants to go to war, it's your job to give him a reason to do so.[68]

In a report entitled "The Constitution in Crisis," Congressman John Conyers wrote:

> A former CIA analyst described the intense pressure brought to bear on the CIA by the Bush Administration in these terms: "The analysts at the C.I.A. were beaten down defending their assessments. And they blame George Tenet"—the CIA director—"for not protecting them . . . from Dick Cheney, who with his sidekick I. Lewis Libby visited CIA headquarters about a dozen times to personally ensure that CIA analysts knew precisely what their instructions were—what conclusions their analysis should yield."[69]

The analysts were right to blame Tenet. James Bamford wrote:

> Normally the CIA Director would protect his people from that kind of pressure. But . . . Tenet decided against intervening directly whenever employees told him that they felt pressure while writing analytical papers on Iraq. . . . Ultimately Tenet lost sight of his role. Instead of the country's apolitical eyes and ears around the world, . . . he simply became the President's cheerleader.[70]

In fact, Cheney and Bush likely retained Tenet from the Clinton administration because of what Sidney Blumenthal called "his chameleon-like quality of adapting to any environment."[71] It was this corrupted CIA to which Powell went to get reliable intelligence to use in his UN speech.

SUCCESS OF BUSH-CHENEY PROPAGANDA

The Bush-Cheney administration's propaganda campaign was enormously successful. Shortly before the war on Iraq was launched, the idea that Iraq had weapons of mass destruction was accepted by 70 percent of the American people. That same percentage believed that Iraq was connected to al-Qaeda, even that Saddam Hussein had played a direct role in the 9/11 attacks. Indeed, a 2006 poll showed that almost 90% of the US troops in Iraq believed that the war was "retaliation for Saddam's role in 9/11."[72]

As a result, pointed out Stefan Halper and Jonathan Clarke, the Bush-Cheney administration was "able to build the environment surrounding the terrorist attacks of September 2001 into a wide moral platform from which to launch a preemptive strike."[73]

Incidentally, the success of this propaganda campaign could have been predicted, based on the observation of Hermann Göring, one of the top Nazi officials: "[I]t is the *leaders* of the country who determine the policy and it is always a simple matter to drag the people along," said Göring. "All you have to do is tell them they are being attacked."[74]

Accordingly, just as the propaganda offensive against Osama bin Laden, al-Qaeda, and the Taliban created almost unanimous acceptance of the war in Afghanistan, the propaganda offensive directed at Saddam Hussein was able to channel this fear, anxiety, and desire for revenge into a widespread feeling that a war to remove Saddam was justified.

However, this propaganda was based almost entirely on lies. On the last page of his *A Pretext for War*, James Bamford wrote:

> [T]he Bush administration's massive disinformation campaign, abetted by a lazy and timid press, succeeded spectacularly. In the end, it was the power of lies, not logic, that was the deciding factor.[75]

Although Republicans and the corporate media still commonly claim that the Bush administration was misled by faulty intelligence,[76] Paul Krugman in an op-ed entitled "Errors and Lies," said that the invasion of Iraq "was worse than a mistake, it was a crime."[77]

DISASTROUS CONSEQUENCES

Like the Afghanistan War, the Iraq War was disastrous for both the United States and the country it attacked.

Consequences for the USA

Although the negative consequences of the Iraq war were most serious for Iraq, this war was also very harmful to the United States.

Death and Injury: The war caused around 4,500 American deaths and hundreds of thousands of serious injuries, including over 320,000 brain injuries. In addition, as much as 35 percent of the returning veterans suffer from PTSD.[78]

Economic Cost: Although the Bush administration predicted the war would cost a total of $50-60 billion, the war had cost $4 trillion by 2014 and may, counting interest to the national debt, come to more than $6 trillion over the following decades.[79]

Opportunity Costs: The devotion of these billions to the war meant that this money could not be used for many important matters, such as curing cancer, rebuilding infrastructure, and especially tackling climate change (see Chapter 10).

Loss of Respect and Status: Juan Cole has written:

> In the aftermath of the invasion and occupation of Iraq, the US was widely seen as an international bully. . . . The US invasion and occupation of Iraq harmed the US in bringing into question its basic competency as a world leader. Almost everything the US did in Iraq was a disaster. . . . It looked dishonest, bumbling. It went into the war having no plans, and the plans the Bush administration made on the fly were mostly poorly thought-out and doomed to fail.[80]

Fueling Islamophobia: Added to the effect of 9/11, the Iraq war did much to fuel Islamophobia (which will be discussed in the following chapter).

Consequences for Iraq

Whereas the Iraq War had negative consequences for the United States, it was *disastrous* for Iraq, in many ways:

Iraqis Killed: Probably most surprising to Americans in general is the sheer number of Iraqis killed in the war, as the government and the media have not reported anything close to the truth. People were not told that during the first month of the war, the US and the UK unleashed over 29,000 bombs and missiles, which killed tens of thousands of civilians.

For the war as a whole, the mainstream media primarily use the Iraq Body Count, which estimates that the war caused 110,000 Iraqi deaths. However, this figure was reached by simply adding up media reports of civilian killings. In 2006, *The Lancet* published a scientific study, which combined violent deaths with deaths caused by war-caused deprivation as well. This study, accepted by most epidemiologists, estimated that 655,000 Iraq deaths had already occurred by 2006. By 2008, a British study said that the figure had risen to over a million. And in 2015, Gideon Polya, using "UN and US Just War Policy" figures, estimated that 2.3 million Iraqi deaths had been caused by the war.[81]

Murder and Genocide: According to Nicolas J.S. Davies (who authored *Blood On Our Hands: The American Invasion and Destruction of Iraq*):

> The US recruited, trained and deployed at least 27 brigades of Iraqi Special Police Commandos, who detained, tortured and murdered tens of thousands of men and boys in Baghdad and elsewhere in 2005 and 2006. At the peak of this campaign, 3,000 bodies per month were brought to the Baghdad morgue and an Iraqi human rights group matched 92% of the corpses to reported abductions by US-backed forces. US Special Forces officers in Special Police Transition Teams worked with each Iraqi unit, and a high-tech command center staffed by US and Iraqi personnel maintained US command and control of these forces throughout their reign of terror. . . . In 2006 and 2007, US forces worked in tandem with the Special Police Commandos (by then rebranded "National Police" following the exposure of one of their torture centers) . . . to complete the ethnic cleansing of Baghdad." The US occupation deliberately targeted the Sunni Arab minority in Iraq, eventually killing about 10% of Sunni Arabs and driving about half of them from their homes. This clearly meets the definition of genocide in international treaties.[82]

Health Crisis: Dr. Margaret Chan of the World Health Organization said in 2015, "The situation [in Iraq] is bad, really bad, and rapidly getting worse."

And according to international health consultant César Chelala, who quoted that statement, added:

> 2.9 million people have fled their homes, 6.9 million Iraqis need immediate access to essential health services, and 7.1 million need easier access to water, sanitation and hygiene assistance. Medical facilities, which in the 1980s were among the best in the Middle East, have deteriorated significantly after the 2003 invasion. As a result of the collapsed sanitation infrastructure, the incidence of cholera, dysentery and typhoid fever has increased. Malnutrition among children and other childhood diseases have also increased. . . . [It] is extremely difficult to find Iraqi doctors willing to work in certain areas because they fear for their security. . . . [P]eople's health [is] being seriously affected by the use of white phosphorus and depleted uranium by American and British forces. . . . We are facing nothing less than the almost total destruction of a country by an ill-advised invasion.[83]

Torture: Torture was more widespread than media reports about Abu Ghraib suggested. A leaked 2004 report from the Red Cross's International Committee documented torture of various types: mock executions, waterboarding, suffocation, electric shocks, beatings, burning, cutting with knives, deadly forms of hanging, injurious use of flexi-cuffs, extreme heat and cold, starvation and thirst, sleep deprivation, sensory deprivation, rape and sodomy, sexual humiliation, threats against family members, and withholding medical treatment.

This torture was carried out with virtual impunity: The most severe punishment was a five-month prison sentence, and even though torture was authorized from the highest levels, no criminal charges were brought against any officer above the rank of Major.[84]

Destruction of Cultural Heritage: In 2015, the Global Policy Forum said:

> The United States and its allies ignored the warnings of organizations and scholars concerning the protection of Iraq's cultural heritage, including museums, libraries, archaeological sites and other precious repositories. Arsonists badly burned the National Library and looters pillaged the National Museum. Looters also damaged or destroyed many historic buildings and artifacts. . . . Coalition forces destroyed or badly damaged many historic urban areas and buildings, while thieves have ruined thousands of incomparable, unprotected archeological sites.[85]

Insurgency and Civil War: Beyond the initial attack on Iraq, many of the consequences listed above resulted from an unbelievably stupid decision made by the Bush-Cheney administration three weeks after that initial attack. As described by Dexter Filkins of the *New York Times:*

> In 2003, the US military, on orders of President Bush, invaded Iraq, and nineteen days later threw out Saddam's government. A few days after that, President Bush . . . decreed the dissolution of the Iraqi Army. . . . Overnight, at least two hundred and fifty thousand Iraqi men—armed, angry, and with military training—were suddenly humiliated and out of work. This was probably the single most catastrophic decision of the American venture in Iraq. In a stroke, the Administration helped enable the creation of the Iraqi insurgency. . . . Many of those suddenly unemployed Iraqi soldiers took up arms against the United States.[86]

Another disastrous decision by the Bush-Cheney administration was its choice of Nouri al-Maliki as the Prime Minister of Iraq in 2006. He was such a partisan Shiite that he made it difficult for Sunnis to get work, allotted less electricity to them, and transformed Baghdad into a largely Shiite city. His sectarianism led to violent conflict, with elements of a civil war between Sunnis and Shias. This conflict led to the rise of various insurgent groups, including al-Qaeda in Iraq.[87]

CONCLUSION

That the Iraq War was not based on faulty intelligence, but on lies, has been declared in the titles of many books and articles, such as: "Lie by Lie: A Timeline of How We Got into Iraq"; "9/11 and Iraq: The War's Greatest Lie;" and *The Five Biggest Lies Bush Told Us About Iraq.*[88]

Once it is agreed that the Bush-Cheney administration lied us into war, one may be led to raise Joseph Wilson's question: Noting in 2003 that the administration lied about an issue as fundamental as going to war, Wilson asked: "[W]hat else are they lying about?"[89]

In any case, the lie about Iraq led to the virtual destruction of that country. Moreover, it also led, in conjunction with the war in Afghanistan, to chaos in much of the Middle East, partly because Al-Qaeda in Iraq turned into ISIS (Islamic State in Iraq and Syria)—which will be discussed in Chapter 6.

5 • ISLAMOPHOBIA

In a 2010 book entitled *Islamophobia: Making Muslims the Enemy*, Peter Gottschalk and Gabriel Greenberg wrote that the term "Islamophobia" calls attention to unjustified discrimination, just as "racism," "sexism," and "anti-Semitism" have drawn attention to other forms of unjustified discrimination.[1] In his edited volume *Islamophobia/Islamophilia*, Andrew Shryock wrote:

> What is most problematic about Islamophobia is its essentializing and universalizing quality, which casts both Islam itself and all Muslims as real or potential enemies in a way that, if similarly applied to Jews or Christians, would seem delusional at best, vile at worst.[2]

To speak of Islamophobia as "universalizing," explained Stephen Sheehi in his book *Islamophobia*, means all Muslims are blamed for the statements of the few.[3]

This universalizing is almost a complete distortion: Islamists who employ violence for political ends are based on Salafism, a "philosophical outlook which seeks to revive the practices of the first three generations of Islam, who are collectively known as the *as-salaf as-saliheen,* or 'pious predecessors,'" explained a 2016 book entitled *Salafi-Jihadism.* The Salafist movement is comprised of three groups: the quietists, the (non-violent) activists, and the jihadists. The jihadist group is by far the smallest, containing only 0.5 percent of the world's Muslims.[4]

ROOTS OF TODAY'S ISLAMOPHOBIA

"Islamophobia" is a fairly new term, which arose in Britain in the 1990s in response to anti-Muslim sentiment, which had grown because of various developments, including the Rushdie affair and the first Gulf War. The first major publication on the issue was *Islamophobia: A Challenge for Us All*, which appeared in 1997. It defined Islamophobia as "an unfounded hostility towards Islam," along with "the practical consequences of such hostility," such as "the exclusion of Muslims from mainstream political and social affairs."[5]

Widespread usage of the term arose even later in the United States, mainly after 9/11. But the phenomenon was much older.

Medieval and Early Modern Roots

The phenomenon goes back at least to the First Crusade in 1095, when Pope Urban II portrayed Muslims as "*the* enemy of Christianity and Christendom: their normative, fundamental, quintessential, universal enemy." At a time of internal strife and violence within, "Christians could unite in peace," explained Tomaž Mastnak, "in a God-willed war against Muslims." Indeed,

> The antagonist difference between themselves and Muslims became at this crucial point a constitutive element of the Latin Christians' collective identity. . . . A defining trait of [the new] global order was the fundamental unacceptability to Western Christians of the existence of Muslims as Muslims.[6]

Four centuries later, a new form of Islamophobia arose in response to the fall of Constantinople to the Turks in 1453. In 1458, the new leader of Western Christians, Pope Pius II, revitalized the image of the Muslim enemy to cultivate European unity.

> When Europe became the reference point for the sense of "us-ness" directed against the Turk, the Muslim became the enemy of Europe. The rallying cry, which transformed Christendom into Europe and Latin Christians into Europeans, was to "liberate Europe," to "chase the Turk out of Europe."[7]

In the following centuries, there were many plans to promote peace and unity among Christian nations by joining forces against Muslims. One of the earliest was the seventeenth-century "Grand Design" of the Duke of Sully, which aimed to "convert the continual wars among its several princes, into a perpetual war against the Infidels"—which could have been termed a "perpetual crusade."[8]

This frame of mind was even shared by leading thinkers of the Enlightenment. For example, Leibniz, considering war within Europe scandalous, proposed a new Teutonic Order that would engage in permanent, unceasing warfare against Turks. Abbé de Saint Pierre, who was eulogized as an "enemy of religious intolerance," wanted to "extirpate Mohammedanism . . . one of the greatest scourges of the human race."[9]

Orientalism

Although the negative image of Islam continued, big changes occurred after the Crusades: The ideal of a Christian Europe was replaced by a new focus on nationalism and a desire of the nations to colonize foreign lands. This desire encouraged the rise of a new field of study, "Orientalism," through which the secrets of the East could be unlocked. Some of the Orientalist scholars saw themselves as agents of empire, while others provided disinterested scholarship. However, said Deepa Kumar in her book *Islamophobia and the Politics of Empire*: "Whether consciously or not, Orientalists produced a body of work that aided the project of imperialism."[10]

In any case, the Orientalist scholars continued to produce negative images of Islam (as well as other Eastern religions). In the nineteenth century, especially, the Orientalists began focusing on differences between the West and the East: Because of its roots in ancient Greece, the West had unique qualities, including "freedom, law, rationality, science, progress, intellectual curiosity, and the spirit of invention, adventure and enterprise."[11]

By contrast, all the civilizations of the East were inferior. The world of Islam, in particular, was characterized as premodern, backward, primitive, despotic, static, undemocratic, and rigid.[12]

One result of this contrast was a paternalistic attitude, as exemplified in Rudyard Kipling's 1899 poem, "The White Man's Burden." Portraying peoples of the Orient as "half devil, half child," it portrayed them as needing protection and guidance. In French, the responsibility to civilize the East was called *mission civilisatrice*.[13]

Edward Said, the great critic of Orientalism,[14] noted in 1980 the tendency of US writings about the Muslim world to present "a series of crude, essentialized caricatures of the Islamic world presented in such a way as to make that world vulnerable to military aggression."[15] The orient, said Deepa Kumar, was portrayed as "unchanging, barbaric, misogynistic, uncivilized, and despotic"—a portrait that implied "the responsibility of the West to intervene in these static societies and bring about change."[16]

American Islamophobia in the 20th Century

Just as Christianity and then Europe had long had a felt need for an enemy, the same has been true of America. In this case, the need was originally filled by the battle to wrest the continent from Native Americans and Europeans, especially Spain. In the 20th century, new enemies were provided by Fascism and then Communism. Scholars of Islamophobia have described how Islam replaced Communism as the arch-enemy. In "The Lies of Islamophobia," John Feffer wrote:

> In the theology of the Cold War, the Soviet Union replaced the Islamic world as the untrustworthy infidel. However unconsciously, the old crusader myths about Islam translated remarkably easily into governing assumptions about the communist enemy.

Although the Cold War ended with the disappearance of the Soviet Union in 1991, Feffer continued, that era's mindset did not disappear. "The prevailing mythology was simply transferred back to the Islamic world."[17] Sheehi wrote:

> With the fall of the Soviet Union and the rise of the United States as the

unchallenged global hegemon, the preexisting forms of Orientalism and Arabophobia were blended into new forms of political Islamophobia. . . . [Arabs] are still identified as the source of all things malevolent within Islam. However, the difference between previous strains of Orientalism and contemporary Islamophobia is that the sins of Arab Muslims are now visited on all Muslims. Now all Muslims are saddled with the failures, irrationalism, and backwardness that Orientalists previously defined as particular to the Semitic Arab culture and history. Islamophobia in North America is Orientalism on steroids.[18]

The transition from Orientalism to Islamophobia was pioneered in America by Bernard Lewis, who came from England to Princeton in 1974. As the neoconservative movement developed, integrating hardline Cold Warriors, American Zionists, and members of the Evangelical Right, Lewis became its in-house academic.

He provided them with a moral argument that reincarnated European colonialism's *mission civilisatrice* into an imperative that would define the necessity for the United States' increased military, political and economic intervention in the Middle East.[19]

To a great extent, it was because of Lewis that, in Sheehi's words: "Islamophobia has emerged as the dominant ideological foil that has underwritten US foreign policy since the end of the Cold War."[20]

In his 1990 essay, "The Roots of Muslim Rage,"[21] Lewis warned of an impending "clash of civilizations," which was then popularized by Samuel Huntington in an essay and book of that title. Portraying Islamic civilization as an especially dangerous threat to the West, Lewis and Huntington prepared the way for defining Islam as the post-Cold War enemy.[22]

Muslim rage, Lewis argued, is based on Arab culture's "acute discomfort with the supremacy of the non-Muslim West as well as an envy of that supremacy." As a result, there has been "a rising tide of rebellion against this Western paramountcy [sic] and a desire to reassert Muslim values and restore Muslim greatness." This rebellion takes the form of *jihad*, or holy war, said Lewis, because Muslims think: "What is truly evil and unacceptable is the domination of infidels over true believers."[23]

Just as aggressive Islamophobia has generally been rooted in imperialistic desires, this has been true in spades for the post-Cold War imperialism of the neoconservatives. The neocons hoped, as discussed in Chapter 2, to create the first truly global empire. Realizing that they would need to win over the American public, they stressed that America's domination of the world would be benevolent, in the interests of all nations. In 1998, neocon Robert Kagan published "The Benevolent Empire," and in June 2001, Charles Krauthammer wrote: "[W]e are not just any hegemon. We run a uniquely benign imperium."[24]

Whereas Lewis had led the transference in intellectual and political circles from Communism to Islam as the arch-enemy, this transference among the general public would require dramatic events in the world. This need was provided by the 444-day confinement in 1979 of members of the American embassy by Iranian students, the deaths in 1983 of hundreds of marines in Lebanon, Ayatollah Khomeini's *fatwa* consigning Salman Rushdie to death in 1989 for his *Satanic Verses,* and the 1993 bombing of the World Trade Center. But something even more dramatic was needed to lead the American public to support the neocon argument that major interventions in the Muslim world were needed.

9/11: NEW BASIS FOR IMPERIALISM

"What better way to promote this ideology," asked Deepa Kumar,

> than to create an over-arching enemy, the Muslim 'evildoers' . . . against whom America, the great and the good, should make war? September 11 provided the neocons with the enemy they needed to promote their vision.[25]

In fact, as pointed out in Chapter 2, the neocon Project for the New American Century (PNAC) had itself said, in its 2000 document *Rebuilding America's Defenses*, that its vision could be realized more quickly if there were "some catastrophic and catalyzing event—like a new Pearl Harbor."[26]

The 9/11 attack did, in fact, end up being considered a New Pearl Harbor. As mentioned in Chapter 2, Bush himself reportedly wrote in his diary the night of the attacks: "The Pearl Harbor of the 21st century took place today."[27] Moreover, commentators very quickly published essays supporting the idea of responding to 9/11 as a new Pearl Harbor. For example, just after Bush's address to the nation on 9/11, Henry Kissinger posted an online article in which he said:

> The government should be charged with a systematic response that, one hopes, will end the way that the attack on Pearl Harbor ended—with the destruction of the system that is responsible for it.[28]

Also fast out of the gate was Robert Kagan, who was one of PNAC's founding directors. On September 12, calling 9/11 "the date that will live in infamy, the day the post-Cold War era ended," Kagan told *Washington Post* readers:

> One can only hope that America can respond to yesterday's monstrous attack on American soil—an attack far more awful than Pearl Harbor—with

the same moral clarity and courage as our grandfathers did. . . : Go to war with those who have launched this awful war against us.[29]

The "new Pearl Harbor" did indeed fast-track the plan to use fear of Islam to justify intervention in Islam-majority nations. As Gottschalk and Greenberg said, "Nothing before [9/11] had so crystallized fears of Muslims and Islam."[30] These fears led, furthermore, to desires for revenge. "What's needed," said a *Time* magazine article the day after 9/11, "is a unified, unifying, Pearl Harbor sort of purple American fury—a ruthless indignation that doesn't leak away in a week or two."[31] One day later, Ann Coulter notoriously said:

> We should invade [Muslims'] countries, kill their leaders and convert them to Christianity. We weren't punctilious about locating and punishing only Hitler and his top officers. We carpet-bombed German cities; we killed civilians. That's war. And this is war.[32]

PNAC's prediction, that a new Pearl Harbor would produce acceptance of its vision, certainly came true. To repeat the senior official of the Bush-Cheney administration quoted by Nicholas Lemann in Chapter 2:

> The reason September 11th appears to have been "a transformative moment" is not so much that it revealed the existence of a threat of which officials had previously been unaware as that it drastically reduced the American public's usual resistance to American military involvement overseas.[33]

Thanks to 9/11, accordingly, a "war on terror," which had long been discussed by American and Israeli leaders—a war against Muslims and Muslim-majority nations—could finally be launched. Although the "Islamic threat" had been hyped by Lewis and others since the 1980s, observed Deepa Kumar, "it was not until the events of 9/11 that this rhetoric became the United States' dominant means of justifying its imperialism."[34]

9/11 AND ISLAMIC TERRORISM

The ideology of America as a benevolent empire in attacking Iraq and other Islamic nations depended on the widespread perception of Islam as promoting terrorism. Although there had been a long history of arguments connecting Islam and terrorism, said Kumar, "these arguments managed to enter the public sphere in a significant way only after the events of 9/11."[35]

The widespread acceptance of these arguments was necessary, because Americans would not have accepted wars launched for obviously imperialistic reasons. In his 1997 book, *The Grand Chessboard*, Zbigniew Brzezinski said:

The pursuit of power and especially the economic costs and human sacrifice that the exercise of such power often requires are not generally congenial to democratic instincts. Democratization is inimical to imperial mobilization. . . . The public supported America's engagement in World War II largely because of the shock effect of the Japanese attack on Pearl Harbor. But the pursuit of power is not a goal that commands popular passion, except in conditions of a sudden threat or challenge to the public's sense of domestic well-being.[36]

"The overarching threat of 'Islamic terrorism,'" observed Kumar, "provides a useful cover for [America's] imperial ambitions."[37] Also, "the War against Terror is not really about terror," said Arundathi Roy. "It's about a superpower's self-destructive impulse toward supremacy, stranglehold, global hegemony."[38]

The widespread perception of Islam as a threatening terrorist religion has been based primarily on the 9/11 attacks. Since 9/11, wrote Greenberg and Gottschalk, "Muslims have become nearly synonymous with the term [terrorism] in the minds of many Americans."[39] But this fact did not result simply from the 9/11 attacks.

ISLAMOPHOBIA PROMOTED BY THE BUSH-CHENEY ADMINISTRATION

There have been claims that the Bush-Cheney administration did not try to promote Islamophobia, but tried to prevent it. These claims have been based on some oft-quoted statements saying that the United States was not hostile to Islam, but only to terrorists who used Islam as a pretext for terrorism. A week after 9/11, Bush met with Muslim religious and civic leaders. "Women who cover their heads," he said, "must not be intimidated in America. That's not the America I know." In a speech to the nation the following week, Bush said that "no one should be singled out for unfair treatment or unkind words because of their ethnic background or religious faith."

Words vs. Actual Policies

These statements by Bush, which suggested that he did not promote Islamophobia, were praised in 2015 by Al Jazeera host Mehdi Hasan in a *New York Times* op-ed headed "Why I Miss George W. Bush." Likewise, during a Democratic presidential debate, Hillary Clinton said that a legacy of friendly discourse "was one of the real contributions—despite all the other problems—that George W. Bush made after 9/11 when he basically said after going to a mosque in Washington, 'We are not at war with Islam.'"[40]

However, the question of whether the Bush-Cheney administration pro-moted Islamophobia does not depend on a few nice statements: As we know, "talk is cheap." Rather, the answer to this question depends upon the policies that administration actually put into effect. In response to the statements by Mehdi Hasan and Hillary Clinton, journalist Glenn Greenwald wrote an article saying: "Let's Not Whitewash George W. Bush's Actual, Heinous Record on Muslims in the US." After mentioning some of Bush's actions outside the US, such as Guantánamo, Abu Ghraib, and the destruction of Iraq, Greenwald mentioned some of his actions on American soil:

[H]e perpetrated a wide array of radical abuses aimed at Muslims in the wake of 9/11. In the weeks after the attack, more than 1,000 Muslims and Arabs were swept up by the FBI and detained without charge, often by abusing the powers allowing for detention of "material witnesses." Thousands of Muslim immigrants were deported from the US in the months following the attack. Bush quickly and secretly implemented an illegal scheme of warrantless domestic eavesdropping aimed largely at Muslims. . . . [T]he Bush DOJ indicted and prosecuted the nation's largest Muslim-American charity (Holy Land Foundation), and then perma-nently smeared the nation's largest Muslim-American civil rights organi-zation (CAIR) by officially labeling them an "unindicted co-conspirator," which meant they had no ability to challenge the accusation. . . . The actual domestic record of Bush on American Muslims—as opposed to his pretty rhetoric—is hideous.[41]

Greenwald's position was seconded in John O'Day's "Bombs Speak Louder Than Words: The Liberal Reinvention of George W. Bush." In a sardonic passage, O'Day wrote:

As the demonization of Muslims once again gains currency in American electoral politics, liberal personalities are joining the call to return to the good old days when Republicans fielded candidates who talked sweetly to the community of over 1.5 billion Muslims around the world while at the same time ordering warplanes to bomb an ever-larger number of them.

Citing a number of liberal politicians and commentators who have praised their former arch-enemy for his sweet talk, O'Day pointed out that Bush's policies, largely continued by his successor, "have kept the nation at war with Muslim peoples for 15 years."[42]

Policy Derived from the Consummate Academic Islamophobe
The stance of the Bush-Cheney administration with regard to Islamophobia can also be evaluated by looking at the main thinker it used to justify its

policies. Bernard Lewis, whose 20th-century work was discussed above, came to be known as the "Bush administration's academic face." Stephen Sheehi also called Lewis "the consummate ideologue of Islamophobia."[43]

Right after 9/11, Paul Wolfowitz, Dick Cheney, and Richard Perle organized a secret "war on terror" caucus in the White House. The "brain trust" of this caucus had three academic members, with Lewis being the central member (along with Fareed Zakaria and Fouad Ajami). This caucus designated the invasion of Iraq and removal of Saddam among the highest priorities.[44]

Lewis' explanation of "Muslim Rage" was very attractive to Cheney, as it provides an explanation of Muslim grievances in terms of an inherently visceral, irrational hate of the West, based on the shortcomings of Islamic religion and society. In other words, in Sheehi's words:

> [T]he reasons for Muslim "rage" toward the United States do not involve the long list of Western policy failures in the region; the US's unquestioning support of Israel; and Washington's "limited" support for authoritarian regimes and their human rights abuses. Nor could the origins of this rage lie in the history of the West's designs on the region's oil.

Rather, said Lewis, "the origins of 'Muslim Rage' spring from Muslims' own feelings of resentment, jealousy and impotence toward the successful West."[45]

Accordingly, said Sheehi, Lewis gave Cheney and the other neocons a moral argument for America's increased political and military intervention in the Middle East. In private dinners with Cheney after 9/11, Lewis urged him to wage war against Muslims, assuring him that "America was taking on a sick civilization, one that it had to beat into submission."[46]

POST-9/11 ISLAMOPHOBIA

The 9/11 attacks, combined with the Bush-Cheney policies, were extremely effective in promoting Islamophobia in America. Increasing Islamophobia is generally reflected in an increase in the number of hate crimes directed at Muslims, and, said Sheehi:

> After September 11, the level of hate crimes, vandalism and even murder of Arabs and Muslims (and other peoples of color mistaken for Arabs or Muslims) exploded in the United States. . . . Human Rights Watch noted that anti-Arab hate crimes spiked 1700 percent.[47]

An FBI report put the increase in hate crimes in absolute terms: "Prior to 9/11, the FBI recorded just 28 hate crimes against Muslims. The following year it increased to 481."[48]

Although 9/11 did not create Islamophobia, it did, Sheehi said, "un-chain the paradigms, hate-speech, hate-acts and political programs and policies that were hinged by political latches and ethical filters."

The anti-Muslim invective sometimes seemed to have no limits, as illustrated by Ann Coulter's previously quoted statement—that America should invade Muslim countries, kill their leaders, and convert them to Christianity.[49] Radio host Michael Savage referred to Arabs as "nonhu-mans" and "racist, fascist bigots," who deserve to be "nuked."[50]

In some cases, the increased Islamophobia clearly arose in reaction to the 9/11 attacks themselves, as it arose right after 9/11. This instantaneous Islamophobia was illustrated by Coulter's murderous outburst—along with another statement the same month: "Not all Muslims may be terrorists, but all terrorists are Muslims—at least all terrorists capable of assembling a murderous plot against America that leaves 7,000 people dead in under two hours."[51]

This instantaneous Islamophobia was also illustrated by well-known writer Christopher Hitchens, who was led by 9/11 to refer to Muslims as "theocratic barbarians" and "Islamofascists" (in his book titled *God Is Not Great*, which ridicules the Arabic refrain *Allah Akbar*, meaning "God is great"). Shortly after the 9/11 attacks, he wrote that he was going to pros-ecute Islam—"the most frightful enemy"—for the rest of his life. Likewise, Sam Harris, another member of the so-called New Atheists, said he started his first book attacking Islam on the day after the 9/11 attacks.[52]

However, although many Americans were converted instantaneously to fear and hatred of Islam by the 9/11 attacks, the Islamophobia in the immediately following weeks, months, and even first four years was not nearly as strong as it would become in following years.

Two months after 9/11, polls showed that 59% of Americans had a favorable impression of Islam, which was higher than before the attacks. Although Americans felt intensely threatened by Islamic fundamentalism, this fear was outweighed by "sympathy for innocent Muslims defamed by the actions of extremists and targeted by retaliatory hate crimes."[53]

However, this response to Muslims did not last. By 2004, only 25% of Americans expressed a positive opinion of Islam, and 46% of them consid-ered Islam more likely than other religions to encourage violence.[54]

In an essay describing anti-Islamic sentiment in the decade after 9/11, Christopher Smith reported that there was "a gradual increase of animos-ity toward Islam during the period from 2002 to 2010," and this increase occurred primarily among people who knew little about Islam. "Largely neutral toward Islam in 2003, the uninformed were overwhelmingly unfa-vorable toward it by 2006."[55]

Prior to 2006, "favorable" responses about Islam outnumbered "unfavorable" ones in virtually every poll. But in 2006 the "unfavorable" responses exceeded 50% and then continued to rise.[56] In 2010, there was an especially large spike in hostility to Muslims and Islam. Reza Aslan, the well-known author of *No God but God,* wrote:

> Ten years after the attacks of 9/11, anti-Muslim sentiment is at an all-time high throughout Europe and North America, far higher than it was in the immediate aftermath of that tragic day in 2001.[57]

But this "all-time high" was soon left behind: In 2015, Al Jazeera provided this report:

> Anti-Islam and anti-Muslim bigotry is worse than ever in America. Tellingly, 73 percent [of] Americans have negative view[s] of Islam and Muslims. Only 27 percent of Americans have a favorable opinion of Muslims, down from 35 percent in 2010. Polls show that nearly half the populations in the United States and Canada hold unfavorable views toward Islam.[58]

This report seems counterintuitive: One would expect Islamophobia to be highest immediately after the 9/11 attacks and then to decline over the following years. How can this counterintuitive fact be explained? The answer is that, as Nathan Lean said in *The Islamophobia Industry,* the increase in anti-Muslim sentiment "is not the result of a naturally evolving climate of skepticism but a product that has been carefully and methodically nurtured."[59]

THE ISLAMOPHOBIA INDUSTRY

In describing the Islamophobia industry, Lean refers to it as a "tight-knit and interconnected confederation of right-wing fear merchants." Since 9/11, the merchants of this "industry of hate" have labored "to convince their compatriots that Muslims are gaining a dangerous influence in the west."[60] This confederation contains many different organizations, such as Zionist groups, fundamentalist Christian churches, and right-wing media, such as Fox News. It also contains various types of individuals.

Native Informants

One of the especially effective types of people in promoting Islamophobia are "native informants," who (allegedly) from their own experience tell the "ugly truth" about Islam.

Ayaan Hirsi Ali: Native informants usually have anti-Muslim books to sell. One of the most popular of these authors has been a woman originally from Somalia who changed her name to Ayaan Hirsi Ali. Beginning with her 2007 best-selling book, "Infidel," in which she explained why she renounced Islam, she provided a prime example of how people can win fame and fortune by fabricating false stories about themselves.

Ali's public story began in 1992, when she was given political asylum in the Netherlands after claiming that she had escaped from the violence of the civil war in Somalia. But this claim was not true: Before that war had broken out, she had moved to Kenya, where she lived securely under the protection of the United Nations, which funded her education in a good girls' school.

After coming to the Netherlands, Ali told audiences that her parents, being fanatical Muslims, forced her into a terrible marriage and said that if she offended their religious honor, they would kill her. These claims were also false: Far from being Muslim fanatics, her parents had sent her brother to a Christian school.[61]

Nevertheless, Ali's story was accepted and she became well-respected in the Netherlands, even being elected to Parliament as a member of the Party for Freedom and Democracy—which knew her story was false but covered it up.

In 2006, however, a television program revealed that Ali's entire story was false. The program's exposé threw Parliament into chaos and led Ali to resign, but her career was saved by the right-wing American Enterprise Institute, which invited her to join it—even though it also knew that her story was false.[62]

After coming to America, Ali was warmly embraced by the Christian right (although she is an atheist), and even by Harvard University. Being a beautiful and eloquent speaker and writer who characterized Islam very harshly, calling it a "destructive, nihilistic cult of death," this atheist must have been regarded by the Islamophobia community in America as a godsend. Especially helpful to anti-Muslim imperialism was her statement that on 9/11, "war had been declared in the name of Islam."[63]

Walid Shoebat: Another star of the Islamophobia circuit is a Palestinian named Walid Shoebat (the son of author Theodore Shoebat, a self-identified "proud fascist"[64]). Having become a fundamentalist Christian, Shoebat teaches that at the "end times," Muslims will join forces with Satan.[65] Before becoming a Christian, Shoebat said, he had been an Islamic terrorist.

On that basis, Shoebat gives a presentation based on his 2007 book, *Why We Want to Kill You: The Jihad Mindset and How to Defeat It.* Besides saying that Islamists are by nature violent, he claims that mainstream Muslim organizations, such as the Islamic Society of North America and the Council on American-Islamic Relations, are terrorist fronts.[66]

People have paid attention to Shoebat on the grounds that, having been a terrorist, he knows Islam from within. "Being an ex-terrorist myself," Walid Shoebat told CNN's *Anderson Cooper 360°*, "is to understand the mindset of a terrorist." The one terrorist attack he reported was the bombing of Israel's Bank Leumi in Bethlehem. However, neither CNN nor anyone else found any support for this story, and many facts suggest its falsity. The bank has no record of such an attack, and Shoebat's own uncle said that it never occurred. Shoebat's claim to have been a terrorist is now generally considered debunked.[67] Nevertheless, he is invited to speak at government-funded events, such as the second annual South Dakota Homeland Security Conference held in Rapid City in 2011.[68]

Ergun Caner: Another lying Christian is Ergun Caner, who after 9/11 became an evangelical celebrity on the basis of his jihadist-turned-Christian story, according to which he was saved by Christ at the last minute from being a jihadist wreaking havoc in America. "I hated you," he told his Christian audiences. He became well-known in right-wing Christian circles through his 2002 book, written with his brother Emir Caner, *Unveiling Islam: An Insider's Look at Muslim Life and Beliefs*, which sold hundreds of thousands of copies.[69] Through his fame, he was invited to become the dean of the theological seminary of Jerry Falwell's Liberty University.

According to Caner's story, he was born in Istanbul as the son of a devout Muslim, who raised him to be an anti-American jihadist. He said that he did not come to America until he was 14 years old.

In 2010, however, the truth came out: He was born in Sweden, came to America when he was three, and went to school in Ohio, where he was a normal American kid, participating in theater, French club, and intramural sports. Although he indeed had a Muslim father, his parents were divorced and he lived with his Swedish mother most of the time. Caner was soon removed from his deanship at Liberty University's theological seminary.[70]

"The 9/11 Mosque"

It was mentioned above that in 2010, American attitudes toward Islam became considerably more negative, with the amount of anti-Muslim hate speech and crimes rising significantly. The major cause of this was propaganda around the so-called "9/11 Mosque." This name was used by some Islamophobes to inflame people about a planned Muslim community center in lower New York City, which had been unanimously approved by the Mayor and the New York City Community Board.

This community center, called Park51, was the idea of Imam Feisel Abdul Rauf, a demure but charismatic religious leader who wanted to build it to "push back against the extremists." Intended to send a message opposite to that of the 9/11 attacks, the community center would be a family-oriented complex, having an auditorium, a movie theater, a performing arts center, a swimming pool, child care, restaurants, and a mosque. The mosque was to "encourage dialogue, harmony, and respect among all people regardless of race, faith, gender, or cultural background."

However, Islamophobes claimed that the mosque, which was to be built on property only two blocks from the World Trade Center, was to be a command center for Islamic terrorism built on this sacred land, where thousands of Americans had been killed by Muslim terrorists.

A campaign named Stop the 9/11 Mosque was begun by Pamela Geller, who in 2005 had started an anti-Muslim blog named Atlas Shrugged, after which in 2010 she started an organization called Stop Islamization of America.

Geller's campaign to disallow the community center received much support. The *New York Post* falsely claimed that the center's opening day would be September 11, 2011. Tea Party blogger Mark Williams wrote:

> The animals of allah for whom any day is a great day for a massacre are drooling over the positive response that they are getting from New York City officials over a proposal to build a 13 story monument to the 9/11 Muslims who hijacked those 4 airliners.

"The monument," Williams continued, would include "a Mosque for the worship of the terrorist's monkey-god."[71] Neocon Frank Gaffney, who pushed a claim that Muslims wanted to put American courts under Sharia law, declared: "Ground Zero mosque is designed to be a permanent, in-our-face beachhead for Sharia, a platform for inspiring the triumphalist ambitions of the faithful."[72]

Some national politicians lent support. "Nazis don't have the right to put up a sign next to the Holocaust Museum in Washington," said Newt Gingrich. "There is no reason to accept a mosque next to the World Trade Center."[73] Even liberal Democrat Howard Dean, a former governor and presidential candidate, said that building an Islamic center two blocks from the World Trade Center would be a "real affront to people who lost their lives" there on 9/11.[74]

"From Left to Right, religious to atheism," said Stephen Sheehi, "Islamophobia pervades all levels of American life."[75]

A Lucrative Industry

In speaking of an Islamophobia *industry*, Nathan Lean means in part that people have been using it to make a living, perhaps even to get wealthy, as documented in a 2015 report entitled "Fear, Inc. 2.0." To give a few examples:

- Neocon Frank Gaffney, a Fox News regular, receives $300,000 a year, which he pays himself from the approximately $3 million his Center for Security Policy receives yearly.

- David Horowitz, who has been called "the godfather of the modern anti-Muslim movement," was given a salary of $525,000 in 2013 out of the $7.2 million in gross receipts received by his Freedom Center.

- Robert Spencer has written 12 books (two of which became *New York Times* best-sellers), beginning with his 2002 book, *Islam Unveiled*.[76] He also directed Jihad Watch, which he began, as well as co-founding two organizations with Pamela Geller: Stop Islamization of America and the Freedom Defense Initiative. In addition to his other ways of making money, he has been given a $150,000 salary for his Jihad Watch from Horowitz's Freedom Center.

- Pamela Geller has received about $200,000 a year from her Stop Islamization of America (also called the American Freedom Defense Initiative), which in 2013 received almost $1 million in gross receipts.[77]

Why is Islamophobia stronger today than it was shortly after 9/11? In the conclusion of his book, Lean said:

> The Islamophobia industry is a growing enterprise, one that is knowledgeable about the devastating effects of fear on society and willing to produce and exploit it. They may be a relatively small group, but the scope of their reach and the consequences of their program . . . are not of little consequence.

The fact that the Islamophobia industry's products are "not of little consequence" is illustrated by the 2011 terrorist attacks in Norway, as discussed in the following section.

TERRORISM: ISLAMIC BY DEFINITION?

One reason why "Islam" and "terrorism" are so closely related, explained Max Hussain, is that in the public rhetoric of America and its allies, "Terrorism means nothing more than violence committed by Muslims." Therefore, he said:

The US and its allies can, by definition, never commit Terrorism even when it is beyond question that the purpose of their violence is to terrorize civilian populations into submission.

Having quoted Hussain's statement, Greenwald supported it by reference to the 2011 Norwegian attacks, in which 77 people were killed and many more injured. At first, assuming that the attacks had been carried out by a Muslim, US newspapers treated the event as an act of terrorism. But then it was learned that the attacker was Anders Breivik, a blond Norwegian, who had been influenced by Muslim-hating blogs and books, including those of Robert Spencer and Pamela Geller (both discussed in the previous section[78]). So the murderous rampage, explained the press, turned out not to be terrorism, but merely extremism. Accordingly, Greenwald said, terrorism is simply "violence committed by Muslims whom the West dislikes."[79]

Besides not being the work of a Muslim, the Norwegian attacks, it was soon learned, were carried out by a self-identified Christian. When asked about his religious beliefs, Breivik replied: "I am a militant Christian; to prevent the de-Christianization of Europe is very important."[80] Accordingly, it would seem, he was a Christian terrorist. That logical conclusion, however, led to much discussion in the mainstream press, such as an article in the *Christian Science Monitor* asking: "Norway attacks: Was Breivik a Christian terrorist?"[81]

Can There Be Christian Terrorists?

Some opinion-makers declared that he definitely was not, because he said and did non-Christian things. "Anders Breivik is Not Christian but Anti-Islam," stated the title of an article in the *Guardian*. Bill O'Reilly of Fox News declared:

> Breivik is not a Christian. That's impossible. No one believing in Jesus commits mass murder. The man might have called himself a Christian on the net, but he is certainly not of that faith.[82]

However, if that standard were to be applied consistently, then the 9/11 attacks, which resulted in a huge spike in Islamophobia, were not examples of Islamic terrorism. Mohamed Atta, known as the ringleader of the alleged 9/11 hijackers, violated many basic principles of Islam (as discussed below in Chapter 15).

But the attempts to withhold the label "Christian terrorist" from Breivik, several writers have pointed out, do not work. For example, *Media Matters* had an article headed, "Sorry, O'Reilly: Anders Breivik Is a Christian."[83] Religion professor Stephen Prothero explained:

Yes, [Breivik] twisted the Christian tradition in directions most Christians would not countenance. But he rooted his hate and his terrorism in Christian thought and Christian history, particularly the history of the medieval Crusades against Muslims, and current efforts to renew that clash.

Another religion professor, Mark Juergensmeyer, said: "If bin Laden is a Muslim terrorist, Breivik and [Timothy] McVeigh are surely Christian ones."[84]

The same is true of Radovan Karadžić, the Bosnian Serb leader who in March 2016 was convicted of being responsible for genocide—up to 8,000 deaths—in the 1995 Srebrenica massacre. Was Karadžić a Christian? He called his war "holy" and was proclaimed by Greek bishops a "Christian hero," being "one of the most prominent sons of our Lord Jesus Christ working for peace."[85]

Double Standards Encouraged by Corporate Press

Nevertheless, the American public is not given much encouragement by politicians and the mainstream press to use logic consistently with regard to terrorism. So there is much resort to double standards, using violence by Muslims to show Islam to be a violent religion, while not using the attacks by the Ku Klux Klan, the Aryan Nations, or any of the new "Christian Identity" groups—such as the Army of God, the Phineas Priesthood, or the Church of the Almighty God—to show Christianity to be a violent religion.[86] In spite of these and similar groups, the Crusades, Breivik, Karadžić, and countless other examples self-identified Christians engaging in religious based violence, "religious terrorism" is by and large assumed to be *Islamic* terrorism.

This assumption has been promoted by the corporate press, including the *New York Times*. In 2016, a major study of the headlines of NYT stories from 1990 to 2014 showed that Islam and Muslims were "associated with negative terms" almost two thirds of the time, with less than 10 percent of the headlines being positive. In fact, the NYT, as one story about the study put it, "Presents Islam More Negatively than Cancer and Cocaine."[87]

The study, which asked, "Are Muslims Collectively Responsible?" concluded that "the average reader of the NYT is likely to assign collective responsibility to Islam/Muslims for the violent actions of a few." Although NYT headlines had been presenting Islam and Muslims negatively during the decade prior to 9/11, the rate increased afterwards: Whereas in 1990 such headlines appeared only once every five days, they began appearing "about once every two days after September 11th." Moreover, "since 9/11 the increase in headlines per day has been enduring and pronounced."[88] Accordingly, the NYT has been furthering the image of Islam as a terrorist religion.[89]

EFFECTS OF ISLAMOPHOBIA ON MUSLIMS

The Bush-Cheney administration's anti-Muslim policies—in conjunction with its failure to prevent the 9/11 attacks—were very successful in greatly increasing Islamophobia in America. By cultivating the fear and hatred of Muslims and Islam, the administration was able to advance its goals, especially the goal of getting the American public to support military attacks on Afghanistan and Iraq, even though these attacks were illegal. This Islamophobia has had very negative effects for Muslims:

- Besides ruining both countries, the US invasions of Afghanistan and Iraq resulted in an enormous number of deaths.

- Besides resulting in so many deaths, the increased Islamophobia has also led the public and the media to be quite unconcerned with the deaths of Muslims. In 2015, Jack Balkwill wrote: "The mass media in the US have covered up the most important fact in America's ongoing wars: the number of people slaughtered." Citing Polya's estimate, Balkwill wrote: "[W]hy is it that few seem aware of these numbers? After all, anyone you ask on the street can tell you 6 million Jews died in the Holocaust. Why aren't 7 million Muslims important enough to notice?"[90]

- During the Republican presidential campaign in 2016, Ted Cruz—while talking about destroying ISIS (which will be discussed in Chapter 6)—said that he would find out whether "sand will glow in the dark," which appeared to mean that he would use nuclear weapons on cities controlled by ISIS.[91] With reference to the indifference to this statement shown by Washington's political class, Scott McConnell in the *American Conservative* commented: "If someone thought to ask do Muslim Lives Matter, Washington's answer was not very much."[92]

- In 2015, *Salon* had an article entitled "Thirty Percent of GOP Voters Support Bombing Any Arab-Sounding Nation—Even Fictional Lands." The basis for the reference to "fictional lands" was to a poll showing that "30 percent of Republican primary voters nationally support bombing Agrabah," the made-up home of Walt Disney's Aladdin.[93]

- More generally, the American opinion of Muslims has declined drastically. For a brief period after 9/11, polls suggested that it increased: Whereas a Pew Research poll before 9/11 showed that 24 percent of Americans had an unfavorable view of Muslims (while 31 percent expressed no opinion), a Pew poll two months after 9/11 showed that only 17 percent had negative views, evidently due largely to President Bush's call for tolerance. But by August 2007, those with unfavorable opinions of Muslims had increased to 29 percent. Then, by 2010, a poll by *Time* magazine showed that the unfavorable view of Islam had risen to 43 percent.[94] And in 2015, this percentage had increased to 73 percent and hate crimes were 78 percent higher than the previous year—given the notion, fostered by the press and the Islamophobia industry, to blame Islam for the actions of a few Muslims. This very high percentage of people with negative views of Islam was also fueled by the Islamophobic campaign of Donald Trump.[95]

- While Americans in general have negative attitudes toward atheists, a poll in 2016 showed that Muslims are unique in receiving an even more negative evaluation than atheists.[96]

- Polls in 2016 showed that in many states, over 60 percent of the Republican voters favored Donald Trump's call to ban the entry of Muslims to the US. A Fox News poll showed that 45 percent of the Democrats among those polled favored the ban, as long as it was not identified as originating with Trump.[97]

- This unfavorable view of Islam has led Americans to consider the religious rights of Muslims to be less important than those of the members of any other religion.[98] This is significant, said Sheehi, because the media have "saturated American public space with reports and analysis that would be viewed as blatantly racist and prejudicial if it were any other religion under discussion."[99] For example, "Mohammad is demonized in ways that would be viewed as outrageous and unacceptable if referring to any other religion's most holy figures."[100] Whereas TV hosts who have denigrated Jews and Blacks have lost their shows, anti-Islamic commentators— such as Ann Coulter and Michael Savage—have flourished.

- Some people even deny that Islam is a religion. A state representative in Oklahoma has endorsed the views of a man named Paul Hollrah, who argues: "Islam is not a religion, subject to First Amendment protections, as we in western cultures understand the term.

Rather, it is a complete political, legal, economic, military, social, and cultural system with a religious component." Although 95% of the Muslims are "moderate," they will not keep "their radicalized brethren in check," so we have no choice but to prohibit them "from residing anywhere within the civilized nations of the Earth."[101]

- The denigration of Islam and Muslims has, if anything, been even worse in television series. Using *24* and *Homeland* as examples, one commentator wrote: "It seems that Hollywood knows no limits when it comes to dehumanizing Middle Eastern peoples and adherents of Islam." He continued: "How come the level of political correctness in the US is often so high, for better or for worse, yet these over the top racial stereotypes of, and racist slurs towards, Arabs and Muslims are business as usual?"[102] Accordingly, Muslims in America can scarcely watch TV without being reminded that their fellow citizens likely have negative views of them and their religion.

- This denigration of Muslims leads them to be treated terribly, perhaps especially on airplanes. In April 2016, a man was removed from an airplane for speaking Arabic. The next month, a passenger approached a female passenger and ordered: "Take it off! This is America!" When she didn't, "he proceeded to pull her hijab [head scarf] all the way off, leaving the woman's head exposed."[103] But not only on airplanes. On September 16, the holiest day for Muslims, "A 36-year-old woman dressed in traditional garb was set on fire on Fifth Avenue in Manhattan."[104]

- The public and legal effects of Islamophobia have increased the insecurity of Muslims. "Arab and Muslim Americans have lived in fear in the years following 9/11," wrote Sheehi. The demonization of Muslims, added Kumar, has led them to be treated as "guilty until proven innocent." Commenting on the extent to which law officials have infiltrated and spied on Muslims, Abdul Malik Mujahid, a leader of the Muslim Peace Coalition, wrote: "The Muslim community in the United States has been living in a virtual internment camp ever since 9/11."[105]

CONCLUSION

The extreme Islamophobia unleashed by the Bush-Cheney administration has played an essential role in that administration's ruination of America, the world, and the lives of Muslims: "It is a nightmare for an entire religious tradition," said Joshua Stanton, "to be put on the stand as a collective for the actions of an extreme few."[106] It also must be a nightmare to live in a country in which one of the major political parties nominated a notorious Islamophobe to be its candidate for the presidency. The nightmare became even worse when that Islamophobe became the US president.

As this book was going to press, President Trump's proposed ban on Muslims entering the country was causing chaos.[107] Trump was rightly blamed for his ignorant and dangerous policy. But equally to blame was the Bush-Cheney administration, which created the image of Muslims as being so dangerous that they could be abused with impunity.

Likewise, the Islamophobia unleashed by the Bush-Cheney administration has been a nightmare for Muslim-majority nations—at least those in the Middle East—as is discussed in the following chapter.

6 · GLOBAL CHAOS

The wars in Afghanistan and Iraq, as devastating as they were, turned out to be merely the first two countries in the Bush-Cheney administration's war for the Greater Middle East—"a vast swath of territory stretching from North and West Africa to Central and South Asia." This characterization is provided by Andrew Bacevich in his 2016 book, *America's War for the Greater Middle East*. The Greater Middle East runs from Morocco and Libya in the West through Turkey, Syria, and Iraq in the middle to Iran, Afghanistan and Pakistan in the East.[1]

AMERICA'S WAR FOR THE GREATER MIDDLE EAST: BEGINNINGS

America's war for the Greater Middle East can be said to have begun in 1953, when the United States, along with Great Britain, engineered regime change in Iran by replacing a democratically-elected government with a dictator, the Shah of Iran, who would sell Iran's oil to the US and the UK for less than what the elected government had charged. That seemed to American leaders a satisfactory solution until 1979, when the Shah was deposed by an anti-American cleric, Ayatollah Khomeini. After classifying Persian Gulf oil as one of our "vital interests" (meaning one we felt we could not live without), American leaders announced the Carter Doctrine:

> An attempt by any outside force [such as the Soviet Union] to gain control of the Persian Gulf region will be regarded as an assault on the vital interests of the United States of America, and such an assault will be repelled by any means necessary, including military force.[2]

This was an incredible claim—as if the Soviet Union, deciding that it needed Alaska's minerals, had said that it would go to war to protect them.

In any case, this development occurred during a period when national security thinkers such as Paul Wolfowitz-were arguing that the United States could solve all of its problem by means of its military power.[3]

THE BUSH-CHENEY ADMINISTRATION'S DREAMS FOR THE GREATER MIDDLE EAST

Early in the Bush-Cheney administration, as mentioned in Chapter 3, it developed a list of seven countries in which it would bring about regime change. To repeat: General Wesley Clark, the former supreme commander of NATO, reported that a three-star general in the Pentagon told him that the Pentagon was "going to take out seven countries in five years," starting with Iraq and ending with Iran. The other five countries were identified as Syria, Lebanon, Libya, Somalia, and Sudan (the decision to attack Afghanistan had already been made).[4]

As also reported in Chapter 3, the truth of Clark's report was confirmed in 2008 by neocon Douglas Feith, who had been the under-secretary of defense for policy. On September 30, 2001—two weeks after Bush had approved the military operation in Afghanistan—Rumsfeld sent a letter to Bush, revealed Feith, saying that the United States should seek to establish "new regimes" in those seven countries.[5]

Although these seven countries were supposedly chosen because they harbor terrorists, the list did not, Clark observed, include some of the countries most supportive of terrorism, such as Saudi Arabia, Egypt, and Pakistan, all of which were considered US allies. These exclusions suggest that the "war on terror" was really a pretext for attacking countries that, besides having oil and gas, are not in harmony with US policy.

This list of countries also illustrates a comment by Bacevich: "To undertake a 'global war' was to remove limits on the exercise of American power."[6]

The limits were perceived to be removed, of course, by the demise of the Soviet Union. According to Clark, Wolfowitz in 1991 had lamented to him the fact that President George H.W. Bush had not removed Saddam in 1991. "But," Wolfowitz added, "we did learn one thing that's very important. With the end of the Cold War, we can now use our military with impunity."[7]

This sense of impunity, along with America's overwhelming military superiority, led the Bush-Cheney administration to believe that it could take control of the Middle East. Its attack on Iraq was meant to be simply the first phase of this process. As one member of the Bush-Cheney administration said, "The road to the entire Middle East goes through Baghdad."[8]

THE BUSH-CHENEY DREAMS BECAME NIGHTMARES

In seeking to begin taking control of the Greater Middle East, the Bush-Cheney administration created chaos. Just as it had done this in Afghanistan and Iraq, it intended to do the same with the other countries on their list. As Wesley Clark said of the neocons: "They wanted us to destabilize the Middle East, turn it upside down, make it under our control."[9]

Crazies in the Basement

For people who knew the reputation of Cheney, Rumsfeld, and the other neocons in the Bush administration, this had not been surprising. George Bush Sr. had referred to the neocons—especially Cheney, Rumsfeld, Perle, and Wolfowitz—as the "crazies in the basement." This term stuck: Former CIA briefer Ray McGovern has used this term with approval, and Colin

Powell, during a phone conversation with the British foreign secretary (Jack Straw), referred to these neocons as the "fucking crazies."[10]

Ruining the Middle East

Although learning about the use of this term is amusing, there is nothing funny about the ways in which these neocons meant to exploit the 9/11 attacks. As the title of an essay cited in the Introduction said: "9/11 Hurt America, But It Destroyed the Middle East."[11]

After having created chaos in Afghanistan and Iraq, the Bush-Cheney administration's policies led to chaos in Pakistan, Syria, Libya, and Yemen. This chaos, moreover, provided the conditions for new terrorist organizations, such as al-Qaeda in the Arabian Peninsula (AQAP) and the Islamic State in Iraq and Syria (ISIS), to be formed.

Creative Destruction

Chaos is generally regarded as a bad thing, almost by definition. But neocons, as already suggested, have promoted chaos as a means to achieve their goals. In 1996, for example, David Wurmser, a Richard Perle protégé, made a case for "expediting the chaotic collapse" of the Iraqi and Syrian governments.[12]

Chaotic collapse can also be described as "creative destruction." Neocon philosopher Michael Ledeen, who during the Reagan administration was involved in the Iran-Contra affair, was in 2003 called "the driving philosophical force behind the neoconservative movement," whose "ideas are repeated daily by such figures as Richard Cheney, Donald Rumsfeld and Paul Wolfowitz." Saying that "[c]reative destruction is our middle name," Ledeen suggested that America's manifest destiny is violence in the service of spreading democracy. In June 2003, Ledeen said:

> Iraq is not what it's all about. We have been at war for twenty years with a terror network supported by Iraq, Iran, Syria and Saudi Arabia. . . . Now, like it or not, we're in a regional war, and we can't opt out of it. We have to bring down these regimes and produce free governments in all these countries. . . . Undermining the governments of other countries? No big deal.[13]

In line with his idea of foreign policy through violence, Ledeen had been critical of the State Department and the United Nations for preferring diplomacy, rather than violence, to solve conflicts.[14] Ledeen, therefore, reinforced Cheney's own inclinations.

The idea of "creative destruction" was employed in a proposal, by Secretary of State Condoleezza Rice in 2006, to replace the term "Greater Middle East" with "New Middle East." This term was then heralded by Rice and Ehud Olmert, Israel's Prime Minister, during the Israeli siege of Lebanon, which was intended to begin redrawing the map of the New Middle East. Geopolitical analyst Mahdi Darius Nazemroaya described the plan thus:

> This project, which has been in the planning stages for several years, consists in creating an arc of instability, chaos, and violence extending from Lebanon, Palestine, and Syria to Iraq, the Persian Gulf, Iran, and the borders of NATO-garrisoned Afghanistan. The "New Middle East" project was introduced publicly by Washington and Tel Aviv with the expectation that Lebanon would be the pressure point for realigning the whole Middle East and thereby unleashing the forces of "constructive chaos." This "constructive chaos"—which generates conditions of violence and warfare throughout the region—would in turn be used so that the United States, Britain, and Israel could redraw the map of the Middle East in accordance with their geo-strategic needs and objectives.[15]

LIBYA

Chaos has certainly been created in Libya and Syria. Like Iraq, Libya was on the Bush-Cheney administration's list of countries to be targeted for regime change. But in 2003, the Libyan leader, Muammar Gaddafi (sometimes spelled Qaddafi), renounced terrorism and handed over all of his weapons of mass destruction. As a reward, the Bush-Cheney administration established full diplomatic relations with Libya. As *Time* magazine put it, "Gaddafi's Now a Good Guy."[16] However, the US government's perception of him as a good guy did not last.

The Attack on Gaddafi

Although Gaddafi was appreciated by most of his people—for one thing, he had given them the highest standard of living in Africa and shared profits from his country's oil with them—he did have enemies. In 2010, some of these enemies began protests against him, and these protests soon turned into an insurrection, led by Islamic extremists, including Al Qaeda's North African affiliate. In response, Gaddafi in 2011 counter-attacked and, within a month, had the rebels almost completely defeated, with remarkably little loss of life. He needed only to defeat the rebels in Benghazi, which was the stronghold of the al-Qaeda, anti-Gaddafi forces. However, anti-Gaddafi fighters, neocons, and members of the Obama administration began making false claims, especially the claim that Gaddafi had pledged to create a bloodbath in Benghazi.[17]

Neocons and others began pressuring President Obama to take action. A letter demanding immediate military action to depose Gaddafi was signed by 40 members of the neocon Foreign Policy Initiative (which succeeded the Project for the New American Century).[18] The *Washington Post* supported this demand. "Clearly pining for the days of George W. Bush's muscular unilateralism," wrote Robert Parry, "the [Washington] Post's editors demanded that Obama take the lead in implementing a military strategy that ensures regime change in Tripoli."[19]

The drive to remove Gaddafi was led by Secretary of State Hillary Clinton, who is sometimes labeled a "humanitarian interventionist" but is also considered a neocon by many political thinkers. In 2016, Robert Parry said, "Yes, Hillary Clinton Is a Neocon," and several others have said the same.[20] That claim may be too strong. She is surely not a card-carrying neocon, but her policies have shown her to be a fellow-traveller. (Parry at one time referred to her as "a neocon-lite."[21]) One of the founders of the Project for the New American Century, Robert Kagan, endorsed her presidential bid, saying: "If she pursues a policy which we think she will pursue it's something that might have been called neocon." (By contrast, Donald Trump, said Parry, had "disdain for neocon strategies that he views as simply spreading chaos around the globe.")[22]

In any case, Clinton in 2011 argued strongly for a R2P ("Responsibility to Protect") intervention. Speaking on ABC News, with a reference to the Rwanda massacre (which her husband had allowed to happen), Clinton said:

> Imagine we were sitting here and Benghazi had been overrun, a city of 700,000 people, and tens of thousands of people had been slaughtered, hundreds of thousands had fled. ... The cries would be, "Why did the United States not do anything?"[23]

Reportedly accepting this argument, Obama asked the UN Security Council to authorize a military intervention in order to save the lives of peaceful, "pro-democracy" protesters, because Gaddafi was poised to commit a "bloodbath" in Benghazi.[24]

Although the case for a R2P intervention was also made to Obama by Susan Rice (then the US ambassador to the UN) and Samantha Power (then serving on the National Security Council), it is widely agreed that Clinton's argument was so pivotal in persuading the president that it is sometimes known as "Hillary's War."

In any case, the Security Council gave the authorization for force, with NATO providing air support for the rebels. (Although it was officially a NATO operation, the United States provided all of the planes and drones.[25]) After a seven-month battle, the rebels, with continued Western support, conquered the country and killed Gaddafi (with Clinton crowing on CBS, "We came, we saw, he died").[26]

Another Attack Based on Lies

However, the attack was based on lies. There were claims that large numbers of peaceful citizens were targeted; that Gaddafi's airforce had bombed and strafed civilians in Tripoli and Benghazi; that Gaddafi "adopted a rape policy, and even distributed Viagra to troops." All of these claims proved to be false. For example, although there was some indiscriminate violence, most of those killed or injured were fighting-age males; there were few women and children.[27]

Most important, the claim about an impending bloodbath had no basis. Whereas a Saudi news channel claimed that Gaddafi had killed 10,000 people in the first few days, Human Rights Watch documented only 233 deaths. Also, far from promising a bloodbath, Gaddafi had pledged to protect Benghazi's citizens; he even promised that no harm would come to rebels who disarmed. Gaddafi's warning about his impending violence was directed only at rebels who refused to disarm—rebels who, Gaddafi had warned, were mainly al-Qaeda terrorists.[28]

"Obama's Libya Debacle," as Alan Kuperman has called it, was even more deplorable because of the reports given by objective witnesses monitoring the situation. The Defense Intelligence Agency, besides calling it highly unlikely that Gaddafi would have risked alienating the international community with a bloodbath, also reported that there was no evidence to support the fear of such an outcome. Rather, said the DIA, Clinton's case for intervention rested "more on speculative arguments of what might happen to civilians than on facts reported from the ground."[29]

In fact, Clinton's drive for war had little if anything to do with facts. As secret recordings reveal, Gaddafi's son Saif, along with other high-level members of the regime, let it be known that they wanted to negotiate a resolution, but Clinton ordered a general in the Pentagon to refuse to take a call from them. An intelligence asset working with the Joint Chiefs of Staff told Saif: "Secretary Clinton does not want to negotiate at all."[30]

It was later confirmed, moreover, that the conviction that the US attacked Libya for humanitarian reasons was a lie, as then-Secretary of Defense Leon Panetta admitted in his memoirs, "our goal in Libya was regime change."[31]

It seems that at least one motive was that Clinton wanted Gaddafi out of the way so that the CIA, then under the leadership of its new director, General David Petraeus, could have a free hand to send Gaddafi's weapons to the anti-Assad "rebels" in Syria.[32] Another motive was evidently to forestall Gaddafi's plan to use his gold to create a single African currency, which would be needed to buy Libyan oil, thereby threatening the dollar.[33]

Overall Consequence of the Attack: Chaos

With the operation seeming like a success, Clinton and her people were anxious to brag that it was her operation. A *New York Times* account said: "Mrs. Clinton had taken a triumphal tour of the Libyan capital, Tripoli, and for weeks top aides had been circulating a 'ticktock' that described her starring role." The timeline, said her top policy aide, demonstrated Mrs. Clinton's "leadership/ownership/stewardship of this country's Libya policy from start to finish."[34]

However, this operation worked out no better than the neocons' regime changes in Afghanistan and Iraq. The term most commonly used for post-Gaddafi Libya is *chaos*.

- Ellen Brown, pointing out that Clinton's victory lap was premature, said that "as the country dissolved into chaos, leading to a civil war that would destabilize the region," the State Department relegated Libya to the back burner.[35]

- Ralph Nader wrote: "Gates had warned about the aftermath. He was right. Libya has descended into a ghastly state of chaotic violence that has spilled into neighboring African nations."[36]

- "[T]he cascading Libyan chaos has turned the 'regime change,' from a positive notch on Clinton's belt,'" said Robert Parry, "into a black mark on her record."[37]

- Jo Becker and Scott Shane of the *New York Times* wrote: "Libya's descent into chaos began with a rushed decision to go to war, made in what one top official called a 'shadow of uncertainty' as to Colonel Qaddafi's intentions."[38]

- With Gaddafi's death, "A peaceful and prosperous country descended into chaos," wrote Diana Johnstone in her book about Hillary Clinton, *Queen of Chaos*.[39]

- Finally, a 2016 book, entitled *Sowing Chaos: Libya in the Wake of Humanitarian Intervention*, was written by an Italian author, who referred to the "ever-destructive Hillary Clinton."[40]

Without using the term "chaos," Glenn Greenwald gave a similar verdict in a comment about a *New York Times* story entitled "US Tactics in Libya May Be a Model for Other Efforts," which appeared just after the killing of Gaddafi.[41] Writing in 2016, Greenwald said:

Libya—so predictably—has all but completely collapsed, spending years now drowning in instability, anarchy, fractured militia rule, sectarian conflict, and violent extremism. . . . This was supposed to be the supreme model of Humanitarian Intervention. It achieved vanishingly few humanitarian benefits, while causing massive humanitarian suffering.[42]

Particular Consequences for Libya of NATO's Attack

In addition to the general chaos created by the attack on Gaddafi, the attack resulted in many particular consequences.

- When NATO intervened, the civil war was about to end, as Gaddafi had the rebels in retreat. But thanks to NATO's intervention, the rebels regained the offensive and the war continued for another eight months. As a result, although only about 1,000 people had been killed before NATO intervened, at least 10,000 more people were killed after the intervention.[43]

- Arguing that Clinton's NATO intervention was not really "humanitarian intervention," Dan Kovalik, a professor of international rights law, said: "[T]he human rights situation in Libya is a disaster, as 'thousands of detainees [including children] languish in prisons without proper judicial review,' and 'kidnappings and targeted killings are rampant.'"[44]

- Libya quickly became a failed state, having two warring governments and roughly 400,000 Libyans fleeing their homes.[45]

- Greenwald wrote, "Just as there was no al Qaeda or ISIS to attack in Iraq until the US bombed its government, there was no ISIS in Libya until NATO bombed it." The chaos in Libya, moreover, allowed ISIS to establish its most important outpost there.[46]

- Indeed, "The branch in Libya," said CIA Director John Brennan in 2016, "is probably the most developed and the most dangerous."[47]

- Whereas Gaddafi had been effective in limiting the territory controlled by terrorists, the militants by 2016 were trying to take control of the entire country.[48]

- After having attained, through Gaddafi's leadership, the highest standard of living in all of Africa, Libya after the NATO attacks went into free fall, leaving cities with power outages much of the time, along with other problems.[49]

- Gaddafi had created the world's largest irrigation system, the Great Man-Made River. Called by Libyans the "eighth wonder of the world," it was built to provide free fresh water to all Libyans and to make their country self-sufficient in food production. Committing a war crime, the US-led NATO destroyed it, leaving Libya with a national water crisis.[50]

Consequences of NATO's Attack for the Region

Just as the US intervention created chaos in Libya, complete with a host of ruinous internal consequences, the intervention was also ruinous for the larger region.

- When Gaddafi was taken out, his enormous arsenal of arms was not secured, with the result that they started "turning up in Syria, Tunisia, Algeria, Mali, Niger, Chad, Nigeria, Somalia, Sudan, Egypt and Gaza, often in the hands of terrorists."[51]

- The effort to reduce the world's nuclear and chemical weapons programs was undermined by the fact that Gaddafi was attacked after he had voluntarily given up these programs. For example, North Korea said that, having learned from Libya's experience, it would not fall for the US attempts to get it to abolish its own programs.[52]

- By 2016, about 100,000 Libyans left Libya for Europe, thereby adding to its refugee crisis (to be discussed below). By August of that year, "Obama's Libya Debacle" led him to authorize a month-long bombing campaign against ISIS in the formerly "peaceful and prosperous country" of Libya.[53]

Conclusion

Although the Bush-Cheney administration was not directly responsible for Libya's chaos, it was *indirectly* responsible, as it started the project of bringing about regime change in a number of named countries in the Middle East, with Libya being one of the "seven countries in five years" that the Pentagon, under Cheney and Rumsfeld, was to "take out." The idea of removing Gaddafi from power was advocated by the same mindset that was behind the removal of Saddam. And the result was the same: disaster, chaos. And in 2016, the U.K. Parliament report on the war in Libya said that it was based, like the Iraq war, on *lies*.[54] Moreover, the lies were virtually identical with the lies to be employed in the attempt to bring about regime change in Syria.

SYRIA

In Syria, the goal of creating chaos has succeeded in spades. Mnar Muhawesh wrote:

> [F]oreign powers have sunk the nation into a nightmare combination of civil war, foreign invasion and terrorism. Syrians are in the impossible position of having to choose between living in a warzone, being targeted by groups like ISIS and the Syrian government's brutal crackdown, or faring dangerous waters with minimal safety equipment only to be denied food, water and safety by European governments if they reach shore.

Of course, many Syrians were unable, or chose not to try, to reach Europe. Continuing her discussion of the refugee crisis created by the destabilization of Syria, Muhawesh added:

> Other Syrians fleeing the chaos at home have turned to neighboring Arab Muslim countries. Jordan alone has absorbed over half a million Syrian refugees; Lebanon has accepted nearly 1.5 million; and Iraq and Egypt have taken in several hundred thousand. . . . Turkey has [by 2015] taken in nearly 2 million refugees.[55]

By the end of 2015, the conflict in Syria had "displaced 12 million people, creating the largest wave of refugees to hit Europe since World War II."[56]

Planning to Destabilize Syria

Some neocons had come into office with preformed ideas about destabilizing Syria. As mentioned earlier, Richard Perle and other neocons had prepared a 1996 paper for Israeli Prime Minister Benjamin Netanyahu, entitled "A Clean Break: A New Strategy for Securing the Realm." It suggested that Israel seek peace with *some* neighbors while beginning to topple the regimes of its enemies, especially Iraq, Iran, and Syria. Although regime change in Iraq would be the first goal, it would be achieved primarily for the sake of "weakening, containing, and even rolling back Syria," ultimately overthrowing Bashar al-Assad. In other words, the road to Damascus would run through Baghdad.[57]

When Bush and Cheney took control of the White House, a new largely neocon document, "Navigating through Turbulence: America and the Middle East in a New Century," had the same message: "The two main targets" of the new administration, the document said, "should be Syria and Iraq."[58] In 2001, a week after the 9/11 attacks, 40 members of the Project for the New American Century, led by Bill Kristol, wrote a letter to President Bush saying:

We believe the administration should demand that Syria and Iran immediately cease all military, financial and political support for Hizbollah [sic] and its operations. Should Iran and Syria refuse to comply, the Administration should consider appropriate measures of retaliation against these known state sponsors of terrorism.[59]

A few months later, Assistant Secretary of State John Bolton accused Syria of developing chemical and biological weapons and warned Damascus that it might be included in the "axis of evil." Shortly thereafter, the State Department declared Syria to be a sponsor of terrorism, after which Congress made most US dealings with Syria illegal.[60]

The Bush-Cheney Hostility to Syria

The Bush-Cheney administration was hostile to Syria partly because Israel was hostile to Syria, and especially to its president, Bashar al-Assad. Syria had opposed Israel and especially Zionism; Syria had been aligned with Iran, which Israel considers its major threat.

More generally, Assad is an Alawite, which is a branch of Shiite Islam, and Assad has been viewed as, said Parry,

the centerpiece of the "Shiite crescent" stretching from Iran through Iraq and Syria to Lebanon. Since Israeli leaders (and thus the American neocons) see Iran as Israel's greatest enemy, the goal of collapsing the "Shiite crescent" has concentrated on bringing down Assad.[61]

More particularly, Israel has been hostile to Syria because it had supported Lebanon's paramilitary fighting force, Hezbollah, which defeated Israel militarily in 2006; and although Israel in the 1967 war took Syria's Golan Heights—which now provides 15 percent of Israel's water—Syria wants it back. More generally, Syria, with the assistance of Hezbollah, had prevented Israel from realizing its goal of taking control of land that, it claims, belongs to it by divine right.

There have been, in addition, several other reasons for the US hostility to Syria, Assad in particular. An overarching one is that Syria has remained independent of the US-dominated global order. For example, Syria has its own state-owned bank and has no IMF loans through which it could be ordered around. And Syria has refused to be included within the American empire. The document "Navigating through Turbulence" complained that "[m]aintaining a strong alliance with Israel" had not prevented "every state on Israel's border, except Syria, from accepting America as their principal source of military aid and matériel."[62]

As to why Syria did not want to be absorbed into the American empire:

American politicians and media do not remind the world that four years before the CIA overthrew Iran's elected government in 1953, it had overthrown Syria's government for the same reason—the price of oil.[63]

For a variety of reasons, "ousting the Assad dynasty," said Parry, had been "a top neocon/Israeli goal since the 1990s," so the Bush-Cheney administration was from the beginning intent on destabilizing Syria. In 2002, Under-Secretary of State John Bolton named Syria as one of the "rogue states" that "can expect to become our targets."[64]

Knowing how he was regarded, Assad made many attempts to develop better relations. In 2004, Assad started secret peace talks in Turkey with Israel, offering what Israel's leading newspaper called "a far reaching and equitable peace treaty that would provide for Israel's security."[65]

Although the talks were supported by a large number of senior Israelis, "the Bush administration nixed them"— not surprisingly, because Cheney was "an implacable opponent of engagement with Syria."[66] In 2007, the Bush-Cheney administration, discussing "a new strategic alignment in the Middle East," distinguished between "reformers" and "extremists," placing Syria, along with Iran and Hezbollah, in the latter category. According to Seymour Hersh's 2007 article "The Redirection," the US participated in clandestine operations aimed at Syria as well as Iran.[67]

Information about what went on behind the scenes in the Bush-Cheney administration has been provided by WikiLeaks, which had obtained the cables of William Roebuck, the political counselor for the US Embassy in Damascus. These cables are discussed by Robert Naiman in a chapter of Julian Assange's *The WikiLeaks Files,* entitled "WikiLeaks Reveals How the US Aggressively Pursued Regime Change in Syria, Igniting a Bloodbath." Roebuck's cables show, according to Naiman,

> that regime change had been a long-standing goal of US policy; [and] that the US promoted sectarianism in support of its regime-change policy, thus helping lay the foundation for the sectarian civil war and massive bloodshed that we see in Syria today.[68]

Some commentators today suggest that the US hostility to Assad began with his brutal response to the Arab Spring protests in 2011. However, "as far back as 2006—five years before 'Arab Spring' protests in Syria," reported Naiman, the cables show that "destabilizing the Syrian government was a central motivation of US policy," and Roebuck's cables suggested strategies for doing this. Accordingly, said Naiman:

> We are told in the West that the current efforts to topple the Syrian government by force were a reaction to the Syrian government's repression

of dissent in 2011, but now we know that "regime change" was the policy of the US and its allies five years earlier.

According to these cables, Naiman summarized,

> the top US diplomat in Syria believed that the goal of US policy in Syria should be to destabilize the Syrian government by any means available; that the US should work to increase Sunni-Shia sectarianism in Syria...; the US should try to strain relations between the Syrian government and other Arab governments, and then blame Syria for the strain; that the US should seek to stoke Syrian government fears of coup plots in order to provoke the Syrian government to overreact...; the US should work to undermine Syrian economic reforms and discourage foreign investment; that the US should seek to foster the belief that the Syrian government was not legitimate; that violent protests in Syria were praiseworthy.[69]

The 2011 Protests and the Obama Administration

The Obama administration publicly gave the same reason for hostility to Assad, namely, his excessive reaction to the 2011 uprising against him—a reaction that led to major protests, which soon turned into a civil war between Assad and rebel forces.

The Need for a Balanced View: However, that was a very limited understanding of the events: The conflict resulted from a complex interplay of factors, some of which were Assad's fault, some of which were not. One of the factors that was not his fault was the beginning in 2006 of a drought in Syria, which some climate scientists said to be the worst in 900 years; other scientists even call it the worst since agricultural civilization began many thousands of years ago.[70] Describing the context for the war, William Polk wrote:

> In some areas, all agriculture ceased. In others crop failures reached 75%. And generally as much as 85% of livestock died of thirst or hunger. Hundreds of thousands of Syria's farmers gave up, abandoned their farms and fled to the cities and towns in search of almost non-existent jobs and severely short food supplies. Outside observers including UN experts estimated that between 2 and 3 million of Syria's 10 million rural inhabitants were reduced to "extreme poverty."

Also, added Polk, "hundreds of thousands of Palestinians and Iraqis had in previous years taken refuge there, so that the new Syrian refugees had to compete with them for jobs, water, and food."[71]

By 2008, the representative of the UN's Food and Agriculture Organization had described the situation as "a perfect storm," which threatened Syria with "social destruction."[72]

However, Assad made the effects of the drought worse by poor governance. Central to this was what Francesco Femia and Caitlin Werrell called *criminal mismanagement* of Syria's natural resources, which contributed to water shortages for farmers. Favoring the big farmers over the poor farming communities, Assad's regime subsidized wheat and cotton, which are water-intensive, and it also allowed unsustainable farming and irrigation techniques. It even allowed the big farmers to take all the water they wanted from the aquifer (although this was illegal), while the government's wasteful use of water also meant that rural people needed to drill for water, thereby emptying the aquifers. Moreover, Assad gave no aid to the increasingly poor farmers, and even raised their expenses: While subsidizing the wheat and cotton farmers, Assad damaged ordinary farmers by cutting subsidies for diesel and fertilizers.[73]

Because of the severe drought and Assad's mismanagement, almost a million people, having lost their livelihoods by 2009, were forced to move to the slums, and many more were to follow. By 2011, about a million people had insufficient food. There is little room for doubt, therefore, that the beginnings of the Syrian opposition movement were originally rooted in Assad's own destructive policies (in conjunction with the drought).[74]

An important factor in this insufficient food supply was another feature of criminal mismanagement: "Lured by the high price of wheat on the world market, it sold its reserves." Accordingly, Polk said:

> [T]ens of thousands of frightened, angry, hungry and impoverished former farmers constituted a 'tinder' that was ready to catch fire. The spark was struck on March 15, 2011, when a relatively small group gathered in the town of Dara'a to protest against government failure to help them.[75]

The protest in Dara'a began after a group of children had "painted some anti-government graffiti on a school wall" and then were arrested and tortured by city police. Some protesters were shot. This excessive response by the government led to protests in the city. Assad made several attempts to calm the situation: He fired government and security officials for their roles in the overreaction; he assured the residents that the shooters would be prosecuted; and he announced several national reforms. But his response did not satisfy the protestors and they continued destroying property and attacking police and soldiers. Dara'a was declared a "liberated zone." And the protests spread to other towns.[76] But why did the protests turn violent?

The Turn of Violence: The standard portrayal of the protest movement, summarized independent researcher Jonathan Marshall, was that "the protest movement in Syria was overwhelmingly peaceful until September 2011."[77] The Syria government rejected this view from the beginning, but its claim was long dismissed. But Marshall has provided evidence that the government's view was essentially correct on this point. In an essay entitled "Hidden Origins of Syria's Civil War," Marshall said, "opposition to the government had turned violent almost from the start." For example, unknown gunmen in Dara'a reportedly killed 19 Syrians; in addition "nine Syrian soldiers on their way to quell demonstrations in Banyas were ambushed and gunned down on the highway outside of town."[78]

Professor Joshua Landis, the head of Center for the Middle East Studies at the University of Oklahoma, reported that video footage of the fighting showed that the government account was correct: "the soldiers stationed in the town were overrun by armed and organized opposition."[79]

The protests in other towns also involved armed men. In one city, about 140 members of the police and security forces were massacred. But media largely ignored this side of the story. After studying the protests and the press's coverage of them, Landis concluded: "Western press and analysts did not want to recognize that armed elements were becoming active. They preferred to tell a simple story of good people fighting bad people."[80]

It is important to recognize that this method of setting up a leader to be overthrown was an oft-repeated modus operandi by the US government. Besides being used in Libya as well as Syria, it was previously used in the 1990s, recalled William Engdahl, when the Bill Clinton administration wanted to split up Yugoslavia into its six republics. Making a deal with Bosnia to start a war with Serbia, the Washington propaganda machine began demonizing the Serbs as Nazis, and made up fake stories claiming that they not only bombed civilians and hospitals but also raped thousands of Muslim women.[81]

In any case, at some point the Syrian government cracked down ruthlessly on the protestors, and several hundred protestors were reportedly killed. But even here it appears that the press, as well as giving a one-sided account, exaggerated. The private intelligence firm Stratfor, sometimes called the "Private CIA," warned their clients not to be misled by opposition propaganda. "Although it is certain that protesters and civilians are being killed," said Stratfor, "there is little evidence of massive brutality compared to . . . other state crackdowns in the region."[82]

Some human rights organizations also, pointed out Jonathan Marshall, acknowledged that armed opposition forces had begun committing crimes against civilians. For example:

Human Rights Watch sent an "open letter" to leaders of the Syrian opposition, decrying "crimes and other abuses committed by armed opposition elements," including the kidnapping and detention of government supporters, the use of torture and the execution of security force members and civilians, and sectarian attacks against Shias and Alawites.[83]

Not incidentally, this same pattern—armed elements joining a largely peaceful protest and shooting police as well as civilians—would occur with the protest leading to the coup d'etat in Ukraine as discussed in Chapter 9. In fact, said Engdahl,

Washington's Arab Spring protests often used secret CIA and mercenary snipers to enflame and anger the population against their government by creating innocent martyrs and blaming the killings on the regime.[84]

Accordingly, the beginning of the opposition was due not only to the drought, Assad's mismanagement of the country's natural resources, his foolish and immoral responses to the drought, and his neo-liberal economic policies. The 2011 violence did begin with the Assad regime's brutal response to the protests, but this response was stimulated by armed elements. Accordingly, whereas Western propaganda has portrayed Assad as almost uniquely evil, said Marshall, "the deadly provocations against Syrian government forces put an entirely different cast on the origins of the conflict."[85]

In sum, the Obama administration's interpretation of the origins of the anti-Assad movement was one-sided to the point of being false.

US Contributions to the anti-Assad War: An adequate understanding of the war in Syria requires an expanded discussion of the role played by the United States. Some of this role was played by the Bush-Cheney administration.

In 2008, that administration withdrew its ambassador from Damascus as part of an effort to weaken and isolate Assad.[86] It also played a role in the Assad regime's failure to prevent the drought from resulting in so much social destruction. In November 2008, the representative of the UN Food and Agriculture Organization in Syria appealed to USAID for assistance, noting that Syria's minister of agriculture said that the economic and social fallout from the drought was "beyond our capacity as a country to deal with." However, the Bush-Cheney USAID director said (in a cable that was later published by WikiLeaks), "we question whether limited USG resources should be directed toward this appeal at this time."[87]

More generally, as pointed out above, the Bush-Cheney administration had begun talking about how to destabilize Syria, such as undermining its attempts at economic reform, toward the goal of bringing about regime change.

But the actual beginning of the war in Syria occurred during the Obama administration. This administration made part of its contribution to the war by its false interpretation of the origins of the anti-Assad movement—by saying that that the civil war arose out of a spontaneous and peaceful uprising against Assad. But like Marshall, Muhawesh said that it was not entirely spontaneous: Wikileaks cables "reveal CIA involvement on the grounds in Syria to instigate these very demonstrations as early as March 2011."[88] That is, of course, what should be expected, given Naiman's report of the Wikileaks cables during the Bush-Cheney administration about ways to destabilize Syria.

Robert Parry also agreed with Marshall's account of the instigation of violence: "Since the start of the Syrian conflict in 2011," wrote Parry,

> the powerful role of Al Qaeda and its spinoff, the Islamic State, has been a hidden or downplayed element of the narrative that has been sold to the American people. That storyline holds that the war began when "peaceful" protesters were brutally repressed by Syria's police and military, but that version deletes the fact that extremists, some linked to Al Qaeda, began killing police and soldiers almost from the outset.[89]

The Number of Protesters

Another issue raised by Muhawesh relates to the reports by major media outlets, such as the BBC and the Associated Press, that "the demonstrations that supposedly swept Syria were comprised of only hundreds of people." Writing in 2015, she asked:

> How did demonstrations held by "hundreds" of protesters demanding economic change in Syria four years ago devolve into a deadly sectarian civil war, fanning the flames of extremism haunting the world today and creating the world's second largest refugee crisis?

She replied:

> Just a few months into the demonstrations which now consisted of hundreds of armed protesters with CIA ties, demonstrations grew larger, armed non-Syrian rebel groups swarmed into Syria, and a severe government crackdown swept through the country to deter this foreign meddling. It became evident that the United States, United Kingdom, France, Qatar, Saudi Arabia and Turkey would be jumping on the opportunity to organize, arm and finance rebels to form the Free Syrian Army as outlined in the State Department plans to destabilize Syria.[90]

In other words, without the intervention of the United States and other countries, the protestations could have never turned into a civil war.

Regarding the Free Syrian Army, the BBC said that by 2013 there were "believed to be as many as 1,000 armed opposition groups in Syria, commanding an estimated 100,000 fighters."[91] The most powerful of these groups were ISIS and al-Qaeda's al-Nusra Front (which had joined ISIS only briefly). Can anyone say that Assad did not have the right to defend his democratically-elected government against these outside forces?[92]

As for the United States in particular, its CIA started sending large shipments of weapons by 2012. "The CIA," reported Seymour Hersh, "was responsible for getting arms from Gaddafi's arsenals into Syria."[93] In fact, Chris Stevens, who had become the American ambassador in Libya, was killed in Benghazi after he had come there to negotiate a transfer of several hundred tons of Gaddafi's weapons to Syria. In what Hersh called a "rat line," these weapons were sent from Libya to Syria via southern Turkey, in an operation headed by General David Petraeus, the then-director of the CIA, under the supervision of Secretary Clinton. Indeed, the "consulate" where Stevens was killed was really only a mission, which existed merely "to provide cover for the moving of arms," according to a former intelligence officer.[94]

In 2013, during a Congressional investigation of the Benghazi attack, Clinton swore under oath that she knew nothing about the weapons shipments to Syrian rebels prior to the attack. But in 2015, Judicial Watch obtained previously classified documents from the State Department and DOD that provided the first official confirmation that the US government knew about the shipments of arms from Benghazi to Syria.[95]

In 2016, moreover, Julian Assange reported that Clinton's claim was disproven by 1,700 hacked emails about Libya in Wikileaks' Hillary Clinton collection. These emails included, said Assange, proof that Clinton pushed for weapons to be sent to "jihadists within Syria, including ISIS."[96] This would seem to mean that she had lied under oath.

In any case, the CIA, beginning in 2012, spent $1 billion a year and trained some 10,000 "moderate" rebel forces.[97] This was done in spite of the fact that then-DIA director Michael Flynn, reported Hersh, "had sent a constant stream of classified warnings to the civilian leadership about the dire consequences of toppling Assad. The jihadists, he said, were in control of the opposition." His reports, Flynn told Hersh, "got enormous pushback" from the Obama administration. "I felt," said Flynn, "that they did not want to hear the truth." The Joint Chiefs of Staff likewise believed, reported one of their advisors, "that Assad should not be replaced by fundamentalists."[98]

Indeed, the idea that the United States and its allies were funding only *moderate* rebels—ones who were fighting both against Assad and the al-Qaeda jihadists—was increasingly regarded as a myth. Many observers provided evidence that *there were now no moderate rebels in Syria.*[99]

In fact, Vice President Biden admitted this. Saying that America had been trying to identify a moderate middle for a long time, he added:

> [T]he idea of identifying a moderate middle has been a chase America has been engaged in for a long time. The fact of the matter is . . . there was no moderate middle, because the moderate middle are made up of shopkeepers, not soldiers.[100]

Admitting that the jihadists had been armed by America's allies, Biden went on to say that America's "allies in the region were our largest problem in Syria." Turkey, Saudi Arabia and the United Arab Emirates, he explained, had "poured hundreds of millions of dollars and tens, thousands of tons of weapons into anyone who would fight against Assad." The result, Biden added, was that "the people who were being supplied were Al Nusra and Al Qaeda and the extremist elements of jihadis coming from other parts of the world." Biden thereby contradicted the Obama administration's public posture, according to which, in Secretary Kerry's words, armed "legitimate opposition groups" exist separately from Al Qaeda's Nusra Front.[101] (Gareth Porter called this "Obama's 'Moderate' Syrian Deception."[102])

The administration's claim, that the Free Syrian Army (FSA) consisted of non-terrorist rebels, was contradicted by many facts. A 2016 story reported that al-Nusra (which had changed its name to Jabhat Fatah al-Sham [Conquest of Syria Front], claiming that it was breaking ties with the al-Qaeda network[103]) reportedly took orders from Israel. Alastair Crooke, who had been a senior figure in British intelligence, said that "the FSA is little more than a cover for the al-Qaeda-affiliated al Nusra."[104]

In any case, besides starting to fund so-called moderate anti-Assad rebels covertly, Obama declared that Assad needed to step down. After it was learned in 2012 that Assad had chemical weapons, Obama announced that using them would be a "red line," to which America would respond militarily. Then in 2013, there was a chemical attack, using deadly sarin gas, which reportedly killed seven hundred civilians. Arguing that Assad was responsible, neocons and other hawks pressured Obama to carry through with his "red line" declaration, and he planned a major attack on Assad's military.

At the last minute, however, Obama cancelled the attack order. There were evidently two reasons for this cancelation. On the one hand, President Vladimir Putin convinced Assad to destroy his chemical weapons, thereby giving Obama a face-saving out.[105] On the other hand, Obama became convinced, according to Seymour Hersh, that there was insufficient evidence to claim that Assad had been responsible for the sarin gas. There seem to have been three reasons for Obama's reevaluation of the evidence:

- James Clapper, the director of national intelligence, told Obama that the intelligence community lacked "slam dunk" evidence of Assad's responsibility.

- A "vector" analysis, which supposedly showed that the rockets carrying the sarin gas could have come only from Damascus, broke down, showing that they could have come from rebel territory. Relevant to this possibility is the fact that, Hersh reported, "the US and its allies knew from highly classified CIA and allied intelligence reporting throughout the spring and summer of 2013, that the jihadist opposition to Assad (primarily al-Nusra) had the ability to manufacture a crude form of sarin."[106]

- A British laboratory showed that, in Hersh's words, "the gas used didn't match the batches known to exist in the Syrian army's chemical weapons arsenal." The sarin gas, Hersh concluded, was a false-flag attack launched by Turkey "to instigate an event that would force the US to cross the red line."[107]

It is good that Obama resisted the temptation to support an attack on Syria as a "humanitarian intervention." But his decision not to start a war against Syria led to great pressure on him to reverse it. In 2015, for example, 51 members of the State Department—which Hillary Clinton had headed for four years, during which she gave important posts to neocons[108]—issued a "dissent," saying against Obama's policy that the US should bomb Syria until it agrees to our wishes. The dissent's argument was based on an extremely superficial understanding of the reasons for the Syrian war. "The government's barrel bombing of civilians," the dissent said (according to a summary by the *New York Times*), "is the 'root cause of the instability that continues to grip Syria and the broader region.'"[109]

This interpretation was rejected by Veteran Intelligence Professionals for Sanity, who said:

It's true that the initial phase of the Syrian Spring seems to have been largely spontaneous. Facts show, however, that outside interveners—primarily the United States, the United Kingdom, Turkey, Israel and Saudi Arabia—cooperated in lighting the match that brought the inferno of civil war. Covert funding and provision of weapons and other material support to opposition groups for strikes against the Syrian Government provoked a military reaction by Assad—which created a pretext for our enlarged support to the rebel groups.[110]

Besides evidently not understanding what had been going on in Syria in 2011, the State Department "dissenters" ignored the fact that they had suggested a policy that would be completely illegal under international law.[111] Moreover, they also seemed to be unaware of how terribly unwise their proposed policy would have been.

In an article asking the question "Risking Nuclear War for Al Qaeda?" Parry pointed out that for Obama to have followed the urging of Turkey, Saudi Arabia, and Hillary Clinton to permit a full-out attack on Syria would have been insane. If these powers attacked Syria while Russia's troops were there, Russia—having insufficient ground forces and conventional weapons to protect them—might have been tempted to resort to tactical nuclear weapons, and this response could easily have led to a nuclear showdown. The insanity is that "the United States [is] being urged to take on that existential risk for all humankind on behalf of preserving Al Qaeda's hopes for raising its black flag over Damascus."[112] (An extensive discussion of the threat of nuclear war is reserved for Chapter 9.)

The Main Reason for Attacking Assad

If the US desire for regime change in Syria was not based on Assad's crackdown on rebels, we must deal with the question about the real reason (aside from the desire of neocons in general and Hillary Clinton in particular to help Israel—see the section on Israel below). Mnar Muhawesh said that what has been driving the chaos is "control over gas, oil and resources."[113] Wesley Clark—in his report on the Bush administration's plan to take out seven regimes, including Syria's—indicated that this strategy was fundamentally about the region's oil and gas.[114] Chris Floyd likewise wrote:

> Vast interests in oil and natural gas—both existing and potential—are in play. . . . Competing pipelines—one favoring the West, undercutting Russia, the other bolstering Moscow and Tehran—are in the mix.[115]

Dmitry Minin, an independent analyst, wrote:

> A battle is raging over whether pipelines will go toward Europe from east to west, from Iran and Iraq to the Mediterranean coast of Syria, or take a more northbound route from Qatar and Saudi Arabia via Syria and Turkey.[116]

Minin based his ideas primarily upon "renowned researcher on energy issues F. William Engdahl." Engdahl is, in fact, the researcher who—along with Pepe Escobar, the author of *Empire of Chaos*[117]—has over the years written the most about gas pipelines in relation to Syria.

F. William Engdahl on the Syrian Pipeline War

"In a fundamental sense the entirety of the five-year-long war over Syria," Engdahl wrote in 2016, "has been about control of hydrocarbon resources— oil and natural gas—and of potential hydrocarbon pipelines to the promising markets of the European Union."[118] Political assessments, he had said in 2012, had not fully appreciated "the dramatically rising importance of the control of natural gas to the future." This importance had been greatly enhanced in the European Union by its mandate to reduce CO_2 emissions significantly by 2020, and natural gas has been considered far less polluting than coal (even if that is questionable[119]). The importance of this situation to the Middle East was enhanced still further by the discovery of huge natural-gas sources in Syria as well as Israel and Qatar.[120]

The movement toward the Syrian war as a pipeline war began in 2009, Engdahl said, after "it became clear to some geopolitical Washington strategists that Qatar could play a strategic role in pushing Russia out of the EU natural gas game and put a US-controlled supplier, Qatar, in the dominant role." Accordingly, the Emir of Qatar, which owns the world's largest gas field, went to Damascus in 2009 to propose to Bashar al Assad the construction of a natural gas pipeline that would begin in Qatar, cross Saudi Arabia and Syria, then end up in Turkey, where the gas would be sold to EU markets.

However, Assad declined the offer, saying that he wanted "to protect the interests of [his] Russian ally, which is Europe's top supplier of natural gas." Engdahl continued: "This was the beginning of the NATO decision to militarily destroy the Assad regime." That this decision was made in 2009—rather than after Assad's 2011 response to the protesters—was made clear by Ronald Dumas, a former French Foreign Minister, who in 2009 "revealed that British military were preparing for invasion of Assad's Syria." Also, the previously mentioned intelligence firm, Stratfor, reported that by 2011, "US and UK special forces' training of Syrian opposition forces was well underway." [121]

In any case, Syria chose a competing project, an Iran-Iraq-Syria pipeline. Iran would get its natural gas from its part of the Pars field (Qatar gets its gas from its portion of the same field) then cross Iraq and end up in Syria. "The deal was formally announced in July 2011," pointed out Pepe Escobar, "when the Syrian tragedy was already in motion."[122]

Then in July 2012, the three countries signed a Memorandum of Understanding to construct a pipeline from Iran through Iraq to Syria.

This route, sometimes called the Shi'ite Pipeline, would leave Turkey and Qatar out in the cold, so they began doing everything they could to thwart the construction of that pipeline, including arming the anti-Assad rebels. The signing of this Memorandum was also, Engdahl added, "the precise point when the US gave the green light to Saudi Arabia, Qatar and Turkey to back regime change in Damascus—mad pipeline geopolitics."[123]

Victory would open the door for the Qatar-Saudi Arabia-Turkey gas pipeline to Europe, with its huge natural gas import market. Besides bringing riches to Qatar, Saudi Arabia, and Turkey, the war would intend, said Dmitry Minin, to accomplish three goals: "to break Russia's gas monopoly in Europe; to free Turkey from its dependence on Iranian gas; and to give Israel the chance to export its gas to Europe by land at less cost."[124]

The first of these goals was most important to Washington. Whereas Russia had been filling 40 percent of the EU's natural gas demand, Washington wanted it and her allies to control much of the gas to meet this demand. Here we find "the true agenda behind Washington's five-year-long war for regime change in Damascus," said Engdahl, "a war with terrorist groups such as ISIS or Al Nusra Front-Al Qaeda in Syria financed largely by money from Qatar."[125]

In sum, from the perspective of Engdahl and the other researchers discussed in this section, the Syrian War has been primarily about energy and money (not good and bad people). Indeed, Escobar's 2015 essay on the war in Syria as a pipeline war began by stating, "Syria is an energy war."[126]

The Extreme Moral Charges against Assad Contributed to Chaos

The claim that Assad was unbearably evil, like the claims about Saddam and Gaddafi, was used to get politicians and others in America and Europe to support the US drive, begun by the Bush-Cheney administration, to bring about regime change in Syria.

But even if he were as evil as he was portrayed by US officials, this would not have justified the attempt to depose him. Colin Powell, referring to his "old Pottery Barn rule," cautioned:

> I think you have to be extremely careful. We thought we knew what would happen in Libya. We thought we knew what would happen in Egypt. We thought we knew what would happen in Iraq, and we guessed wrong. In each one of these countries the thing we have to consider is that there is some structure . . . that's holding the society together. And as we learned, especially in Libya, when you remove the top and the whole thing falls apart. . . you get chaos.[127]

This chaos has resulted in a tragedy for the Syrian people. In July 2016, international lawyer Franklin Lamb wrote:

> The conflict here has, according to some NGO estimates, now claimed the lives of nearly half a million Syrians, out of a pre-war population of 22 million. More than 11 percent of the Syrian population is estimated to have been killed or injured. More than five million have fled the country while approximately 8 million are internally displaced. The UN estimates that nearly 12 million people are in urgent need of humanitarian assistance, more than six million being children ranging from infants to age 12.[128]

The Syrian chaos resulted primarily from the Bush-Cheney administration and its neocon attitudes, which continued significantly in the Obama administration. Robert Parry observed:

> In Neocon Land, it goes without saying that once the United States judges some world leader guilty for having violated international law or human rights or whatever, it is fine for the US government to "take out" that leader. . . . In this view, the "exceptional" United States has the right to invade any country of its choosing and violently remove leaders not to its liking.[129]

Unless this neocon way of thinking can be overcome, there will be little hope that the United States will quit causing chaos in the Greater Middle East. When this book was first planned, it appeared that the Queen of Chaos herself would be the next US president. She made it clear, said Parry, that she was "eager to use military force to achieve 'regime change' in countries that get in the way of US desires."[130] Indeed, argued Andre Damon, "There is little doubt that talks were underway between the Clinton campaign and the Obama administration, and planning was well advanced, for a massive US military escalation in Syria to be launched after the expected election victory of the Democratic candidate.[131]

Evidently realizing that the United States under Obama and Clinton was going to continue its assault on Syria, rather than helping to achieve a tolerable resolution to the Syrian situation, Russia, Iran, and Turkey set up talks without inviting the United States.[132] Excluding the United States, at least under the neocon-inspired Democrats, seemed necessary to begin bringing the ruination of Syria to an end.

Moreover, the ruination resulting from the neocon ideology of the Bush-Cheney administration, continued by Obama and Secretaries Clinton and Kerry, has not been limited to the Greater Middle East. As a 2016 *Newsweek* article said, "The Tide of Syrian Refugees Is Unraveling Europe"[133]—a problem to be explored after a discussion of ISIS and Russia.

ISIS

As mentioned in Chapter 5, a great increase in Islamophobia came about in 2015, mainly because of a number of attacks attributed to an organization known as ISIS, about which the public had known little.

ISIS took responsibility for four major attacks in 2015—the Charlie Hebdo attack in Paris, which killed 12 people; the mosque bombing in Yemen, which killed 130; the downing of a Russian plane in Egypt, which killed 224; and the Paris attacks at the end of the year, which killed 130. Then in 2016, ISIS took credit for the Brussels bombing, which killed 32. ISIS was also credited with having conducted, or at least inspired, some 70 attacks in 20 countries around the world (not including its activities in Iraq, Libya, and Syria)—such as the 2015 shootings in San Bernardino.[134] ISIS especially impressed itself on the public's consciousness by televising apparent beheadings.

Questions about ISIS

There has been much confusion about ISIS, with the most common questions being: (1) Where did ISIS come from? (2) Why is ISIS sometimes called ISIL, sometimes simply the Islamic State? (3) Who was responsible for the rise of ISIS? (4) How did the Obama administration treat it?

(1) *Where Did ISIS Come From?* Although ISIS seemed to many people to have come out of nowhere, it actually came out of a series of developments after the US attack on Iraq. The basic development was the decision of the Bush-Cheney administration to ban the Baath party, which was largely Sunni, and to disband the Iraqi military. This twofold purging left hundreds of thousands of men, mainly Sunni, with no jobs and no pensions. But the members of the military were allowed to keep their weapons. The purged military officers formed the core of the Sunni insurgency, which began a civil war between Sunnis and Shias. Many members of the Sunni insurgency would then end up joining ISIS.

As for the leadership of ISIS: Shortly after the invasion of Iraq in 2003, a Jordanian named Abu Musab al-Zarqawi—who had previously run a paramilitary camp in Afghanistan—set up an anti-Shia organization called the Party of Monotheism and Jihad, which organized many suicide bombings in Iraq. Then in 2004, merging his organization with Osama bin Laden's, he changed his organization's name to Al-Qaeda in Iraq (AQI). In 2006, al-Zarqawi was killed, and Abu Bakr al-Baghdadi took over the leadership.

Al-Baghdadi was one of thousands of Iraqis incarcerated in Camp Bucca, which served as a "pressure cooker for extremism." He and several other al-Qaeda military leaders made new plans for the organization, now called the Islamic State of Iraq (ISI).[135] Then in 2013, al-Baghdadi opened a second front in Syria and enlarged the name to the Islamic State of Iraq and Syria (ISIS). In 2014, proclaiming a worldwide caliphate, Baghdadi changed the name to simply the Islamic State (IS), although the media also still use the name ISIS.[136]

(2) *Why Is ISIS Sometimes Called ISIL?* Whereas most people have thus far used the abbreviation ISIS, President Obama and others spoke of ISIL (Islamic State in Iraq and Levant). The reason some prefer this name is based on the fact that the name "Syria" can refer either to the modern state or to the area that was historically known as "Sham," usually translated "Greater Syria." This region includes at least Lebanon, Jordan, Israel, and Palestine, as well as modern Syria. This Greater Syria has been known as the Levant.

When the name al-Qaeda in Iraq (AQI) was replaced in 2013, the organization renamed itself "Islamic State in Iraq and al-Sham." Accordingly, the final "S" in ISIS means Greater Syria, so the more accurate translation would be "Islamic State in Levant." However, because the term "ISIS" has become so widespread, it is arguably best to continue using it while remembering that the final "S" means "Greater Syria." Alternatively, some have given up both "ISIS" and "ISIL" in favor of Baghdadi's newly preferred term, "Islamic State" (and still others use an Arabic acronym, "Daesh").[137]

(3) *Who Was Responsible for the Rise of ISIS?* On this question, there is great unanimity:

- "The rise of ISIS," wrote Stephen Zunes, "is a direct consequence of the US invasion and occupation of Iraq. While there are a number of other contributing factors as well, that fateful decision is paramount."[138]

- The aforementioned Lt. General Michael Flynn, the former director of the Defense Intelligence Agency, said: "As brutal as Saddam Hussein was, it was a mistake to just eliminate him; [his fall] presented an opportunity for groups like ISIS to grow."[139]

- "Were it not for Bush's invasion of Iraq," said Andrew Bacevich, "ISIL would not exist—that's a fact. Responsibility for precipitating the rise of this vile movement rests squarely with Washington."[140]

- Even President Obama said: "ISIL is a direct outgrowth of Al Qaeda in Iraq that grew out of our invasion, which is an example of unintended consequences."[141]

(4) *What was the Obama Administration's Attitude toward ISIS?* On this question, there have been different views. On the one hand, the Obama administration from virtually the beginning portrayed ISIS as an extremely serious threat, against which the United States needed to devote great resources.

- The rise of ISIS reportedly led Obama to give up his dream, stated in 2013, that he would be able to get the United States off the "perpetual wartime footing" by the time he left office.[142]

- Although Obama resisted the call to have US ground forces fight ISIS, he did in 2014 start using air power against it.

- The financial cost of this air war was great, with the United States spending about $11 million a day, for a total of over $5.5 billion by 2016, in fighting against ISIS.[143]

On the other hand, many writers provided evidence that US forces long attacked ISIS only half-heartedly, because they wanted ISIS to help overthrow Assad. For example, David Swanson published an article entitled "The US Wants the Islamic State Group to Win in Syria."[144] Chris Floyd said: "ISIS keeps Assad tied down and weakened, which neatly serves our [US and UK] leaders' purposes."[145]

ISIS as Covert Western Asset

Some commentators go even further. For example, Eric Margolis, who was long a correspondent for the *Toronto Sun,* referred to ISIS as a covert western asset and called the US war against it a "big charade." Likewise, former CIA contractor Steven Kelly said: "The US has always been the main sponsor and creator of Daesh (Arabic acronym for IS), so this charade that they are having anything to do with fighting Daesh in Syria is completely a farce."[146]

Nowadays, most knowledgeable researchers, as illustrated by Engdahl, take for granted that ISIS and al Qaeda's al-Nusra front (aka Fatah Al-Sham) were used by the US against the Assad regime. The contention that ISIS was a covert Western asset was confirmed at the beginning 2017, when an audio of Secretary Kerry's conversation with members of Syria's opposition was leaked (see below).

RUSSIA, SYRIA, AND ISIS

Near the end of 2015, Russia's airforce intervened in Syria to protect Assad—at Assad's invitation. This invitation made Russia's intervention legal, according to international law, whereas any US intervention in Syria would be illegal. (Secretary Kerry has even admitted this in private.[147])

Russia's intervention allowed Assad to take the offensive against ISIS and the other jihadists. The success of this intervention led the Obama administration to drop its public insistence that Assad had to go, but it continued to try to protect al-Nusra and other jihadists.[148]

Russia tried to work out a plan in which it and the United States would join forces against ISIS and other jihadists, but it soon concluded that the US was not going to cooperate but instead wanted to use ISIS against Assad's government. So Russia, along with Syria and Hezbollah, launched "a three-prong attack intended to dispose of the US-backed jihadists."[149]

The effort to clean the jihadists out of Syria focused first on Aleppo—in particular, East Aleppo, which had been under the control of al-Nusra since 2012. Not appreciating the successful beginning of this effort, the United States used this as an opportunity to claim that Russia and Syria, having deliberately targeted children and hospitals, were guilty of war crimes. The US corporate press, being almost unanimous in repeating these charges, evidently convinced most Americans that these claims were true.

The White Helmets

However, Finian Cunningham pointed out that these press claims should not be accepted at face value, because claims of Russian and Syrian "war crimes" made by Western reporters were based on "rebel sources," not on interviews with ordinary citizens in Aleppo. Also, much of the "information" that got reported came from the so-called "volunteer aid" group known as the White Helmets, which made many false claims about itself.

For one thing, it called itself the Syria Civil Defense, but it is not Syrian. Rather, it was created by the U.K. and the USA; it was established in Turkey; and its "volunteers" were mainly trained in Turkey and Jordan. In addition, whereas the *real* Syria Civil Defense has existed since 1953, the White Helmets was formed in 2013 by James Le Mesurier, a former British intelligence officer who was involved in NATO's interventions in Bosnia and Kosovo. He then "moved into the lucrative private mercenary industry," where he became "a mercenary with the Olive Group, a private contracting organization that is now merged with Blackwater-Academi."[150]

The *real* Syria Civil Defense, which was founded in 1953, is the only one. "The White Helmets," said the International Civil Defense Organization, "are not even civil defense concretely. We are working . . . only with official governments… , not the White Helmets."[151]

The real Syria Civil Defense no longer operated in East Aleppo. Journalist Vanessa Beeley, who probably wrote the most about the White Helmets, said that in an interview with the real Syrian Civil Defense, inside West Aleppo, she was told that, in 2012, when various militant factions infiltrated East Aleppo, they drove out the real Syria Civil Defense crew—they massacred many, they kidnapped others, they stole equipment, including all of the ambulances and three to five fire engines.[152]

Another false claim by White Helmets was that it was composed of "volunteers" and that it is "fiercely independent and accepts no money from governments." In truth, it received funding from various governments, especially the U.K. ($65 million) and the US ($23 million), which had collaborated with Le Mesurier in creating the White Helmets. In particular, calling themselves "impartial," the White Helmets claimed, "We're not being paid by anybody to pursue a particular line."[153] However, Abdulrahman Al Mawwas, the chief liaison officer of the White Helmets, confirmed that the group was sponsored by the Western governments.[154]

In any case, this organization did have a very particular, twofold purpose: First, to demonize Assad as a butcher, who killed his own people indiscriminately, so as to argue the need for a no-fly zone (which was, of course, how the attacks on Iraq and Libya began). In campaigning for a no-fly zone, the White Helmets were working together with the public relations organization Avaaz, which had delivered a petition with 1,203,000 signatures to the UN for the Libya no-fly zone. In 2015, Avaaz began trying for a million signatures for a "Safe Zone" petition for Syria.[155]

Second, although the White Helmets served as a terrorist support group, "in the sense of bringing equipment, arms, even funding, into Syria," said Beeley, their "primary function is propaganda," as investigative journalist Rick Sterling explained.[156]

Whereas the US press willingly accepts such propaganda, which supports our government's negative description of Assad and hence Putin, independent journalists who have spent time in Syria, where they have talked to ordinary Syrians, have presented views of Assad that disagree radically with the claims of White Helmets and the US press. See, for example, interviews of journalist Eva Bartlett, who said, "The Media Is Lying to You!" and Vanessa Beeley, who said, "Everything the US Media Says about Aleppo Is Wrong."[157]

Similarly, the highly respected journalist Stephen Kinzer wrote a *Boston Globe* article entitled "The Media Are Misleading the Public on Syria." Although the truth about Aleppo was being reported by "brave correspondents in the war zone," Kinzer said, their reports do "not fit with Washington's narrative. As a result, much of the American press is reporting the opposite of what is actually happening."[158]

Russia vs. America

Thanks to its support from Russia, along with Iran and Hezbollah, Assad's forces were able to defeat the so-called rebels in Aleppo and some other parts of Syria. Turkey then supported the idea of giving up all hope of removing Assad and even joined Russia in fighting against the US-supported jihadists. It became possible, therefore, that the war might be ended, with all jihadists in Syria defeated or removed.

This radical change in the situation was, however, no reason to lose interest in this several-year war. One reason is indicated by a *New York Times* story headed: "Assad Has Won in Syria. But Syria Hardly Exists."[159] The authors wrote:

> Nearly 70 percent of Syrians live in extreme poverty, meaning they cannot secure basic needs. . . . The unemployment rate is close to 58 percent, with a significant number of those employed working as smugglers, fighters or elsewhere in the war economy. Life expectancy has dropped by 20 years since the beginning of the uprising in 2011. About half of children no longer attend school—a lost generation. The country has become a public health disaster. Diseases formerly under control, like typhoid, tuberculosis, Hepatitis A and cholera, are once again endemic. And polio—previously eradicated in Syria—has been reintroduced, probably by fighters from Afghanistan and Pakistan. Upward of 500,000 are dead from the war, and an untold number of Syrians have died indirectly from the conflict (the price for destroying hospitals, targeting health care professionals and using starvation as a weapon). With more than two million injured, about 11.5 percent of the prewar population have become casualties. And close to half the population of Syria is either internally or externally displaced.

A second reason not to forget this war is that, in spite of the fact that the United States, in violation of international law, is significantly responsible for the destruction of Syria, its government and major media—ignoring the evidence and even lying about it—continued to claim that Assad and Putin were the ones guilty of war crimes, thereby suggesting that the US was looking for a way to continue the war.

But at the beginning of 2017, a leaked audio recording of a conversation of Secretary Kerry with so-called rebels confirmed that the strategic aim of the war that the Obama Administration led since 2011 against the Arab Syrian Republic was to topple the regime; that the Obama administration was hoping that ISIS would be able to step into its place to take down the Syrian Arab Republic; and that the Obama administration provided ISIS with arms to topple the Syrian Arab Republic.[160]

This recording made clear that it was Obama, Clinton, and Kerry, not Assad and Putin, who were guilty of crimes against humanity.

EUROPE'S REFUGEE CRISIS

One of the most discussed problems arising out of Bush-Cheney policies has been the aforementioned refugee problem in Europe. Although it is technically a *migrant* problem, as there are many migrants who have not received refugee status, the term "refugee" is here used broadly to refer to all who have sought refuge, so the terms "migrants" and "refugees" are here used interchangeably.

The number of refugees who have come to Europe from the Greater Middle East is large and getting larger. Whereas in 2013, there were 60,000 of them, that number jumped to 280,000 in 2014 then to over a million in 2015.[161]

Most of the refugees have come from countries that have been attacked by the United States: Afghanistan (from which an increasing number of people are trying to leave),[162] Iraq, Libya, and especially Syria, which accounts for about half of them.[163] And unless peace comes to Syria, the number of Syrian refugees wanting to come to Europe is certain to grow, because there are now four million Syrian refugees in Jordan, Lebanon, and Turkey, and there are another 6.5 million Syrians who are internally displaced.[164]

The US-NATO attack on Libya, besides adding to the number of refugees wanting to come to Europe (61,000 came in 2011 alone), added to the problem by removing Gaddafi, because he had helped prevent people from making it to Europe.[165] Adding to the tragedy is the fact that many of those trying to reach Europe died en route, with over 10,000 dying between 2014 and mid-2016.[164]

Dimensions of the Crisis

The number of migrants has become so great that two writers at the Migration Policy Institute said: "[E]ven the best-prepared European countries have reached a breaking point in their ability to meet European Union (EU) standards for receiving and processing applicants." Indeed, they added:

> In the face of seemingly endless spontaneous arrivals, systems are caving under pressure, and trust and solidarity are eroding—between Member States, between publics and their governments, and within the global-protection system as a whole.[167]

For example, the strain on Greece "has become intolerable," explained a *Newsweek* article in February 2016: "There are over 12,000 migrants stranded in Greece, a country that is simply unable to cope financially, politically, or socially with the influx." By August, after the European Union quit allowing large numbers of newcomers to enter, the number of migrants trapped in Greece had increased to 57,000.[168]

With regard to coping financially, the expense can be crippling. By 2015, for example, Turkey—which is treated here as part of Europe—had spent over $6 billion to deal with new refugees.[169]

Another dimension of the crisis involves the unfairness in the acceptance of migrants. "Frontline states such as Greece and Italy [and Turkey] bear a disproportionate responsibility for receiving new arrivals." Although most of the migrants want to move further north, there are many countries who are unwilling to receive their fair share of migrants. Indeed, only Germany, Sweden, and Turkey have been very welcoming. Although Germany has "urgently demanded the solidarity of the rest of the EU," many of the countries are refusing. Indeed, Hungary and some other countries have built high razor-wire fences along their borders.[170]

Saying that "the disregard for agreed decisions experienced during the refugee crisis is a worrying phenomenon," Stefan Lehne said that, although the EU has sought an "ever closer union among the peoples of Europe," the refugee crisis is threatening to lead to "an ever looser union"—a statement that is quoted in the *Newsweek* article about the unraveling of Europe.[171] "Who would have thought," asked Robert Parry, "that the neocons would have succeeded in destabilizing not only the Mideast but Europe as well."[172]

Indeed, after the above stories were written, Britain left the European Union in the so-called Brexit affair, with the migrant crisis widely considered a major factor, and other countries may follow.[173]

Responsibility for the Refugee Crisis

Although it would seem obvious that the primary responsibility for this crisis is the United States, especially the Bush-Cheney and Obama administrations, "American politicians and the US media," observed Bill Van Auken, "are deliberately silent on Washington's central role in creating this unfolding tragedy on Europe's borders." For example, in an editorial entitled "A Refugee Crisis of Historic Scope," the *Washington Post* said that Europe "can't be expected to solve on its own a problem that is originating in Afghanistan, Sudan, Libya and—above all—Syria." Likewise, the *New York Times*, speaking of the "roots of this catastrophe," located those roots in Syria, Iraq, and Libya.[174]

Other people, however, have stated the responsibility clearly: In an essay entitled "A Refugee Crisis Made in America," former CIA case officer Philip Giraldi wrote:

Significantly, the countries that have generated most of the refugees are all places where the United States has invaded, overthrown governments, supported insurgencies, or intervened in a civil war.[175]

Another person capable of stating the obvious is Andrew Bacevich. In spite of Powell's "Pottery Barn Rule," Bacevich said, "the US adamantly refuses to accept anything like ownership of the consequences stemming from Bush's recklessly misguided act." Moreover, Bacevich pointed out, the US has admitted far fewer refugees than have the European countries.[176]

ISRAEL/PALESTINE

Although a discussion of Israel/Palestine is placed last in this chapter, it is arguably second in importance to none. Today's chaos in the Middle East is rooted, Arabs and impartial scholars agree, in what Palestinians call the "catastrophe," when in 1947 the UN General Assembly recommended partitioning Mandate Palestine. The recommendation, which was accepted and put into law by the Security Council, allocated over half of the land to the Jewish state, which then began forcibly taking more and more of the remaining land. Within two years, some 700,000 Palestinian Arabs became refugees, having been forced by the onslaught of Israeli fighters to flee for their lives.

By now, there are over 7 million Palestinian refugees and internally displaced persons, who legally have the right to return. But Israel has passed laws forbidding them to return. Although the United States has never officially endorsed Israel's position, it has tried to convince the refugees that they should settle for symbolic return.[177]

Terrorism and the Occupation

The fact that Palestine has long been occupied is considered by many people, both Arab and not, as the main source of instability and terrorism in the region. For example, this view was stated in 2015 by speakers at the UN's annual International Day of Solidarity with the Palestinian People.

- "The continued Israeli occupation of Arab and Palestinian territory," said Nabil al-Arabi (secretary-general of the Arab League), "represents the main cause for the spread of terrorism and extremist ideology in the region."

- "Failure to find a just solution to the Palestinian cause—as the core issue in the Middle East," said Iyad Ameen Madani (secretary-general of the Organization of Islamic Cooperation)—is "fueling conflicts in the region," threatening to affect international peace and security.[178]

- Except for Arabs and Muslims, however, writers for a long time seldom commented on the connection between terrorism and the occupation. "It is simply extraordinary," remarked Palestinian-American Edward Said in 1996,

that Israel's history, its record—from the fact that it is a state built on conquest, that it has invaded surrounding countries, bombed and destroyed at will, to the fact that it currently occupies Lebanese, Syrian, and Palestinian territory against international law—is simply . . . never addressed as playing any role at all in provoking 'Islamic terror.'[179]

However, increasingly Americans have been speaking out. For example, the website *If Americans Knew* says: "The Israeli-Palestinian conflict is one of the world's major sources of instability."[180] Francis Boyle, University of Illinois professor of international law, wrote:

As matters of fact and of law, the gross and repeated violations of Palestinian rights by the Israeli army and Israeli settlers living illegally in occupied Palestine constitute war crimes.[181]

Richard Falk, in his final report as UN Special Rapporteur on Human Rights in the Palestinian Territories, said:

Through prolonged occupation, with practices and policies of apartheid and segregation, ongoing expansion of settlements, and continual construction of the wall arguably amounting to de facto annexation of parts of the occupied Palestinian territory; the denial by Israel of the right to self-determination of the Palestinian people is evident.

In this report, Falk charged Israel with apartheid, inhuman and degrading treatment, torture, systematic oppression, and murder.[182]

However, what provokes terrorism against the United States is not simply Israel's policies, but the fact that the United States allows these policies and even finances them.

America's "Unwavering Support for Israel"

In 2006, the University of Chicago's John Mearsheimer and Harvard University's Stephen Walt published a major study entitled "The Israel Lobby," in which they said that "the centrepiece of US Middle Eastern policy has been its relationship with Israel." Its "unwavering support for Israel," they wrote, has "inflamed Arab and Islamic opinion and jeopardized not only US security but that of much of the rest of the world."[183] In explaining how this support has jeopardized US security, they wrote:

Support for Israel is not the only source of anti-American terrorism, but it is an important one. . . . [M]any al-Qaeda leaders . . . are motivated by Israel's presence in Jerusalem and the plight of the Palestinians. Unconditional support for Israel makes it easier for extremists to rally popular support and to attract recruits.

Moreover, although during the Clinton administration, "Middle Eastern policy was largely shaped by officials with close ties to Israel," the situation was "even more pronounced in the Bush administration."[184]

Going to War for Israel: In illustrating how decisions of the Bush-Cheney administration were influenced by its complete support for Israel, Mearsheimer and Walt quoted a statement by Philip Zelikow (who was discussed in Chapter 3 above), explaining why Iraq was attacked. Pointing out that Iraq was no threat to America, Zelikow said that the "real threat" was "the threat against Israel."[185] In other words, the Bush-Cheney administration attacked Iraq, at least in part, to help Israel.

Similarly, WikiLeaks in 2016 published a 2012 email letter laying out Hillary Clinton's State Department's support for attacking Syria for the sake of Israel. The letter, which was wrongly dated 2010,[186] has generally been attributed to Clinton herself, but Jason Ditz of AntiWar.com determined that it was a policy statement written by James Rubin. (Rubin had served in Bill Clinton's State Department as Assistant Secretary of State for Public Affairs; he then served as the department's Chief Spokesman; and he later worked for Hillary Clinton's 2008 presidential campaign.)[187] In any case, whether the letter was by Rubin or Clinton herself, it can probably be treated as her thinking.

The document's opening line states: "The best way to help Israel deal with Iran's growing nuclear capability is to help the people of Syria overthrow the regime of Bashar Assad." Pointing out the connection between Iran's nuclear program and Syria's civil war, it said:

For Israeli leaders, the real threat from a nuclear-armed Iran is not the prospect of an insane Iranian leader launching an unprovoked Iranian nuclear attack on Israel. . . . What Israeli military leaders really worry about—but cannot talk about—is losing their nuclear monopoly. An Iranian nuclear weapons capability would. . . result [in] a precarious nuclear balance in which Israel could not respond to provocations with conventional military strikes on Syria and Lebanon, as it can today.[188]

Continuing the explanation, the document said:

It is the strategic relationship between Iran and the regime of Bashar Assad in Syria that makes it possible for Iran to undermine Israel's security—not through a direct attack, . . . but through its proxies in Lebanon, like Hezbollah, that are sustained, armed and trained by Iran via Syria. The end of the Assad regime would end this dangerous alliance.[189]

Summarizing the benefits to Israel if the United States brings about regime change in Syria, the document said:

Bringing down Assad would not only be a massive boon to Israel's security, it would also ease Israel's understandable fear of losing its nuclear monopoly. . . . With Assad gone, and Iran no longer able to threaten Israel through its proxies, it is possible that the United States and Israel can agree on red lines for when Iran's program has crossed an unacceptable threshold.

Unfortunately, the document added, the mission to change the regime in Syria will need to be carried out by a coalition, because "Russia will never support such a mission, so there is no point operating through the UN Security Council." Likewise, it said, the regime would not agree to a diplomatic solution. "With his life and his family at risk, only the threat or use of force will change the Syrian dictator Bashar Assad's mind."[190]

And so, the United States would need to go to war: "Unlike in Libya, a successful intervention in Syria would require substantial diplomatic and military leadership from the United States."

So after the United States had destroyed Iraq, partly for the sake of Israel, its State Department, under the leadership of Hillary Clinton, was ready to do the same for Syria. In addition, it was ready to destroy Iran's nuclear program whenever it and Israel agreed that the time was ripe.

Supporting Israel's Occupation Financially

Alison Weir, who runs the above-mentioned website *If Americans Knew,* pointed out that the case for which Mearsheimer and Walt argued was stated matter-of-factly by Daniel Shapiro, the Obama-appointed Ambassador to Israel. Speaking to a Jewish institute, Shapiro said:

The test of every policy the Administration develops in the Middle East is whether it is consistent with the goal of ensuring Israel's future as a secure, Jewish, democratic state. That is a commitment that runs as a common thread through our entire government.

Giving an example of America's support for Israel, Shapiro said:

Israel will receive over $3 billion in US funding for training and equipment in the coming fiscal year. This assistance allows Israel to purchase the sophisticated defense equipment it needs to protect itself, by itself, including the world's most advanced fighter aircraft, the F-35 Joint Strike Fighter.

At that time, said Shapiro in 2011, the administration was "doing everything we can" to oppose the Palestinian bid for UN membership that was coming up that month.[191]

Protecting Israel in the Security Council: One of the main ways in which the United States supports Israel's continued oppression of Palestinians is using its veto power to block resolutions critical of Israel or otherwise opposed by it. Here is the list of such resolutions since the beginning of the Bush-Cheney administration:

- **2001** To send unarmed monitors to the West Bank and the Gaza Strip.

- **2002** Condemns the killing of a UN worker from the United Kingdom by Israeli forces.

- **2003** Condemns a decision by the Israeli parliament to "remove" the elected Palestinian president, Yasser Arafat.

- **2003** Condemns the building of a wall by Israel on Palestinian land.

- **2004** Condemns the assassination of Hamas leader Sheik Ahmad Yassin.

- **2004** Condemns the Israeli incursion and killings in Gaza.

- **2006** Calls for an end to Israeli military incursions and attacks on Gaza.

- **2007** Calls for the right of self determination for the Palestinian people.

- **2008** Calls for a treaty on children's rights

- **2008** Condemns racial discrimination.

- **2008** Affirms the sovereignty of Palestinians over the occupied territories and their resources.

- **2008** Affirms the right of the Palestinians to self determination.

- **2008** Calls on Israel to pay the cost of cleaning up an oil slick off the coast of Lebanon caused by its bombing.

- **2008** Resolutions concerning Palestine, its people, their property, and Israeli practices in Palestine, including settlements.

- **2009** Calls for an end to the twenty-two-day-long Israeli attack on Gaza.

- **2011** Calls for a halt to the illegal Israeli West Bank settlements. (Prime Minister Netanyahu said, "Israel deeply appreciates the decision by President Obama to veto the Security Council Resolution."[192]

The list of Obama's vetoes need not be continued, given a *New York Times* story of 2016 saying: "Over seven years, Mr. Obama has not permitted passage of any Security Council resolution specifically critical of Israel."[193]

In vetoing resolutions critical of Israel, the United States allowed Israel to violate international law with impunity. For example, the Fourth Geneva Convention of 1949, which deals with "belligerent occupation," applies to the West Bank, the Gaza Strip, and the entire City of Jerusalem, in order to protect the Palestinians living there. In 2000—just before the installation of the Bush-Cheney administration—the Security Council passed a resolution that:

> Calls upon Israel, the occupying Power, to abide scrupulously by its legal obligations and its responsibilities under the Fourth Geneva Convention relative to the Protection of Civilian Persons.

The vote, said Boyle, "was 14 to 0, becoming obligatory international law."[194]

The Palestinian People living in this Palestinian Land, Boyle continued, are "protected persons," whose "rights are sacred under international law." The Fourth Geneva Convention has 149 articles spelling out these rights. However, although violations of the Fourth Geneva Convention are war crimes,

> The Israeli Government is currently violating, and has since 1967 been violating, almost each and every one of these sacred rights of the Palestinian People recognized by the Fourth Geneva Convention.[195]

And yet, the United States continued to protect Israel from needing to abide by any such obligations of international law. One can see why Palestinians, both inside and outside the country, along with other Arabs and Muslims, are enraged by both Israel and the United States.

Israel's treatment of Palestinians, of course, causes violence within Israel itself as well as in the larger region. Ron Huldai, the mayor of Tel Aviv, had the courage to speak about this after four Israelis were shot in his city by a Palestinian teenager. Saying that such violence results from the Israeli Occupation, Huldai explained:

We, as a state, are the only ones in the world with another people living among us under our occupation, denying them any civil rights. . . . The problem is that when there is no terrorism, no one talks about it [the occupation].

Commenting about Huldai's statement, Ben Ehrenreich, who wrote a book subtitled *Life and Death in Palestine*, said: "As long as this oppressive system stands, and the United States continues to support it with billions of dollars a year in military aid, despair will spread, and with it death."[196]

Israel, to be sure, claims that its actions against Palestinians are justified as self-defense. But it takes only a few comparisons to see the absurdity of this claim:

- Between 2000 and 2015: There were 1,224 Israelis killed by Palestinians, while 9,370 Palestinians were killed by Israelis.

- During that same period, 139 Israeli children were killed by Palestinians, while 2,112 Palestinian children were killed by Israelis.

- Between 1967 and 2015: At least 48,888 Palestinian homes were demolished by Israelis, while no Israeli homes were demolished by Palestinians.

- During that same period, 11,755 Israelis were injured by Palestinians, while 87,305 Palestinians were injured.

- Israel currently has 261 (illegal) settlements and outposts on confiscated Palestinian land, whereas Palestinians have no settlements on Israeli land.

- Currently, no Israelis are imprisoned by Palestinians, while 7,000 Palestinians are imprisoned by Israel.

- The Israeli unemployment rate is 5.6%, while the Palestinian unemployment rate in the West Bank is 17.7% and 44% in Gaza.

- During Fiscal Year 2014, the US provided Israel with at least $10.2 million in military aid per day, while it provided $0 to Palestinians.[197]

- Reflecting the differences of their military budgets: Palestinian weapons are limited to stones, knives, rockets, and a few guns, whereas Israel has one of the best-equipped militaries in the world, having up-to-date pistols, rifles, assault weapons, grenade launchers, missiles, artillery, drones, fighter planes, and nuclear weapons—as well as its Iron Dome, which intercepts rockets.[198]

Accordingly, America's totally one-sided treatment of Israel and Palestine can by itself provide an answer to the question, "Why do they hate us?"

One Exception

At the end of 2016, the United States broke with its record of allowing Israel to violate international law with impunity. A US Security Council resolution condemned Israeli settlement construction, and for the first time the Obama administration abstained, rather than veto it. This event cannot, however, be seen as the beginning of a new way to deal with Israel, as President Trump has promised to be even more supportive of Israel's wishes than previous presidents.

CONCLUSION

There are still more features of the chaos unleashed in the Greater Middle East by the Bush-Cheney administration—such as its inauguration of drone killings in Yemen (to be discussed in the next chapter) and its 2006 airstrikes in support of Somalia—which turned that poor country into an even worse basket case and turned al-Shabaab into a major terrorist organization.[199]

But the above examples are sufficient to illustrate some of the ways that the Bush-Cheney administration, whose policies here were continued by the Obama administration, ruined much of the world, beyond what it did to Afghanistan and Iraq. This type of summary is important insofar as Bacevich's observation is correct, namely: "We Americans are in something approaching complete denial about how truly horrible our nation's recent impact on the rest of the world has been."[200]

Indeed, it could have been even more horrible if Cheney had been able to attack another of the targets on the list of seven countries he wanted to attack: Iran. Along with other neocons, Cheney fervently wanted to attack Iran (as illustrated by the quip going around, "everyone wants to go to Baghdad; real men want to go to Tehran"[201]). Cheney evidently gave up this plan only because of extreme pressure, including a threat by Democrats that Bush would be impeached if he attacked Iran without permission from Congress,[202] plus a 2007 National Intelligence Estimate (based on America's 16 intelligence agencies), which declared "with 'high confidence' that a military-run Iranian program intended to transform that raw material into a nuclear weapon has been shut down since 2003."[203] One of the most important achievements of Obama as president was working out a nuclear deal with Iran that might stop the incessant drive by Israeli and American hawks to attack Iran (Cheney continued to call for war with Iran after he left office).[204]

Unfortunately, with regard to the major ways in which the United States has recently used its military power to dominate the Greater Middle East, Obama, rather than curtailing it, expanded it not only in Libya and Syria but also in still another respect—as discussed in the next chapter.

7 • DRONE WARFARE AND INTERNATIONAL LAW

The global chaos discussed in the previous chapter followed significantly from the Bush-Cheney administration's unilateral rejection, or modification, of international law with regard to war, as discussed in Chapter 3. According to traditional international law, as formulated after the creation of the United Nations, one nation may legally attack another nation preemptively only under one condition: If nation A knows *with certainty* that an attack on it by nation B is *imminent*—too imminent for the issue to be sent to the UN Security Council for arbitration.

According to the Bush Doctrine, by contrast, the United States will act against emerging threats "before they are fully formed."[1] In other words, if the United States sees that another country may sometime in the future acquire the ability to harm our country, the United States may attack it now. This new doctrine was enunciated, of course, in the interests of defending and expanding the American empire.

Some defenders of the Bush-Cheney administration have claimed that the Bush Doctrine was no big change, because the United States and other countries have often attacked others without permission from the United Nations. However—said Stefan Halper and Jonathan Clarke in their 2005 book on neoconservatives and global order—no president had ever "set out a formal national strategy *doctrine* that included [preventive] preemption."[2] This doctrine stated explicitly that the basic principle of international law, as embodied in the United Nations, did not apply to the USA.

Besides being used to attack Iraq, this new doctrine implied that the United States would have the right to attack any other states to prevent them from developing the means to threaten America or its interests. Of course, the United States would not extend this privilege to any other countries. The United States has this privilege only because it is militarily so much more powerful than any of the other countries, so it would be able to inflict unacceptable retribution on them. As this doctrine shows, the Bush Doctrine rests on the principle, from which the United Nations was created to protect us, that *might makes right*.

DRONE WARFARE AND 9/11

Since the first few years of the wars in Afghanistan and Iraq, the Bush Doctrine has become most important with regard to the military use of drones—technically: unmanned aerial vehicles. This type of warfare is very different from the traditional type: Rather than being exercised against armies, military drones are used to kill individuals, who may or may not be in war zones. In other words, drone warfare seems to involve assassination.

Unmanned aerial vehicles (UAVs) had been in existence for several decades, but they started to be used extensively by the military only during the first Gulf War of 1990-1991, where they were used primarily by the CIA. "Before September 11, the CIA," pointed out the author of *Drone Warfare*, Medea Benjamin, "only used drones for surveillance." However:

> Post-9/11, everything changed. The agency asked for, and received from President Bush, a secret memorandum giving it the right to target Al Qaeda virtually anywhere in the world. With the green light to kill, the CIA began putting its drones to work.

As a result, "the 9/11 World Trade Center attacks," said Benjamin, "led to an explosion in the US military's use of drones."[3] However, this explosion began slowly. The Bush-Cheney administration started an assassination-by-drone program in 2005, with only a few strikes in the first few years.[4] But in the administration's final year, wrote Mark Mazzetti—the author of *The Way of the Knife*[5]—it "really started ramping it up,"with the result that this administration ended up conducting a total of 51 strikes.[6]

But then a second explosion occurred in the administration of Barack Obama, which continued the Bush-Cheney policies on this issue—as it did on many other issues—and, in Mazzetti's words, "ramped it up even further."[7]

In fact, drone warfare became the primary means through which the United States sought to enforce its will in the Greater Middle East. In 2015, Lt. General Michael Flynn, who had been head of the Defense Intelligence Agency, said: "Our entire Middle East policy seems to be based on firing drones."[8]

The centrality of drones in today's military battles is discussed in a documentary film entitled *National Bird*. It suggests that, to many people around the world, "America's new national symbol is not the bald eagle," said Peter Van Buren, "but a gray shadow overhead armed with Hellfire missiles."[9]

The use of drones to attack alleged "bad guys" has become very popular among US political and military leaders. The main attraction is that US warriors can kill enemies with no risk to themselves. These "cubicle warriors" can, while sitting in an office somewhere in the United States, program drones to kill people in Afghanistan, Pakistan, Iraq, Syria, Yemen, Somalia, or anywhere else. President Obama reportedly became "enraptured by their potential for risk reduction."[10]

Another attraction is that this way of fighting the "war on terror" solves what had been the most long-standing problem for America resulting from the wars in Afghanistan and Iraq: What to do with prisoners. Drones cannot capture people, but they can kill them, thereby avoiding debate about what to do with prisoners. As Stalin reportedly said, "No man, no problem."[11]

ARE DRONE KILLINGS ACCEPTABLE?

However, in spite of these perceived advantages, America's use of drones militarily has evoked an enormous amount of criticism. A growing number of writers have suggested that America's drone warfare is unacceptable.

Assassination

The main reason for this view is the fact that killing by drone seems to be *extrajudicial killing*, which is the intentional taking of life that has not been authorized by a judge. The Bush and Obama administrations have used drone strikes, said Jeremy Scahill in a major study known as the "Drone Papers," to kill people they have "deemed—through secretive processes, without indictment or trial—worthy of execution."[12]

When carried out by a government, extrajudicial killing is usually called *assassination*. In the United States, however, governmental assassination has long been considered unlawful. Presidents Gerald Ford, Jimmy Carter, and Ronald Reagan issued orders making assassination by anyone acting on behalf of the US government illegal. (The executive order signed by Reagan in 1981, for example, said. "No person employed by or acting on behalf of the United States Government shall engage in, or conspire to engage in, assassination.") This policy was restated as late as two months before 9/11, when Martin Indyk, the US ambassador to Israel, criticized that country's targeted killing of Palestinians. "The United States is very clearly on record as against targeted assassinations," he said.[13]

But after 9/11, the Bush-Cheney and Obama administrations have treated drone killing as legal. How could this fact be reconciled with the prohibition of assassination? At first, the Obama administration had sought to avoid the charge by simply not acknowledging that it engaged in drone killings. But after they became known as one of "the worst kept secrets in Washington," Obama finally in 2012 admitted their existence.[14] From then on, his administration's approach was to say that drone killings are not "extrajudicial killing" or "assassination," but merely "targeted killings."

In 2013, the NYT's public editor dealt with an article by Scott Shane entitled "Targeted Killing Comes to Define War on Terror." Responding to a reader's question, she asked: "If it's premeditated assassination, why call it a 'targeted killing?'" Shane replied:

> "Assassination" is banned by executive order, but for decades that has been interpreted by successive administrations as prohibiting the killing

of political figures, not suspected terrorists. . . . Were we to use "assassination" routinely about drone shots, it would suggest that the administration is deliberately violating the executive order, which is not the case.[15]

Shane is certainly correct that the prohibition of assassination was about *political* assassination; in fact, in the original order, given by President Ford, the term used was "political assassination."

However, the term "assassination" is not used only for the extrajudicial killing of *politicians*. Rather, said Judge Abraham Sofaer, "the word *assassination* is used in the twenty-first century to describe murders committed for political reasons."[16] Most extrajudicial killings by drone are carried out for political reasons. *So most drone killings are assassinations.* As retired US Army Colonel Ann Wright said in 2011:

> These drones, you might as well just call them assassination machines. That is what these drones are used for: targeted assassination, extrajudicial ultimate death for people who have not been convicted of anything.[17]

Drone warfare, wrote Eugene Robinson, "is, put simply, war by assassination."[18]

Murder

Moreover, Shane's argument completely lost cogency when he turned to the term "murder," saying:

> "Murder," of course, is a specific crime described in United States law with a bunch of elements, including illegality, so it would certainly not be straight news reporting to say President Obama was "murdering" people. This leaves "targeted killing," which I think is far from a euphemism. It denotes exactly what's happening: American drone operators aim at people on the ground and fire missiles at them. I think it's a pretty good term for what's happening, if a bit clinical.[19]

"Targeted killing" is indeed an accurate term. But Shane ignores the question of why targeted killing is not also *murder*, at least as this process is used by the US government.

In explaining why he renounced his commission, Army Chaplain Captain Chris Antal said that the US government "claims the right to kill anyone, anywhere on earth, at any time, for secret reasons, based on secret evidence, in a secret process, undertaken by unidentified officials."[20] If that is not murder, what would be?

As Judge Abraham Sofaer said, assassination is wrong not only because it is government officials killing politicians, but more fundamentally because it is *murder*:

> Assassination is widely defined as murder, and is for that reason prohibited in the United States by executive order. US officials may not kill people merely because their policies are seen as detrimental to our interests.[21]

In other words, assassinations are wrong most fundamentally because they are murder, against which there are laws, both domestic and international. As Rebecca Gordon said:

> Such killings—at least when they take place outside a declared war zone—are almost certainly illegal; that is, they are murders, plain and simple.[22]

To be sure, Sofaer added, "killings in self-defense are no more 'assassinations' in international affairs than they are murders when undertaken by our police forces against domestic killers." Extrajudicial killing is not murder or assassination if it is lawful.[23]

But if targeted killing is not self-defense or lawful for some other reason, it is murder. So unlawful targeted killing is illegal whether it be defined as assassination or not. America's prohibition of assassination simply made clear that extrajudicial killing cannot be excused on the grounds that it was carried out on behalf of one's government.

To emphasize the fact that US policy in the Greater Middle East is now oriented around drone killings, Paul Craig Roberts wrote an article headed, "Murder Is Washington's Foreign Policy."[24]

In an essay entitled "How Extrajudicial Executions Became 'War' Policy in Washington," Rebecca Gordon wrote:

> The technical advances embodied in drone technology distract us from a more fundamental change in military strategy. . . . Drone technology is really a Trojan Horse, a distracting, glitzy means of smuggling an illegal and immoral tactic into the heart of US foreign relations.[25]

Self-Defense

An attempt to defend the government's targeted killing by drone was provided in 2010 by State Department advisor Harold Koh, who argued that the Obama administration's use of lethal force against specific individuals cannot be called *unlawful extrajudicial killing* on the grounds that they do not "provide adequate process." Why? Because a state engaged in an armed conflict or in legitimate self-defense is "not required to provide targets with legal process."[26]

However, the United States has not declared war on most of the countries in which it has used drone strikes, so drone fighters are not engaged in "armed conflict" in the legal sense. Also, drone killings are seldom if ever used in "self-defense" in the generally accepted sense, according to which the need for self-defense is "instant, overwhelming, and leaving no choice of means and no moment of deliberation."[27] US drone strikes are usually based on planning that took days, weeks, or even months. Far from being self-defense in any meaningful sense, drone strikes are usually assassinations to prevent actions that are contrary to US imperial interests. That cannot legitimately be called "self-defense."

Koh used the same two bases for arguing that drone killing does not constitute "assassination." But whether or not this term be used, targeted killing by drone typically involves extrajudicial killing that is unlawful because it is not committed in self-defense.

UN Authorization

The Bush-Cheney and Obama administrations were heavily based on a self-defense argument resting on the Authorization for Use of Military Force (AUMF) passed after 9/11, which said:

> [T]he President is authorized to use all necessary and appropriate force against those nations, organizations, or persons he determines planned, authorized, committed, or aided the terrorist attacks that occurred on September 11, 2001, or harbored such organizations or persons, in order to prevent any future acts of international terrorism against the United States by such nations, organizations or persons.

There are two reasons why this authorization cannot be used to legalize US military strikes from Afghanistan to Iraq to Syria to Libya to Yemen and Somalia.

First, although the authorization document did not have a termination date on it, Congress and the UN Security Council did not mean to authorize a war to last forever. Second, even if the invasion on Afghanistan *were* justifiable as self-defense (which Chapter 2 argued was not the case), it is illegitimate to use the AUMF not only for the original al-Qaeda but also for "associated forces." In a 2013 speech at the National Defense University (NDU), President Obama said:

> This is a just war—a war waged . . . in self-defense. We were attacked on 9/11. Under domestic law, and international law, the United States is at war with al-Qaeda, the Taliban, and their associated forces.

According to Charlie Savage's summary, the Obama administration defined an associated force as "(1) an organized, armed group that (2) aligned itself with al-Qaeda, and (3) entered the fight against the United States and its coalition partners."[28]

The Obama administration, therefore, said that targeted killings of members of "al-Qaeda and associated forces" are not assassinations, just as the Bush-Cheney administration claimed that the president had the right to take "legal action against members of al-Qaeda and any affiliated groups."[29]

However, neither Bush's term "affiliated groups" nor Obama's term "associated forces" is found in the AUMF. So, even if the AUMF could be used to authorize an ongoing battle against al-Qaeda today, it cannot be used to authorize battling against "associated forces" (even if the administration would finally specify which forces these are[30]).

Moreover, even if one were to accept the claim that AUMF can apply to "associated forces," not all of the groups being attacked by the United States can reasonably be called associated forces. This difficulty is most important in relation to ISIS, which in 2015 became the Obama administration's primary focus (at least after it reduced its drive to get rid of Assad). The problem is that in 2014, the new leader of al-Qaeda, Ayman al-Zawahiri, ex-communicated al-Baghdadi's group (ISIS) from al-Qaeda. So ISIS can hardly be called one of al-Qaeda's "associated forces." Nevertheless, in order to justify using the AUMF as legalizing its war with ISIS, the Obama administration— as Savage put it—employed the "Islamic State war equals al-Qaeda war" claim.[31] The claim that Somalia's al-Shabaab is an associated force is especially problematic, given the fact that in 2001, it did not exist.[32]

Accordingly, because the 2001 AUMF cannot be used to justify war 15 or more years later, and because there is no basis for enlarging it to apply to "associated forces," all drone (as well as air) strikes today would require new authorization from the UN Security Council. The Obama administration did not ask for this, however, probably because they didn't anticipate approval. Also, the executive branch claimed that it did not need it: Cheney's neocon argument that the United States can ignore the United Nations was embraced, if only implicitly, by the Obama administration.

Sure enough, near the end of Obama's administration, the *New York Times* told us: "The administration has decided to deem the Shabab, the Islamist militant group in Somalia, to be part of the armed conflict that Congress authorized against the perpetrators of the Sept. 11, 2001, terrorist attacks."[33] How does one "deem" that al-Shabab was part of the armed conflict in 2001, even though it did not exist? By the end, the Obama administration evidently felt that it should just declare anything it wanted.

In any case, the Bush-Cheney and Obama administrations, all in all, appealed to the AUMF a total of 37 times in 14 different countries

(Afghanistan, Cuba, Djibouti, Eritrea, Ethiopia, Georgia, Iraq, Kenya, Libya, the Philippines, Somalia, Syria, Turkey, and Yemen).[34]

International Law

Insofar as Americans do not accept the neocon view of the Bush-Cheney and Obama administrations, according to which America can ignore international law, it is important to recognize that experts in this branch of law have indicated that most drone killings are unacceptable.

- Professor Philip Alston, UN special rapporteur on extrajudicial executions, said drone killings may be lawful in the context of authorized armed conflict. But the use of drones "far from the battle zone," he added, "is almost never likely to be legal."[35]

- Professor Mary Ellen O'Connell has pointed out that, under the charter of the United Nations, international law authorizes nations to kill people in other countries only in self-defense against an armed attack, or if authorized by the UN, or if invited to aid another state in the lawful use of force. "Outside of war, the full body of human rights applies, including the prohibition on killing without warning."[36]

In sum, whether or not killings by drones be technically called "assassinations," they are unacceptable insofar as they fit the definition of murder according to both international and domestic law.

DO DRONE STRIKES RARELY KILL CIVILIANS?

Aside from the issue of assassination, many other questions have been raised about the government's claims about drone strikes. The central one has been about the killing of innocent people.

From the beginning, US officials have spoken of drone strikes as very *precise*, so that they would result in little collateral damage:

- In a speech to cadets at The Citadel less than a month after 9/11, President Bush said that the Predator drone can "transmit information instantly back to commanders, then fire on targets with extreme accuracy."[37]

- In 2012, in first publicly acknowledging the reality of drone assassinations, President Obama said: "Drones have not caused a huge number of civilian casualties. For the most part they have been very precise precision strikes against Al Qaeda and their affiliates.[38]

- That same year, John Brennan, the president's top counterterrorism advisor, acknowledged that there have been instances when "civilians have been accidentally injured, or worse, killed in these strikes." However, he said, "It is exceedingly rare."[39]

- In 2016, Michael Hayden, who had served under both Bush and Obama (as director of the NSA and then the CIA), described drone warfare as "the most precise and effective application of firepower in the history of armed conflict."[40]

Evidence Disproves the Government's Claims

However, evidence has been accumulating that drone strikes have been less precise, and have killed far more civilians, than those statements would suggest.

In 2006, a drone launched by the Bush-Cheney administration hit an Islamic school, resulting in about 80 deaths. Although the US and Pakistani governments claimed that all those killed were militants, "An eyewitness told the BBC that the madrassa was filled with about 80 local students who had resumed studies after the Muslim Eid holidays." This consequence was evidently no exception, as suggested by this report:

> More than a third of all Bush drone strikes appear to have resulted in the deaths of children. On only one occasion during Bush's time in office did a single child die in a strike. Multiple deaths occurred every other time.[41]

Obama's drone attacks were also problematic from the beginning. On the third day he was in office, he raised no objection to a CIA drone strike in Pakistan that was about to take place. Shortly thereafter, he learned that there had been a mistake:

> Instead of hitting the CIA's intended target, a Taliban hideout, the missile had struck the compound of a prominent tribal elder and members of a pro-government peace committee. The strike killed the elder and four members of his family, including two of his children.[42]

One of the family members who survived was 14 year-old Faheem Qureshi, a promising student who planned a career in chemistry. The drone attack destroyed Qureshi's plans, as well as most of his family:

> Shrapnel had punctured his stomach. Lacerations covered much of his upper body. Doctors operated on the entire left side of his body, which had sustained burns, and used laser surgery to repair his right eye. They could not save his left. His family kept the worst from him while he recuperated. Two of Qureshi's uncles, Mohammed Khalil and Mansoor

Rehman, were dead. So was his 21-year-old cousin Aizazur Rehman Qureshi, who was preparing to leave the family's North Waziristan home for work. . . . Fourteen of Qureshi's cousins were left fatherless. Barely a teenager, Qureshi was suddenly an elder male within his family, tasked with providing for his mother, brothers and sisters.[43]

On the same day as the strike that struck Qureshi and his family, a second drone strike approved by Obama did not work out any better: The attack "leveled another house," killing "between five and ten people, all civilians."[44]

Although these deadly mistakes, which reportedly angered Obama, increased his skepticism about drone attacks, he soon became an advocate. "When Obama accepted the Nobel Peace Prize in December 2009, he had authorized more drone strikes than George W. Bush had approved during his entire presidency."[45]

Obama defended them on the grounds given by Brennan and himself—that civilian deaths from drone strikes are "exceedingly rare," so they have "not caused a huge number of civilian casualties." Likewise, Hillary Clinton, when she was the Secretary of State, said:

> The numbers about potential civilian casualties I take with a somewhat big grain of salt, because there has been other studies which have proven there not to have been the number of civilian casualties.[46]

However, reports have demonstrated that they are not rare at all. According to a 2014 story in the *Guardian*:

- In 2006, the government started using drones in Pakistan to try to kill the al-Qaeda leader, Ayman Zawahiri, but he is still alive, while 105 people not targeted—29 adults, 76 children—were killed.

- In 2008, the government started targeting Oari Hussain, an officer in the Pakistani Taliban. After several attempts, in which 128 non-targeted people (including 13 children) were killed, he was finally eliminated in 2010.

- Some 24 men targeted in Pakistan resulted in the deaths of 874 people, 142 of whom were children.

- In 2016, the UN condemned a strike in Afghanistan of some 15 men who had "gathered in a village to celebrate the return of a tribal elder from the Hajj pilgrimage to Mecca" while they were sleeping. This slaughter occurred "almost a year to the day," reported the *Guardian*, "after another US airstrike destroyed a Doctors Without Borders hospital in Kunduz, killing 42."[47]

As these stories illustrate, significant evidence of the falsity of the government's rosy descriptions of drone attacks had been accumulated by 2014. The press had also discovered details about the program, such as the fact that the administration has selected from a number of people proposed for assassination by the Pentagon, and that the "kill list" has no geographic limits, so that the US can assassinate people from anywhere on the planet. The selection is made from some of Obama's advisors and, when there is disagreement among the advisors, by Obama himself.[48]

The Drone Papers

But then in 2015, a much fuller and more damning amount of evidence became available through the release by The Intercept of an 8-part series of reports, called "The Drone Papers." These papers were based on information provided—reported journalist Jeremy Scahill in the first of the papers—by "a source within the intelligence community."

This source decided to provide these documents because, in Scahill's words, "he believes the public has a right to understand the process by which people are placed on kill lists and ultimately assassinated on orders from the highest echelons of the US government." This process of "assigning [people] death sentences without notice, on a worldwide battlefield," said the source, "was, from the very first instance, wrong."[49]

In the first of the papers, entitled "The Assassination Complex," Scahill said that the papers "lay bare the normalization of assassination as a central component of US counterterrorism policy."[50] They also show that the assassinations typically kill more people than the number who had been targeted. For example, during a five-month stretch of a campaign in Afghanistan dubbed "Operation Haymaker," drone strikes resulted in 19 "jackpots" and at least 136 other people classified as "enemies killed in action," abbreviated EKIA; over a 14-month period of that operation, there were some 35 jackpots out of 219 people killed.

As one of the Drone Papers explains: When drone operators hit their target, killing the person they intend to kill, that person is called a "jackpot." When they miss their target and end up killing someone else, they label that person EKIA, or "enemy killed in action"—or, more precisely, as the *New York Times* had explained in 2012, all military-age males "unless there is explicit intelligence posthumously proving them innocent." Given this explicit intelligence, the killed people are called "civilian"; otherwise they are called "enemies killed in action" (not mistakes).[51]

This practice is one of the ways in which the government can claim that drone strikes result in very few civilian deaths. Without that dishonest method of counting, the Drone Papers show—reported *New York*

Magazine—that in Afghanistan, Yemen, and Somalia, "For every targeted individual assassinated, another five or six non-targeted individuals are killed."[52]

These papers give the lie, wrote an article in *Consortium News*, "to the Obama administration's long-standing claims of careful, precision killing of specific targets in order to avoid killing civilians."[53]

Change of Policy?

In the NDU speech in May 2013, Obama indicated that his previous picture had been too rosy; he should have made clear that his statement about few civilian casualties was less a claim than an aspiration:

> [O]ver the last four years, my administration has worked vigorously to establish a framework that governs our use of force against terrorists— insisting upon clear guidelines, oversight and accountability that is now codified in Presidential Policy Guidance that I signed yesterday.

Admitting that "that US strikes have resulted in civilian casualties," he announced his new policy: "[B]efore any strike is taken, there must be near-certainty that no civilians will be killed or injured."[54]

There was some evidence, reported at the end of 2013, that Obama's new policy was resulting in fewer civilian deaths.[55] But if the policy change did reduce civilian deaths, it evidently did not do so significantly. In early 2015, the Bureau of Investigative Journalism published a report headed, "US Airstrikes in Afghanistan Killing Civilians at Greatest Rate for Seven Years." (This report appeared just before the day, incidentally, in which Michael Hayden described drone warfare as "the most precise and effective application of firepower in the history of armed conflict.")[56]

Moreover, the new policy did not last long: In 2016, because of Obama's focus on defeating ISIS, he established a more relaxed policy, according to which drone strikes would be allowed in areas in which as many as 10 civilian casualties might occur.[57] A way in which this extra-immoral policy might be reversed has been suggested by Medea Benjamin, "If Americans Can Sue Saudis Over 9/11, Drone Victims Should Be Able to Sue the US."[58]

Signature Strikes

Accordingly, Obama's assassination-by-drone program went on killing a lot of civilians. One reason for this ongoing killing was the fact that the Obama administration continued "signature strikes," in which, rather than targeting specific persons, the strikes target individuals who "match a pre-identified 'signature' of behavior that the US links to militant activity."[59] In other words, these people look like they might be terrorists, so we will kill them as if we knew they were.

Signature strikes were begun in the final year of the Bush-Cheney administration and then continued by Obama. He was reportedly advised by Michael Hayden: "You could take out a lot more bad guys when you targeted groups instead of individuals."[60] Continuing these are almost certain to cause a large number of civilian deaths.[61] A likely example of a signature strike gone terribly wrong is provided by one in 2013 that turned a wedding party into a funeral. According to the story by Democracy Now!:

> [A] US drone targeted a wedding procession going toward the groom's village outside the central Yemeni city of Rad'a. According to HRW [Human Rights Watch], "some, if not all those killed and wounded were civilians" and not members of the armed group al-Qaeda in the Arabian Peninsula (AQAP), as US and Yemeni government officials initially claimed. The report concluded that the attack killed 12 men . . . and wounded 15 others.

The father of one of the young men who were killed said:

> We were having a traditional marriage ceremony. According to our traditions, the whole tribe has to go to the bride's tribe. We were in about 12 to 15 cars with 60 to 70 men on board. He had lunch at the bride's village at Al Abu Saraimah. Then we left to head back to the groom's village. . . . One of the missiles hit the car. The car was totally burned. Four other cars were also struck. . . . Blood was everywhere, and the people killed and injured were scattered everywhere.[62]

Although the United States never offered an explanation, it seems likely that a motorcade transporting dozens of men was considered a signature for a bunch of al-Qaeda terrorists.

In any case, another signature strike in Pakistan in 2011, reported Arianna Huffington, was even more deadly, killing 42 people, showing Obama's criterion about "near-certainty" to be empty rhetoric.[63]

In 2013, Obama's aides had said they were going to phase out signature strikes. But in 2016, the administration "abandoned any pretense of reining in its use of signature strikes."[64] However, recognizing how controversial they had become, the Obama administration changed the name to "terrorist attack disruption strikes" (TADS).[65] As long as signature strikes, a.k.a. TADS, continue, it is certain that there will continue to be a high number of citizen casualties—of "men, women and children," in Bill Van Auken's words, "who are not deliberately targeted but nonetheless blown to pieces."[66]

ARE DRONE STRIKES USED ONLY WHEN CAPTURE IS IMPOSSIBLE?

The Obama administration stated emphatically and repeatedly that, in seeking to prevent militants from harming Americans, it preferred to capture them if possible; it resorted to drone strikes only when capture was impossible.

- In response to the charge that the government "prefer[s] to kill suspected terrorists, rather than capture them," John Brennan said: "This is absurd, and I want to take this opportunity to set the record straight. . . . [W]henever it is possible to capture a suspected terrorist, it is the unqualified preference of the administration to take custody of that individual so we can obtain information that is vital to the safety and security of the American people."[67]

- In his NDU speech, Obama said: "America does not take strikes when we have the ability to capture individual terrorists; our preference is always to detain, interrogate, and prosecute."[68]

- In a 2013 document stating "US Policy Standards and Procedures" for drone strikes, the White House said: "The policy of the United States is not to use lethal force when it is feasible to capture a terrorist suspect, because capturing a terrorist offers the best opportunity to gather meaningful intelligence and to mitigate and disrupt terrorist plots."[69]

This issue is one of the central matters of dispute about drone warfare, as illustrated by the fact that Daniel Klaidman wrote an entire book about it, *Kill or Capture: The War on Terror and the Soul of the Obama Presidency*.[70]

The administration's claim—that the operating policy of the Obama administration is to prefer capture—has been roundly disputed by journalists, as illustrated by the titles of some articles and programs:

- In 2013, Micah Zenko wrote an article for *Foreign Policy* asking: "Why Did the CIA Stop Torturing and Start Killing?"[71]

- That same year, Democracy Now! had a program entitled: "The Way of the Knife: NYT's Mark Mazzetti on the CIA's Post-9/11 Move from Spying to Assassinations."

- In 2015, Joshua Keating wrote an article in *Slate* entitled: "Obama Says He'd Rather Capture Terrorists Than Kill Them. Then Why Doesn't He Do That?"[72]

These titles were based on facts, one of which is the ratio of kills to captures. Between Brennan's 2011 statement—in which he declared the charge that the government preferred killing to capturing "absurd"—and 2015, there were about 215 drone strikes compared with "fewer than a dozen known cases of US troops capturing terrorist suspects in foreign countries."[73]

Another fact is that some of the intended victims could easily have been captured. In explaining why most terrorists must be killed rather than captured, Brennan said:

> These terrorists are skilled at seeking remote, inhospitable terrain, places where the United States and our partners simply do not have the ability to arrest or capture them. At other times, our forces might have the ability to attempt capture, but only by putting the lives of our personnel at too great a risk.[74]

But there are many cases where this reason clearly did not apply.

- Pointing to the too-ignored problem of "the targeting of suspects who are within the reach of the law," the *Washington Post* relayed a story from Yemen, where US drone strikes support the government: In 2013, a school teacher named Ali Saleh al-Qawili and his cousin, a university student, were killed after Ali allowed two men to hitch a ride home in his truck. These two men, Rabia Laheb and Naji Saad, were evidently supporters of al-Qaeda in the Arabian Peninsula. But they were, as the *Washington Post* put it, "hardly fugitives," being well-known members of the community. They could have easily been captured: Living a few miles outside the capital, they regularly passed through military checkpoints, and when they were killed, they were just 500 meters from a checkpoint.[75]

- Another example involves a man named Bilal el-Berjawi, about whom the Drone Papers have a long report. Berjawi had been a British citizen until his citizenship was taken away. Prior to being killed in 2012, Berjawi had been under surveillance for several years as he traveled back and forth between the U.K. and East Africa. However, rather than arresting him, the US waited to inflict death by drone on him in Somalia, right after he had called a London hospital to talk to his wife, who had just given birth.[76]

- In 2013, Human Rights Watch provided case studies of four more examples, one of which involved a cleric, with seven children, who "had long preached against AQAP's [Al-Qaeda in the Arabian Peninsula's] violent methods."[77]

A third fact is that Lt. Gen. Michael Flynn, who had been the head of the Defense Intelligence Agency, told Intercept:

The drone campaign right now really is only about killing. When you hear the phrase "capture/kill," capture is actually a misnomer. In the drone strategy that we have, "capture" is a lower case "c." We don't capture people anymore.[78]

Micah Zenko confirmed this fact in different words, saying:

Other than invading Afghanistan and Iraq, this shift from capturing suspected terrorists to killing them was the most important and enduring counterterrorism policy decision made since 9/11.[79]

According to Mark Mazzetti, this decision was made by Cheney, who at a White House meeting right after 9/11 authorized the CIA to "create hit teams to kill terror suspects." In addition, Mazzetti said, "the United States shifted markedly from capture to kill in George W. Bush's second term," a policy that then "expanded markedly under President Obama's watch."[80]

In sum: It appears that the claim that drone strikes are used only when the targets cannot be captured is no more true than the claim that very few civilians are killed.

ARE DRONE STRIKES USED ONLY FOR IMMINENT THREATS?

In his NDU speech, Obama said that America takes drone strikes only "against terrorists who pose a continuing and imminent threat to the American people." There are many problems with this claim.

One problem is posed by the use of signature strikes. If people are targeted simply because they fit a profile of likely terrorists, no one can know whether these people present an imminent threat.

A second problem is that the word "imminent" has been defined so as to make it meaningless. According to Obama's Justice Department:

[T]he condition that an operational leader present an "imminent" threat of violent attack against the United States does not require the United States to have clear evidence that a specific attack on US persons will take place in the immediate future.[81]

As Jameel Jaffer of the ACLU observed, the memo "redefines the word imminence in a way that deprives the word of its ordinary meaning." Conor Friedersdorf of *The Atlantic* agrees, saying that the government has "defined the term in a way that excludes its only actual meaning!" And James Downie, the *Washington Post* digital opinion editor, said: "You don't need a dictionary to know that 60 days is not 'imminent.'"[82]

As William Saletan has pointed out in *Slate*, the redefinition of "imminent" is only one part of a bigger problem: In justifying drone strikes, "the United States has redefined every legal term that got in the way." In discussing the term "imminent" in particular, Saletan pointed to a 2011 statement by Brennan, in which he had said:

> [A] more flexible understanding of "imminence" may be appropriate when dealing with terrorist groups, in part because threats posed by non-state actors do not present themselves in the ways that evidenced imminence in more traditional conflicts.

With this definition, said Saletan, all potential attacks by al-Qaeda "would now be classified as imminent."[83]

Interestingly, although Saletan intended his statement to be a *reductio ad absurdum*, it actually stated the position of the Obama administration. According to its "broader concept of imminence," any person judged to be "continually planning terror attacks [on America] presents an imminent threat." In other words, as Charlie Savage put it in his *Power Wars*, "al-Qaeda operatives who were essentially in the business of trying to attack the United States pose a *continuous and imminent threat*," so they "could be targeted whenever spotted."[84] As Rebecca Gordon put it,

> once a person has been identified as an al-Qaeda or allied group "leader," he is by definition "continually planning attacks," always represents an imminent danger, and so is a legitimate target. Q.E.D.[85]

Moreover, given the Bush-Obama enlargement of "al-Qaeda" in the AUMF to "al-Qaeda and affiliated groups or associated forces," the "broader definition" of *imminent threat* gives the government the right to target any member of al-Qaeda or anyone belonging to any group in the world that the US president judges to be an affiliated (or associated) organization—without providing a list of what these organizations are.

Accordingly, the US president has the right to be judge, jury, and executioner—just what the US Constitution meant to rule out.

In any case, the government's claim here, that it uses drone strikes to kill people only when they present an imminent threat, is correct only if the term "imminent" is redefined so that it does not mean *imminent*.

Looking at the legality of the Obama administration's drone warfare, international lawyer Marjorie Cohn said:

> Like his predecessor, Obama defines the whole world as his battlefield, reserving for himself the role of judge, jury and executioner. Compliance with due process (arrest and fair trial), which the US Constitution

guarantees all persons, not just US citizens, has not been a priority in the Obama administration's "war on terror."[86]

DO DRONE STRIKES HELP DEFEAT TERRORISM?

According to the government's narrative about the drone program, it "makes the US safer from 'global terrorism' with minimal downsides."[87] However, there is a lot of evidence suggesting that this narrative is not true.

One downside is that the drone program, which has terrified people in Pakistan, Somalia, and other places, has made them hate the United States. A Pew Center Poll in 2012 showed that 74% of Pakistanis consider the US an enemy.[88] This is to a great extent because America has killed so many civilians.

- "When you're trying to win a battle of hearts and minds," pointed out Jane Mayer in 2009, killing innocent civilians while trying to kill terrorists is counterproductive, because this killing will have "inflamed anti-American sentiment."[89]

- Lt. General Michael Flynn, who had been Obama's former top military intelligence official, said the same. "When you drop a bomb from a drone," said Flynn, "you are going to cause more damage than you are going to cause good."[90]

- In the Drone Papers, Jeremy Scahill made the same point, saying that drone killings have been "exacerbating the very threat the US is seeking to confront."[91]

Moreover, drones create hate for America not only because they kill civilians but also because they terrorize the people. In an article entitled "'Every Person Is Afraid of the Drones': The Strikes' Effect on Life in Pakistan," Conor Friedersdorf provided some examples of this terrorism:

- A father of three said, "drones are always on my mind. It makes it difficult to sleep. They are like a mosquito. Even when you don't see them, you can hear them, you know they are there."

- Another man said, "I can't sleep at night because when the drones are there . . . I hear them making that sound, that noise. The drones are all over my brain, I can't sleep. When I hear the drones making that drone sound, I just turn on the light and sit there looking at the light. Whenever the drones are hovering over us, it just makes me so scared.

- A third Pakistani man said, "Because of the noise, we're psychologically disturbed, women, men, and children. . . . Twenty-four hours, a person is in stress."

- A journalist who photographs drone strike craters said that children are "perpetually terrorized."

- According to a Pakistani politician, people "often complain that they wake up in the middle of the night screaming because they are hallucinating about drones."[92]

Yemen has been afflicted by the same effects. "The people of Yemen can hear destruction before it arrives. In cities, towns and villages across this country, the air buzzes with the sound of American drones flying overhead," said an article in *Mother Jones*. "Such quite literal existential uncertainty is coming at a deep psychological cost," continued the article. "Yemenis widely describe suffering from constant sleeplessness, anxiety, short-tempers, an inability to concentrate and, unsurprisingly, paranoia."[93]

According to forensic psychologist Peter Schaapveld, continued the article, the fear of drones "is traumatizing an entire generation." Indeed, he reported, "92 percent of the population sample he examined was found to be suffering from PTSD—with children being the demographic most significantly affected."[94]

Discussing the psychological effects on Pakistanis, Clive Stafford Smith, director of the human rights group Reprieve, said:

An entire region is being terrorized by the constant threat of death from the skies. Their way of life is collapsing: kids are too terrified to go to school, adults are afraid to attend weddings, funerals, business meetings, or anything that involves gathering in groups."[95]

Besides killing and terrorizing people, the drone program has been creating hate for America that inspires a desire for revenge. In response to the fact that a US drone strike had killed his friend and his friend's siblings and father, a young man named Abdullah said:

They have targeted them because they are simply killing Muslims. I simply hate America. . . . It is like they [are] showing their power and we are helpless. But one day we will have power and teach them.[96]

This hatred will surely be increased by learning that the US has apologized to and financially compensated families of civilians—one American, one Italian—who were killed by drone strikes. The ACLU said: "No other victim's family has received official acknowledgement and an apology, let alone been promised an investigation or compensation. That's fundamentally unfair, and it increases the hostility against the United States."[97]

It seems, therefore, that the attempt to fight terrorism with terrorism—which was started by the Bush-Cheney administration and intensified by Obama's—is entirely counterproductive (as well as wholly immoral). During a period in which drone strikes were killing about 15 terrorist leaders in Pakistan, they were killing several hundred civilians, said David Kilcullen, who had been a counterinsurgency advisor to Gen. David Petraeus. Also Andrew McDonald Exum, a former Army officer, wrote that "every one of these dead non-combatants represents an alienated family, a new revenge feud, and more recruits for a militant movement."[98]

This observation is confirmed by the titles of numerous articles. For example:

- "How Drones Create More Terrorists" *(The Atlantic)*

- "Obama's Drone War a 'Recruitment Tool' for Isis, Say US Air Force Whistleblowers" *(Guardian)*

- "How Drones Help Al Qaeda" (*New York Times*)

- "Retired General: Drones Create More Terrorists Than They Kill" *(Intercept)*

- "Secret CIA Report: Drone Strikes and Targeted Killings 'Boost Support for Terror Groups'" *(International Business Times)*

As Tom Engelhardt has observed, "the drone has produced not an effective war on terror, but a war that seems to promote terror."[99]

Accordingly, if the US Government really wants to reduce terrorism, as it says, it should eliminate the drone assassination program. Of course, we can only hope that the government really wants to eliminate terrorism, rather than, as some critics allege, protect the Pentagon's budget and the war industry's profits.

DON'T DRONES AT LEAST KEEP AMERICAN WARRIORS SAFE?

It is generally thought that, even if drones inflict an enormous amount of pain and death on people in Muslim countries, it at least keeps America's own warriors safe. But it turns out that even this is not entirely true. Inflicting death by drone does prevent our fighters from being killed by guns, missiles, and roadside bombs. But this does not necessarily mean that drone warfare is not destructive to them.

In an essay entitled "Killing Someone Else's Beloved," Mattea Kramer said:

> Once in a while a drone operator comes forward to reveal the emotional and psychic burden of passing 12-hour shifts in a windowless bunker on an Air Force base, killing by keystroke for a living.

One day, after having sent a missile, the operator saw a figure that looked like a child. This sight would not have bothered those operators who "refer to targeted images of children on computer screens," as Mark T. Harris put it, "prior to being obliterated, as 'fun-sized terrorists.'" But the trauma of fear that he had killed a child led this operator to leave the military. "After his resignation, he spent a bitterly cold winter in his home state of Montana getting blackout drunk and sleeping in a public playground in his government-issued sleeping bag."[100]

The aforementioned documentary film *National Bird* tells the stories of four drone operators. One of them, Heather Linebaugh, reported that a significant percentage of her fellow-workers became alcoholic and that, in fact, alcohol is sometimes called "drone fuel." Linebaugh also reported that many of her colleagues had suicidal feelings. She herself, besides developing crippling PTSD, was diagnosed as suicidal. Two of her friends and colleagues did commit suicide.[101]

After Heather resigned, she wrote an opinion piece for the *Guardian* entitled: "I Worked on the US Drone Program. The Public Should Know What Really Goes On." She wrote:

> Few of these politicians who so brazenly proclaim the benefits of drones have a real clue of what actually goes on. I, on the other hand, have seen these awful sights first hand. . . . What the public needs to understand is that the video provided by a drone is not usually clear enough to detect someone carrying a weapon, even on a crystal-clear day with limited cloud and perfect light. This makes it incredibly difficult for the best analysts to identify if someone has weapons for sure. . . . I may not have been on the ground in Afghanistan, but I watched parts of the conflict in great detail on a screen for days on end. I know the feeling you experience when you see someone die. Horrifying barely covers it. And when you are exposed to it over and over again it becomes like a small video, embedded in your head, forever on repeat, causing psychological pain and suffering that many people will hopefully never experience. UAV troops are victim to not only the haunting memories of this work that they carry with them, but also the guilt of always being a little unsure of how accurate their confirmations of weapons or identification of hostile individuals

were. . . . [T]he suicide statistics in this career field aren't reported, nor are the data on how many troops working in UAV positions are heavily medicated for depression, sleep disorders and anxiety.[102]

According to another article, written in 2015: "The US drone war across much of the Greater Middle East and parts of Africa is in crisis: drone pilots are quitting in record numbers," with 240 of them quitting in one year because of PTSD. The article also said that "the Air Force is at a loss to explain the phenomenon."[103]

Perhaps its generals and the President should watch *National Bird*, read Heather Linebaugh's article, and interview some of the other people who have quit.

IS AMERICA NOW A NATION OF ASSASSINS?

Jeremy Scahill has charged that the acceptance of drone killings has made America a "nation of assassins." Has it?

Scahill could not mean, of course, that all Americans support drone assassinations, because many of us explicitly oppose it and many others do not even know about it. He primarily means that America's political leaders support it: The executive branch aggressively promotes it; the courts have not subjected it to judicial review; and the legislative branch has supported it—Scahill pointed out that proposed legislation "opposing the assassination of US citizens abroad without due process received only six votes in the House of Representatives."[104] But it also means that, once the public was informed about the drone program, a majority of Americans turned out to approve it.[105]

To whatever degree America has become a nation of assassins, this fact adds to the ruination of our country. As Chris Floyd has said, the government's program of assassination by drone "taints and stains us all."[106]

There is no doubt that the American government is now an assassin. What better term could be used for its claim to have the right, as the above-quoted Army chaplain said, "to kill anyone, anywhere on earth, at any time, for secret reasons, based on secret evidence, in a secret process, undertaken by unidentified officials."[107] The American government would not, of course, grant that the governments of other countries have the right to assassinate American citizens. This asymmetry is a clear illustration of the fact that our country is now fully operating on the principle that might makes right.

CONCLUSION

The US drone program arguably raises the most serious questions for Obama's legacy, American democracy, and international relations.

- Obama's drone program is likely to be widely regarded as one of the most destructive parts of his presidency. For example, James Downie, the *Washington Post's* digital op-ed editor, recently wrote, "Obama's Drone War Is a Shameful Part of His Legacy."[108] Arguably, what should most disturb Obama is the fact that, whereas the *Washington Post's* Eugene Robinson wrote about "President Obama's Immoral Drone War," that newspaper's uber-neocon Charles Krauthammer wrote a vigorous defense of the administration's drone policy.[109]

- With regard to the United States itself, the main question is whether our country will allow the drone policy of the Bush-Cheney and Obama administrations to finish destroying Constitutional rule, which was so deeply wounded by various policies of the Bush-Cheney administration. The likelihood that it will is arguably increased by Obama's order, near the end of his presidency, that the number of targeted killings by airstrikes, including drone strikes, outside of war zones will be reported annually. As Charlie Savage and Scott Shane wrote in the *New York Times,* this order "further institutionalized and normalized airstrikes outside conventional war zones as a routine part of 21st-century national security policy."[110]

- Although in 2013 Obama had promised to make the drone policy transparent, his administration did not immediately make the Presidential Policy Guidance public. In did so only in 2016 because of a court order in response to an FOIA request. However, complained Marjorie Cohn, "much of it is redacted, or blacked out. That is the opposite of transparent."[111]

- According to Paul Craig Roberts, "the US government has become an unaccountable, lawless, criminal organization and is a danger to the entire world and its own citizens."[112] We now have, Jeremy Scahill told Amy Goodman, "a global assassination program" run under a parallel legal system, in which "the president and his advisers serve as the judge, jury and executioner of people across the globe."[113] The president and his advisors, therefore, are overseeing a program of murder—a fact emphasized by the titles of some articles, such as "Obama's Drone Order: Institutionalizing a

State Murder Operation," and "Obama's Drone-Missile Machinery of Murder."[114]

- Continuing the present use of military drones will increase the chaos already existing in the world. Just as other countries did not allow the United States to retain a monopoly on nuclear weapons for very long, the same will be true of weaponized drones. And, said the current UN special rapporteur on extrajudicial executions, Christof Heyns, the behavior of the United States "raises the question why other States should not engage in the same practice."[115] Unless the United States quickly reforms itself, some of them surely will. And, as the former UN special rapporteur on extrajudicial executions, Philip Alston, said, "If other states were to claim the broad-based authority that the United States does, to kill people anywhere, anytime, the result would be chaos."

For these and still more reasons, the US drone killing program, begun under the Bush-Cheney administration and expanded during Obama's, has done much to ruin America and its reputation. People in many countries now agree with Noam Chomsky's view, according to which the "worst terrorist crimes going on right now are the drone campaigns."[116]

In addition, the program of drone killing as practiced by the United States violates the Fifth Amendment of the Constitution, according to which no citizen shall "be deprived of life . . . without due process of law"—as discussed in the following chapter.

However, it appears that, in spite of all the solid objections to the drone program, the US government does not plan to cancel or even curtail it, as evidenced by the US military's plan to build a $100 million drone base in Africa.[117]

8 • SHREDDING THE CONSTITUTION

How did the Bush-Cheney administration ruin America? The answer most obviously involves the shredding of the US Constitution. Asking "Does The United States Still Exist?" Paul Craig Roberts said:

> Clearly what differentiates the US from other countries is the US Constitution. The Constitution defines us as a people. Without the Constitution we would be a different country. Therefore, to lose the Constitution is to lose the country.[1]

In other words, to change America so that its laws are no longer consistent with the Constitution is to ruin America. Many experts agree that this ruination resulted from 9/11:

- Peter van Buren, distinguishing between three eras of America—PreConstitutional, Constitutional, and PostConstitutional—said. "[T]he essence of the Constitutional era, ended when those towers came down on September 11, 2001." Accordingly, insofar as people celebrate America today, he said, they are "celebrating a land that no longer exists."[2]

- Law professor Jonathan Turley said: "Since 9/11, we have created the very government the framers feared: a government with sweeping and largely unchecked powers resting on the hope that they will be used wisely."[3]

Of course, this fundamental change was not brought about by the 9/11 attacks themselves, but by the way they were used by the Bush-Cheney administration. Near the tenth anniversary of 9/11, Vincent Warren, executive director of the Center for Constitutional Rights, wrote a piece for CNN entitled "How 9/11 Began the Decline in Our Democracy." And then four days later, on 9/11 itself, Warren wrote an essay entitled "The 9/11 Decade and the Decline of US Democracy," in which he said:

> In response to the terrorist attacks on September 11, 2001, George W. Bush shredded the US Constitution. . . . [T]he Bush administration engineered and presided over the most sustained period of constitutional decay in our history.[4]

This shredding had quickly become obvious to legal minds. In an op-ed in early December 2001, international lawyer John V. Whitbeck wrote that "the Bush Administration appears to be feeding the US Constitution and America's traditions of civil liberties, due process and the rule of law into a shredder."[5]

On the 13th anniversary of 9/11, Paul Craig Roberts said:

> 9/11 was used to fundamentally alter the nature of the US government and its relationship to the American people. Unaccountable executive power has replaced due process and the checks and balances established by the US Constitution. . . . Essentially, Americans today have no rights if the government targets them.[6]

In attributing this shredding of the Constitution to Bush, to be sure, one has to mean the Bush-Cheney administration, in which the assault on the Constitution was led by Dick Cheney—who, as discussed in this book's introductory chapter, was essentially the president during this administration's first term.

When commentators speak of shredding the Constitution, they typically focus on violations of the Bill of Rights, especially Amendments 1, 4, and 5. The shredding of the Constitution does consist of, to a great extent, these violations. However, these violations of the Bill of Rights were based on Dick Cheney's long-held view of the inherent powers of the presidency. This chapter begins with a discussion of Cheney's view of the powers of the presidency, which Obama largely continued. The second part of the chapter deals with the violations of the Bill of Rights by the Bush-Cheney and Obama administrations.

THE PRESIDENT AS HAVING INHERENT POWERS

In describing Cheney's view of the presidency, writers have often said that he held the view of the "unitary executive." However, that view may mean merely that the president has responsibility for the entire executive branch.

However, much less innocuous was Cheney's version of this doctrine, according to which the president has *inherent* executive powers. "'Inherent' is sometimes used as synonymous with 'implied,'" explained Constitutional scholar Louis Fisher, "but they differ fundamentally."[7]

"Inherent powers," explained *Black's Law Dictionary,* are "powers over and beyond those explicitly granted in the Constitution or reasonably to be implied from express grants."[8] As this definition indicates, inherent powers are distinct from implied as well as express powers. The express powers, of course, are those expressly stated in the Constitution. An implied power is one that can be reasonably drawn from an express power. For example, said Fisher, "Because it is an express duty of the President to see that the laws are faithfully executed, any executive officer who prevents a law from being carried out can be removed by the President."[9]

Inherent powers, if they exist, are over and above both express and implied powers. Indicating that this was Cheney's view, Charlie Savage said: "He embraced a belief that presidents have vast 'inherent' powers, not spelled out in the Constitution, that allow them to defy Congress."[10]

This extreme view of presidential power was enunciated by John Yoo, a young lawyer brought into the Office of Legal Counsel. Yoo said that the president has plenary powers to determine the country's foreign relations and to interpret international law. "Beginning on September 11," said Barton Gellman, Yoo was "empowered to turn beyond-the-edge arguments into the law of the executive branch."[11] According to these arguments, "the president could disregard laws and treaties prohibiting torture, war crimes, warrantless eavesdropping, and confinement without a hearing."[12]

Yoo was encouraged to take these positions by Cheney's legal counsel David Addington, who was the power behind Cheney's vice-presidential throne, and who wrote the regulations and executive orders coming out of the Bush-Cheney administration. Cass Sunstein, before he became a member of the Obama administration, suggested that Yoo's task was "to create a kind of 9/11 Constitution."[13]

Inherent Powers as Unconstitutional

Having quoted the definition of inherent executive power in *Black's Law Dictionary*, Louis Fisher wrote: "The model of a unitary executive, if properly understood, is compatible with the Constitution. Inherent executive power is not."[14]

This view was endorsed by the Supreme Court in 1972. Nixon had declared that he had the inherent authority to approve warrantless surveillance. After a lower court "expressly dismissed the claim of broad 'inherent' presidential power," the Supreme Court affirmed this conclusion unanimously.[15]

In explaining why the claim of inherent executive powers is not Constitutional, Fisher wrote:

> Presidents who claim inherent powers move a nation from one of limited powers to boundless and ill-defined authority, undermining the doctrine of separated powers and the system of checks and balances.[16]

Doctrine of Separated Powers

According to the separated powers doctrine, there are three equal branches of government, each of which has its role. As stated in Articles 1, 2, and 3 of the Constitution, the legislative branch makes laws, the judicial branch interprets them, and the executive branch enforces them.

In interpreting the separation of powers, the Supreme Court enunciated a "nondelegation" doctrine, derived from Article 1, which says: "All legislative powers herein granted shall be vested in a Congress of the United States." According to this doctrine, one branch cannot delegate any of its functions to another branch. For example, the legislative branch, which has the power to pass laws, cannot delegate these powers to the executive (except that the legislature, after formulating a law, could delegate details to the executive).[17]

Article 1 assigns many more powers to the legislative branch, including the power to declare war. Presidents Truman, Johnson, and Nixon all challenged this doctrine, claiming that the commander-in-chief had "inherent" power to take the country to war on his own. Cheney believed they were right.

- In 1990, when Cheney was the Secretary of Defense, he urged President H.W. Bush to launch a war against Saddam Hussein without asking Congress for authorization.

- In 1987, Cheney was the top Republican on the committee investigating the Iran-Contra scandal, which centered around Reagan's violation of the Boland Amendment, which had banned any assistance to the anti-Marxist Nicaraguan Contras. Cheney was a leading member of a small group of Republicans (including David S. Addington, later to become Vice-President Cheney's legal counsel) who wrote a minority report—which has been called "Mr. Cheney's Minority Report"—that rejected the committee's conclusion that Reagan had broken the law. According to this report, "the President's inherent powers" had historically allowed the executive to act "when Congress was silent, and even, in some cases, where Congress had prohibited an action."[18]

- Cheney himself said: "I personally do not believe the Boland Amendment applied to the president." The real lawbreakers were those members of Congress who supported the Boland Amendment, because the Constitution "does not permit Congress to pass a law usurping Presidential power."[19]

Cheney's passion to strengthen the presidency evidently originated at the time of the Watergate Crisis, which allowed Congress to recover the powers it had lost during the "imperial presidency" of Richard Nixon (who claimed that he had the "inherent authority" to spy on people he considered enemies and who declared, "when the president does it, that means that it is not illegal"). The post-Watergate recovery of Congressional powers involved passing the War Powers Act, according to which a president could not take the country to war without the approval of Congress.

Cheney resented these developments, which he considered the "erosion" of the president's inherent powers.[20] So when he was in position to shape the presidency of George Bush, he and his White House legal team took various steps to demonstrate the inherent powers of the president to decide everything related to war and other national security matters—such as authorizing the NSA to engage in surveillance far more extensive than the kind of spying for which Nixon was criticized.

The Bush-Cheney Administration

According to the Bush-Cheney administration, the president's inherent power to protect national security means that if he decides to go to war, Congress does not need to authorize it nor the courts to declare it legal. 9/11 gave the administration an opportunity to make this claim publicly. After Congress passed the Authorization for Use of Military Force, John Yoo wrote a Justice Department memo that stated:

> The historical record demonstrates that the power to initiate military hostilities, particularly in response to the threat of an armed attack, rests exclusively with the President. . . . In both the War Powers Resolution and the Joint Resolution, Congress has recognized the President's authority to use force in circumstances such as those created by the September 11 incidents. Neither statute, however, can place any limits on the President's determinations as to any terrorist threat, the amount of military force to be used in response, or the method, timing, and nature of the response. These decisions, under our Constitution, are for the President alone to make.[21]

In other words, the memo said, thanks anyway: The President did not require any authorization from Congress.

This position entails a total rejection of the doctrine of separated powers, which provides, as Fisher emphasized, a system of "checks and balances" on the power of government. The main purpose, of course, is to prevent the president from becoming a new king. In explaining the importance of this doctrine, Fisher quoted James Madison, who said:

> The accumulation of all powers, legislative, executive, and judiciary, in the same hands, whether of one, a few, or many, and whether hereditary, self-appointed, or elective, may justly be pronounced the very definition of tyranny.[22]

It is for good reason, therefore, that Fisher declared Cheney's idea of inherent executive powers, which trump the doctrine of separated powers, unconstitutional.

Although Cheney was the reason the Bush-Cheney administration was based around the idea that the presidency possesses inherent powers, one might wonder whether Bush was enthusiastic about this position. Fisher wrote:

> [T]here are clear examples of presidents who invoked inherent, extra-constitutional, and exclusive power. Still, at no time in America's history have inherent powers been claimed with as much frequency and breadth as the presidency of George W. Bush.[23]

The Obama Presidency

The claim of the present chapter, that the Bush-Cheney administration ruined America by shredding its Constitution, could not be made if the following administration had quickly reversed the Bush-Cheney position on the inherent authority of the president. This reversal would have entailed the return to the separation of powers doctrine and the recovery of momentarily lost civil rights. In 2008, while he was still the dean of Yale Law School, Harold Koh said:

> [T]he last eight years [since 9/11] are far less important than the next 8 years: For the next eight years will determine whether the pendulum of American policy will swing back from where it has been pushed, or whether it will stay stuck in the direction in which it has been pushed for the last 8 years? In the next eight years, we simply cannot allow our policy toward international law and human rights be subsumed entirely under the War on Terror.[24]

However, the pendulum did not swing back.

As discussed in the previous chapter, Obama continued to assume the right to order drone assassinations. He even increased the rate of drone killings, many of which must be called murder—contrary to a later statement by Koh, who while serving as State Department advisor said that the Obama administration's drone strikes "comply with all applicable law."[25]

With regard to inherent executive power: Although Obama, unlike Cheney and Bush, did not trumpet the idea, he did continue to act in accord with it.

Prior to becoming president, Obama said that he would not justify actions on the basis of constitutional (i.e., inherent) executive powers. Having criticized the Bush-Cheney administration on this point, he said: "I will not assert a constitutional authority to deploy troops in a manner contrary to an express limit imposed by Congress and adopted into law" but instead "follow existing law." However, complained Louis Fisher,

> That understanding of the Constitution disappeared when Obama took

office. . . . Over the years, the Obama administration frequently claimed the right to decide various matters based solely on independent presidential powers, even in the face of restrictive statutory provisions. . . . [Obama had a] pattern of claiming presidential authority that cannot be restricted by statute.[26]

Obama illustrated this pattern most dramatically in his behavior *vis-à-vis* Congress in the attack on Libya. First, he started the war without obtaining (or even seeking) authority from Congress. Such authorization was necessary, because as he himself had said in 2007:

The President does not have power under the Constitution to unilaterally authorize a military attack in a situation that does not involve stopping an actual or imminent threat to the nation.[27]

But Obama's attack on Libya was based on "humanitarian" grounds, not on preventing a threat to the United States.

Insofar as he recognized the need for authorization, Obama said that the attack had been authorized by the United Nations and NATO, but of course neither the UN or NATO existed when the Founders wrote the US Constitution—which spoke only of the Congress as authorizing war.

Obama's second demonstration of acting on the basis of inherent power was his refusal to abide by the War Powers Resolution, which said that, if a president does introduce armed forces into hostilities without obtaining Congressional authorization, the armed forces may not remain for more than 60 days. However, rather than ending after two months, the war continued for eight months.

To argue that Obama had not violated the War Powers Resolution, his lawyers used the same kind of argument-by-redefinition that they used with regard to drone strikes. They first argued that the action in Libya was not really a war, because that term refers only to "prolonged and substantial military engagements, typically involving exposure of US military personnel to significant risk over a significant period." However, as Louis Fisher pointed out, "The War Powers Resolution does not speak of 'risk.' It speaks of 'hostilities.'"[28]

They next argued that "US military operations [in Libya] are distinct from the kind of 'hostilities' contemplated by the Resolution's 60 day termination provision." In making this argument, the lawyers said:

US operations do not involve sustained fighting or active exchanges of fire with hostile forces, nor do they involve the presence of US ground troops, US casualties or a serious threat thereof.

However, as Fisher points out, this redefinition of "hostilities" ignores the context in which the War Powers Resolution was passed:

> Part of the momentum behind passage of the statute concerned the decision of the Nixon administration to bomb Cambodia. The massive US air campaign did not involve "sustained fighting or active exchanges of fire with hostile forces," the presence of US ground troops, or substantial US casualties.

Fisher concluded:

> The decision to act unilaterally without seeking congressional authority eventually forced the administration to adopt legal interpretations that were not only strained, but in several cases incredulous. Weak or not, those legal precedents are likely to broaden presidential power for future military actions.[29]

The arguments by the White House lawyers were extremely weak. Their real argument was expressed in a response to a Congressional complaint that the President had not sought authorization from Congress: "[T]he President had constitutional [inherent] authority, as Commander in Chief and Chief Executive and pursuant to his foreign affairs powers, to direct such limited military operations abroad."[30]

According to Fisher, the doctrine of the president's inherent executive powers provides the basis for tyranny.[31] The truth of this claim can be judged by looking at some of the consequences of that doctrine, as employed by the Bush-Cheney and Obama administrations, for the Bill of Rights.

These consequences were made evident shortly after 9/11, especially on October 26, when the USA PATRIOT Act was published. Commonly called the Patriot Act, this document is *anti*-patriotic because it is anti-Constitutional. This document, which was quickly approved by Congress—most members did not read it—announced significant restrictions on freedom of association, information, and speech; right to freedom from unreasonable searches; and right to legal representation and speedy-and-public trial. These restrictions primarily involve Amendments 1, 4, and 5.

VIOLATIONS OF THE FIRST AMENDMENT

Besides saying that Congress shall make no law establishing or prohibiting religion, the First Amendment says that it will also make no law "abridging the freedom of speech, or of the press; or the right of the people peaceably to assemble, and to petition the government for a redress of grievances."

Nevertheless, the Bush-Cheney administration passed a law, known as the "material support statute," that seems to abridge free speech. After 9/11, said David Cole of Georgetown University's Center for Constitutional Rights and James X. Dempsey of the Berkeley Center for Law & Technology, this statute became "the Justice Department's most popular charge in anti-terrorism cases."[32]

The present statute was a revised version of a law, called the "Antiterrorism and Effective Death Penalty Act of 1996," which was intended to prevent terrorist organizations with charitable or humanitarian arms to raise funds that could be used to further their terrorist activities. The law outlawed "material support or resources," including money, goods, materials, personnel, and training. In 2001, the USA PATRIOT Act included "expert advice or assistance." Human rights groups and some courts have found "personnel," "training," and "expert advice or assistance" to be unconstitutionally vague. In 2004, the "Intelligence Reform and Terrorism Prevention Act," providing more detailed definitions of these terms, was passed. But human rights groups and lawmakers still found the law a threat to free speech.

- The reason why the material support law is so popular, said Cole and Dempsey, "is easy to see: convictions under the law require no proof that the defendant engaged in terrorism, aided or abetted terrorism, or conspired to commit terrorism. But what makes the law attractive to prosecutors—its sweeping ambit—is precisely what makes it so dangerous to civil liberties."[33]

- The American Civil Liberties Union said that the "material support" statute allows "the government to secure convictions without having to show that any specific act of terrorism has taken place, or is being planned, or even that a defendant intended to further terrorism."[34]

- Jeanne Theoharis, Brooklyn College professor of political science, wrote: "Material support laws are the black box of domestic terrorism prosecutions, a shape-shifting space into which all sorts of constitutionally protected activities can be thrown and classified as suspect, if not criminal. Their vagueness is key. They criminalize guilt by association and often use political and religious beliefs to demonstrate intent and state of mind."[35]

- Senator Patrick Leahy said: "I have long urged reform of our laws governing so-called material support for terrorism. The current law is so broad as to be unworkable. Aid workers trying to provide relief to starving Somalis fear they could be prosecuted if some of it were to end up in the hands of al-Shabab. . . . And so while the situation in Somalia grows more desperate each day, with children dying needlessly, the delivery of food and medicines is hampered ... by our overly restrictive laws."[36]

- Professor David Cole said: "This provision has already served as the basis for the prosecution of a college student for running a website that happened to have links to other websites which in turn featured speeches by Muslim sheikhs advocating violent jihad. The prosecution's theory was that the student was providing material support in the form of 'expert advice or assistance' by running the website and linking it to such statements. ... On that understanding of the law, the *New York Times* could be prosecuted for featuring a link to Osama bin Laden's latest taped statement in connection with a story about the statement."[37]

A 2004 case called *Humanitarian Law Project v. Ashcroft* clearly illustrates how the law can restrict free speech because of the vagueness of the terms "training" and "expert advice or assistance," combined with the fact that it is generally interpreted to mean that no terrorist support needs to be involved.

A doctor and six organizations had been trying to help Sri Lanka's Liberation Tigers and the Kurdistan Workers Party, both of which have been classified by the US State Department as terrorist. The plaintiffs were assisting the groups only with their nonviolent activities, such as offering training in how to use international law to resolve disputes peacefully. But they were taken to court by the Justice Department and convicted. The plaintiffs took the case to the Supreme Court, but it upheld the lower court's conviction, with Chief Justice Roberts saying:

> [P]laintiffs simply disagree with the considered judgment of Congress and the executive that providing material support to a designated foreign terrorist organization—even seemingly benign support—bolsters the terrorist activities of that organization.[38]

However, Justice Roberts misinterpreted the "considered judgment of Congress," because it said:

> [The provision of "expert advice or assistance"] will only be a crime if it is provided 'knowing or intending that [the expert advice or assistance] be used in preparation for, or in carrying out,' any 'Federal terrorism offense' . . . or any of the crimes related to terrorism.[39]

So, although the law as written by Congress would not have criminalized efforts to provide benign advice to groups that that have been added to the US list of terrorist organizations, this statute as interpreted by the

Bush-Cheney and Obama administrations does criminalize some kinds of free speech. Dia Kayyali of the Electronic Frontier Foundation wrote:

> [The Supreme Court's] decision, signing off on the government's broad interpretation of material support, allows the government to apply the statute to activities that would otherwise be protected under the First Amendment—and that could actually help prevent terrorism, instead of supporting it. The material support laws have made it difficult for many Muslim-Americans to know where exactly they can make donations. This is a particularly big burden for Muslims, since zakat (essentially charitable giving) is one of the "five pillars" of Islam.[40]

VIOLATIONS OF THE FOURTH AMENDMENT

In an essay entitled "Shredding the Fourth Amendment in Post-Constitutional America," Peter Van Buren said: "If the First Amendment's right to speak out publicly was the people's wall of security, then the Fourth Amendment's right to privacy was its buttress." But the Bush-Cheney and Obama administrations have also threatened the Fourth Amendment to the Constitution, which states:

> The right of the people to be secure in their persons, houses, papers, and effects, against unreasonable searches and seizures, shall not be violated, and no Warrants shall issue, but upon probable cause.

This threat arose because the Bush-Cheney administration had secretly authorized the NSA to monitor—*without search warrants*—phone calls, Internet activity, and text messages.

Bush-Cheney Authorization of Warrantless Searches

The historical background to this threat goes back to the Nixon administration, during which the NSA had violated the Fourth Amendment by spying on Americans. The hearings headed by Senator Frank Church led to a law preventing the NSA from being directed at Americans. The government could spy on foreign spies in the United States only with a warrant from the newly-created Foreign Intelligence Surveillance (FISA) Court. In describing the report, Church said that tyranny would result if the agency "were to turn its awesome technology against domestic communications." As a result of the law, the NSA developed a culture of respect for the Fourth Amendment, even displaying posters quoting it.[41]

Cheney, however, believed this law to be a mistake and asked NSA director Michael Hayden what, if the NSA were "unleashed"—that is, if it forgot about the law—it might do differently. On the basis of his answer, he, Cheney, and Addington worked up a new surveillance program (which came to be called simply "the program"). Less than one month after 9/11, Bush authorized the program, which was kept secret from the FISA Court and for which no authorization from Congress was requested.[42]

Because it remained secret, the program went along with no problems until 2003, when a lawyer named Jack Goldsmith was put in charge of the Office of Legal Counsel. Quickly deciding that the program "was the biggest legal mess I'd seen in my life," he described the mess to Attorney General Ashcroft, who said it had to be fixed so as to be legal.

After great resistance from Addington, Goldsmith brought into the conversation Ashcroft's new assistant, Jim Comey, who became very disturbed. He, Goldsmith, and Ashcroft agreed that the Justice Department would not re-certify the program unless changes were made. Cheney refused and so did Bush, so Comey, Goldsmith, FBI Director Robert Mueller, and many more members of the Justice Department planned to resign. After having authorized the program on his own, Bush cancelled it.[43]

This story is important because it shows how strongly these lawyers felt about being a party to violations of the Fourth Amendment.

Edward Snowden's Revelations

Feeling just as strongly about these violations was Edward Snowden, an NSA computer programmer, whose work gave him access to the details of the NSA operations. He learned, for example, about the history of "the program," such as how Addington and Hayden wrote the authorization and how the Justice Department rebelled until it was properly certified.

In order to document "the program's" violations of the Fourth Amendment, Snowden downloaded many thousands of top secret NSA documents. Knowing that he was risking his freedom and possibly even his life, Snowden in 2013 offered them to Glenn Greenwald, Barton Gellman, and American documentary filmmaker Laura Poitras. After seeing something of what he had, Greenwald and Poitras, along with a veteran *Guardian* correspondent Ewen MacAskill, accepted his invitation to come to his hiding place, a hotel in Hong Kong, where they debriefed him for a week, thinking, said Greenwald, that "it was possible that the door could be barged down at any moment."[44]

Learning details about the program, Greenwald and Poitras were stunned, for example, to learn that Verizon was ordered to turn over its customers' phone records to the NSA. Greenwald later said:

> What this document revealed is that the NSA surveillance system is not directed at very bad people or terrorists, it's directed at the American

citizenry and other citizenries around the world, indiscriminately, in bulk.[45]

This document contradicted testimony that General James Clapper, the Director of National Intelligence, had recently given to Congress. Having been asked whether the NSA "collect[s] any type of data at all on millions or hundreds of millions of Americans?" Clapper replied: "Not wittingly." Greenwald concluded: "Watching President Obama's top national security official go before the Senate Intelligence Committee and outright lie about what the NSA was doing convinced [Snowden] that the only hope for public discussion and reform was for him to do what he was going to do."[46]

Realizing that it had been handed a really big story, the *Guardian* told the White House that, unless it had a good national security reason against it, the paper was going to report the leak. The Deputy National Security Advisor said that it took the administration some time to comprehend how big the leak was and how comprehensive the revelations were. The NSA's Director of Compliance said: "This is going to be a really tough story as it comes out."[47]

Gellman's story for the *Washington Post* indicated how big the story was. It had commonly been claimed that the NSA, besides searching only communications involving foreigners, swept up only "metadata," meaning data about data, not the content of the communications. However, reported Gellman,

> The PRISM program is not about metadata, it's about content. It's the photos and videos you send. It's the words of your emails. It's the sounds of your voice on a Skype call. It's all the files you have stored on a cloud drive service. It's content. It's everything.[48]

However, prior to Snowden's revelations, President Obama had not told the truth about this. In response to a reporter's question, he said:

> What the intelligence community is doing is looking at phone numbers and durations of calls. They are not looking at people's names, and they're not looking at content. . . . Now, with respect to the Internet and emails— this does not apply to US citizens and it does not apply to people living in the United States.[49]

Shortly thereafter, the public would learn that this was not true.

As had been predicted, the story about the documents was sensational, called a "bombshell." The *Guardian* and the *Washington Post* won Pulitzer prizes. Poitras's highly acclaimed documentary, *Citizenfour,* won an Academy Award. But did Snowden's revelations achieve any results?

They certainly confirmed one of Snowden's predictions: In an early letter to Gellman, Snowden said: "I understand that I will be made to suffer for my actions, and that the return of this information to the public marks my end."[50] And indeed, he was quickly charged with two crimes, making it essentially impossible for him to return to America, at least until he is guaranteed a legal and impartial trial.

But what about Snowden's main purpose? In spite of his heroism and the worldwide awareness it raised, his revelations have resulted in very little with regard to bringing American law back into line with the Fourth Amendment. In the years since Snowden's revelations, civil rights advocates have continued to say that America has gone far toward losing the rights guaranteed by this amendment:

- According to Peter Van Buren in 2014, "the Fourth Amendment has by any practical definition been done away with as a part of Post-Constitutional America." Edward Snowden's revelations about the NSA, said Van Buren, are a shock to the Fourth Amendment: "our government spies on us. All of us. Without suspicion. Without warrants. Without probable cause."[51]

- In that same year, Snowden himself said: "All of your private records. All of your private communications, all of your transactions, all of your associations, who you talk to, who you love, what you buy, what you read, all of these things can be seized and then held by the government and then searched later for any reason, hardly without any justification, without any reason, without any real oversight, without any real accountability for those who do wrong." Accordingly, he said, the Fourth Amendment "as it was written no longer exists."[52]

- In a 2015 essay, attorney Andrew Napolitano said that, under the influence of Obama's lawyers, "judges actually did the unthinkable," namely, they issued *general warrants*, which had been "used against the colonists by the British and are expressly prohibited by the Fourth Amendment," which specifies that a warrant must be based on probable cause about a specific person or organization. Moreover, when Michael Hayden was head of the NSA, he was told that "the line between privacy and unbridled government surveillance" was moveable, so he moved it. "In such a world," concluded Napolitano, "our Constitution has become a worthless piece of paper."[53]

However, those statements were made prior to the passage on June 2, 2015, of the USA FREEDOM Act (a revised version of the so-called Patriot

Act). Many individuals, organizations, and media outlets have claimed that it fixed the various Fourth Amendment problems. However, civil liberty advocates have said otherwise. For example:

- 30-year NSA cryptographer-turned-whistleblower William Binney, writing shortly before the vote on the bill, said that if it passes, it "won't do anything." He asked: "Why do you think NSA [and other intelligence agencies] support it?"[54]

- The Electronic Frontier Foundation spoke of "the meager intelligence reforms of the FREEDOM ACT."[55]

- Although ACLU legal director Jameel Jaffer had supported the 2013 version of the act (which failed to pass), he said the 2015 version "would make only incremental improvements, and at least one provision—the material-support provision [discussed above in the section on the First Amendment]—would represent a significant step backwards."[56]

- David Segal, the executive director of Demand Progress, wrote: "The Senate just voted to reinstitute certain lapsed surveillance authorities—and that means that USA Freedom actually made Americans less free."[57]

The view that the USA FREEDOM Act has resulted in little or no improvements, or worse, continued in 2016. For example,

- An editorial in a North Carolina newspaper, speaking of the "misnamed and milquetoast USA Freedom Act," said that it "merely added one small inconvenience to the machinations of federal spies."[58]

- Paul Craig Roberts, in his aforementioned essay asking whether the United States still exists, wrote: "The Fourth Amendment is a dead letter amendment. In its place we have warrantless searches, SWAT team home invasions, strip and cavity searches, warrantless seizures of computers and cell phones, and the loss of all privacy to warrantless universal spying."[59]

- Contrary to the claim that Snowden's documents revealed no illegal behavior, Glenn Greenwald wrote: "Multiple courts have now found the domestic metadata spying program in violation of the Constitution and relevant statutes." However, Greenwald added, "illegality was never the crux of the scandal triggered by those NSA revelations. Instead, what was most shocking was what had been legalized: the secret construction of the largest system of suspicionless spying in human history. What was scandalous was not that most of this spying was against the law, but rather that the law—at least as applied and interpreted by the Justice Department and secret, one-sided FISA 'courts'—now permitted the US government and its partners to engage in mass surveillance of entire populations, including their own."[60]

The Fourth Amendment Butchered

If, as Roberts said in March 2016, the Fourth Amendment was dead, three months later it was butchered—thanks to a ruling by the US Supreme Court in *Utah v. Strieff*, which overturned a ruling by the Utah Supreme Court. In the majority's opinion, as summarized by Mark Joseph Stern on *Slate*, "if an officer illegally stops an individual *then* discovers an arrest warrant—even for an incredibly minor crime, like a traffic violation—the stop is legitimized, and any evidence seized can be used in court. The only restriction is when an officer engages in "flagrant police misconduct" (which is not defined).[61]

This ruling, said John W. Whitehead of the Rutherford Institute, "opened the door for police to stop, arrest and search citizens without reasonable suspicion or probable cause."[62] This ruling overturned the Fourth Amendment's long-accepted "exclusionary rule," which has prevented the admission of illegally obtained evidence at trial.[63]

Justice Sonia Sotomayor responded with a scathing dissent. According to this ruling, she explained, "the discovery of a warrant for an unpaid parking ticket will forgive a police officer's violation of your Fourth Amendment rights." Moreover, she said:

> This case allows the police to stop you on the street, demand your identification, and check it for outstanding traffic warrants—even if you are doing nothing wrong. . . . So long as the target is one of the many millions of people in this country with an outstanding arrest warrant, anything the officer finds in a search is fair game for use in a criminal prosecution. The officer's incentive to violate the Constitution thus increases: From here on, he sees potential advantage in stopping individuals without reasonable suspicion—exactly the temptation the exclusionary rule is supposed to remove.[64]

Agreeing with Justice Sototmayor, constitutional lawyer John W. Whitehead said:

> With this ruling, the US Supreme Court has effectively stripped

Americans of their Fourth Amendment rights and provided police with even greater incentives to erode our freedoms, undermine our sovereignty, abuse our trust, invade our privacy and generally operate above the law.

Whitehead continued:

By giving police a green light to illegally stop any American for any reason, arrest them for any minor outstanding violation, and embark on a fishing expedition of one's person and property, the Supreme Court has rendered us completely vulnerable to the whims of any cop on the beat.[65]

Justice Elena Kagan, who like Justice Ruth Bader Ginsburg agreed with Sotomayor, said that the ruling "practically invites" police illegally to stop Americans who are not acting suspiciously.[66]

Driving home the absurdity and Constitution-violating nature of this ruling, Sotomayor added that, according to the majority's opinion:

The mere existence of a warrant not only gives an officer legal cause to arrest and search a person, it also forgives an officer who, with no knowledge of the warrant at all, unlawfully stops that person on a whim or hunch.[67]

The Court's majority argued that its ruling was about an "isolated" event, so that it would not affect many people. However, Sotomayor countered, the Justice Department "recently reported that in the town of Ferguson, Missouri, with a population of 21,000, 16,000 people had outstanding warrants against them." Justice Kagan added: "The state of California has 2.5 million outstanding arrest warrants"- in other words, about 9 percent of California's adult population.[68]

Explaining still further the horribleness of this ruling, Sotomayor said:

If the officer thinks you might be dangerous, he may then "frisk" you for weapons. This involves more than just a pat down. As onlookers pass by, the officer may "feel with sensitive fingers every portion of [your] body. A thorough search [may] be made of [your] arms and armpits, waistline and back, the groin and area about the testicles, and entire surface of the legs down to the feet.[69]

This ruling, Sotomayor concluded, "says that your body is subject to invasion while courts excuse the violation of your rights. It implies that you are not a citizen of a democracy but the subject of a carceral state."[70]

During the 2016 presidential campaign, there was much discussion about whether a Donald Trump White House would issue in fascism.[71] But a prior concern should be what Bush, Cheney, Obama, and the Supreme Court have already done to the Constitution.

VIOLATIONS OF THE FIFTH AMENDMENT

If the First and Fourth Amendments have been ruined, what about the Fifth? According to the most important clause of the Fifth Amendment, no person shall "be deprived of life, liberty, or property, without due process of law." This phrase "due process of law" means: Decided by an impartial judge or jury acting in accord with the Bill of Rights.

The killing of American citizens by drones, as discussed in Chapter 7, clearly violates this amendment. But the Obama administration claimed that the requirement for due process is fulfilled by an executive branch process, which was described in the *New York Times* thus:

> Every week or so, more than 100 members of the government's sprawl-ing national security apparatus gather, by secure video teleconference, to pore over terrorist suspects' biographies and recommend to the president who should be the next to die. This secret "nominations" process is an invention of the Obama administration, a grim debating society that vets the PowerPoint slides bearing the names, aliases and life stories of sus-pected members of Al Qaeda's branch in Yemen or its allies in Somalia's Shabab militia.[72]

But even though this process may be elaborate, it surely cannot count as "due process," because this requirement can only be fulfilled by the judicial branch. The main reason the US Constitution insists on three branches of government is so a king or dictator cannot be judge, jury, and executioner. And yet, the *Times'* story said:

> The Justice Department's Office of Legal Counsel prepared a lengthy memo justifying that extraordinary step, asserting that while the Fifth Amendment's guarantee of due process applied, it could be satisfied by internal deliberations in the executive branch.[73]

This "extraordinary step" was the assassination of an American citizen, Anwar al-Awlaki (also spelled *al-Aulaqi*), who was born in America and lived here for many years until his father moved his family to Yemen, after which Anwar returned to the United States to attend a university. One of the benefits of being an American citizen is that you could not be jailed or killed without due process—until now. In response to the Office of Legal Counsel's ruling, Glenn Greenwald wrote:

> Here we have the Obama administration asserting what I genuinely

believe, without hyperbole, is the most extremist government interpretation of the Bill of Rights I've heard in my lifetime—that the Fifth Amendment's guarantee that the State cannot deprive you of your life without "due process of law" is fulfilled by completely secret, oversight-free "internal deliberations by the executive branch."[74]

How could this have come about? Following in the steps of Bush and Cheney, Obama got lawyers in his Justice Department's Office of Legal Counsel (OLC), David Barron and Martin Feldman, to write a secret memo making the claim about the sufficiency of executive branch deliberations. This memo, Charlie Savage had learned, "provided the justification for acting despite an executive order banning assassinations, a federal law against murder, protections in the Bill of Rights and various strictures of the international laws of war."[75]

Barron and Feldman thereby issued an opinion even more radical than any of the notorious opinions offered by the Bush-Cheney Office of Legal Counsel. Nevertheless, two years later, Obama nominated Barron for an important federal judgeship. In an essay in *The Atlantic* entitled "This Lawyer Enabled the Extrajudicial Killing of an American," Conor Friedersdorf asked: "Should the Constitution be entrusted to a man who thinks Americans can be killed without due process?" Pointing out that this precedent "could allow Americans to be targeted in secret in the future," Friedersdorf wrote:

> I don't want to live in a nation with a judge who so blatantly helped the federal government wriggle out of respecting the Bill of Rights, nor with any senator who would vote to confirm him.[76]

Nevertheless, the Senate confirmed Barron.

Attorney General Eric Holder publicly supported the position of Barron and Feldman, saying:

> "Due process" and "judicial process" are not one and the same, particularly when it comes to national security. The Constitution guarantees due process, not judicial process.

This astounding opinion was rightly ridiculed by Stephen Colbert, who said: "'Due Process' Just Means There's a Process That You Do."[77]

In reality, due process involves having a fair judicial trial with many procedures, including:

> the right to have the assistance of counsel; the right to know one's accuser and the evidence against one; the right to confront and cross-examine that person; the right to have decision based solely upon a record generated in

open proceedings; as well as the right to present argument and evidence on one's own behalf. [78]

Obviously, killing people with drone strikes rules out all of these procedures. Therefore, the Obama administration's claim that due process can be fulfilled by a process within the executive branch completely destroys the most important stipulation of the Fifth Amendment.

The procedures involved in due process can also be described in terms of many other amendments in the Bill of Rights. According to Tom Carter:

> That procedure included indictment by a civilian grand jury (the Fifth Amendment), an arrest warrant issued by a neutral magistrate (the Fourth Amendment), and a speedy and public trial by an impartial jury (the Sixth Amendment), in which the accused has a right to an attorney (the Sixth Amendment), in which evidence cannot be introduced that was obtained through torture or other unlawful means (the Fourth and Fifth Amendments), in which the accused may confront his accusers (the Sixth Amendment), in which the punishment may not be "cruel or unusual" (the Eighth Amendment), and so on. In addition, under principles descended from the English common law, the accused was to be entitled to the presumption of innocence, and the burden of proof was to rest on the prosecution to prove guilt beyond a reasonable doubt.

Accordingly, Carter concluded, "an extrajudicial killing flouts and ignores every single one of the victim's basic legal protections provided by law."[79]

The assassination of Anwar al-Awlaki (whose 16-year-old American son was killed by a drone strike two weeks later[80]) illustrates how fully the American government, beginning with the Bush-Cheney administration and continued in the Obama administration, has erased fundamental principles of both international law and the US Constitution. In both Republican and Democratic administrations, said Medea Benjamin, "US officials have insisted that the government has the right to assassinate anyone, anywhere, who they believe poses a threat to America."[81]

Indicating how far the Democratic Party as well as the Republican Party had come by 2006, Glenn Greenwald referred to a speech by Al Gore, in which he had asked:

> If the president has the inherent authority to eavesdrop on American citizens without a warrant, imprison American citizens on his own declaration, kidnap and torture, then what can't he do?[82]

But today, Greenwald said, we have an even more serious version of the question:

[I]f the US President can openly declare the power to order even the nation's own citizens executed by the CIA in total secrecy, without charges or a whiff of transparency or oversight, what can't he do?[83]

A judge's ruling in 2010, in fact, had already indicated that the president had the power to do what Benjamin and Greenwald criticized. After al-Awlaki had been put on a kill list, his father—who had been both Yemen's agriculture minister and a university president—asked for a judicial review of the Obama administration's claimed right to assassinate his son. This request was supported by the ACLU and the Center for Constitutional Rights. However, Judge John Bates, who had been appointed to the federal judiciary by President Bush, said that the decision was "judicially unreviewable."[84] Jameel Jaffer, Deputy Legal Director of the ACLU, replied:

If the court's ruling is correct, the government has unreviewable authority to carry out the targeted killing of any American, anywhere, whom the president deems to be a threat to the nation. It would be difficult to conceive of a proposition more inconsistent with the Constitution or more dangerous to American liberty.[85]

In 2012, Nasser al-Awlaki took the request for judicial review to another court, saying that the 2011 killing of his son violated "the right not to be deprived of life without due process of law." But the judge, agreeing with the Justice Department request that the case be dismissed, said that the executive must be trusted, because the prospect of a later lawsuit could hinder officials' ability in the future to act "without hesitation in defense of US interests."[86]

These two cases, said Savage, suggest that presidents will have free rein in killing American citizens that they call terrorists.[87] The danger became even more pressing after Donald Trump was declared the victor of the 2016 presidential race, as reported in a story headed: "Trump Is Inheriting Power to Assassinate Anyone, Including US Citizens, With No Oversight."[88]

TORTURE VIOLATES CONSTITUTION

The US Constitution rules out many practices that are not explicitly in the Bill of Rights. Arguably the most important of such practices, in relation to the Bush-Cheney administration, is torture.

The Bush-Cheney Administration

Chief Justice Antonin Scalia, perhaps influenced by his friendship with Dick Cheney, argued that there is nothing in the United States Constitution that prohibits torture of suspected terrorists. "I don't know what article of the Constitution," he said, would contravene it.[89] However, said law professor Marjorie Cohn:

> We have ratified three treaties that all outlaw torture and cruel, inhuman or degrading treatment or punishment. When the United States ratifies a treaty, it becomes part of the Supreme Law of the Land under the Supremacy Clause of the Constitution.

For example, she continued:

> The Convention Against Torture and Other Cruel, Inhuman or Degrading Treatment or Punishment, says, "No exceptional circumstances whatsoever, whether a state of war or a threat of war, internal political instability or any other public emergency, may be invoked as a justification for torture."[90]

Whereas Scalia tried to defend the practices authorized by the Bush-Cheney administration by simply denying that torture is outlawed by the Constitution, John Yoo redefined torture so narrowly that the administration would be off the hook for its practices. To count as torture, said Yoo:

> The victim must experience intense pain or suffering of the kind that is equivalent to the pain that would be associated with serious physical injury so severe that death, organ failure or permanent damage resulting in a loss of significant body functions will likely result.[91]

According to Yoo, therefore, the practices authorized by the Bush-Cheney administration should not be called "torture"—they were simply "enhanced interrogation techniques."

How false it was to claim that these techniques were not torture became evident to the world in April 2004, when CBS News aired *60 Minutes II: Abuse at Abu Ghraib*, which showed photos, and the *New Yorker* published Seymour Hersh's "Torture at Abu Ghraib."[92] These reports were based on documents—written primarily by Yoo and fellow Office of Legal Counsel lawyer Jay Bybee—that provided, as Karen Greenberg put it,

> uniquely tortured definitions of torture that made almost any act in which the infliction of pain didn't rise to the level of "organ failure, impairment of bodily function, or even death" acceptable.[93]

The Obama Administration

Although these reports about extreme torture caused great anger and disgust, they did not prevent the reelection of the Bush-Cheney administration—although perhaps due only to widespread election fraud.[94]

In any case, after promising during the 2008 election campaign to make torture illegal, Barack Obama did so in his first week in office. Moreover, as PolitiFact reported in 2011, there has been wide agreement that "Obama's torture ban has held."[95] Because of these developments, it might appear that we need not fear that the Bush-Cheney policy on torture resulted in any lasting damage to America and the world. However, the Obama administration seemed less than fully committed to ensuring that the Bush-Cheney torture policy would not return.

The administration's lack of total commitment was illustrated by Obama's decision, as Glenn Greenwald complained, "to block the Justice Department from criminally investigating and prosecuting Cheney and his fellow torturers."[96] This was a disastrous decision, because as Rupert Stone (like many others) pointed out: "Laws are futile if they are not enforced." "Not only," Stone continued,

> has the Justice Department declined to prosecute any Bush officials, but it has also repeatedly invoked state-secrets privilege to stop civil litigation brought by torture victims. Without the deterrent provided by possible criminal prosecution, future presidents might feel they can torture with impunity.[97]

Another illustration of Obama's less-than-complete commitment to rule out torture permanently arose, at the end of 2014, with the publication of the 576 page *Senate Intelligence Committee Report on Torture*.[98] Describing the report as "depicting even worse brutality than what was previously understood to have happened and a program that could only be described as sadistic," Jane Mayer was critical of Obama because he "praised C.I.A. officers as 'patriots' and allowed John Brennan, his C.I.A. director, to stop short of calling the tactics 'torture.'"[99]

A critique on MSNBC by Zachary Roth also reported that Obama muted his criticism of the Bush-Cheney administration by saying that it had faced "agonizing choices" about how to stop another terror attack. In discussing the President's cautious tone, Roth said that, "when it comes to torture, Obama's hands aren't entirely clean either." Some have gone further, Roth added, quoting Wells Dixon of the Center for Constitutional Rights, who said: "[Obama's] record on torture has been abysmal, to the point of obstruction, concealment, and ultimate complicity." Taking issue with Obama's mantra, "We want to look forward and not back," Roth said: "[P]rosecuting torture isn't just looking backwards—failing to do so makes it more likely that the program could be resuscitated going forward."[100]

The following year, the House of Representatives unveiled a marble bust of Cheney to reside in Emancipation Hall of the US Capitol. Quoting appreciative statements about Cheney by Vice President Joe Biden, Greenwald said that the Obama administration, having immunized Bush-era torturers, moved to "honoring and gushing over them in public."[101]

To be sure, Obama's response to the torture report was not nearly so bad as Cheney's, who dismissed the report as "full of crap"[102]—a comment that gave Andy Borowitz the basis for a satirical piece:

> Former Vice-President Dick Cheney on Tuesday called upon the nations of the world to "once and for all ban the despicable and heinous practice of publishing torture reports. . . . I ask [them to stand up and] say, 'This is not who we are."[103]

Nevertheless, Obama's failure to prosecute any torturers left his successor, who declared that torture works,[104] with no basis for fear that his administration, if it chooses to reinstate torture, would be prosecuted.

CONCLUSION

The Bush-Cheney administration used the 9/11 attacks to shred the US Constitution with regard to the separation of powers, the Bill of Rights, and the prohibition of torture, almost completely changing the original meanings of the First, Fourth, and Fifth Amendments, as well as torture. And although the Obama administration outlawed torture, it did not do so with the vigor that was needed. And far from repealing the first post-9/11 government's Constitution-changing meanings of Amendments 1, 4, and 5, the Obama administration strengthened and further embedded them in laws.

Paul Craig Robert's claim—that the United States has been lost—is not much of an exaggeration. John W. Whitehead, in a 2016 essay entitled "The Tyranny of 9/11," wrote: "What began with the passage of the USA Patriot Act in October 2001 has snowballed into the eradication of every vital safeguard against government overreach, corruption and abuse."[105] "[T]he most painful truth about the last decade," said Vincent Warren in 2011,

> is that it marks an undoing of democracy so severe that without concerted and deliberate action by the people in this country—and, one hopes, by their elected leaders—the values which defined us, before the events of 9/11 allowed the Bush administration to reshape our perception of executive power, may never be regained.[106]

One reason that they may not be regained is that, as James Zogby has said, "in the post-9/11 era the challenge to constitutional rights has all too often been met with silence—because it was Arabs and Muslims who were the targets."[107] So, recovering the Constitution and overcoming

Islamophobia may be closely related.

In any case, if President Trump decides to move in a fascist direction, the Bush-Cheney and Obama administrations will have made it easy for him. In fact, Ajamu Baraka published an article entitled, "Trump's Neo-Fascism Will Be Built on Neo-Fascism of Obama and Democrat Party."[108]

9 • NUCLEAR HOLOCAUST

As discussed in the previous chapters, the future of America and the world is threatened by many factors—either initiated or at least intensified by the Bush-Cheney administration and continued by the Obama administration. But these threats are dwarfed in importance by another: the threat of human extinction, which could easily come about through a nuclear or an ecological holocaust. The present chapter discusses the possibility of nuclear holocaust, saving the threat of an ecological holocaust for the next chapter.

ARE WE HEADED TOWARD WORLD WAR III?

Commentators from diverse perspectives have suggested that, if we continue the present course, we are headed toward World War III. (A few writers speak of WW IV, on the grounds that the Cold War should be called WW III.[1] But most writers speak of a coming global war as WW III.) Paul Craig Roberts, a former member of the Reagan administration, wrote an essay explaining "Why WW III Is on the Horizon." Australian John Pilger wrote simply: "A World War Has Begun."[2]

As to how a new world war would break out, virtually everyone agrees that it would begin with a war between America and Russia. But what would provoke such a war? The same things that provoked the US wars in Afghanistan, Iraq, and Libya, along with the almost-war in Syria: The fever of the neocons to bring about regime change. Seeing Russia as the primary obstacle to establishing an all-inclusive global empire, the neocons want to bring about regime change in Russia. As Roberts said in his essay about why WW III is on the horizon:

> When the Soviet Union fell, something new was born, something utterly new a unipolar world dominated by a single superpower unchecked by any rival and with decisive reach in every corner of the globe. . . . [T]he dangerous situation facing the world is the product of the neoconservative's arrogant policy of US world hegemony.[3]

WW III might also begin between the United States and China. On the occasion of Obama's visit to Hiroshima in 2016, Gregory Kulacki, the China Project Manager for the Union of Concerned Scientists' global security program, wrote of the "growing risk of nuclear war with China."[4] Summarizing a new UCS report,[5] Kulacki discussed several ways in which "the United States and China could become involved in a military conflict that escalates rapidly and ends in a nuclear exchange."

This has been a concern of many experts, such as Noam Chomsky and former secretary of defense William Perry, who mention China and Russia together in relation to the possibly of a nuclear conflict with the United States.[6] Referring to Chomsky, Perry, and "other sentient observers of the neoconservatives' aggressive policies toward Russia and China," Roberts wrote that, by following neocon recommendations, "the US is pushing a policy that means the end of life."[7]

Although the relations with either China or Russia could lead to nuclear war, the present chapter focuses primarily on Russia, discussing China only near the end.

CHENEY AND RUSSIA

Major Todd E. Pierce, who retired as a defense counsel in the Army's Judge Advocate General Corps, argued that "Dick Cheney's ideology of US global domination has become an enduring American governing principle regardless of who is sitting in the Oval Office." As discussed above in Chapter 2, this ideology was first fully stated in the 1992 draft of the Defense Policy Guidance (DPG), which was to provide "American foreign policy after the Cold War."[8] Although this draft was attributed primarily to Cheney's assistant Paul Wolfowitz, the ideas were primarily Cheney's. Indeed, as mentioned in Chapter 2, one critic called it "Dick Cheney's Song of America."[9]

In speaking of this ideology as *enduring*, Pierce said that "President Obama has cemented Cheney's ideological legacy by continuing his unilateralism and even expanding it." Although there have been changes in details, "there is virtually no deviation in the United States from the core of Cheney's ideology," namely, the "unrelenting pursuit of total US global military domination as outlined in the Defense Planning Guidance."

Referring to this ideology as "Cheneyism," Pierce entitled his essay "We're All Cheneyites Now." In describing Cheneyism, Pierce said that it combines "an un-American, anti-constitutional authoritarianism" with "militarism under a state of permanent war" and "an aggressiveness toward past, present and possibly future adversaries, especially Russia." With regard to Russia in particular, Pierce quoted former CIA director Bob Gates' memoir, *Duty*, which said: "[Cheney] wanted to see the dismantlement not only of the Soviet Union and the Russian Empire but of Russia itself."[10]

Central to the drive of the Bush-Cheney administration to bring about regime change in Russia was a double-cross. In 1989, the first President Bush negotiated with Mikhail Gorbachev about the dissolution of the Soviet Union and the unification of Germany. Gorbachev was fearful that allowing East Germany to be absorbed by West Germany would simply be the first step of the movement of NATO towards Russia.

But Gorbachev accepted the unification on the basis of a deal suggested by Bush: On the one hand, Moscow would not use force to reimpose control over Eastern Europe; on the other hand, NATO would not—in the word's of Bush's secretary of state, James Baker—"leapfrog" eastward over Germany. In fact, promised Baker, NATO would not expand "one inch eastward." Various people have testified that they knew about this promise. One of those was West German Chancellor Helmut Kohl, who intended to keep the promise. But Bush said: "To hell with that! We prevailed, they didn't." On the basis of Bush's dictum, the promise was never mentioned by his and future administrations, so the promise became a non-occurrence.[11]

This promise was first broken by President Bill Clinton, who brought the Czech Republic, Hungary, and Poland into NATO in 1999. (George Kennan, one of America's Wise Men, called this enlargement a "strategic blunder of potentially epic proportions."[12]) This promise-breaking really speeded up during the Bush-Cheney administration, which in 2004 brought Bulgaria, Estonia, Latvia, Lithuania, Romania, Slovakia, and Slovenia into NATO.

Then in the final year of the Bush-Cheney administration, Cheney spoke of bringing Ukraine into NATO, suggesting that Russia had no right to protest this move. Cheney said:

> [T]he Russian government is increasingly antagonistic toward the enlargement of NATO and the advance of democracy. . . . Moscow has opposed every eastward addition to NATO. . . . Russia strongly protested membership in the Alliance for Georgia and Ukraine, now and forever. . . . Let us make clear that the enlargement of NATO will continue as and where the Allies decide.[13]

The following day, Cheney stated this policy in relation to Ukraine in particular, saying:

> Ukrainians have a right to choose whether they wish to join NATO, and NATO has a right to invite Ukraine to join the alliance when we believe they are ready and that the time is right.[14]

Cheney did not mention, however, that Ukraine's relation to Russia was different from that of the aforementioned countries that had been brought into NATO: Russia has a special relation to Ukraine, in which most of the population speak Russian as well as Ukrainian, with Russian dominating in the Southeast part of the country; Crimea had long been part of Russia until 1954 (when Nikita Khrushchev for some reason gave it to Kiev); and Ukraine had long been crucial to Russia's security, such as during WW II, when Ukrainians were central to the Soviet Union's defeat of Nazi Germany's troops. Moreover, Ukraine had never applied for membership in NATO until 2014.

As suggested by Cheney's above-quoted statement, Ukraine would be invited to join it when "the time is right." The Obama administration decided in 2014 that the time was right—although it was only deemed right by Ukraine after the United States engineered regime change there. Before this regime change is described, it must be considered in the context in which it occurred.

NEOCON PLANS FOR REGIME CHANGE IN RUSSIA

Russian leaders believe that the United States wants to bring about regime change in Russia. Whereas some people believe the US is putting pressure on Russia to persuade it to change policies, Russia's foreign minister Sergey Lavrov said no, the US government "wants to secure regime change." Likewise, President Putin said that Moscow must guard against a "color revolution."[15]

Although this may sound like paranoia, many commentators believe there are good grounds for their fears.

- Robert Parry said that the financial crisis being imposed on Russia (to be discussed below) "appears to be another neocon-driven 'regime change' scheme, this time focused on Moscow with the goal to take down Russian President Vladimir Putin and presumably replace him with some US puppet."[16]

- In an essay entitled "US Elite Wants to Destroy Russia at Any Price," Eric Zuesse wrote: "America's aristocracy is determined to take over Russia. Ever since the end of the Soviet Union and of its communism, the Cold War has become replaced by an increasingly hot war in which the US and its allies are expanding NATO right up to Russia's borders."[17]

- In an essay asking "Regime Change in Russia?" Neil Clark said: "Russia is the biggest block on the endless war lobby's plans for world domination, which is why the removal of Putin and his replacement with a marionette who will do exactly what the neocons want is their overriding objective."[18]

Clark added, unsurprisingly, that this scheme was hatched back when Cheney was in charge: "The neocon plans for regime change in Russia," said Clark, can "be traced back to 2003 when it became clear that Vladimir Putin would [unlike Boris Yeltsin] stand up for Russia's legitimate interests."[19]

As to how the regime change would be engineered, there is a consensus that the plan is for a *hybrid war* against it—one that would be both military and economic.[20]

THE MILITARY ROUTE TO REGIME CHANGE

The possible military approach to regime change in Russia involves various dimensions. There are, at least, four facts that could reasonably make Russia fear that the United States is planning to use military means to bring about regime change in Russia.

First, since the latter part of 2014, John Pilger has pointed out, "the greatest build-up of military forces since World War II—led by the United States—[has been] taking place along Russia's western frontier."[21] Hardly anyone believes that Russia would attack America (unless, at least, it feared that the United States was preparing to attack *it*). So what could be the purpose of this build-up, Russia can reasonably ask, unless the United States were preparing to attack it?

Second, the United States and NATO are encircling Russia, so that Russia will be surrounded on virtually all sides by former Warsaw Pact countries that will now be members of NATO. In mid-2016, Philip Giraldi said that "the Obama Administration is already treating Georgia and Ukraine as if they were *de facto* members of NATO." Hillary Clinton, while she was running for the presidency in 2016, pledged to bring both of these nations into the alliance.[22]

Third, besides encircling Russia with allies, the United States is putting missiles in these countries—even though the Soviet Union's placing of missiles in Cuba during the Kennedy administration almost resulted in a nuclear war. The United States seems to believe that Russia will accept a situation that it itself would not.

Fourth, the US has installed an anti-missile shield in Romania (which it could do because of the cancellation of the ABM treaty during the first year of the Bush-Cheney administration). Russia has denounced this shield as a threat, because it undermines the mutually-assured-destruction (MAD) system, which had prevented nuclear war since WW II.[23] This development seems to reflect the switch, noted during the final years of the Bush-Cheney administration, from the era of MAD to the era of *nuclear primacy*.

The development of the shield reportedly infuriated the Russians. According to Reuters:

> Russia is incensed at such a show of force by its Cold War rival in formerly communist-ruled eastern Europe where it once held sway. Moscow says the US-led alliance is trying to encircle it close to the strategically important Black Sea, home to a Russian naval fleet.

But the United States has claimed that Russia has nothing to fear, because the "system is not aimed against Russia," but at Iran.[24]

This claim, however, is absurd: Iran has no nuclear missiles and will not have them for some time, especially given the recent treaty (made possible by Putin himself), preventing Iran from building any nuclear weapons in the near future. The Kremlin said:

> [T]he missile shield's real aim is to neutralize Moscow's nuclear arsenal long enough for the United States to make a first strike on Russia in the event of war.[25]

Moreover, the United States has argued that Russia should not fear an attack from it, because the missiles are purely defensive. However, Putin countered, the defense positions being installed near Russia's borders can be "inconspicuously" transformed into offensive weapons.[26]

Still another dimension of the military threat to Russia is the fact that the United States is developing new nuclear weapons, which could make a nuclear strike seem more doable. One of these weapons is a tiny nuclear bomb—a new model (Model 12) of the long-existing B61. It has a "dial-a-yield" feature, which allows the yield to be dialed down to the level at which it would be only two percent as powerful as the Hiroshima bomb. The B61-12 also has moveable fins, which allow the bomb to be guided much more precisely to the target, so the bomb does not need to be very powerful to take the target out.[27]

One of the reasons why America has never used nuclear weapons since Hiroshima and Nagasaki is that they would have been devastating not only to an enemy but also to America itself and its allies. Powerful nuclear weapons would also likely result in a "nuclear winter," which could bring all life to an end. But the B61-12 could lead American leaders to believe that they could launch a crippling attack on Russia with only an "acceptable" level of collateral damage to it, its allies, and the environment.[28]

In announcing the 2010 Nuclear Posture Review (which includes the B61-12), President Obama said:

> My Administration is taking a significant step forward by fulfilling another pledge that I made in Prague—to reduce the role of nuclear weapons in our national security strategy and focus on reducing the nuclear dangers of the 21st century.[29]

However, many experts question this claim. For example:

- Gen. James E. Cartwright, who as vice chairman of the Joint Chiefs of Staff was an influential nuclear strategist for Obama, likes the fact that precise targeting allows the United States to hold fewer weapons. But "what going smaller does," he added, "is to make the weapon more thinkable."[30]

- Hans M. Kristensen, the director of the Nuclear Information Project, said that he included himself among the critics who say that "the increased accuracy and lower yield options could make the B61-12 more attractive to use because of reduced collateral damage and radioactive fallout."[31]

The most important criticism, however, came from Moscow. The Obama administration defended the development of the B61-12 by saying that it "creates more strategic stability."[32] Russia's deputy defense minister, Anatoly Antonov, condemned a (warheadless) test of the B61-12, which used a F-15E fighter-bomber to carry the bomb. Calling the test "irresponsible" and "openly provocative," Antonov said that the use of the F-15E to carry the bomb "gave grounds to believe that the test was conducted in order to examine the possibility of using the B61-12 atomic bomb by NATO fighter-bombers stationed in Europe." In addition, Russia's Security Council Secretary Nikolay Patrushev said that the test showed that the US missile shield is intended for use against Russia.[33]

Accordingly, it is not paranoid for Russians to fear that the United States is preparing to launch a first strike. American leaders might believe that they could take out virtually all of Russia's nuclear weapons in a first strike by using the B61-12 (possibly along with other low-yield nuclear weapons), while producing relatively little collateral damage. And thanks to the missile shield, they may believe that they can destroy any remaining Russian weapons that survived the first strike. Given how rabid the neocons are about having a completely global empire—Robert Parry has spoken of their "madness," another critic has called them "psychopaths"[34]—they may believe the so-called collateral damage to be worth the price, especially because taking over Russia would give America control of Russia's unequaled natural resources.

If Russia strongly fears that the US is preparing for a first strike on it, its leaders might decide to launch a pre-emptive first strike, believing that it would have a better chance of surviving an American counter-strike than a first strike. Russia's fears could be reduced if the United States would adopt a "No First Use" protocol and persuade Russia to do the same.[35] Obama brought a "no first use" proposal to the National Security Council in August 2016. But this idea was resisted by powerful members of his cabinet, including the secretaries of state, defense, and energy.[36]

For an essay entitled "How the World Ends," Philip Giraldi provided this subtitle: "Baiting Russia Is Not Good Policy." As those of us old enough to remember, America's new "nuclear posture" will bring us back to the kinds of debates about nuclear strategy that we had in the 1980s, which were brilliantly described in Fred Kaplan's *The Wizards of Armageddon*.

THE ECONOMIC ROUTE TO REGIME CHANGE

The second way the United States has attempted to bring about regime change in Russia has been to use economic power. America engaged in, as Mahdi Darius Nazemroava emphasized, a "multi-spectrum war."[37] One dimension of this war is economic. The present discussion is focused on one aspect of the economic war: the placing of sanctions on Russia's economy. As for the reason for the sanctions, Neil Clark in 2014 gave this brief explanation:

> The neocon plan is for the Russian economy to be weakened by sanctions, which they hope will lead to a reduction in support for Putin and make it easier for them to destabilize the country and bring about a "regime change" in Moscow. They want a compliant stooge in the Kremlin who will surrender all of Russia's natural resources, and allow them to get rid of President Assad and the Baathists in Syria—an essential prerequisite before any attack on Iran.[38]

In other words, the Obama White House was following the approach taken in 1973 by President Nixon in bringing about a coup in Chile: "Make the economy scream."[39]

The Russian leaders were, of course, fully aware of this strategy. "Now public figures in Western countries say there is a need to impose sanctions that will destroy the economy and cause public protests," said Foreign Minister Lavrov.[40]

The Obama administration did not try to hide its intentions. At the end of 2014, top White House economist Jason Furman said that the West's sanctions on Russia, combined with the falling price of oil, "put their economy on the brink of crisis." White House press secretary Josh Earnest added: "As long as that sanctions regime remains in place, the costs on the Russian economy will continue to increase."[41]

In 2014, US Assistant Secretary of State Victoria Nuland—the wife of neocon Robert Kagan and an advisor to Vice President Cheney—told the House's Foreign Affairs Committee that (in Nazemroava's paraphrase):

> [T]he objectives of the US economic sanctions strategy against the Russian Federation was not only to damage the trade ties and business between Russia and the EU, but to also bring about economic instability in Russia and to create currency instability and inflation.

The aims of the US, added Nazemroava, did not "appear to be geared at coercing the Russian government to change its foreign policy, but to incite regime change in Moscow."[42]

Two ways in which Putin could be removed from power were suggested by Herbert E. Meyer, who had been a special assistant to the CIA director in the Reagan administration. The goal of US sanctions against Russia, said Meyer, "should be to get the Russians who've been keeping Putin in power, or tolerating Putin in power, to throw that knockout punch." Alternatively, he added:

> If Putin is too stubborn to acknowledge that his career is over, and the only way to get him out of the Kremlin is feet-first, with a bullet hole in the back of his head—that would also be okay with us.[43]

In any case, the Obama administration's approach was to put the screws on Russia's economy and then progressively tighten them with a series of sanctions.

Regime Change in Ukraine

Ukraine had long been divided between the predominantly Russian-speaking East and the predominantly Ukrainian-speaking West. Historically, Ukraine had been associated with Russia, but at the end of 2013, there began a revolution that in early 2014 replaced pro-Russian president Viktor Yanukovych. How and why this occurred is contentious. According to Western politicians and media, the standard account of what happened would go something like this:

> The Yanukovych government was presented with a petition that it sign an association agreement with the European Union. Although Yanukovych originally intended to do this, he changed his mind at the last moment, partly because Russia offered a $15 billion loan, which would allow Ukraine to remain with it (which was Yanukovych's preference). This decision, which caused great anger, sparked a wave of protests in Kiev's central square (so the protests became known as the Euromaidan movement—"maidan" is the Ukrainian word for "square").
>
> The protests were peaceful until the Yanukovych government sent in police to use violence to disperse the protestors. Then pro-Russian groups joined in and soon more than 100 people were killed, many of them by unidentified snipers, probably hired by Yanukovych. In February 2014, Yanukovych suddenly fled to Russia for some unknown reason. Arseniy Yatsenyuk was then named the new prime minister, and he signed the agreement to join Europe.
>
> Eventually, a civil war between the new Ukrainian government and pro-Russian separatists broke out in the southeast region of Ukraine, known as the Donbass, consisting of the Donetsk and Luhansk oblasts (provinces), which came to call themselves people's republics (DPR and LPR). The Minsk Protocol, detailing conditions for a ceasefire, was signed

in 2014, but it did not hold; in 2015, Minsk II was signed, but it also did not hold. By 2016, over 9,000 people had been killed, and this tragedy is Russia's fault for funding the separatists.

In the midst of these developments, Putin used the crisis as an occasion to take over Crimea in order to begin rebuilding the Russian empire.

On the basis of this account, the US government leveled sanctions on Russia for allegedly provoking the conflict, extending the civil war, funding the separatists, and invading Ukraine to occupy Crimea. European countries, under pressure from Washington, did the same.[44]

However, John Mearsheimer, one of our leading political scientists, wrote an article for *Foreign Affairs* entitled "Why the Ukraine Crisis Is the West's Fault," in which he said:

> According to the prevailing wisdom in the West, the Ukraine crisis can be blamed almost entirely on Russian aggression. Russian President Vladimir Putin, the argument goes, annexed Crimea out of a long-standing desire to resuscitate the Soviet empire, and he may eventually go after the rest of Ukraine, as well as other countries in eastern Europe. In this view, the ouster of Ukrainian President Viktor Yanukovych in February 2014 merely provided a pretext for Putin's decision to order Russian forces to seize part of Ukraine.
>
> But this account is wrong: the United States and its European allies share most of the responsibility for the crisis. The taproot of the trouble is NATO enlargement, the central element of a larger strategy to move Ukraine out of Russia's orbit and integrate it into the West. . . . Since the mid-1990s, Russian leaders have adamantly opposed NATO enlargement, and in recent years, they have made it clear that they would not stand by while their strategically important neighbor turned into a Western bastion. For Putin, the illegal overthrow of Ukraine's democratically elected and pro-Russian president—which he rightly labeled a "coup"—was the final straw. He responded by taking Crimea, a peninsula he feared would host a NATO naval base. . . . Putin's pushback should have come as no surprise. After all, the West had been moving into Russia's backyard and threatening its core strategic interests, a point Putin made emphatically and repeatedly.[45]

In the same vein, a *Guardian* article by Seumas Milne declared: "The story we're told about the protests gripping Kiev bears only the sketchiest relationship with reality."[46]

In fact, reality-based reports show that virtually every element in the official account is false, as facts from several sources have shown:

- What happened at Maidan "was not a peaceful democratic regime change, as it was presented in Western media, but a violent *putch* complete with murderous acts by hired assassins," reported professor Vlad Sobell of New York University's campus in Prague. He said that there were some 20 snipers, who killed both policemen and demonstrators on both sides to provoke chaos.[47]

- The coup was not evoked by outrage about Yanukovych's refusal to sign the agreement. Rather, the coup was planned by Victoria Nuland, the sister-in-law of neocon Frederick Kagan, who had strongly advocated for Ukraine's reorientation toward Europe. Nuland had been made Assistant Secretary of State for European Affairs by Hillary Clinton. To indicate that she was to be in charge, Nuland reminded Ukrainian business leaders that America had invested $5 billion in their "European aspirations," and at the beginning of the coup, she was even in the Maidan passing out cookies to the anti-Yanukovych agitators.[48]

- Three weeks before the coup, Nuland told Geoffrey Pyatt, the US Ambassador in Kiev, that when Yanukovych is replaced by a new president, the new prime minister should be Arseniy Yatsenyuk. In a four-minute intercepted phone call between Nuland and Pyatt, she can be heard saying (now on YouTube), "Yats is the guy who's got the economic experience." Also, expressing her view that the regime change should be mediated by the UN rather than the European Union, she said "Fuck the EU!"[49]

- Catherine Ashton, the EU's foreign-affairs chief, had asked Urmas Paet to investigate the cause of the violence that brought down Yanukovych's government. Although she had assumed that the snipers had been sent by Yanukovych, Paet told her that "behind the snipers, it was not Yanukovych, but it was somebody from the new coalition." This conversation, which was hacked by security service officers loyal to Yanukovych, can be heard on YouTube.[50]

- The coup, said Ray McGovern, was "spearheaded by well-organized neo-Nazi militias."[51] For the months of the Euromaidan conflict, added Robert Parry, the commandant was Andriy Parubiy, a well-known neo-Nazi, who directed the acts of neo-Nazi storm troopers, including the snipers.[52]

- In an essay on the "snipers' massacre," Ivan Katchanovski of the University of Ottawa pointed out that the conclusion "that the massacre was perpetrated by government snipers and special police units on a Yanukovych order has been nearly universally accepted by the Western governments [and] the media." However, Katchanovski said: "This academic investigation concludes that the massacre was a false flag operation, which was rationally planned and carried out with a goal of the overthrow of the government and seizure of power. . . . Concealed shooters and spotters were located in at least 20 Maidan-controlled buildings or areas. The various evidence that the protesters were killed from these locations include some 70 testimonies, primarily by Maidan protesters, [and] several videos of 'snipers' targeting protesters from these buildings."[53] (The use of snipers is what should be expected in a US-arranged protest-turned-violent, given William Engdahl's statement, quoted in Chapter 6, that "Washington's Arab Spring protests often used secret CIA and mercenary snipers to enflame and anger the population."[54])

- Contrary to the claim that Russia was behind the breakout of civil war in the Donbass, Russia scholar Paul Robinson said: "No plausible evidence has been produced to indicate that members of the Russian army were involved at the start of the uprising."[55]

- Intent on making Putin and Russian-speaking Ukrainians the instigators of the violence, the Western media have hidden what really happened. *The New York Times* in particular continued to deny that there was a coup.[56] But even George Friedman, the head of Stratfor, called the Euromaidan event the "most blatant coup in history."[57]

- With regard to Crimea: Putin knew immediately that the regime change in Ukraine was illegal and, as correspondent Pepe Escobar said, Russian intelligence knew quickly "that Maidan would be replicated in Crimea, so the Kremlin acted swiftly."[58] Naturally, Putin was not going to allow an illegal coup to separate him from Crimea, which had been part of Russia since the 18th century and provides its only warm-water port. Contrary to the claim that Putin had "invaded" Ukraine, Russian troops were already stationed inside Crimea at the Russian naval base at Sevastopol. But Putin did not annex Crimea until there was a referendum, which showed that 96% percent of the Crimeans wanted to secede from Ukraine.[59] The US press claims that that high vote shows that the referendum was rigged, but exit polls showed that about 93%

of the voters said they voted for secession.[60]

- "[T]he consistent pattern of the mainstream US news media," wrote Parry, has been "to white-out the role of Ukraine's brown-shirts." However, a few comments did make it through the US and UK censors.[61] (a) A *New York Times* article cited a leader of the neo-Nazi Right Sector, who bragged that Ukraine's revolution would never have happened without this group.[62] (b) A *Telegraph* article reported that the Kiev regime recruited neo-Nazis to serve as storm troopers, some of whom carried banners with the Wolfsangel symbol, which the SS had on its banners.[63] (c) The *BBC* provided a video showing how neo-Nazis spearheaded the seizure and occupation of government buildings, then forced Yanukovych and his aides to flee for their lives. (Accordingly, it is not true that Yanukovych fled for "some unknown reason.")[64]

Given the overwhelming evidence that the regime change in Ukraine was a false-flag operation, organized by members of the Obama administration, it was outrageous that the other G7 countries used the 2013-14 events in Ukraine as an excuse to put sanctions on Russia.[65]

Discussing the extreme danger of America's behavior in Ukraine, Parry wrote:

> If you wonder how the world could stumble into World War III much as it did into World War I a century ago all you need to do is look at the madness that has enveloped virtually the entire US political/media structure over Ukraine where a false narrative of white hats vs. black hats took hold early and has proved impervious to facts or reason.[66]

However, WW III could also result from the incautiousness of the belligerent regime the US installed in Ukraine. The Deputy Foreign Minister of Ukraine, Vadym Prystaiko, announced on CBC Radio that authorities in Kiev were seeking "a full-scale war" with Russia. He added: "Everybody is afraid of fighting with a nuclear state. We are not anymore, in Ukraine." He continued: "However dangerous it sounds, we have to stop [Putin] somehow." Seeking lethal weapons from the West, Prystaiko called on the West to "stiffen up in the spine a little."[67]

The Downing of MH17

On July 17, 2014, Malaysia Airlines flight MH17, travelling from Amsterdam to Kuala Lumpur, crashed near the Ukraine-Russia border, killing all 298 people aboard. According to the official report, the plane was brought down by a Russian-made ground-to-air missile.

Although the official report, written by the Dutch government, said there was no evidence that the missile was fired by pro-Russian separatists, the US argued that this was indeed the case and that Russia had provided the means.[68] In spite of the lack of any good evidence,[69] the US media accepted this claim as a flat fact.[70] Accordingly, with the support of their media, the US and the EU, shortly after having placed sanctions on Russia in relation to the regime-change events, imposed even more crippling sanctions.

But, as Dave Lindorff explained, neither Russia nor Russian separatists "had anything to gain (and everything to lose) by such a horrific act of terror."

> Pro-Russian separatist forces were trouncing Ukrainian military forces trying to conquer the rebellious Donbass region. The last thing they or their backer, Russia, needed was to do something that would be guaranteed to turn all of Europe against them, and hand the US government a perfect justification for providing more offensive military support to Ukraine. On the other hand, Ukraine and its military had every reason to commit such a heinous act if they thought they could pin the blame on Russia, and win more support from the US.[71]

In any case, the official claim about MH17—that it was shot down by a ground-to-air missile, and that the missile was sent up by Russian separatists—was made the very next day by the US ambassador to the UN, Samantha Power, who said the plane was "likely downed by a surface-to-air missile, an SA-11, operated from a separatist-held location."[72] The first part of this claim is contradicted by at least three types of evidence.

- Machine gun-like holes in the cockpit were reported by a German pilot and airlines expert, Peter Haisenko.[73] They were also reported by OSCE (the Organization for Security and Cooperation in Europe), which said—in a story carried by the *Wall Street Journal*—that "shrapnel-like, almost machine gun-like holes" were found in "two separate pieces of the fuselage."[74]

- Radar data showed a Ukrainian Su-25 Fighter Jet trailing MH17, and a Spanish air traffic controller also reported the existence of a Ukrainian military jet in the area.[75]

- In 2014, the BBC produced a video containing interviews of three eyewitnesses, all of whom reported that, after seeing a military aircraft following MH17, they heard an explosion in the air. One of the eyewitnesses said: "[T]here was another aircraft, a military one, beside it. Everybody saw it." Although the BBC quickly deleted the video, a copy of the report was found and made public.[76]

There was also evidence against the claim that an anti-aircraft weapon was fired from eastern Ukraine by the ethnic Russian rebels. According to the report provided by the Netherlands, the rebels had some surface-to-air missiles, but due to their limited range, "they do not constitute a danger to civil aviation at cruising altitude." Rather, said the report, the only anti-aircraft weapons in eastern Ukraine capable of bringing down an airline at MH-17's altitude (33,000 feet) was possessed by the (post-coup) Ukrainian government. Moreover, satellite imagery showed that a Ukrainian weapon with that capability was present in eastern part of the country.[77]

Unwilling to give up the US claim that Russia had provided the rebels with a missile launcher, the *New York Times* in mid-2016 endorsed an amateur report claiming that Russia had faked the satellite imagery that seemed to show the presence of Ukrainian anti-aircraft missile batteries in eastern Ukraine that day. However, well-known computer imaging expert Neal Krawetz said of the report touted by the *Times:* "'Bad analysis' is an understatement. This 'report' is outright fraud." Another expert said, "This is either amateur hour or supposed to deceive audiences without tech background." Krawetz replied: "Why 'or'? Amateur hour *and* deceptive."

In 2016, the BBC produced a new version of their MH17 documentary, advance reports of which said that it would involve the following elements:

- Exploration of the idea that that the plane was brought down by a Ukrainian fighter jet.

- "[A]nalyze the possibility that the downing of the jet was a CIA plot to pin the blame on Russia."

- Discuss German investigative reporter Billy Six, who interviewed 100 eyewitnesses, seven of whom reported seeing a fighter jet.

- Discuss private investigator Sergey Sokolov, who said: His 100 agents investigating the site found no shrapnel from a Russian-made missile; he was provided with a phone intercept between two CIA agents about planting two bombs on MH-17; and this act was "a pretext for firstly intensifying sanctions on Russia, secondly to show the world that Russia is a barbarian country and thirdly to strengthen the presence of NATO in Europe, particularly Ukraine."[78]

Ukraine: Coup, Lies, and Sanctions

The Euromaidan affair had a double benefit for the US government: Besides moving Ukraine, at least much of it, from the East to the West, it provided an excuse for imposing economic sanctions on Russia. Likewise, the claim that pro-Russian separatists had used a missile-launcher to bring down MH17 provided a basis for even more sanctions to be placed on Russia, thereby weakening its economy still further.

But both of these claims were contrary to the evidence, just as was the case with the US claims that Saddam was involved in 9/11 and had weapons of mass destruction, that Gaddafi was planning to launch a bloodbath in Libya, and that Assad had used chemical weapons. And yet European countries went along with sanctions against Russia based on US claims that are devoid of evidence and even contrary to the evidence. In the present case, the entire G7 endorsed a US document stating that: "Sanctions can be rolled back when Russia meets these commitments," meaning the commitments the US demands that Russia make, based on the assumption that the US charges against Russia were correct.[79] But by mid-2016, fortunately, there were signs that European countries would start eliminating the sanctions.[80]

The Threat of War with Russia

As many astute commentators have pointed out, America's pressing of Russia, both militarily and economically, is not rational. In an article entitled "Neoconservatives' Hegemonic Goal of Making Sovereign Countries Extinct Is Bringing the Extinction of Planet Earth," Paul Craig Roberts said:

> Unless Russia and China are content to be Washington's vassal states, for the neoconservatives, who control Washington and, thereby, the West, to press these two powerful countries so hard can only lead to war. As Washington is not a match for Russia and China in conventional warfare, the war will be nuclear, and the result will be the end of life on earth. . . . [The desire of American neoconservatives] for hegemony over the world is driving the world to extinction.

Parry added that the neocon desire for an all-inclusive empire has caused Washington and the American press to go mad.[81]

In his essay "How the World Ends," Philip Giraldi said that, according to Mearsheimer, "if the United States has but a single foreign policy imperative it would be to maintain a solid working relationship with Russia."[82] But the United States was doing the opposite, seemingly doing everything it can to humiliate and anger it. Putin wrote:

[T]here is a limit to everything. And with Ukraine, our Western partners have crossed the line. If you compress the spring all the way to its limit, it will snap back hard. . . . Russia has its own national interests that need to be taken into account and respected."[83]

Speaking to this point, Giraldi wrote:

No one but Victoria Nuland and the Kagans actually want a war but Moscow is being backed into a corner with more and more influential Russian voices raised against détente with a Washington that seems to be intent on humiliating Russians at every turn as part of a new project for regime change. Many Russian military leaders have quite plausibly come to believe that the continuous NATO expansion and the stationing of more army units right along the border means that the United States wants war.

This dynamic, pointed out Giraldi, has "the potential to become the greatest international catastrophe of all time." The "nearly constant animosity directed against Russia by the Obama Administration," Giraldi added, "should be seen as madness as the stakes in the game, a possible nuclear war, are, or should be, unthinkable."[84]

The diagnosis of the US by both Giraldi and Parry as mad was also offered by William Engdahl in his recent book *The Lost Hegemon: Whom the Gods Would Destroy.* The subtitle is a reference to a dictum of Euripides, "Those whom the gods wish to destroy they first make mad." Engdahl's thesis is that the desperation of America's elite class to hold onto its empire, and even to create a *global* empire, has driven it mad—as witnessed by its willingness to risk nuclear holocaust.[85]

In his essay "A World War Has Begun," John Pilger referred to the fact that "the US military is deploying combat troops, tanks, [and] heavy weapons" in "Latvia, Lithuania and Estonia—next door to Russia." This is, Pilger pointed out, "extreme provocation of the world's second nuclear power."[86] Similarly, Robert Parry, referring to the coup in Ukraine, pointed out that this risk "occurred on the border of Russia, a nuclear-armed state that— along with the United States—could exterminate all life on the planet."[87]

If the United States keep pushing, the worst could happen. The seriousness with which Putin takes this threat was illustrated by Russia's national nuclear preparedness exercises in October 2016.[88]

In an essay entitled "The Looming US War on Russia," Irish journalist Finian Cunningham wrote of the "burgeoning US-led aggression towards Russia—in the form of provocative political campaigns to demonize and vilify with false accusations, economic sanctions and the spurning of diplomacy and dialogue, as well as the expansion of military forces, including the deployment of missile systems."

Cunningham's essay was published in the context of NATO's provocative war games in June 2016, the "largest war games since Soviet Russia dissolved in 1991," explained Stephen Lendman.[89] Russian Deputy Foreign Minister Alexei Meshkov, who said that the exercises "carry a serious destabilizing component," said that their "main goal is to continue the aggravation of tensions."[90] Robert Bridge, an American journalist living in Moscow, wrote:

> For those who still aren't convinced that Russia has some serious grounds for concern as the US-led war machine grinds ever closer, let's put the situation into its proper perspective. Let's imagine that the geopolitical chessboard were suddenly flipped and it is Russia that is now busy hatching a 28-member military alliance near America's border, for example, in Latin America . . . .
>
> But why stop there? Let's roll the dice and see what Washington's reaction would be if Russia had just dispatched three TU-160 Blackjack bombers to South America to participate in war games with the likes of Cuba, Venezuela and Brazil, for example, just weeks after Moscow dropped a missile defense system—which could go offensive with the flick of a switch—in, say, Colombia. Yikes! I dare say there's not a straitjacket in the world that could restrain the writhing neocon convulsions that would break out across the Beltway.[91]

More seriously, does anyone believe that neocons and many others in Washington, convinced that Russia was getting ready to launch a nuclear attack on America, would not argue that we should strike first? Can anyone be certain that this is not what the Kremlin would do, if we continue to threaten and humiliate Russia?

Saying that Vladimir Putin came to consider the United States an "immoral, power-crazed entity that will destroy the planet before it gives up its goal of hegemony over the entirety of the Earth," Roberts asked: "Do you believe the Russians will sit there awaiting a nuclear strike, or will they pre-empt it with a strike of their own?"[92]

This threat could be removed if the United States as mentioned above would adopt a no-first-use policy, as Obama proposed. The urgency of this issue was increased when Donald Trump reportedly asked, "If we have [nuclear weapons], why can't we use them?"[93] In a *New York Times* op-ed, James E. Cartwright—former commander of the US Strategic Command and a former vice chairman of the Joint Chiefs of Staff—argued for ending the US first-use policy. Among the reasons he gave, he said: "Leaders of other countries would be calmed by the knowledge that the United States viewed its own weapons as deterrents to nuclear warfare, not as tools of aggression."[94] But as reported above, Obama's advisors opposed the idea.[95]

The threat of war with Russia over Ukraine was increased by the situation in Syria, which was discussed in Chapter 6. In 2014, the United States started (illegally) making airstrikes in Syria, supposedly going only after ISIS.[96] Although US planes sometimes struck Syrian troops, the strikes could be interpreted as accidental. But with the attack on Syrian forces at Deir Ez-Zor on September 17, 2016, the attack was clearly deliberate (even though the US government and its press maintained the fiction that it was a mistake). From then on, the two countries did and said things that suggested that they were headed to war. On the US's side, there were a number of threats and belligerent actions:

- Less than two weeks after the attack on Deir Ez-Zor, US-led coalition warplanes destroyed two main bridges on the Euphrates River in the same province.[97]

- After former CIA deputy director Mike Morell had said on the *Charlie Rose* TV show in August that the US should start killing Russians to give them a message, State Department spokesman John Kirby gave Russia a veiled threat, saying that unless it "stops the violence" in Syria, "more Russian lives will be lost, more Russian aircraft will be shot down."[98]

- Senator John McCain, chairman of the Committee on Armed Services, declared: "If Russia continues its indiscriminate bombing, we should make clear that we will take steps to hold its aircraft at greater risk. And we must create safe zones for Syrian civilians."[99]

- Mark Milley, the US Army's chief of staff, threatened Russia over Syria, saying "We'll beat you anywhere. . . . We will beat you harder than you have ever been beaten before."[100]

- Hillary Clinton's call for a "no-fly zone" or "safe zones" became widely echoed after Russia and Syria, in order to remove all the jihadist rebels from Aleppo, began bombing it (after the Deir Ez-Zor attack), with the result that many citizens as well as rebels were killed. During the 2016 vice-presidential debates, both Tim Kaine and Mike Pence endorsed safe zones, although it was not clear that they understood that they would—in addition to knocking out the enemy's air-defenses to establish a no-fly zone— require US ground troops. Perhaps they did not understand about ground troops because Clinton, while advocating a no-fly zone, had said that putting ground troops in Syria would be "a very serious mistake." However, Secretary Kerry had told a Senate panel that creating safe zones would require 15,000 to 30,000 ground troops.[101] Also, in spite of having given the impression that setting up a no-fly zone was a simple matter, which would not take many lives, Clinton in a leaked 2013 speech had explained: "To have a no-fly zone you have to take out all of the air defenses, many of which are located in populated areas. So our missiles, even if they are standoff missiles so we're not putting our pilots at risk—you're going to kill a lot of Syrians."[102] In addition, said General Joseph Dunford, chairman of the Joint Chiefs of Staff, imposing a no-fly zone "would require us to go to war against Syria and Russia." [103] So Clinton's plan to remove Assad, if she had won the White House and been able to carry it out, could very well have led to nuclear war.

On the Russian side: Having made developments enabling its defense of Syria, it also become more of a factor in the Middle East more widely and made statements warning the US not to attack Syria or try to prevent it from doing so. Some of these moves were made expressly in response to the Deir Ez-Zor attack:

- In early October, Russia let it be known that it will "take down any airplane or missile targeting [the] Syrian Army."[104]

- Russian Foreign Minister Lavrov, having learned that US policymakers were considering targeting Syrian airfields to cripple Damascus's airstrikes against rebels,[105] announced that "Russia will protect its assets if [the] US strikes Syrian bases."[106]

- It was then reported that Russia planned to expand its small naval base in Tartus, Syria, thereby making it usable by larger warships, and also turn it into a permanent base, demonstrating that it will not give up on Syria.[107]

- Russia also let it be known that it planned to create a military base there, complete with air and naval bases.[108]

These developments, wrote Ian Greenhalgh, "represent a major strategic shift by Russia where they are gaining a foothold in the eastern Mediterranean and a permanent presence in the Middle East." South Front said: "Washington's actions to counter the Russian efforts in Syria have only pushed Moscow to expand its military presence in the Middle Eastern region."[109] More generally, these and other developments demonstrated Russia's determination not to be pushed around.

DONALD TRUMP ON RUSSIA

Dick Cheney famously said that, if there is even a 1% chance that something truly awful will happen, one should act as if it were a certainty.[110] This doctrine should be applied to the possibility that America's aggressiveness towards Russia might result in a nuclear holocaust. "But the neocons," said Parry, "apparently think the risks are well worth it." This is, as he observed, madness. But what is particularly shocking, he added, "is how virtually everyone in US officialdom and across the mainstream media spectrum has bought into this madness."[111]

As a result, most Americans have no idea, or a false idea, of what has been going on in Ukraine, because, Parry said, much of the US media has "behaved as essentially a propaganda organ for the new regime in Kiev and the State Department."[112] Likewise, Dave Lindorff pointed out that a *New York Times* columnist, while complaining that Americans are ignorant about Ukraine, contributed to this ignorance by spreading the false propaganda about it.[113]

This madness can be diagnosed as a neoconservative virus, which infected the brains of journalists and editors, along with Washington politicians and their staff during the Bush-Cheney years and then continued to grow, as exemplified by Hillary Clinton and her appointee Victoria Nuland—who apparently shares the same worldview as Robert Kagan, to whom she is married—and Dick Cheney, for whom she previously worked. This virus, inherited from the Bush-Cheney administration, could ruin civilization—literally and completely. It is possible that the defeat of Clinton in the 2016 presidential election might lead this virus to become less virulent.

To put the point positively: During the presidential campaign, Donald Trump said that he was in favor of better relations with Vladimir Putin. So a good result from Trump's surprising victory may turn out to be a lessening of the danger of a war with Russia. Two days after the election, Stephen Kinzer wrote about this possibility. Although Trump had not spoken much about foreign policy, Kinzer said, he had enunciated a couple promising ideas.

> [H]e wants to de-escalate our spiraling conflict with Russia. . . . [H]e has rejected the [Washington] playbook view that President Vladimir Putin is a mad thug whose policies threaten our national security. If he remains firm and pulls us out of the spiral of US-Russia confrontation, he will be stepping back from the conflict that has seemed more likely than any

other to explode into nuclear war. . . . His election could allow NATO to escape from American control and pursue the less aggressive policies that France, Germany, and Italy would prefer.[114]

Unlike Kinzer, however, most of the corporate press reacted very negatively to Trump's statement that he did not want war with Russia. Indeed, as mentioned in the preface to this book, Trump's statement turned him from "media darling, to the devil incarnate."[115] The intelligence community essentially told Trump if he was to succeed as president, he would have to get tough with Russia.[116]

Trump soon got the message, fired his Russia-friendly national security advisor, made military strikes on Syria and Afghanistan, reversed his view that NATO was obsolete, and reported that he "was not getting along with Russia at all."[217] Trump also announced that he was delegating decisions about military actions to the Pentagon. In fact, he may have had no choice, if the fear that he has lost control over the Pentagon is true. In any case, the election of Donald Trump may prove to make the United States more dangerous that it was, rather than less.[118]

THE PUSH TOWARD WAR WITH CHINA

Australian John Pilger has warned about the threat from the US pressure on Russia, saying that in 2015, "the greatest build-up of military forces since World War II—led by the United States—is taking place along Russia's western frontier. Not since Hitler invaded the Soviet Union have foreign troops presented such a demonstrable threat to Russia."[119]

But in a film entitled "The Coming War on China," Pilger gave equal emphasis to the US provocations of that country. Saying that the war with China has already begun, he explained: "At present, it is a war of propaganda, of lies and distraction, but this can change instantaneously with the first mistaken order, the first missile."[120]

The immediate occasion for this concern was Obama's so-called "pivot to Asia," in which he ordered almost two-thirds of US naval forces to be transferred to Asia and the Pacific. This transfer represented the greatest build-up of American military forces since the Second World War, aimed at China. Somewhat like what American bases did to Russia, they "form a giant noose encircling China with missiles, bombers, warships all the way from Australia through the Pacific to Asia and beyond."[121]

In 2015, the US staged Talisman Sabre, its biggest single military exercise since the Cold War. It involved an armada of ships and long-range bombers that rehearsed an "Air-Sea Battle Concept for China," blocking sea lanes in the Straits of Malacca and cutting off China's access to oil, gas and other raw materials from the Middle East and Africa[122]—something like what America did in the 1940s to provoke Japan to attack Pearl Harbor.[123]

In response, China began "feverishly building strategic airstrips on disputed reefs and islets in the Spratly Islands in the South China Sea—the chokepoint through which its lifelines run." The US has portrayed this building as evidence of new Chinese aggression, threatening the "freedom of navigation" in the South China Sea. According to Obama's secretary of defense, Ashton Carter, the threat comes from those "who see America's dominance and want to take that away from us." Like Russia, said Pilger, the rise of China as an economic power has been declared "an 'existential threat' to the divine right of the United States to rule and dominate human affairs."[124]

Unsurprisingly, Hillary Clinton was central to this claimed threat. While Secretary of State in 2010, she "declared China's claim on the Spratly Islands—which lie more than 7,500 miles from the United States—a threat to US 'national security' and to 'freedom of navigation.'" By giving millions of dollars in arms and military equipment to the Philippines, she convinced it to break off talks with China and to persuade the UN Permanent Court of Arbitration to rule against China's claim of sovereignty over the islands.[125]

In spite of the fact that the US has clearly been the aggressor, it has propagandized "the threat of China," with the media "beating the drums of war as the world is being primed to regard China as a new enemy."[126]

This became especially important when Donald Trump, who had spoken very negatively about China during his campaign, was elected president. Although Obama's attempt to thwart China was a failure, the Trump presidency began with commentators having no idea of what he might try to do.[127] This resulted in a dangerous situation, given the fact that, in response to US moves, "China is discussing putting its nuclear missiles on high alert so that they can be launched quickly on warning of an attack."[128] Whether or not the election of Trump reduces the threat of a nuclear holocaust in relation to Russia, the threat might grow in relation to China.

10 • ECOLOGICAL HOLOCAUST

The threat from a nuclear holocaust is real, and should be taken much more seriously in today's world than it has been. Many commentators, however, point out that the possibility of an ecological holocaust, resulting in human extinction, is at least equally serious.

- In a 2016 essay entitled "Human Extinction Isn't That Unlikely," the first words were: "Nuclear war. Climate change." Referring to a recent report by the Global Challenges Foundation, the author—the *Atlantic*'s Robinson Meyer—said: "The report holds catastrophic climate change and nuclear war far above the rest."[1]

- Reporting on a recent interview with Noam Chomsky, Amy Goodman gave it this title: "Climate Change & Nuclear Proliferation Pose the Worst Threat Ever Faced by Humans."[2]

- "Pointing out that several decades ago, the "two superpowers made 'end times' a human possession for the first time in history," Tom Engelhardt observed that "while an instant apocalypse loomed, a slow-motion version of the same, also human-made, was approaching, unrecognized by anyone."[3]

It is well known, at least among people who accept scientific evidence, that the major threat to the planet's life, aside from nuclear weapons, results from humanity's burning too many fossil fuels, which release excessive greenhouse gases into the atmosphere, especially carbon dioxide (CO_2) and methane (CH_4). The main resulting problems are global warming and its "evil twin," ocean acidification.[4]

Just as the Bush-Cheney administration and other people infected by the neocon virus have made nuclear war more possible, they also moved us closer to an ecological holocaust. In fact, taking office at the beginning of the 21st century, just as the world was waking up to the global-warming issue, Bush and Cheney were just about the worst possible people to have in charge of the US government.

THE RESPONSIBILITY OF
THE BUSH-CHENEY ADMINISTRATION

This section does not seek to give a complete history of the Bush-Cheney administration's treatment and effects on environmental issues, but merely to recount some episodes to give a sense of its destructiveness.

Cheney's Hostility

Cheney had long been hostile to efforts to spend money to protect the environment. During the George H.W. Bush administration, while Cheney was secretary of defense, he worked to quash the widely endorsed idea after the end of the Soviet Union for a "peace dividend," according to which the money being spent on the Cold War could be switched to domestic matters, such as health, education, and the environment. Calling this talk "irresponsible," Cheney succeeding in "putting a Department of Defense claim on every penny that might have gone to the peace dividend."[5]

Bush's Reversal on Regulating CO_2

Bush may not have been so bad on the environment had he not chosen Cheney as his vice president. During his race for the presidency against Al Gore, Bush said: "We will require all power plants to meet clean-air standards in order to reduce emissions of carbon dioxide within a reasonable period of time." But two months after entering the Oval Office, Bush reneged. What had happened was that Cheney sent a memo to his aides, saying that they should nudge Bush toward the position that "the current state of scientific knowledge about causes of and solutions to global warming is inconclusive." Sure enough, when Bush announced that he would *not* regulate CO_2 emissions, he explained that, besides the fact that doing so would impose rising costs upon Americans, current knowledge about the causes of global climate change was incomplete.[6]

Bush on the Watsons

Another illustration of the Bush-Cheney administration's aid to the oil-and-gas industry involved its acceptance of the ExxonMobil recommendations about two men named Watson. In the first month of Bush's presidency, the IPCC's new report stated that global warming was definitely caused by human activity. Bush accepted ExxonMobil's suggestion that he get the IPCC's (excellent) chief, Robert Watson, replaced.[7]

At the same time, ExxonMobil asked Bush to appoint Harlan Watson (no relation)—who had been President's George H.W. Bush's climate negotiator at Rio and who worked closely with members of Congress opposing action on global warming—as the new climate negotiator. Revelations about this request led Greenpeace to ask, "Who can now doubt that US policy is being steered by the world's largest oil company?"[8]

Eliminating the Need for GCC

The support for oil by the Bush-Cheney administration was so extensive that that Global Climate Coalition—which had been formed in 1989 to resist the anti-fossil fuel policies of the newly formed IPCC (Intergovernmental Panel on Climate Change)—disbanded in 2002, saying that, because of the Bush administration's new policies, it was no longer needed.[9]

The Appointment of Philip Cooney

In 2007, *Rolling Stone* published an article on "the Bush administration's secret campaign to deny global warming."[10] One segment of the article dealt with Bush and Cheney's appointment of Philip Cooney to be the chief of staff for the White House's Council on Environmental Quality (CEQ). Being a lawyer with no scientific credentials, Cooney used his role to censor and even distort government reports "so as to exaggerate scientific uncertainty about global warming." As an example of distortion, Cooney claimed the 20th century was not unusually warm. Rick Piltz, a Senior Associate in the Climate Change Science Program, resigned in protest.[11]

Refusal to Help Syria's Agriculture

As is now well known, one of the causes for the war in Syria was the lengthy and devastating drought that began afflicting that country in 2006.[12] To repeat an episode reported in Chapter 6: Appealing to the USAID program for help, the Syrian minister of agriculture said that the economic and social fallout from the drought was "beyond [Syria's] capacity as a country to deal with." But the Bush-Cheney administration's director of USAID said—in a cable that was later published by WikiLeaks—"we question whether limited USG resources should be directed toward this appeal at this time."[13]

Conclusion

After the journalists who had supported the Bush-Cheney administration's claims about weapons of mass destruction became aware of the truth, some of them felt anguish about having used "'evidence' now known to be bogus" to support the push for war. "The lethal fallout from misinformation a decade ago," wrote *Guardian* journalist Stephen Lewandowsky, "primarily affected the people of Iraq," but "the fallout from misinformation about climate change is likely to affect us all."[14]

At the end of 2008, a survey of over 100 historians showed that almost two thirds of them ranked Bush as the worst US president ever. Still more serious was the judgment of the International Institute for Environment and Development's Saleem Huq—who had been one of the authors of the IPCC's 2007 report—that Bush was possibly the president "who has doomed the planet."[15]

GLOBAL WARMING

Although many people might not be able to conceive how an ecological holocaust could occur, the frightening truth is that, just as there are many ways a nuclear war might begin, there are many ways in which an ecological holocaust could occur.

To begin with global warming: There has been much confusion about it. The idea of "global warming" is often taken to mean that the weather is getting warmer always and everywhere (allowing a Republican senator to refute global warming by bringing a snowball to the Senate floor). But global warming merely means that the planet's *average temperature* is going up. Global warming, thus understood, results in many phenomena in addition to heat, such as more intense hurricanes, longer droughts, and worse snowstorms as well as rainstorms at places. Nevertheless, global warming does result in more intense heat waves, and they can be deadly.

Heat

People often think of hurricanes and tornadoes as the most serious types of extreme weather, but according to the National Weather Service, "Heat is the number one weather-related killer in the United States."[16] And really intense heat waves can kill many thousands of people: 35,000 to 70,000 in the European heat wave of 2003, and 50,000 in the 2010 Russian heat wave.

Moreover, "by the middle of this century," said Stanford University's Noah Deffenbaugh, "even the coolest summers will be hotter than the hottest summers of the past 50 years."[17] If the global temperature continues to rise, scientists say, temperatures will *exceed livable limits*.[18]

But could global warming bring about human extinction? Climate scientists now say that, at the current rate of greenhouse emissions, it will not be long before the global temperature will be 4°C to 7°F higher than it was in pre-industrial days. This will occur when the percentage of CO_2 in the atmosphere reaches 550 ppm (parts per million). During the industrial age, which began about the middle of the 19th century, the atmosphere's CO_2 has risen from 270 to over 400 ppm, most of which has occurred since 1950, when the burning of fossil fuels really speeded up. So the world is already almost half-way to 550 ppm, and the rate of burning fossil fuels has continued to rise. So unless there is a rapid transition from fossil-fuel to clean energy (such as solar, wind, and geothermal energy), the global temperature will rise 4°C by about the end of this century. Some scientists, including Joe Romm at Climate Progress and those at the World Bank, even believe that the world may rise 4°C by the 2060s.[19]

Climate scientists have given much attention to the question of what the world will be like if it rises 4°C.[20] According to Kevin Anderson of

England's Tyndall Centre for Climate Change Research:

> A global mean surface temperature rise of 4°C equates to around 5-6°C warming of global mean land surface temperature. . . . [A] 4°C world would likely see the hottest days in China being 6-8°C [9-14°F] warmer than the hottest days experienced in recent heat waves with which China has struggled to cope; Central Europe would see heat waves much like the one in 2003, but with 8°C [14°F] on top of the highest temperatures; during New York's summer heat waves the warmest days would be around 10-12°C [18-21.6°F] hotter.[21]

As to what this would mean for the human race, Anderson said: "I think it's extremely unlikely that we wouldn't have mass death at 4°C. . . . [Y]ou might have half a billion people surviving."[22]

Unfortunately, Anderson is considered an optimist by some other climate scientists, who will be discussed after this chapter looks at some other ways that an ecological holocaust might occur.

Sea-Level Rise

Some scientists believe that "sea level rise will likely be the first to produce a human catastrophe on a global scale."[23] Shanghai, China's largest city with its more than 14 million people, is less than 2 meters (7 feet) above sea level. In 2010, some experts said the sea level might rise that much by the end of the century. They were considered extremists, but by 2016, this had become the consensus view.[24] Adding the population of Shanghai to that of much of the rest of southeast China tells us that a significant portion of the human race will need to move. And of course that 7-feet rise will also deluge cities on the coasts of the United States and many other countries.

But this will be only the start, if global warming continues. The Greenland and Antarctic ice sheets, long considered stable, are now melting rapidly. The complete melting of the Greenland ice sheet would raise the sea level by 23 feet; the melting of West Antarctica, 19 feet; and East Antarctica, a whopping 197. This would leave relatively little land left for some 9 billion people, who are already too crowded in many places.

Food Shortage

In 2009, Lester Brown wrote an article in *Scientific American* asking, "Could Food Shortages Bring Down Civilization?"[25] Answering yes, he wrote a book entitled *Full Planet, Empty Plates*, in which he said: "Food is the weak link in our modern civilization—just as it was for the Sumerians, Mayans, and many other civilizations that have come and gone. They could not separate their fate from that of their food supply. Nor can we."[26]

Already a billion people a year are going hungry or even starving to death. But the situation is fated to become much worse, especially if global warming continues. The amount of food produced can be reduced by many dimensions of climate change produced by global warming: wildfires, fresh-water shortage, sea-level rise, storms (especially hurricanes, tornadoes, and extreme rain with flooding), and especially—at least thus far—heat and drought. (As one plant biologist in Illinois said: "It's like farming in hell."[27])

Former UN Secretary-General Kofi Annan said that climate change is having a devastating effect on food production. A 2012 Oxfam report said that "the food security outlook in a future of unchecked climate change is bleak."[28] Writing in the *Guardian*, Nafeez Ahmed said in 2013 that "if we don't change course, this decade will go down in history as the beginning of the global food apocalypse."[29]

OCEAN ACIDIFICATION

Although food availability will be increasingly reduced by global warming, it will be even more drastically reduced by ocean acidification. Although it is not simply a dimension of global warming, ocean acidification results from the same excessive CO_2. It has reached a crisis stage because about 30 percent of civilization's CO_2 emissions have been absorbed by the ocean.

Ocean acidification involves a decrease in the ocean's pH, which had held steady for at least the past 600,000 years. But since the industrial revolution, there has been a whopping 30 percent increase in acidity, and the acidifying is now the fastest in 300 million years.[30]

The absorption of increasingly more CO_2 is destructive because when it is combined with sea water, it produces carbonic acid—which is the ingredient that, besides giving soft drinks their fizz, eats out limestone caves. It also does this to animals with chalky skeletons, ones that calcify, "which make up more than a third of the planet's marine life." Elevating the percentage of carbonic acid makes it increasingly difficult for calcifying organisms to make their skeletons—organisms such as plankton, corals, sea butterflies, molluscs, crabs, clams, mussels, oysters, and snails.[31]

Most important for the cycle of life, however, is plankton, which, being capable of photosynthesis, is at the base of the marine food web. Besides providing about half of the biosphere's oxygen, phytoplankton also "account for about half of the total organic matter on Earth." They "ultimately support all of our fishes." Therefore, a reduction in the ocean's phytoplankton would be extremely serious. And unfortunately, there has been a 40 percent decline in the phytoplankton since the 1950s. Marine ecologist Boris Word said he could not think of a biological change that would be bigger. Fellow marine ecologist Daniel Boyce said that "a decline of phytoplankton affects everything up the food chain."[32]

The more the acidification goes up, so the pH goes down, the more difficult it is for phytoplankton and the other organisms mentioned above—corals, sea butterflies, molluscs, crabs, clams, mussels, oysters, and snails—to calcify.[33]

CO_2 is now at about 400 parts per million. If it reaches roughly 500 ppm, thereby driving the pH down a lot more, said Danish marine biologist Ove Hoegh-Guldberg, "you put calcification out of business in the oceans."[34] If and when this occurs, phytoplankton will die and so will the rest of the calcified sea creatures. We should, as urges the subtitle of a film: *Imagine a World without Fish.*

If that is difficult, it would be even harder for the planet's people to *live* without seafood: Besides being the world's largest source of protein, with over 2.6 billion people depending on it as their main source of protein, the ocean also serves as the primary source of food for 3.5 billion people.[35] How would we survive if three and a half-billion people can no longer rely upon what has always been their primary source of food? "Global warming is incredibly serious," said Ove Hoegh-Guldberg, "but ocean acidification could be even more so."[36]

EXTINCTION

The previous section discussed various processes that could lead to an ecological holocaust, wiping out billions of human beings. But what about the possibility of global extinction? This unhappy topic has been broached by several climate scientists and science writers.

New Yorker writer Elizabeth Kolbert, in her 2014 book, *The Sixth Extinction*, asked, "In an extinction event of our own making, what happens to us?" Many people, she observed, seem to think that we self-named *Homo sapiens* are so wise and powerful that nothing could drive us to extinction. However, she pointed out, "When a mass extinction occurs, it takes out the weak and also lays low the strong." The famous anthropologist Richard Leakey, she added, warned that "*Homo sapiens* might not only be the agents of the sixth extinction, but also risks being one of its victims."[37]

In 2013, Paul and Anne Ehrlich wrote: "Humankind finds itself engaged in what Prince Charles described as 'an act of suicide on a grand scale.'"[38] In the following year, Tom Engelhardt said that climate change, besides being a "crime against humanity," is also a crime "against most living things," hence "terracide."[39]

Kolbert and the Ehrlichs did not make predictions about how soon human beings would suffer extinction. But Australian microbiologist Frank Fenner, who had become famous decades ago for announcing the eradication of smallpox, said in 2010: "Homo sapiens will become extinct, perhaps within 100 years." The extinction, he said, would come about because of the combination of climate change, declining resources, and overcrowding.[40]

But is there any kind of process that could conceivably lead to extinction? Actually, there are several such processes.

Climate War

It has now become widely accepted that global warming is a factor making war more likely. Canadian journalist Gwynne Dyer discussed this idea in his 2010 book, *Climate Wars: The Fight for Survival as the World Overheats*.[41] Joe Romm, who had long argued that drought was the weather phenomenon that will have the worst direct effects on people, said in 2013 that "war, conflict, competition for arable and/or habitable land [may well] affect far more people both directly and indirectly."[42] (He made this point while discussing the war in Syria, which is now acknowledged to have been significantly influenced by climate change.)

This issue was also acknowledged by Secretary of State John Kerry, who said that the challenge of climate change is "not just an environmental issue and it's not just an economic issue. It is a security issue."[43]

Admiral Samuel Locklear, the Commander of the US Pacific Command, has said that significant upheaval related to global warming "is probably the most likely thing that . . . will cripple the security environment."[44]

In addition, the 2014 version of the assessment of climate change by the IPCC (Intergovernmental Panel on Climate Change), having never before mentioned how climate change would contribute to resource wars, said that "human security will be progressively threatened as climate changes." In particular, escalating "breakdown of food systems linked to warming, drought, flooding, and precipitation variability and extremes" will increase the "risks of violent conflicts in the form of civil war and inter-group violence."[45]

On the question of how climate change could lead to war: "There is a probability of wars," said Dyer, "if temperatures rise 2 to 3 degrees Celsius." After saying that "the first and most important impact of climate change on human civilization will be an acute and permanent crisis of food supply," he added that "countries that cannot feed their people are unlikely to be 'reasonable' about it."[46]

The ecological threat of war in many places, especially in the Middle East, is most likely to involve fresh water. General Anthony Zinni, the former head of the US Central Command, said:

You already have great tension over water. These are cultures often built around a single source of water. So any stresses on the rivers and aquifers can be a source of conflict.[47]

In some cases, the conflicts could become nuclear. For example, Gwynne Dyer said that the melting of glaciers and snowpack that have provided water for the rivers that rise in the Himalayas and the Tibetan plateau—including the Ganges, Indus, Mekong, and Yangtze rivers—"will lead to food shortages and cross-border disputes over water in the Indian subcontinent, and nuclear-armed India and Pakistan will face the risk of war over the Indus River."[48]

Indeed, conflicts over water could result in nuclear war between any of the nuclear-armed powers in Asia: India, Pakistan, and China. Just as a nuclear war started over territory could result in extinction, the same would be true of a nuclear war rooted in water or other natural resources.

Ecosystem Collapse

An ecosystem (ecological system) is a network of living organisms (plants, animals, microbes) interacting with nonliving things (including air, water, soil, and minerals), functioning as a unit. An ecosystem can be very small, such as a tiny pond, or very large, such as the ocean. Inclusive of all local ecosystems, the planet as a whole can be considered an ecosystem.[49]

Small local ecosystems can collapse, so that they no longer provide support for animals, as when a pond no longer supports the life of its fish. Larger ecosystems, such as a lake or a sea, can also collapse, as when they no longer support plant and animal life. For example, the Dead Sea is dead because it became so salty that nothing other than microbes can live in it. Because of ocean acidification, the oceanic ecosystem as a whole might collapse.

Finally, earth scientists have begun thinking about an unprecedented ecosystem collapse: the collapse of the *global* ecosystem.

- In 2004, Chris Thomas, a conservation biologist at Leeds University in England, led a team studying "Extinction Risk from Climate Change." The conclusion was that if business as usual continues, 15 to 37 percent of the land plants and animals they studied would, by 2050, be "committed to extinction"—a conclusion that Thomas found "terrifying."[50]

- In 2007, a major article dealt with the plight of four keystone species which are absolutely essential for human survival: plankton, edible fish, bees, and topsoil. The study concluded that all four are in trouble.[51]

- In 2009, an essay on "Planetary Boundaries" was written by 29 major scientists, including James Hansen. The question behind the essay was: "What are the non-negotiable planetary preconditions that humanity needs to respect in order to avoid the risk of deleterious or even catastrophic environmental change at continental to global scales?" Calling these non-negotiable planetary preconditions "thresholds," the authors' idea was that, just as a local ecosystem has thresholds that, if reached will cause that ecosystem to undergo a sudden "state change," the transgression of one or more *global* thresholds might lead to an abrupt state change of the global ecosystem as a whole.

- The team then worked out estimates of "planetary boundaries within which we expect that humanity can operate safely," so there would be no danger of "crossing thresholds that will trigger non-linear, abrupt environmental change within [the global ecosystem]." Settling on nine such thresholds, the team concluded that three of them—atmospheric CO_2 concentration, biodiversity loss, and changes to the nitrogen cycle—have already been transgressed, so that these transgressions need to be reversed quickly.[52]

- In 2012, Anthony Barnosky of the University of California (Berkeley) and 22 other scientists produced a study entitled "Approaching a State Shift in Earth's Biosphere." The *Vancouver Observer* provided this summary:

  > Scientists have reached near-total consensus on climate change. But according to the new study, once you add other variables—such as population growth, over-consumption, agriculture and extinctions—to that mix, the entire ecological system may teeter on the brink. Everything could, in fact, change in the proverbial blink of an eye (at least, on the scale of earth's history). It's called a 'global state change,' and the report estimates it could begin as early as the second half of this century if we stay on our present course.[53]

- One of the participants said that his fellow scientists are "more than pretty worried"—in fact, "some are terrified." Another one of the scientists said that the conclusion "scares the hell out of me."[54]

The Methane Threat

Methane (CH_4) is a greenhouse gas dozens of times more potent than CO_2. Many scientists consider the increasing release of methane into the atmosphere the greatest threat to the global ecosystem. Methane release from thawing permafrost in the Arctic, Joe Romm has said, "is the most dangerous amplifying feedback in the entire carbon cycle."[55]

Permafrost (perennially frozen soils) was formed in the Arctic during the most recent glacial period. It contains an enormous amount of carbon from dead plants and animals that were prevented from thawing by the Arctic's extremely cold climate. The carbon exists in methane clathrates (or hydrates), which are crystalline solids, looking like ice, in which water molecules form cage-structures around methane molecules.

"Over hundreds of millennia," explained a 2013 NASA article, "Arctic permafrost soils have accumulated vast stores of organic carbon, . . . about half of all the estimated organic carbon stored in Earth's soils." If that is correct, the Arctic's frozen carbon is more than the carbon that has been emitted by fossil fuels since 1850.[56] Four factors combine to make global warming in relation to permafrost very threatening:

- The Arctic is warming up twice as fast as the rest of the planet except for Antarctica.

- When permafrost thaws, it releases its carbon.

- Most of the carbon is located in thaw-vulnerable topsoils within 3 meters (10 feet) of the surface.

- If the permafrost is on dry land, where the organic material is well-aerated, oxygen-breathing bacteria break down the material into CO_2, but if the permafrost is in the bottom of a lake or wetland, the organic material enters the atmosphere as methane.[57]

One reason many scientists take seriously the possibility that methane will cause human extinction is the evidence that the melting of frozen methane was central to the Permian mass extinction, or "Great Dying," of 250 million years ago, in which about 95 percent of all the planet's species went extinct.[58]

In 2010, scientists discovered that permafrost on the Siberian shelf had already started thawing. In response, the National Science Foundation said: "Release of even a fraction of the methane stored in the shelf could trigger abrupt climate warming." The National Snow and Ice Data Center predicted that, if business as usual continues, the thawing of permafrost will dump 100 billion tons of carbon into the atmosphere by 2100.[59]

Highly regarded glaciologist Jason Box has expressed the fear more graphically, saying: "Even if a small fraction of the Arctic carbon were released to the atmosphere, we're fucked."[60]

The concern about methane extinction was further increased in 2013 when a study of coastal permafrost in the Antarctic suggested that it was melting as fast as Arctic permafrost.[61]

The main reason that the thawing of permafrost could produce extinction is that it is likely to become self-amplifying: The warmer atmosphere thaws some permafrost, which then releases methane into the atmosphere, warming it further. This warmer atmosphere then causes more permafrost to melt, and so on. The thawing of a significant amount of permafrost could, therefore, create runaway global warming, leading to ecological collapse.[62]

Some scientists believe that this process could cause enormous changes very quickly:

- Professor Paul Beckwith of the University of Ottawa said: "It is my view that our climate system is in early stages of abrupt climate change that, unchecked, will lead to a temperature rise of 5 to 6 degrees Celsius within a decade or two."[63]

- Natalia Shakhova of the University Alaska at Fairbanks, who made the discoveries on the Siberian shelf, said that methane emissions tend to be non-gradual; in fact, the transition from frozen to unfrozen methane "is like the difference between a closed valve and an open valve."[64] Shaky conditions throughout the East Siberia Arctic Shelf (ESAS), she said, may bring on extremely dangerous conditions within "only a matter of decades."[65]

- British scientist John Nissen, who heads the Arctic Methane Emergency Group, has suggested that if the summer sea ice loss passes "the point of no return," and "catastrophic Arctic methane feedbacks" kick in, we'll be in an "instant planetary emergency."[66]

Many other scientists, to be sure, do not believe that methane is soon going to run out of control, having catastrophic consequences for the planet's life. Sometimes they even ridicule those who are worried. In relation to this difference of opinion, *Guardian* journalist Nafeez Ahmed, who had carried out an extensive literature search, made an important observation: On the one hand, "none of the scientists rejecting the plausibility of the scenario are experts in the Arctic, specifically the East Siberia Arctic Shelf." On the other hand, there is an emerging consensus among experts on the ESAS that there is "a real danger of unprecedented quantities of methane venting due to thawing permafrost."[67]

Ahmed's observation is supported by environmental journalist Robert Hunziker, who said that "it's the scientists in the field, like Natalia Shakhova, . . . who travels and works the East Siberian Sea who is most alarmed."[68]

In any case, the methane threat has led some climate scientists to believe that it will bring the extinction, or at least near-extinction, of human beings and other animals. For example, Ira Leifer of the University of California at Santa Barbara, who specializes in Arctic methane, commented on the fact that some scientists recommend that "we should make plans to adapt to a 4°C world." Having an even bleaker view than Kevin Anderson, Leifer responded:

> While prudent, one wonders what portion of the living population now could adapt to such a world, and my view is that it's just a few thousand people [seeking refuge] in the Arctic or Antarctica.[69]

Some scientists have suggested that the "catastrophic Arctic methane feedbacks," resulting from what is sometimes called the "methane bomb," will bring about extinction in a matter of decades.

The one who has written the most about this is Guy McPherson, professor emeritus of evolutionary biology at the University of Arizona. In various articles, at a blog called "Nature Bats Last," and in a 2013 book entitled *Going Dark,* McPherson has presented an array of scenarios through which humanity could become extinct, but the one to which he devotes the most time is methane emissions from thawing permafrost.[70] Referring to the evidence that methane was central to the Permian mass extinction, he said: "The importance of methane cannot be overstated."[71]

McPherson has made many provocative statements, especially his claim, based partly on the idea that there will be a large release of methane—sometimes called a "methane burp"—that the "planet will not be habitable for the human species long beyond 2030."[72] Many fellow scientists and other commentators dismiss him as unscientific, but he certainly knows the literature,[73] and some well-informed people, such as Dahr Jamail, take him seriously.[74]

In any case, there are other climate scientists with similar views. The prediction of human extinction through methane emissions has also been central to the thinking of retired Earth-systems scientist Malcolm Light. In 2012, Light wrote that the process of significant methane release, which began in 2010, "will accelerate exponentially, release huge quantities of methane into the atmosphere and lead to the demise of all life on earth before the middle of this century." In 2013, Light said that "the accelerating methane eruptions [will] take us into uncontrollable runaway global warming," with the result that in 2080 the oceans will begin boiling off and by 2096 "the Earth's atmosphere will have reached temperatures equivalent to those on Venus."[75] In 2014, he said:

> There are such massive reserves of methane in the subsea Arctic methane hydrates, that if only a few percent of them are released, they will lead to a jump in the average temperature of the Earth's atmosphere of 10 degrees C and produce a 'Permian' style major extinction event which will kill us all.[76]

One may well be dubious about the idea that methane will bring about human extinction in the near future. And we must hope that human extinction, or even a "hell of a life," is not already fated, so that there is still time to take action. But it is virtually certain that, if business as usual continues, global warming will bring about human extinction in the not-too-distant future, especially as methane becomes increasingly significant in causing global warming. One would think, then, that we would immediately stop all fracking for methane-producing natural gas and, more generally, reduce the use of fossil fuels to virtually zero. But thus far the United States has been too preoccupied with military projects to devote time and money to the boring task of saving civilization.

CONCLUSION

Although the Bush-Cheney administration pushed America and the world toward ruination in several ways, the most destructive of its policies are those that threaten terminal climate change.

In the 1990s, given the end of the Cold War, there was much interest in using more of the US budget for domestic issues, including slowing down global warming and hence climate change. But Cheney apparently did everything he could to prevent more money from being used for non-military matters, and Bush went along with his wishes. Whereas the threat of climate change led many people to conclude that we needed to switch our primary attention to the human-nature relation, the Bush-Cheney administration, especially in its response to the 9/11 attacks, forced the world's attention back to the human-human relation—and not in a good way.

Many climate scientists believe that, if the world at the beginning of the century had begun a crash program to cut way down on civilization's use of fossil fuels, we would have had a chance to prevent global warming and ocean acidification from putting civilization at risk. Such a crash program would have required American leadership. But far from exerting leadership on this issue, the Bush-Cheney administration was the primary impediment to progress. It is not unlikely that the Bush administration "doomed the planet."[77]

The Obama administration was considerably better, but its efforts were too little, too late. It is too late to prevent terrible developments, and it may even be too late to save civilization and even to prevent complete human extinction. While speaking about a different issue, Martin Luther King said:

> We are confronted with the fierce urgency of now. In this unfolding conundrum of life and history there is such a thing as being too late. . . . Over the bleached bones and jumbled residue of numerous civilizations are written the pathetic words: 'Too late.'"[78]

A final question: Which is more likely, a nuclear or an ecological holocaust? The previous chapter shows that a nuclear holocaust cannot be dismissed as impossible or even improbable. But an ecological holocaust is more likely: For a nuclear holocaust to occur, someone would have to do something extraordinary—launch nuclear weapons. But for there to be an ecological holocaust, nobody has to do anything extraordinary. An ecological holocaust will be brought about by simply the continuation of business as usual. As Nafeez Ahmed put it, "we are busily, quietly creating the End of Days by simply going about our daily fossil-fuel-dependent lives."[79]

In any case, the risk for each kind of holocaust is real. Assuming the risks to be equal, one would assume that the United States would be devoting about the same amount of money to avoiding each of them. But that is not the case.

With regard to climate change: Nicholas Stern, the world's leading climate economist, has estimated that to keep the global temperature's increase below 2°C, "a trillion dollars a year around climate orientated investments" will be needed.[80] This would be the figure for all of the rich countries, so the cost to America would be only a fraction of that. Moreover, the cost in the long run would not cost anything, as the trillion dollars spent annually will prevent the rich nations from needing to spend many trillions more in the coming years.[81]

However, the United States has shown no sign of willingness to devote anything close to what would be its fair share. At the 2009 climate conference in Copenhagen, the wealthy countries pledged $10 billion for the first three years, with funding increasing to $100 billion annually by 2020. But in 2013, Obama's chief climate diplomat, Todd Stern, said that the annual $100 billion is unlikely to appear anytime soon. "The fiscal reality of the United States and other developed countries is not going to allow it," said Stern, due to our obligations for "aging populations and other pressing needs for infrastructure, education, health care and the like."[82]

By contrast, when the administration decided upon military spending, the "fiscal reality" did not seem so bleak. The US military budget for 2017 is over $770 billion, which means that America spends more for "defense" than the next seven countries *combined*.[83] On top of that, the Obama administration planned for the United States to spend $1 trillion over the next 30 years to "modernize" the country's nuclear weapons. The upgrade will include "redesigned nuclear warheads, as well as new nuclear bombers, submarines, land-based missiles, weapons labs and production plants."[84]

The trillion-dollar question is, of course, how will this modernization increase our security? The United States has roughly 7,000 nuclear weapons, enough to destroy the human race many times over. Our leaders have always said that the only purpose of our nuclear arsenal is to prevent a nuclear attack. The present nuclear weapons will do that as well as any upgraded arsenal could. The only possible use for the so-called modernization would be to make the smaller and more precise nuclear weapons, discussed in Chapter 9, which the United States might use to attack Russia (or China) without unacceptable collateral damage to itself. And, as discussed in that chapter, this modernization would make nuclear war more likely, not less.

So, whereas the United States is unwilling to spend the tens of billions of dollars needed to prevent ecological holocaust, it willingly spends far more money in relation to nuclear holocaust—not to prevent it, but to increase its likelihood. The Cheyneyite madness has continued.

In *The Assassination Complex*, discussed in Chapter 7, the authors called Obama's drone warfare his "deadly legacy." It is certainly one of them. However, said Zhiwa Woodbury:

> [W]hat he is almost assured to be remembered for most is his unconscionable, and frankly, inexplicable lack of leadership on the most pressing issue of this or any other time in our relatively brief history: the climate crisis. . . . While the window of opportunity for alleviating the anticipated suffering of future generations and stemming the toll of species extinction was closing, Obama was cementing the most lethal legacy of any US president ever, because the Sixth Great Extinction would likely include humans.

Whereas most people have imagined a World War III as a nuclear war involving the United States and Russia and/or China, Bill McKibben has argued that we should think of WW III as our battle with climate change, which we are now losing. The burning of carbon and methane, wrote McKibben, has

> fueled a global threat as lethal as the mushroom-shaped nuclear explosions we long feared. Carbon and methane now represent the deadliest

enemy of all time, the first force fully capable of harrying, scattering, and impoverishing our entire civilization.

Although we commonly use "war" as a metaphor—the war on poverty, on drugs, on cancer—the war on climate change is no metaphor, argued McKibben.

> By most of the ways we measure wars, climate change is the real deal: Carbon and methane are seizing physical territory, sowing havoc and panic, racking up casualties, and even destabilizing governments. . . . It's not that global warming is *like* a world war. It *is* a world war. Its first victims, ironically, are those who have done the least to cause the crisis. But it's a world war aimed at us all. And if we lose, we will be as decimated and helpless as the losers in every conflict—except that this time, there will be no winners, and no end to the planetwide occupation that follows.

The only hope for saving civilization, McKibben maintained, would be if we "mobilize for World War III on the same scale as we did for the last world war." (I have coauthored a little book on this issue.[85]) Just as FDR was able to do much of what was required quickly, through executive action, concluded McKibben, we will lose WW III "without immediate executive action."[86]

Had Bernie Sanders become the president, McKibben believes, he might have led the kind of mobilization needed. Having almost half of the members of the Democratic Platform Committee, Sanders' appointees succeeded in getting the Democratic Party to endorse a call for a World War II–type national mobilization to save civilization. Hillary Clinton's negotiators even agreed to the promise that in her first hundred days, she would convene a climate summit "to chart a course to solve the climate crisis." Whether she would have actually carried through, we will never know.

The election of Donald Trump, a climate-change denier, to the presidency bodes very ill for the prospect of preventing an ecological holocaust, especially given his "America-first energy plan," designed to eliminate virtually every impediment to the exploitation of oil, gas, and coal anywhere in the country or in its surrounding waters"—a plan sure to bring, as Michael Klare put it, "the planetary nightmare to come."[87]

The fact that Washington and the media have not faced the overwhelming importance of dealing with climate change has been demonstrated by the way in which they responded to Trump's nomination of longtime ExxonMobil CEO Rex Tillerson. ExxonMobil has arguably been more responsible for the rise in global warming than any other single company since 1977—when its scientists told it that the continued burning of fossil fuels would endanger the planet's climate. Rather than informing the public about this, ExxonMobil hid the evidence and, instead, became the primary funder of climate-denial organizations.

Washington and the major media, however, were primarily worried that Tillerson had good relations with Moscow and would hence help Trump fulfill his stated goal of developing a good working relationship with Vladimir Putin—the exact opposite of what Hillary Clinton would likely have done. There were many reasons to oppose both Trump and Tillerson, but the possibility that they might ease tensions with Russia—and thus reduce the chance for nuclear holocaust—should not be one of them. It appears that Washington and the media are much more interested, like Cheney, in continuing to expand the American empire than in doing everything possible to prevent the destruction of civilization.

In any case, the disastrous behavior of the National Democratic Party during the nomination, insisting that Hillary Clinton win, even though it was clear that Bernie Sanders would have been far more likely to win the national election, meant that the nation ended up with a president who promised to be one of the worst possible choices to take charge of this most important of all tasks, rather than a man who might well have been the best. This willful error could easily turn out to be the decision that will make it impossible to rescue the climate from runaway global warming, resulting in the collapse of civilization and perhaps human extinction.

If so, this failure will be revealed to be the most fateful feature of the loss of America's greatness produced by the neocon drive for universal empire. While China is going full-speed ahead in financing clean energy,[88] the United States, already a laggard, appears to be getting ready to reverse what meager progress it has made. Bush and Cheney will have indeed, with assistance from the Obama and now the Trump administrations, ruined America and the world.

PART II

9/11: A MIRACULOUS DAY

11 • WHY BUSH AND CHENEY SHOULD NOT BE TRUSTED ON 9/11

"America's fate was sealed when the public and the anti-war movement bought the government's 9/11 conspiracy theory. The government's account of 9/11 is contradicted by much evidence. Nevertheless, this defining event of our time, which has launched the US on interminable wars of aggression and a domestic police state, is a taboo topic for investigation in the media. It is pointless to complain of war and a police state when one accepts the premise upon which they are based."—*Paul Craig Roberts*, How America Was Lost[1]

INTRODUCTION

It is now generally accepted, as discussed in Chapter 4, that the Bush administration, under the leadership of George W. Bush and Vice President Dick Cheney, told big lies in order to lead the nation into the 2003 attack on Iraq.[2] Joe Wilson, having experienced these men's lies about Iraq's having received yellowcake from Niger, asked if they would lie to start a war, "what else are they lying about?"[3]

The most important answer to that question is the claim that the 9/11 attacks were engineered by Muslims. The present chapter does not offer evidence for that conclusion but simply gives reasons why Bush and Cheney's statements should not be trusted.

One example is that the Bush-Cheney administration claimed that it had certain evidence that Osama bin Laden was behind the 9/11 attacks, but it never provided any such evidence. Indeed, as mentioned in Chapter 2, the FBI never included 9/11 in the list of bin Laden's terrorist attacks, and when asked why not, the FBI's chief of investigative publicity replied. "[B]ecause the FBI has no hard evidence connecting Bin Laden to 9/11."[4]

Both the US and UK governments promised to provide proof, but neither did. As to why, Seymour Hersh said it was because they *had* no proof. The Bush-Cheney administration then said there was no need to provide proof, because they found a video in which bin Laden confessed.[5] But there were many questions about whether it was a fake. Both the BBC and the CBC aired shows dealing with this question.[6]

To try to answer it, a first question would be whether the Bush-Cheney administration would have had a fake video made. We can answer this by recalling the false evidence it gave to get support for the attack on Iraq, such as the backdated fake letter from Tahir Jalil Habbush to Mohamed Atta.

A second question would be whether making the video would have been technically possible. When the *Guardian* asked Sean Broughton, one of Britain's leading experts on visual effects, he replied that it would be relatively easy for a skilled professional to fake a video of Bin Laden. Moreover, the BBC learned from Dr. Peter French, a forensic expert who specializes in audio, speech, and language, that "today, using digital equipment, it's possible to edit or fabricate in ways that completely defy forensic detection."[7]

A third question is whether there is any evidence that the CIA or Pentagon have ever engaged in such deception. Yes.[8] The "confession video" is, in fact, regarded as a fake by many people, including (as mentioned in Chapter 2) America's leading bin Laden expert, Bruce Lawrence, who answered the question in two words: "It's bogus."[9] There are many good reasons for Lawrence's opinion:

- This was the first statement in which bin Laden allegedly confessed; he had repeatedly—on September 12, 16, 17, and 28—stated that he had had nothing to do with the attacks.[10]

- In the last clearly authentic video of bin Laden, which was produced sometime after November 16, his beard was white, he had a "gaunt, frail appearance," and his "left arm hung limply by his side," said CNN medical correspondent Dr. Sanjay Gupta, adding that the limp left arm (likely from a stroke) and the "frosting of the appearance" suggested that bin Laden was in the final stages of kidney failure.[11]

- Besides looking to Gupta that bin Laden was near death, there is strong evidence that he actually died about December 13, 2001. His death and funeral were reported in Pakistan's *Observer* on December 25, in an Egyptian newspaper and *Fox* News on December 26, and in the *New York Times* six months later.[12]

- By contrast, the bin Laden of the confession video had darker skin and hair and looked heavier and healthier; his nose had a different shape; his hands were shorter and heavier; he lifted his left arm over his head; and he wrote with his right hand (whereas bin Laden was left-handed).[13]

- The man playing bin Laden in the confession video also said several things the real bin Laden would not have said.[14]

However, there are three good questions about how the claim that bin Laden died in 2001 could be true. One of those questions is: *If bin Laden died in 2001, how did he keep appearing in videos in the following years?* The answer is that he did not. As careful examination of these videos shows, they are all fakes, some of them very obviously so.[15]

The second question is whether the US government would have been so deceitful as to have fake videos made. The answer is provided by a recent report from the Bureau of Investigative Journalism. Entitled "Pentagon Paid for Fake 'Al Qaeda' Videos," the report said that the payment, to a U.K. PR firm, was about $540 million.[16]

The third question is: *If bin Laden died in 2001, how could President Obama's SEALs have killed him in 2011?* The answer is: They did not. Paul Craig Roberts and several others have shown that the whole story had to have been a hoax.[17]

In any case, there is very good evidence that the Bush-Cheney administration lied about having good evidence that bin Laden was responsible for the 9/11 attacks, as well as later lying about more matters to get authorization to attack Iraq.

However, while granting that the Bush-Cheney administration told big and disastrous lies, which led to millions of deaths, most mainstream commentators have considered the idea that this administration engineered the 9/11 attack to be so absurd that they can render judgment without checking the evidence.

The Bush administration, said David Corn of *The Nation*, would not have been evil enough to do this. "This is as foul as it gets—to kill thousands of Americans, including Pentagon employees."[18] Dave Gilson in *Mother Jones* said that nothing had convinced him that "George W. Bush and his neocon cronies were either evil or, more important, smart enough to have orchestrated the terrorist attacks on the United States."[19] Tucker Carlson, when he had a MSNBC program, told a guest that "it is wrong, blasphemous, and sinful for you to suggest, imply, or help other people come to the conclusion that the US government killed 3,000 of its own citizens."[20] The editor of the Southern Cross Review wrote:

> There is widespread distrust of the current US administration under President George W. Bush—and rightly so. . . . But to extrapolate this mistrust to the point of accusing him and/or other individuals or organizations in the US government of conspiring to destroy the World Trade Center and the thousands of people in it at the time is . . . absurd, irrational and ignorant.

Another author in the same journal said:

> Whatever one's criticisms of the administration and its approach to the war on terrorism, one would have to be awfully cynical to believe that it would kill or allow thousands (at the least) of Americans to die, simply to accumulate additional powers.[21]

DOES THE MORALITY OF BUSH AND CHENEY
LIFT THEM ABOVE SUSPICION?

Is it really implausible to think that Cheney—who was essentially in charge of the Bush-Cheney administration at the time—would have been evil enough to have arranged the 9/11 attacks? In an essay in a series on "the worst people in America," Sean Murphy said:

> On my rather long list of most despicable people to pollute the planet during my lifetime, Dick Cheney goes straight to the top, no one particularly close to second place. In terms of rapacity combined with cowardice (nothing quite like a chicken hawk who actively avoided battle, blithely sending young soldiers to die and okaying the obliteration of hundreds of thousands of innocent civilians; nothing like being in bed with Big Oil and profiting from policies that devastate the environment; nothing like being head of the company that wins the sole right to "rebuild" the infrastructure you did the most to help destroy, etc.) it's difficult to imagine an American who has done greater harm while getting his pale bloated paws over as much filthy lucre as he could count.[22]

If this criticism is not wholly unjust, would it be unreasonable to suspect that such a man, besides lying to start the war in Iraq, would have also lied to orchestrate the event that was used as the pretext for the wars in Afghanistan and Iraq?

Wars are always deadly affairs. These two wars have killed over 6,500 Americans and left over 600,000 disabled. These wars have also led to the deaths of millions of Iraqis and Afghans—seven million by one estimate.[23] Is it unreasonable to suggest that Cheney and Bush would not have blanched at engineering a false-flag attack that would take a few thousand American lives?

Grounds for suspicion are also provided by the relation of Bush and Cheney to the 9/11 Commission.

THE CREATION OF THE 9/11 COMMISSION

The first investigation of the 9/11 attacks was carried out by the select intelligence committees of the US Senate and the US House of Representatives, which were to study the pre-9/11 intelligence. Many believed that Congress should have a full-scale investigation into the attacks, but Senate Majority Leader Tom Daschle accepted the request by Bush and Cheney that the investigation would be limited to pre-9/11 intelligence failures (which presupposed, of course, that the attacks happened because of intelligence failures). Bush and Cheney made their request on the grounds that a broader inquiry would take resources and personnel "away from the war on terrorism."[24]

However, in spite of the extreme limitations of this Joint Inquiry, it provided enough damaging revelations to leave Bush with little choice but to authorize a full-scale investigation of the 9/11 attacks. Bush had little choice because of the campaigning of family members of victims of the attacks, especially the Family Steering Committee, led by some widows dubbed the "Jersey Girls."[25]

Bush finally set up the 9/11 Commission—formally, the National Commission on Terrorist Attacks upon the United States—on November 27, 2002, 441 days after the 9/11 attacks (whereas the bodies to investigate the Pearl Harbor attack and the assassination of President Kennedy had each been set up within 7 days). Bush agreed to authorize this commission, moreover, only on the condition that he would appoint the chairman.[26]

Bush's Choices for 9/11 Commission Leaders

Bush's first choice was Henry Kissinger, who many doubted would guide the work in an independent and impartial way.[27] "Indeed," said the *New York Times*, "it is tempting to wonder if the choice of Mr. Kissinger is not a clever maneuver by the White House to contain an investigation it long opposed."[28] In any case, Kissinger's tenure was short-lived: Although Bush said that Kissinger would not need to reveal his business clients, the Congressional Research Service disagreed, so Kissinger resigned.[29]

Bush then replaced Kissinger with New Jersey governor Thomas Kean, who had no Washington political experience and who, being the president of Drew University, would have limited time to devote to the Commission. Kean had been recommended by Bush's political advisor, Karl Rove, who had led the White House effort to prevent the creation of a 9/11 commission. After that effort failed, Rove became according to John Lehman (one of the Republican members of the Commission)—the White House's "quarterback for dealing with the Commission."[30] In that role, Rove recommended that Kissinger be the chair and then, after Kissinger resigned, recommended Kean.[31]

The position of vice chairman of the Commission went to former Democratic congressman Lee Hamilton—a Washington insider who had often been helpful to Republicans. As chairman of the House Permanent Select Committee on Intelligence, for example, he chose in 1987 not to investigate President Reagan's role in the Iran-Contra Affair, saying that going through another impeachment trial would not be good for the country. In 1992, as chair of the task force to investigate the 1980 "October Surprise"—which helped Reagan defeat Jimmy Carter for the presidency—Hamilton covered up the evidence for the Republican plot.[32] During the Iran-Contra investigation, Hamilton worked closely with Dick Cheney, who was then the ranking Republican on the House Intelligence Committee. During that investigation, the two men started a friendship that continued after Cheney became vice president.[33]

The Choice of Philip Zelikow as Executive Director

Even more problematic than the choices of Kean and Hamilton to be the chairs of the 9/11 Commission was their choice of Philip Zelikow to be the 9/11 Commission's executive director. In their preface to *The 9/11 Commission Report*, Kean and Hamilton said that they had "sought to be independent, impartial, . . . and nonpartisan."[34] If those were truly their central concerns, however, Zelikow was an absurd choice.

Zelikow was essentially a member of the Bush-Cheney administration. He had worked with Condoleezza Rice on the National Security Council (NSC) in the administration of the first President Bush. When the Republicans were out of office during the Clinton years, Zelikow and Rice co-authored a book. Then when Rice was named National Security Advisor for the second President Bush, she had Zelikow help her make the transition to the new NSC.[35]

In 2002, moreover, Rice had the task of producing a new statement of *The National Security Strategy of the United States of America (NSS 2002)*. After finding the draft by the State Department's Richard Haass insufficiently bold, Rice "ordered the document be completely rewritten," wrote James Mann in *The History of the Vulcans*, and "turned the writing over to her old colleague . . . Philip Zelikow."[36] The result was a bellicose statement, justifying the preemptive action Bush had advocated in his address at West Point in June 2002.

Zelikow's *NSS 2002* declared that, in light of the 9/11 attacks, American behavior would no longer be constrained by the basic principle of international law as embodied in the charter of the United Nations. According to that principle, one country could not launch a preemptive attack upon another country unless it had certain knowledge that an attack on itself by that country was imminent—too imminent to be taken to the UN Security Council. In rejecting this principle, Zelikow had formulated what became known as the Bush Doctrine. "Never before," wrote Stefan Halper and Jonathan Clarke in their *America Alone*, "had any president set out a formal national strategy *doctrine* that included preemption."[37]

In writing NSS 2002, moreover, Zelikow was putting into policy ideas that he had expressed in a 1998 document he had co-authored with John Deutch (who had recently been the CIA director) and Ashton Carter (who in 2015 would become the secretary of defense). Speaking about Pearl

Harbor and a 1993 World Trade Center attack, this document, written three years *before* 9/11, said:

> If the device that exploded in 1993 under the World Trade Center had been nuclear. . . , the resulting horror and chaos would have exceeded our ability to describe it. Such an act of catastrophic terrorism would be a watershed event in American history. It could involve loss of life and property unprecedented in peacetime and undermine America's fundamental sense of security, as did the Soviet atomic bomb test in 1949. Like Pearl Harbor, this event would divide our past and future into a before and after. The United States might respond with draconian measures, scaling back civil liberties, allowing wider surveillance of citizens, detention of suspects, and use of deadly force.[38]

This document uncannily predicted what would turn out to be the actual effects of 9/11: After beginning by speaking of the World Trade Center, this document predicted that this catastrophic terrorist act would undermine America's sense of security; that it would be like a new Pearl Harbor; that it would divide our history into "before and after" (just as the Bush administration would contrast pre-9/11 and post-9/11 mindsets); that the government would respond with "draconian measures," namely, "scaling back civil liberties, allowing wider surveillance of citizens, detention of suspects, and use of deadly force." A conspiracy theorist might conclude that Carter, Deutch, and Zelikow seemed to know that a 9/11-type attack was coming.

In any case, after writing *NSS 2002*, Zelikow was appointed by Bush to the President's Foreign Intelligence Advisory Board. In light of this appointment and the previous list of facts about Zelikow, it is no exaggeration to say that he was essentially a member of the Bush-Cheney administration. One wonders if, after choosing Zelikow to be the 9/11 Commission's executive director, Kean and Hamilton had been able to write with a straight face that they had sought to make the Commission independent, impartial, and nonpartisan.

Knowing about Zelikow's conflicts of interest, the Family Steering Committee demanded that, unless he resigned, he be fired. But Kean and Hamilton refused, explaining later in their 2006 book, *Without Precedent*, that they "had full confidence in Zelikow's independence."[39]

It appears that the idea of replacing Zelikow with someone else was out of the question. In *Without Precedent*, Kean and Hamilton reported that Zelikow had been the only candidate they seriously considered.[40] Although they "review[ed] the résumés of about twenty candidates, including those proposed by the White House"—wrote *New York Times* reporter Philip

Shenon in his book *The Commission*—they decided that "there wasn't anybody even close to Zelikow."[41] Given all of his conflicts of interest, it is difficult to believe that they considered him likely to run an independent, impartial, and nonpartisan investigation of the 9/11 attacks. It seems much more probable that Bush, perhaps prodded by Rice, Rove, and Cheney, insisted that Kean and Hamilton choose Zelikow.

The idea that Kean and Hamilton were committed to Zelikow, no matter what, is reinforced by the fact that, even after they found out that Zelikow had concealed his most serious conflicts of interest, they did not fire him. These concealed facts included Zelikow's role in helping Rice make the transition from the Clinton to the Bush National Security Council and, most important, his authorship of *NSS 2002*. Shenon commented:

> When commission staffers learned that Zelikow was the principal author, many were astounded. It was arguably his most serious conflict of interest in running the investigation. It was in his interest, they could see, to use the commission to try to bolster the administration's argument for war— a war that he had helped make possible.[42]

Kean and Hamilton did not even replace Zelikow after they learned that he had predetermined the nature of the 9/11 Commission's final report before the staff had even begun work. In their 2006 book about the 9/11 Commission's work, Kean and Hamilton claimed that, unlike conspiracy theorists, they started with the relevant facts, not with a conclusion: they "were not setting out to advocate one theory or interpretation of 9/11 versus another."[43] However, they knew that, when Zelikow gave the various teams the topics they were to research, he told one team to "tell the story of al Qaeda's most successful operation—the 9/11 attacks."[44] What could have been a stronger "theory or interpretation" than the idea that the attacks were organized by al-Qaeda?

Even worse, Kean and Hamilton learned that Zelikow and his former professor Ernest May had prepared an outline of the final report at "the outset of [the Commission's] work."[45] Shenon wrote: "By March 2003, with the commission's staff barely in place, the two men had already prepared a detailed outline, complete with 'chapter headings, subheadings, and sub-subheadings.'"[46]

However, rather than firing Zelikow for behaving in this totally partisan and dishonest way, Kean and Hamilton conspired with Zelikow to conceal from the Commission's 80-some staff members this fact—that their "investigative work" would largely be limited to filling in the details of conclusions that Zelikow had reached in advance.

When the staff did learn about this outline a year later, some of them circulated a two-page parody entitled "The Warren Commission Report— Preemptive Outline." One of its chapter headings read: "Single Bullet: We Haven't Seen the Evidence Yet. But Really. We're Sure."[47] The meaning, of course, was that a chapter of Zelikow's outline could be headed: "Osama bin Laden and al-Qaeda: We Haven't Seen the Evidence yet. But Really. We're Sure."

The fact that Zelikow was a completely inappropriate choice to be the executive director—unless he was chosen to protect the Bush-Cheney administration—was further illustrated by his behavior. For one thing, he insisted on virtually total control of the Commission's work:

- None of the Commissioners, including Kean and Hamilton, were given offices in the K Street office building used by the Commission's staff. As a result, said Shenon, "most of the commissioners rarely visited K Street. Zelikow was in charge."[48]

- Even though the Commission would not have existed had it not been for the efforts of the families of the 9/11 victims, "the families were not allowed into the commission's offices because they did not have security clearances."[49]

- "Zelikow had insisted that there be a single, nonpartisan staff." This meant that each commissioner would not, as they had assumed, "have a staff member of their own, typical on these sorts of independent commissions." This structure, Shenon pointed out, "would prevent any of the commissioners from striking out on their own in the investigation." Zelikow himself even admitted that this was his intention, saying: "If commissioners have their own personal staff, this empowers commissioners to pursue their own agenda."[50]

- "Zelikow's micromanagement meant," said Shenon, "that all information was funneled through Zelikow, and he decided how it would be shared elsewhere."[51] Accordingly, "he controlled *how and if the evidence was shared elsewhere*."[52]

- "[M]ore than anyone else," Shenon concluded, Zelikow "controlled what the final report would say."[53] He could exert this control because, although the first draft of each chapter was written by one of the investigative teams, "Zelikow rewrote virtually everything that was handed to him—usually top to bottom."[54]

Accordingly, *The 9/11 Commission Report* was written by a man who, besides being virtually a member of the Bush-Cheney administration, had three years before 9/11 imagined the effects of a Pearl Harbor-like attack on the World Trade Center; who wrote *NSS 2002*, with its doctrine of pre-emptive warfare; and who outlined the Commission's report in advance.

In addition, Zelikow proved himself to be duplicitous about his relation to the White House. "Zelikow had promised the commissioners he would cut off all unnecessary contact with senior Bush administration officials to avoid any appearance of conflict of interest."[55] But he had continuing contacts with both Karl Rove and Condoleezza Rice. This information was confirmed by the executive secretary for the Commission's front office, Karen Heitkotter, who had long served as an executive secretary in the State Department. With regard to Rice, Shenon wrote:

> While Zelikow was telling people how upset he was to cut off contact with his good friend Rice, Heitkotter knew that he hadn't. More than once, she had been asked to arrange a gate pass so Zelikow could enter the White House to visit the national security adviser in her offices in the West Wing.[56]

With regard to Rove, Shenon reported, Heitkotter's logs reveal that he called the office "looking for Philip" four times in 2003.[57] When this continuing contact became widely known after a staff member saw Rove's name in Heitkotter's logs, Zelikow ordered her to quit keeping logs of his contacts with the White House.[58] Although Zelikow claimed that he did not discuss the Commission's work with Rove, this claim was contradicted by a senior White House official with whom Shenon talked.[59]

Additional Obstacles

Besides being saddled with leadership not well-suited to do any real investigation of the attacks, the Commission had many more obstacles placed in front of it by the Bush-Cheney administration. First the administration authorized only $3 million for it and then turned down the Commission's request for an additional $11 million.[60] (This request was finally accepted, but $14 million, or the $15 million that it turned out to be, to investigate the worst terror attack in America was a tiny amount, compared with the almost $80 million that had been spent on investigations of the Clintons.[61])

In addition, after insisting that the investigation be completed by May 2004, the Bush administration was very slow in issuing security clearances and the needed documents, so the Commission was unable to start its work until the middle of 2003, leaving it less than a year to carry out its work.[62] One of the Commissioners, Republican Slade Gorton, told Shenon said that "the lack of cooperation" would make it "very difficult" for the commission to complete its work by the deadline. "It's obvious that the White House wants to run out the clock here," added Commissioner Max

Cleland: "[W]e're still in negotiations with some assistant White House counsel about getting these documents—it's disgusting."[63]

The Jersey Girls also became disgusted with these obstacles, along with the appointment of Zelikow. In 2004, one of them, Kristin Breitweiser, said: "We've had it. It is such a slap in the face of the families of victims."[64] "What we're left with after our journey are no answers," said another one of them, Monica Gabrielle. "I've wasted four years of my life."[65] By 2007, another Jersey Girl, Patty Casazza, said: "It's hard for us to come to any other conclusion than that the 9/11 Commission was a political cover-up from the word go."[66]

No Reason to be Trusted

Because the press has generally not reported the many problems with the 9/11 Commission, most Americans have assumed that its Report was basically correct. For example, near the end of 2015, a columnist for the *Boston Globe* expressed surprise that a group of architects, who belong to an organization called Architects and Engineers for 9/11 Truth, assert that "the events of September 11, 2001, haven't been fully explained." This columnist said: "I don't agree."[67] He evidently meant that this explanation had been provided by Zelikow's report.

But there is no reason for people who want the truth to trust the report by the 9/11 Commission, which Bush and Cheney engineered with their choice of Kean and Hamilton and thereby Zelikow. If "9/11 was an inside job," as the 9/11 Truth Movement holds, there was no chance that this fact would be exposed by the 9/11 Commission.

SUSPICIOUS BEHAVIOR BY BUSH AND CHENEY ON 9/11

In addition to the reasons to suspect that Bush and Cheney wanted a 9/11 commission that would conceal, rather than reveal, the truth, both Bush and Cheney behaved suspiciously on the day of 9/11 itself.

President Bush

On September 11, 2001, President Bush arrived at a classroom in Florida at 8:55 AM, where he was to read a book with grade school students (as a photo opportunity to publicize his new educational policy). Being told that a plane had hit the World Trade Center (WTC), he dismissed it as an accident and went ahead with the reading session. Shortly thereafter, Andrew Card, Bush's chief of staff, reportedly told him: "A second plane hit the second Tower. America is under attack."[68]

When any such event occurs, the Secret Service is supposed to hustle the president to a secure location.[69] But in this case, it allowed Bush to remain in the classroom, said the *Tampa Tribune*, for "for eight or nine minutes." Indeed, reporting that the president "lingered until the press was gone," Bill Sammon, a pro-Bush journalist for the *Washington Times*, called him "the dawdler in chief."[70]

Evidently realizing that the president's lingering in that situation did not look good, the White House started telling a different story. Andrew Card told the press that after he told the president that the country was under attack, Bush "excused himself very politely to the teacher and to the students and he left"; Karl Rove gave essentially the same account.[71]

Unfortunately for this new story, there appeared in 2004 a videotape of this event showing that—reported the *Wall Street Journal*—Bush "followed along for five minutes as children read aloud a story about a pet goat." Shortly thereafter, this videotape became widely known, thanks to Michael Moore's film *Fahrenheit 9/11.*[72]

When the White House was asked by the *Wall Street Journal* about this contradiction, it simply changed the story. Confirming that the president remained in the classroom for at least seven minutes, White House spokesperson Dan Bartlett explained that Bush had not left immediately because his "instinct was not to frighten the children by rushing out of the room."[73]

The *Journal* evidently did not ask the White House to explain why it had attempted to sell a false account. This attempt, however, highlighted the even more basic question. The *St. Petersburg Times* wrote: "One of the many unanswered questions about that day is why the Secret Service did not immediately hustle Bush to a secure location, as it apparently did with Vice President Dick Cheney."[74]

This question is important, because the Secret Service's behavior, combined with the "dawdling" of the president, suggests that he and/or his Secret Service knew that there was no danger, because they knew that the 9/11 attacks were not carried out by foreign terrorists.

Vice President Cheney

Given the fact that the president was down in Florida, Cheney was in charge at the White House. He took charge of the response to the 9/11 attacks, it is agreed, after he descended to the Presidential Emergency Operations Center (PEOC), which is also called the "shelter conference room" or simply the "bunker." There is disagreement, however, as to the time he entered the PEOC. According to *The 9/11 Commission Report*, Cheney arrived "shortly before 10:00, perhaps at 9:58."[75]

However, Secretary of Transportation Norman Mineta told the 9/11 Commission in 2003 that when he reached the PEOC at about 9:20, Cheney was already in charge there. Mineta said this while reporting an ongoing conversation between Cheney and a young man, which took place when "the airplane was coming into the Pentagon."[76] That plane was the one that was said to have struck the Pentagon at about 9:38. Accordingly, Cheney would have been in the PEOC at least 18 minutes prior to the attack on the Pentagon. But the 9/11 Commission's timeline, according to which Cheney did not reach the PEOC until almost 10:00, implies that he was not in charge during that event.

Unfortunately for the account given in *The 9/11 Commission Report*, many people had given reports that fit with Mineta's account. In his 2004 book *Against All Enemies,* counter-terrorism advisor Richard Clarke reported that Cheney, along with National Security Advisor Condoleezza Rice, had descended to the PEOC prior to Mineta's arrival at the White House (which occurred before 9:20).[77] In an ABC program, Cheney's White House photographer David Bohrer described a scene in which Secret Service agents took Cheney down to the PEOC shortly after 9:00. According to this ABC program, the Secret Service also said to Rice: "You have to leave now for the bunker. The Vice President's already there."[78]

Most surprisingly, one of the people reporting Vice President Cheney's early descent to the PEOC was Cheney himself. Speaking to Tim Russert on NBC's *Meet the Press* five days after 9/11, Cheney said that, after talking to the president, "I went down into . . . the Presidential Emergency Operations Center. . . . [W]hen I arrived there within a short order, we had word the Pentagon's been hit."[79] So Cheney, according to his own statement, was in the PEOC considerably earlier than the 9/11 Commission claimed.

The reports that Cheney was in the PEOC fairly early that morning, perhaps before 9:20, became a problem after Mineta's testimony to the 9/11 Commission in May 2003. Having stated that Cheney was already in charge at the PEOC at about 9:20, Mineta added:

> During the time that the airplane was coming in to the Pentagon, there was a young man who would come in and say to the Vice President, "The plane is 50 miles out." "The plane is 30 miles out." And when it got down to "the plane is 10 miles out," the young man also said to the Vice President, "Do the orders still stand?" And the Vice President turned and whipped his neck around and said, "Of course the orders still stand. Have you heard anything to the contrary?"[80]

This report was problematic, of course, because Cheney's "orders" could have been understood to refer to orders to stand down—that is, *not* to intercept the plane heading toward the Pentagon.

The 9/11 Commission Report, under Zelikow's leadership, solved this problem by simply ignoring Cheney's *Meet the Press* interview and the reports, from Clarke to Bohrer, according to which Cheney had entered the PEOC long before the Pentagon attack. Instead, the *Report* relied entirely on a *Newsweek* article by Evan Thomas, which was dated December 31, 2001. According to Thomas in this story, it was not until 9:35 that the Secret Service came into Cheney's office to take him down to the underground corridor that leads to the PEOC. According to this account, Cheney remained in the corridor for some time, during which he had a long conversation with the president and then learned about the Pentagon attack just after Lynne Cheney arrived. Thomas then said: "Shortly before 10 AM, the Cheneys were led into the PEOC conference room. . . . [T]hey looked up at the TV screens. It was 9:58 AM."[81]

This story by Thomas was evidently the source for *The 9/11 Commission Report*. As to where Thomas got this information, *Newsweek* had interviewed Condoleezza Rice on November 1 (2001); Lynne Cheney on November 9; and then Vice President Cheney on November 19.[82] To write this story, Thomas had to ignore not only the contrary reports by Bohrer, the ABC report about the Secret Service statement to Rice, Clarke's book, and Cheney's own statement on *Meet the Press*, and even Thomas's *Newsweek* story of September 24, according to which when the Secret Service at 9:30 told staffers to leave the West Wing quickly, "Vice President Dick Cheney had already been hustled into a bunker designed to withstand the shock of a nuclear blast."[83]

It appears that, although it had been well known that Cheney had gone down to the PEOC fairly early, Rice and Cheney decided that it would be better for the public to believe that he had not gotten there until almost 10:00, so that he could not be blamed for failing to prevent the attack on the Pentagon. Once Thomas had published his revisionary account to this effect, the 9/11 Commission, under the leadership of Rice's colleague Zelikow, was able to change the time of Cheney's arrival at the PEOC, as indicated in earlier reports, by simply citing Thomas's *Newsweek* story of December, while admitting that there was "conflicting evidence." While not pointing out that this conflicting evidence included reports by ABC, Bohrer, Clarke, along with earlier statements by Thomas and Cheney themselves, the 9/11 Commission claimed that it drew its conclusion "from the available evidence."[84] It did not mention that this "available evidence" was provided only by Thomas's new account, based on interviews with Rice, Lynne Cheney, and the vice president.

This distorted picture evidently included Lynne Cheney as well as her husband. During an interview in 2006, Mineta repeated his assertion, saying that, after getting down to the PEOC fairly quickly after the second WTC strike (which occurred at 9:03 AM), "the Vice President was already there."[85] Then in an informal interview in 2007, Mineta was asked if, when he got to the PEOC at 9:30, Cheney was already there. Mineta said "absolutely," adding that "Mrs. Cheney" was also there. When Mineta was told that the Commission had said that Cheney did not arrive until 9:58, Mineta expressed surprise and said: "Oh no, no, no; I don't know how that came about." Mineta added that he might have been mistaken about the exact time that he himself got to the PEOC, but that Cheney was clearly there before the Pentagon was struck.[86]

For a long time, the mainstream press has refused to deal with the evidence from Mineta's account that Cheney and the 9/11 Commission were lying. Reporters and editors might have justified this refusal by saying that they do not support claims by "conspiracy theorists," and they might have justified ignoring Mineta's testimony on the grounds that he was a Democrat, who might have given his account for partisan reasons. But more recently, declassified documents show that Mineta's account was accurate.

- One document is a memorandum from the Technical Services Division (TSD) of the Secret Service headed "Actions of TSD Related to Terrorist Incident." According to this memorandum, Dick Cheney was in the bunker before 9:30 AM. When Danny Spriggs, the Secret Service assistant division chief, entered the PEOC at 9:30, said the memorandum, Cheney and Condoleezza Rice, along with ten other "Presidential and Vice Presidential staff," were already there.[87]

- Mineta's account is also confirmed by statements made in 9/11 Commission interviews of members of the Secret Service. According to the 9/11 Commission reports marked "Commission Sensitive," Carl Truscott, the Special Agent In Charge, escorted Condoleezza Rice down to the PEOC shortly before 9:30 AM. "Upon arrival at the shelter the VP and Mrs were present; VP on the phone."

- The 9/11 Commission was also given information about Special Agent In Charge, Anthony Zotto. Being in charge of Cheney's safety, Zotto accompanied him everywhere. According to the declassified report, Cheney was in the PEOC at least eight minutes prior to the attack on the Pentagon.[88]

- In 2015, a great number of photos of Cheney and other officials in the White House were released in response to a Freedom of Information request. One episode of the PBS program *Frontline* had a program showing some of these photos. Its comment about one of the photos from Cheney's office says: "Vice President Cheney watches as the first reports of terrorist attacks appear on television. Within minutes he would be frog-marched by Secret Service agents to the basement elevator of the White House."[89]

Now that this additional evidence is available, which shows that Cheney, as well as *The 9/11 Commission Report,* lied about Cheney's location when the Pentagon was struck, we should be able to assume that the mainstream press would report it. But at this writing, the press has had this information for over two years and has continued to cover up the truth.

THE ANTHRAX ATTACKS

In addition to the fact that Bush and Cheney lied about their activities on 9/11, there is another major reason to suspect that their story about the 9/11 activities may be false: An examination of the anthrax attacks, which caused 5 people to die and sickened 17 others, suggests that Bush and Cheney were not merely spectators.

There are two ways in which the letters containing anthrax suggest that they originated with the Bush-Cheney administration: The timing of the letters, and the attribution of responsibility for the letters.

The Timing of the Letters

Letters containing anthrax came during the period in which the Bush-Cheney administration was demanding support for an anti-terrorism bill—which came to be called the USA PATRIOT Act. On September 17, one week after 9/11, Attorney General John Ashcroft announced that he was sending the proposed legislation to Congress, which he wanted enacted four days later, by September 21. Given the enormous size of the bill, Graeme MacQueen commented, "He wanted Congress to act with blazing speed and to make an Olympian leap of faith."[90]

The same day, September 17, the *Washington Post* published an article entitled "Bioterrorism: An Even More Devastating Threat," which warned about huge problems posed by "a disease like anthrax."[91] It is interesting that this possibility of anthrax in particular was mentioned two weeks before the first reported case of anthrax.[92] (This was somewhat similar to the way in which in 2002, the *New York Times* would print a story about "a-bomb parts" in Iraq just before the Bush-Cheney administration was to began its media blitz about the need to remove Saddam Hussein, as discussed in Chapter 4.)

On September 17 or 18, right after Ashcroft's announcement, anthrax letters were put in the mail. One of those letters was addressed to Tom Brokaw of NBC (other letters were addressed to ABC, CBS, the *New York Post,* and the *National Enquirer).* With printed block letters and a word misspelled, the letter was evidently meant to suggest that it was written by a foreign Muslim. The letter read:

09-11-01
THIS IS NEXT
TAKE PENACILIN [sic] NOW
DEATH TO AMERICA
DEATH TO ISRAEL
ALLAH IS GREAT

However, this letter had no immediate impact, because it was not opened until later (October 12).

In the final week of September, anthrax had not yet caused panic, and Congress was not ready to act quickly, so Ashcroft kept pushing, insisting that terrorism was a clear and present danger. On September 25, Bush and Cheney themselves got involved. Saying "we're at war," Bush said that "we must make sure the law enforcement men and women have got the tools necessary." Cheney urged Republican senators to get the legislation through Congress by his new deadline, October 5.[93]

Then on September 30, other members of the administration spoke out, with Secretary of Defense Donald Rumsfeld, along with Ashcroft and Bush's chief of staff, Andrew Card, warning that more terrorist attacks were likely.[94]

Pressure to act quickly also started coming from the press. On September 26, *New York Times* columnist Maureen Dowd, saying that people should be prepared for "Muslim martyrs dispersing biological toxins," reported that upper middle-class women in New York were carrying Cipro in their "little black Prada techno-nylon bags," because of widespread fears of an anthrax attack. The following day, the *Times* published an article entitled "Anthrax Scare Prompts Run on an Antibiotic."[95]

Again, it is remarkable that so much discussion about anthrax, by both the media and the Bush-Cheney administration, occurred before there had been any cases of anthrax, and even letters containing anthrax spores, had appeared.

It is not surprising, therefore, that in spite of the pressure by the administration and the media, the Senate was not ready to act fast enough to meet Cheney's October 5 deadline. The delay was due primarily to Vermont Senator Patrick Leahy, the chairman of the Senate Judiciary Committee, who was trying to work out a compromise position that he and his committee could live with. After thinking that Ashcroft had accepted his suggested compromise, Leahy found that it had been *rejected* by Ashcroft, so he would not accept the bill.

Senate Majority Leader Tom Daschle, supporting Leahy, said on September 26 that he "doubted the Senate could take up the legislation before next week."[96] On October 9, Democratic Senator Russell Feingold blocked the attempt to rush the bill for the PATRIOT Act through the Senate with little debate and no opportunity for amendments.[97]

At about the same time—perhaps the very day that Feingold blocked the bill (October 9)—letters containing lethal doses of anthrax were posted to Senators Daschle and Leahy.[98] When the letter to Daschle was opened by his office on October 15 (the Leahy letter had been misdirected), it was found to contain aerosolized anthrax spores, which can become airborne and enter into people's lungs, resulting in inhalation anthrax (the most deadly form of anthrax). This letter exposed 28 people in the Hart Senate Office Building to anthrax, resulting in the closing of this building for almost three months.[99] The letter said:

> 09-11-01
> YOU CAN NOT STOP US.
> WE HAVE THIS ANTHRAX.
> YOU DIE NOW.
> ARE YOU AFRAID?
> DEATH TO AMERICA.
> DEATH TO ISRAEL.
> ALLAH IS GREAT.[100]

MacQueen commented: "Allah's advocates, it seemed, had taken a sudden dislike to Democratic senators who violated the Vice-President's deadlines."[101]

In any case, the letter to Daschle turned out to be unnecessary for him and Leahy to be convinced to accept the bill. They were persuaded, evidently, by an FBI report on October 11, which said that "additional terrorist acts could be directed at US interests at home and abroad over the 'next several days'"—interests such as the Capitol. The FBI also mentioned that the media had informed the public that crop-duster planes were an effective way to deliver large quantities of anthrax.[102]

However, there still needed to be a harmonization of the House and Senate versions of the bill, so the Daschle letter may have helped the senators to give the administration everything it wanted in the final bill, which the Senate passed on October 25 (with all members except Feingold voting for it).

As this account shows, the way in which the PATRIOT Act was passed could easily persuade people that the anthrax letters were sent by someone in Cheney's office. In addition, there is one more fact suggesting that Bush and Cheney were not simply spectators to the anthrax attacks: They and members of their staff had started taking Cipro, which was the recommended antibiotic against anthrax, on 9/11 itself.[103]

In May 2002, incidentally, Judicial Watch sued to receive relevant documents, saying: "One doesn't simply start taking a powerful antibiotic for no good reason. The American people are entitled to know what the White House staffers knew nine months ago."[104]

The Attribution of Responsibility

As we saw in Chapter 4, the Bush-Cheney administration argued that Iraq, not only al-Qaeda, was responsible for the 9/11 attacks. The administration had already made this case with regard to the anthrax attacks, arguing for what MacQueen calls the Double Perpetrator Hypothesis. This hypothesis was based partly on the fact of the two kinds of anthrax—one that was quite simple, which could have been produced by a low-tech organization, and another that was very sophisticated aerosolized anthrax, which was in the letter to Senator Daschle.

"The idea was that," summarized MacQueen, "although Bin Laden's group delivered the spores, behind this group stood a state, Iraq." A CIA source was quoted by the *Guardian* as saying of aerosolized anthrax, "they aren't making this stuff in caves in Afghanistan." As the *Wall Street Journal* put it, "Bin Laden couldn't be doing all this in Afghan caves. The leading supplier suspect has to be Iraq."[105]

In this vein, US officials appealed to the tale about Mohamed Atta meeting an Iraqi agent in Prague, meant to link Iraq with both 9/11 and the anthrax attacks. The above-quoted *Guardian* article began:

> American investigators probing anthrax outbreaks in Florida and New York believe they have all the hallmarks of a terrorist attack—and have named Iraq as prime suspect as the source of the deadly spores. Their inquiries are adding to what US hawks say is a growing mass of evidence that Saddam Hussein was involved, possibly indirectly, with the 11 September hijackers.

This article went on to say: "Last autumn Mohamed Atta is said by US intelligence officials to have met in Prague an agent from Iraqi intelligence."

Shortly thereafter, a *New York Times* front-page story, entitled "Czechs Confirm Iraqi Agent Met With Terror Ringleader," gave this story and its relevance for the anthrax attacks much more prominence. "The public linkage of Iraq's intelligence service and the Al Qaeda terrorists," said the *Times* writers, "raises the question of whether those ties suggest Iraqi complicity . . . in the attacks last month."[106] (This story, as documented in Chapter 4, was shown in 2002 to be baseless.)

Although there was an enormous amount of discussion of the idea that Iraq provided the most deadly type of anthrax, it was realized by year's-end that the source of the attack was in the United States. In mid-December, White House press secretary Ari Fleisher said that it was "increasingly looking like it was a domestic source."[107]

Given that development, the FBI had the task of finding a plausible suspect—other than someone in the Bush-Cheney administration. For some years, it tried but failed to implicate Steven Hatfill. The FBI then turned to Dr. Bruce Ivins, who worked at the US Army Medical Research Institute of Infectious Diseases at Fort Detrick, Maryland. After Ivins died in 2010, whether by suicide or assassination, the Department of Justice declared him guilty. But the case, always weak, was completely undermined when the former FBI agent in charge of the case reported that the bureau, wanting to "railroad" the prosecution, kept secret "a staggering amount of exculpatory evidence."[108]

The realization that neither Hatfill nor Ivins was responsible for the anthrax letters should open the way to considering the most likely source, as suggested by the evidence: The Bush-Cheney administration. Evidence for this conclusion would suggest, moreover, that it was responsible for the 9/11 attacks.

CONCLUSION: REEXAMINING THE EVIDENCE

As this chapter shows, there are many reasons to suspect that claims made by Bush and Cheney about 9/11 should not be trusted. Although these suspicions do not constitute proof, they should provide sufficient bases for examining closely the purported evidence that the official account of 9/11, which originated from Bush and Cheney and their agencies, is false.

One of the strongest types of evidence for this conclusion consists of declassified official accounts refuting central features of the Bush-Cheney account of 9/11, such as the above-mentioned testimony of Secret Service agents.

But the strongest type of evidence is provided by the fact that the official account of 9/11 depends on miracle stories.[109] The term miracle is used here in the sense employed by Eighteenth-century philosopher David Hume, which is the sense in which it is used in scientific and philosophical circles. In his *Enquiry Concerning Human Understanding,* Hume wrote:

A miracle is a violation of the laws of nature; and as a firm and unalterable experience has established these laws, the proof against a miracle, from the very nature of the fact, is as entire as any argument from experience can possibly be imagined.

Accordingly, Hume held, miracles—defined as violations of the laws of nature—cannot possibly occur (unless, of course, one affirms supernatural interventions into the laws of nature).

12 • THE MIRACULOUS DESTRUCTION OF THE TWIN TOWERS

Matthew Rothschild has been one of our leading progressive thinkers; he was, in fact, the editor of *The Progressive* for two decades. Like many other progressive thinkers, he has assumed that those who reject the official account of 9/11 are unscientific, even irrational. In a 2006 essay entitled "Enough of the 9/11 Conspiracy Theories Already," Rothschild wrote:

> Here's what the conspiracists believe: 9/11 was an inside job. . . . [T]he Twin Towers fell not because of the impact of the airplanes and the ensuing fires but because [of] explosives. . . . I'm amazed at how many people give credence to these theories. . . . At bottom, the 9/11 conspiracy theories are profoundly irrational and unscientific. It is more than passing strange that progressives, who so revere science on such issues as tobacco, stem cells, evolution, and global warming, are so willing to abandon science and give in to fantasy on the subject of 9/11.[1]

However, a look at the evidence shows that many people who accept science on tobacco, evolution, and global warming accept miracles, implicitly, on the subject of 9/11, especially in relation to the World Trade Center (WTC). The present chapter examines this issue in relation to the example Rothschild gave, the Twin Towers.

THE FEMA REPORT ON THE TWIN TOWERS

The first official report on the destruction of the WTC was released in 2002 by the Federal Emergency Management Agency (FEMA), which put its name on a study produced by some members of the American Society of Civil Engineers. However, these engineers were not allowed to do a real investigation: FEMA refused to give them "basic data like detailed blueprints of the buildings," and it "refused to let the team appeal to the public for photographs and videos of the towers."[2] FEMA barred them from Ground Zero (except for a brief "tourist trip").[3] For example, the engineers told the House Committee on Science that they did not have the authority "to impound pieces of steel for examination before they were recycled."[4]

FEMA's report, entitled *World Trade Center Building Performance Study*, was severely criticized by the editor of *Fire Engineering* magazine, who said that "the 'official investigation' blessed by FEMA and run by the American Society of Civil Engineers is a half-baked farce that may already have been commandeered by political forces whose primary interests, to put it mildly, lie far afield of full disclosure."[5]

THE 9/11 COMMISSION REPORT ON THE TWIN TOWERS

In spite of the fact that the destruction of the Twin Towers is for most people the central feature of the 9/11 attacks, the 9/11 Commission had remarkably little to say about this destruction. Moreover, much of what little it said was false.

To be fair, the Commission had a very difficult task. On the one hand, the Twin Towers were steel-framed buildings, and steel-framed high-rise buildings had never collapsed because of airplane strikes and/or fire.[6] Prior to 9/11, all such buildings that had collapsed were brought down by explosives.

On the other hand, official reports about the Twin Towers had to explain the collapses of these buildings without referring to explosives, because the Bush-Cheney administration had said that the Twin Towers were brought down entirely by airplanes flown by al-Qaeda terrorists and the resulting fires. The first such report was issued in 2002 by the Federal Emergency Management Agency (FEMA).[7] The 9/11 Commission had to do the same. This task led the Commission to imply the occurrence of miracles—violations of the laws of nature.

Why the Towers Collapsed: Hollow Core

One of the most basic questions about the Twin Towers is why they collapsed. The Commission suggested an answer by saying:

> [T]he outside of each tower was covered by a frame of 14-inch-wide steel columns. . . . These exterior walls bore most of the weight of the building. The interior core of the buildings was a hollow steel shaft, in which elevators and stairwells were grouped.[8]

But this was a ridiculous claim (perhaps due to a misunderstanding of the meaning of the "tube in tube construction"[9]). Rather than being a "hollow steel shaft," the core of the building consisted of 47 massive steel columns, in between which were elevators and stairwells. At its base, each column was 14 by 36 inches, having 4-inch-thick walls. It then tapered up to 1/4-inch walls in the upper floors, which had far less weight to support. It was these massive steel columns that "bore most of the weight of the buildings."

This fact undermines the hypothesis of a "pancake" collapse, which the Commission accepted.[10] According to this hypothesis, the airplanes, by striking the buildings near the top, caused the upper floors to come down, which then brought down all the floors beneath them. This hypothesis might seem credible if the core of each tower were indeed a hollow steel shaft. But because the core of each building consisted of 47 steel columns, a pancake collapse would have left these columns sticking up hundreds of feet in the air. Given the pancake theory, the fact that each tower suffered *total* collapse, leaving debris only a few stories high, would have been a miracle.

Why the Towers Collapsed: Super-Heated Jet Fuel

According to 9/11 Commission co-chair Lee Hamilton, "the super-heated jet fuel melted the steel super-structure of these buildings and caused their collapse."[11] However, fires based on jet fuel, which is essentially kerosene, can at most rise to about 1700° Fahrenheit, whereas steel does not even begin to melt until it reaches about 2770° F.[12] For steel to be melted by jet fuel would be a miracle, as it could not occur apart from divine intervention.

Could the Airplane Impacts Explain the Collapses?

People advocating the official account usually say that it was not just the fires, but the fires combined with the impacts of the airplanes. For example, Rothschild's above-quoted litany of false views held by "9/11 conspiracy theorists" includes this one: "[T]he Twin Towers fell not because of the impact of the airplanes and the ensuing fires but because [of] explosives." In calling that view false, Rothschild was saying that the towers *did not* come down because of explosives. He implied, therefore, that they came down because of the plane impacts and the ensuing fires. But the more than 2,500 Architects and Engineers for 9/11 Truth, some of whom are leading members of their fields, hold that this would be impossible.[13]

Given the fact that a steel-framed high-rise building has never come down without the use of explosives, those who claim this happened on 9/11 should provide some evidence that such an event would even be possible. There could be no historical evidence, of course, because such a collapse would be unprecedented. Is there any evidence on the other side— that an airplane impact and its resulting fire would do nothing toward bringing down a steel-framed high rise? Although the Empire State Building was very different from the Twin Towers, it provides the closest analogy we have.

The 79th floor of the Empire State Building, which had 102 floors, was struck in 1945 by a B-25 bomber. This strike created a hole 18 feet wide and 20 feet high, after which "[t]he plane's high-octane fuel exploded, hurtling flames down the side of the building and inside through hallways and stairwells all the way down to the 75th floor." The plane crash killed 14 people (including the three crewmen) and injured 26 others, but "the integrity of the Empire State Building was not affected." Not even a single floor collapsed.[14]

It is true, of course, that the planes hitting the towers were much bigger than a B-25. But it is also true that the each of the towers was much bigger. So what little historical evidence we have, therefore, suggests that airplane strikes resulting in exploding jet fuel could not have brought down the Twin Towers.

In sum, we have no evidence that the Twin Towers could have been brought down by airplane impacts and fires, apart from miraculous assistance.

Why Did the South Tower Collapse First?

Another problem is the order in which the towers collapsed. If they had been brought down by the heat of their fires, the North Tower (WTC 1) should have collapsed first: It was struck seventeen minutes earlier than the South Tower (WTC 2), and it had larger and hotter fires, and yet the South Tower collapsed 29 minutes earlier than the North Tower (as the Commission acknowledged[15]).

In other words, although the South Tower had smaller fires, it collapsed after only 56 minutes of burning, whereas the North Tower stayed up for 102 minutes after being struck. If the buildings had been brought down by the airplane impacts and the resulting fires, the much earlier collapse of the South Tower would be very puzzling—even if not, strictly speaking, a miracle.

Total Collapse in Ten Seconds

Still another serious problem for the 9/11 Commission's view involves the time it took for the Twin Towers to come down. On the one hand, the Commission said that, to its knowledge, "none of the [fire] chiefs present believed that a total collapse of either tower was possible."[16] On the other hand, the Commission said that the "South Tower collapsed in 10 seconds."[17] To go from an evidently impossible collapse to one that occurred in 10 seconds: This would definitely be a miracle—unless, of course, explosives had been used to remove the 287 steel columns.

Conclusion

Most people who accept the physical sciences agree that, if people have a theory that contradicts the laws of physics, they should give up that theory. Accordingly, although Rothschild claimed that those who reject the official theory about the Towers are ipso facto "profoundly irrational and unscientific," those adjectives actually describe those who accept the theory offered by the 9/11 Commission, because this theory requires a miraculous destruction of the Twin Towers.

NIST ON THE TWIN TOWERS

To some extent, it is not surprising that the 9/11 Commission's treatment of the destruction of the Twin Towers was so terrible, because not a single one of the people chosen to be commissioners was a scientist. The task of developing an adequate explanation of the destruction of the Twin Towers was given to the National Institute of Standards and Technology (NIST). NIST's explanations were to be provided by a team of scientists under lead investigator Shyam Sunder.

However, these scientists were no more independent than the engineers who provided the FEMA report and the members of the 9/11 Commission. NIST did claim to be independent, saying: "Since NIST is not a regulatory agency and does not issue building standards or codes, the institute is viewed as a neutral, 'third party' investigator."[18] However, far from being a neutral, independent organization, NIST is an agency of the US Department of Commerce. While NIST was writing its report, therefore, it was an agency of the Bush-Cheney administration. The name of Carlos Gutierrez, Bush's secretary of commerce, was on the first page of NIST's *Final Report*, and all of NIST's directors were Bush appointees.[19]

It would not be surprising to find the NIST report to contain fraudulent science, given the fact that by 2007, a statement charging the Bush administration of engaging in "distortion of scientific knowledge for partisan political ends" had been signed by over 12,000 scientists (including 52 Nobel Laureates and 63 recipients of the National Medal of Science).[20]

In fact, a former NIST employee, who had worked on the WTC project, reported in 2007 that NIST had been "fully hijacked from the scientific into the political realm." As a result, scientists working for NIST "lost [their] scientific independence, and became little more than 'hired guns.'" With regard to 9/11 related issues, this whistleblower said:

> By 2001, everyone in NIST leadership had been trained to pay close heed to political pressures. There was no chance that NIST people "investigating" the 9/11 situation could have been acting in the true spirit of scientific independence. . . . Everything that came from the hired guns was by then routinely filtered through the front office, and assessed for political implications before release.[21]

Therefore, NIST's report on the WTC must be viewed as a political, not a scientific, document.[22] Nevertheless, we should evaluate NIST as if it were a scientific document, asking how its scientific claims hold up.

Of course, we can suspect in advance that its claims will not hold up, because the NIST team had the same impossible task as did the authors of the FEMA report and *The 9/11 Commission Report*: To explain the collapses of the towers while denying that explosives helped. Accordingly, Sunder's team argued that the towers came down because of three and only three causes: (i) the airplane impacts, which caused structural damage; (ii) the ensuing fires, which were initially fed and spread by jet fuel from the planes; and (iii) gravity. Here, now, are several miracles endorsed by the NIST report.

The Miracle of Free Fall

The difficulty of providing a plausible hypothesis can be seen by considering a statement by Dr. David A. Johnson, an internationally known architect and city and regional planner:

> [A]s a professional city planner in New York, I knew those buildings and their design. . . . So I was well aware of the strength of the core with its steel columns. . . . When I saw the rapid collapse of the towers, I knew that they could not come down the way they did without explosives and the severing of core columns at the base. . . [T]he official explanation doesn't hold water.[23]

In other words, Johnson said, the official story required a miracle.

The miracle to which he referred is implicit in NIST's acknowledgment that both Towers came down "essentially in free fall."[24] Each tower, as stated above, had 287 steel support columns—240 perimeter columns and 47 massive core columns. A steel-frame building can come down rapidly, as Johnson pointed out, only if the core columns have been severed, and this severing could only be done with explosives. But NIST insisted that there were no explosives.

In trying to explain how an essentially free-fall descent could have been possible, NIST said that each airliner took out several perimeter and core columns at its area of impact and also created huge fires, which began weakening the steel. After a period of time, "the massive top section of [each] building at and above the fire and impact floors" fell down on the lower section, which "could not resist the tremendous energy released by [the top section's] downward movement."[25] Accordingly, NIST's report said:

> Since the stories below the level of collapse initiation provided little resistance to the tremendous energy released by the falling building mass, the building section above came down essentially in free fall, as seen in videos.[26]

But this would be miraculous, in the sense of violating the laws of physics. As researcher Jim Hoffman said, NIST's hypothesis "requires us to believe that the massive steel frames of the [lower structure of the] towers provided no more resistance to falling rubble than [would] air."[27]

A more technical explanation was provided by structural engineer William Rice, who said that NIST's account "violates Newton's Law of Conservation of Momentum." This law, he explained, requires that, "as the stationary inertia of each floor is overcome by being hit," the speed of descent must decrease.[28]

A 2016 report by Architects and Engineers for 9/11 Truth, entitled "World Trade Physics," is oriented around this law, as shown by its subtitle: "Why Constant Acceleration Disproves Progressive Collapse."[29] As a paper by Graeme MacQueen and Tony Szamboti explained, the fall of the top section would have needed to produce "one powerful jolt" to the lower structure in order to initiate its collapse, and this jolt would have caused a great deceleration in the collapse. But by tracking the fall of the roof, one can see that there was no slowing down: The building came down with constant acceleration. Hence NIST's theory is false. The constant acceleration can only be explained by the use of explosives to cut all the steel columns supporting the building: The "towers provided no more resistance to falling rubble than [would] air" because the rubble *was* falling through the air.[30]

Just how remote NIST's theory is from reality has been described by mechanical engineer Gordon Ross. His analysis of the collapse of the North Tower showed that, far from failing to retard the downward movement of the building's upper portion, the lower portion would have quickly and completely *stopped* the top portion's descent. To be precise, the "vertical movement of the falling section would [have been] arrested," Ross said, "within 0.02 seconds after impact. A collapse driven only by gravity would not continue to progress beyond that point."[31]

Even if a miracle had gotten the first floor beneath the impact point to start down, more miracles would have been needed to keep the remaining floors coming down in virtual free fall.

The South Tower's Mid-Air Miracles

Whereas the free-fall miracle involved both towers, there was a miracle unique to the South Tower (WTC 2). This tower was struck at the 80th floor, so its upper portion consisted of a 30-floor block. As videos of the beginning of this building's collapse show, this block began tipping toward the corner that had been most damaged by the airplane's impact. According to the law of the conservation of angular momentum, this section should have fallen to the ground far outside the building's footprint. "However," Jim Hoffman and fellow 9/11 researcher Don Paul observed, as the top then began to fall, the rotation decelerated. Then it reversed direction [even though the] law of conservation of angular momentum states that a solid object in rotation will continue to rotate at the same speed unless acted on by a torque.[32]

And then, as if this were not miraculous enough, physicist Steven Jones added:

> We observe that approximately 30 upper floors begin to rotate as a block, to the south and east. They begin to topple over, not fall straight down. The torque due to gravity on this block is enormous, as is its angular momentum. But then—and this I'm still puzzling over—this block turned mostly to powder *in mid-air*! How can we understand this strange behavior, without explosives?[33]

If someone were to ask how even explosives could explain this behavior, we could turn to a statement by Mark Loizeaux, the president of Controlled Demolition, Inc. In response to an interviewer's question as to how he made "doomed structures dance or walk," Loizeaux said:

> [B]y differentially controlling the velocity of failure in different parts of the structure, you can make it walk, you can make it spin, you can make it dance. We've taken it and moved it, then dropped it or moved it, twisted it and moved it down further—and then stopped it and moved it again. We've dropped structures 15 storeys, stopped them and then laid them sideways. We'll have structures start facing north and end up going to the north-west.[34]

If we suppose that explosives were used, therefore, we can understand the mid-air dance performed by the upper portion of the South Tower.

However, NIST explicitly rejected "alternative hypotheses suggesting that the WTC towers were brought down by controlled demolition using explosives."[35] Accordingly, NIST is stuck with another major miracle: Although the upper block was rotating and tipping in such a way that its angular momentum should have caused it to fall down to the side, it somehow righted itself by disintegrating.

This disintegration, incidentally, further undermines the official theory, according to which the "tremendous energy" of this block's downward momentum caused the lower part of the South Tower to collapse. This theory requires that the upper part smashed down, as a solid block, on the lower part. Videos show, however, that it did not. As Jones and his colleagues pointed out:

> [T]he upper portion of WTC 2 did not fall as a block upon the lower undamaged portion, but instead disintegrated as it fell. Thus, there would be

no single large impact from a falling block . . . [but only] a series of small impacts as the fragments of the disintegrating upper portion arrived.[36]

Given this disintegration of the 30-floor upper block, the rapid collapse of the rest of the building, without explosives, was even more miraculous.

Horizontal Ejections from the Twin Towers

Dwain Deets, former director of the research engineering division at NASA's Dryden Flight Research Center, wrote that the "massive structural members being hurled horizontally" from the Twin Towers "leave no doubt" that "explosives were involved."[37]

Deets was referring to the fact that the collapse of each of the Twin Towers began with a massive explosion near the top, during which huge sections of perimeter columns were ejected out horizontally, so powerfully that some of them traveled 500 to 600 feet. Although this feature of the collapses was not mentioned in NIST's (2005) report on the Twin Towers, there could be no doubt about it, because some of these sections of steel implanted themselves in neighboring buildings, as can be seen in videos and photographs.[38]

These ejections are now, in any case, part of the official account, because NIST found them necessary to explain how, as discussed in the next chapter, fires got started in Building 7 of the World Trade Center (WTC 7). NIST's report on WTC 7 said: "The fires in WTC 7 were ignited as a result of the impact of debris from the collapse of WTC 1, which was approximately 110 meters (350 feet) to the south."[39] NIST thereby admitted that debris had been thrown out horizontally from the North Tower at least 350 feet.[40] This report also stated:

When WTC 1 collapsed at 10:28:22 AM. . . , some fragments [of debris] were forcibly ejected and traveled distances up to hundreds of meters. Pieces of WTC 1 hit WTC 7, severing six columns on Floors 7 through 17 on the south face and one column on the west face near the southwest corner. The debris also caused structural damage between Floor 44 and the roof.[41]

Debris that caused such extensive damage, including the severing of seven steel columns, had to be quite heavy. NIST granted, therefore, that sections of steel columns had been hurled at least 650 feet (because "hundreds of meters" would mean at least 200 meters). Enormous force would be needed to eject large sections of steel that far out.

What could have produced this force? According to NIST, as we saw earlier, there were only three causal factors in the collapse of the Twin Towers: the airplane impacts, the fires, and gravitational attraction. And none of these could explain the ejections:

- The airplane impacts had occurred 56 minutes (South Tower) and 102 minutes (North Tower) earlier, so they no longer had kinetic energy.

- Fire could, to be sure, produce horizontal ejections by causing jet fuel to explode, but the jet fuel had burned up within "a few minutes," NIST reported, so jet-fuel explosions could not occur during events happening 102 minutes later.[42]

- Gravitational attraction pulls things straight down.[43]

Therefore, although NIST admitted that these horizontal ejections occurred, it suggested no energy source to explain them.

However, these ejections could be explained by explosives (such as RDX) or incendiaries (such as nanothermite). According to NIST, however, neither explosives nor incendiaries contributed to the destruction of the Twin Towers. Those who accept NIST's account must, therefore, regard these horizontal ejections as constituting further miracles.

Inextinguishable Fires

Besides having the power to produce the miraculous effects already reported, the World Trade Center fires were also miraculously inextinguishable. The fact that fires continued burning in the Ground Zero rubble for many months, in spite of every attempt to put them out, was widely reported. The title of a *New York Times* story in the middle of November, two months after the attacks, referred to the "Most Stubborn Fire." A *New Scientist* article in December was entitled "Ground Zero's Fires Still Burning." Very hot fires continued to burn in the Ground Zero debris piles, these stories reported, even though heavy rains came down, millions of additional gallons of water were sprayed onto the piles, and a chemical suppressant was pumped into them.[44]

According to Greg Fuchek, vice president of a company that supplied computer equipment to identify human remains at the site, the working conditions at Ground Zero remained "hellish" for six months, because the ground temperature ranged from 600 to 1,500 degrees Fahrenheit.[45]

These inextinguishable fires were a mystery. Assuming the truth of the official account of the destruction of the World Trade Center, there would have been nothing in the debris pile other than ordinary building materials, and these materials can burn only in the presence of oxygen. There would have been little oxygen available in the densely packed debris piles and, wherever oxygen was available, the fires should have been easily suppressed by the enormous amounts of water and chemical suppressants pumped into the piles. The fires' seemingly miraculous power to keep burning could not be explained by the airplanes' jet fuel, because it would have all burned out, as mentioned above, within a few minutes.

A non-miraculous explanation is suggested by the discovery of a large amount of nanothermite residue in the WTC dust, which was reported in a peer-reviewed scientific journal in 2009.[46] Being both an incendiary and a high explosive, nanothermite is one among several types of "energetic nanocomposites"—described by an article in *The Environmentalist* as "chemical energetic materials, which provide their own fuel and oxidant and are not deterred by water, dust or chemical suppressants."[47] The discovery of nanothermite residue in the dust provided, therefore, an empirical basis for a non-miraculous explanation of the long-lasting fires at Ground Zero.

According to the official account, however, the buildings were all brought down without the aid of any incendiaries or explosives. The Twin Towers, claimed NIST, were brought down through the combined effects of the airplane impacts, the ensuing fires, and gravity. Accordingly, the inextinguishable underground fires at Ground Zero imply that the World Trade Center fires must have had supernatural powers.

THE QUESTION OF EXPLOSIVES IN THE TWIN TOWERS

With regard to the Twin Towers, the main concern of those in charge of spreading the official story was to convince people that there had been no explosives in the buildings. But this was no mean feat, because there had been dozens of television and newspaper reports of explosions. Here are a few of the television reports on the day of 9/11.

- A Fox News reporter said: "I was making my way to the foot of the World Trade Center. Suddenly while talking to an officer who was questioning me about my press credentials, we heard a very loud blast explosion. We looked up and the building literally began to collapse."[48]

- Fox News interviewed a man who said: "I was down in the basement, all of sudden we heard a loud bang. And the elevator doors blew open, some guy was burnt up, so I dragged him out, his skin was all hanging off."

- Pat Dawson of NBC News reported: "Just moments ago I spoke to the Chief of Safety for the New York City Fire Department, Chief Albert Turi. . . . He tried to get his men out as quickly as he could, but he said that there was another explosion which took place, and then. . . there was another explosion that took place in one of the towers here. He thinks that there were actually devices that were planted in the building."[49]

- At 10:13 AM, a headline on CNN Live said: "Breaking News: Third Explosion Collapses World Trade Center In New York."

- MSNBC reporter Ann Thompson said: "I tried to leave the building. But as soon as I got outside I heard a second explosion. . . . I ran inside the building. . . . And then a fire marshal came in and said we had to leave, because if there was a third explosion this building might not last."[50]

- After both buildings collapsed, CNN's Lou Dobbs said: "[T]his was the result of something that was planned. This is not, it's not accidental that the first tower just happened to collapse and then the second tower just happened to collapse in exactly the same way."[51]

On the next day, September 12, there were many such newspaper reports. For example:

- *The Guardian* said: "[P]olice and fire officials were carrying out the first wave of evacuations when the first of the World Trade Centre towers collapsed. Some eyewitnesses reported hearing another explosion just before the structure crumbled. Police said that it looked almost like a 'planned implosion.'"[52]

- A story in the *Los Angeles Times* said: "At 9:50 AM, . . . the first World Trade Center tower collapsed . . . . There were reports of an explosion right before the tower fell. . . . Not long afterward, . . . the second tower of the World Trade Center collapsed. The top of the building exploded with smoke and dust. There were no flames, just an explosion of debris."[53]

- Being interviewed by ABC's Peter Jennings, an injured woman said: "I got on the . . . freight elevator. And I heard the first explosion. And the elevator blew up. The doors blew up. And it dropped."[54]

By that day, however, there were no more TV reports about explosions, and by the next day, September 13, there were no more such newspaper stories. Thanks to this cooperation by the media, the 9/11 Commission and NIST could ignore the reports of explosions and any talk about planned explosions. *The 9/11 Commission Report* made no mention of testimonies of explosions in the towers, except to say that when the South Tower collapsed, some firefighters in the North Tower, not realizing what had happened, falsely "surmised that a bomb had exploded."[55]

According to NIST, "the aircraft impacts and subsequent fires led to the collapses of the towers after terrorists flew jet fuel laden commercial airliners into the buildings."[56] NIST addressed the question of explosives in only one sentence (although it was repeated three times):

> NIST found no corroborating evidence for alternative hypotheses suggesting that the WTC towers were brought down by controlled demolition using explosives planted prior to September 11, 2001.[57]

In 2006, Lee Hamilton, vice chairman of the 9/11 Commission, had an interview with Evan Solomon of CBC News, during which Solomon asked about the theory "that the buildings were brought down by controlled explosion, controlled demolition." Hamilton replied: "We of course looked at that very carefully—we find no evidence of that."[58]

Besides not mentioning the television and newspaper reports of explosions, neither the 9/11 Commission nor NIST mentioned the fact that about 500 members of the Fire Department of New York provided oral histories of 9/11, almost one fourth of which included descriptions of phenomena suggestive of explosions going off in the Twin Towers, before and during their collapses—explosions that could not be explained as resulting from the airplane impacts and fires.[59] For example:

- Speaking of the South Tower, Firefighter Richard Banaciski said: "[T]here was just an explosion. It seemed like on television [when] they blow up these buildings. It seemed like it was going all the way around like a belt, all these explosions."[60]

- Fire Chief Frank Cruthers said: "[T]here was what appeared to be at first an explosion. It appeared at the very top, simultaneously from all four sides, materials shot out horizontally. And then there seemed to be a momentary delay before you could see the beginning of the collapse."[61]

- Firefighter Kenneth Rogers said: "[T]here was an explosion in the south tower. . . . Floor after floor after floor. One floor under another after another and when it hit about the fifth floor, I figured it was a bomb, because it looked like a synchronized deliberate kind of thing."[62]

- Captain Dennis Tardio said: "I hear an explosion and I look up. It is as if the building is being imploded, from the top floor down, one after another, *boom, boom, boom.* I stand in amazement. I can't believe what I am seeing. This building is coming down."[63]

- Captain Karin Deshore, an emergency medical worker, said that an orange and red flash came out of the middle of the building. "Initially it was just one flash. Then this flash . . . would just go all around the building on both sides as far as I could see. These popping sounds and the explosions were getting bigger, going both up and down and then all around the building.[64]

In ignoring and even denying the testimonial evidence that the towers were brought down by explosives, NIST and the 9/11 Commission provided still more reason not to trust the Bush-Cheney administration with regard to 9/11.

MIRACLES OF THE TWIN TOWERS: A SUMMARY

By accepting the basic truth of the official account of the 9/11 attacks, Matthew Rothschild and a host of others have, probably unbeknownst to themselves, endorsed an account of the Twin Towers that is miraculous through and through. They probably have not realized this because they have been persuaded that critics of the official account are "profoundly irrational and unscientific," so they do not even bother to look at the evidence.

But if people will look at the evidence, they will see that the Bush-Cheney account of the destruction of the Twin Towers requires at least six miracles:

1. The Twin Towers, with their 287 steel columns, were brought down solely by a combination of airplane strikes, jet-fuel fires, and gravity—and hence without explosives or incendiaries.

2. Besides being the first steel-framed buildings to come down without the aid of explosives or incendiaries, the Twin Towers came down in virtual free fall.

3. The upper 30-floor block of the South Tower changed its angular momentum in mid-air.

4. This 30-floor block then disintegrated.

5. Steel columns from the North Tower were ejected out horizontally for at least 500 feet.

6. The fire in the debris from the Twin Towers could not be extinguished for many months.

Moreover, another possible miracle occurred when the South Tower, which was struck later and had smaller fires than the North Tower, came down much earlier. If that should not be technically called a miracle, it is at least exceedingly strange and probably inexplicable.

Finally, there would clearly be a seventh miracle: metals were melted by office fires, which could not possibly get hot enough to melt these metals. This seventh miracle is discussed in the following chapter.

AN INTERVENTION BY A FORMER MEMBER OF NIST

In the summer of 2016, *Europhysics News,* known as "the magazine of the European physics community," published an article entitled "15 Years Later: On the Physics of High-Rise Building Collapses." Written by physicist Steven Jones and three other researchers, the article concluded: "[T]he evidence points overwhelmingly to the conclusion that all three buildings were destroyed by controlled demolition."[65]

Because *Europhysics News* is a magazine, not a peer-reviewed journal, some writers dismissed the paper as unimportant. However, a letter to the editor by Peter Michael Ketcham, a former NIST employee, made it clearly important. Reporting that he had not contributed to NIST's WTC investigation, Ketcham said that in August of 2016, he began looking at some of NIST's reports on the WTC and watching documentaries challenging its findings. In summarizing his response, he said:

> I quickly became furious. First, I was furious with myself. How could I have worked at NIST all those years and not have noticed this before? Second, I was furious with NIST. . . . The more I investigated, the more apparent it became that NIST had reached a predetermined conclusion by ignoring, dismissing, and denying the evidence.[66]

CONCLUSION

Unless the laws of physics and chemistry were supernaturally over-ridden on 9/11, the official account, provided by NIST, is impossible, as Ketcham indicated. Given how disastrous the official account has been for America and the world in general, perhaps some newspapers or TV networks will have the courage to point out that the Bush-Cheney account of 9/11, like the Bush-Cheney argument for attacking Iraq, was a lie.

13 • THE MIRACULOUS DESTRUCTION OF WTC 7

Although the 9/11 Commission and NIST were able to seem to explain—at least partly—the collapse of the Twin Towers (WTC 1 and 2) only by implicitly appealing to miracles, the task of providing an explanation for WTC 7 was even more difficult. In fact, the 9/11 Commission did not even try: The 571 pages of *The 9/11 Commission Report* did not contain a single sentence mentioning that three WTC buildings, not simply two, had come down that day. Lee Hamilton, the 9/11 Commission's vice chairman, was evidently not even aware that Philip Zelikow, as executive director of the 9/11 Commission, had not included a discussion of WTC 7.

During Hamilton's interview by Evan Solomon of CBC News (which was mentioned in the previous chapter), Solomon asked, "why didn't the Commission deal with the collapse of Building 7?" Hamilton replied, "Well, of course, we did deal with it." After other issues were discussed, Solomon came back to this question:

- *Solomon*: I just want to clarify something that you said earlier. You said that the Commission Report did mention World Trade Center Building 7 in it, what happened? It did mention it or it didn't?

- *Hamilton*: The Commission reviewed the question of the Building 7 collapse. I don't know specifically if it's in the Report, I can't recall that it is.

- *Solomon*: I don't think it was in the report.

- *Hamilton*: OK, then I'll accept your word for that.[1]

This interview illustrated, among other things, the fact that *The 9/11 Commission Report* was not written by Kean and Hamilton.

In any case, the fact that the 9/11 Commission did not mention the destruction of WTC 7 fit with the general strategy of the Bush-Cheney administration to keep silent about this event. Again, the media cooperated: Just as American television networks quit discussing explosives in the World Trade Center, they also quit showing footage of the collapse of WTC 7. At the same time, television networks showed the collapses of the Twin Towers endlessly. There would be little mention of the collapse of WTC 7 until 2008, when NIST finally published its report on this building.

THE SPECIAL DIFFICULTY PRESENTED BY WTC 7

The difference was that the airplane strikes on the Twin Towers provided an explanation for the collapses that most people found plausible (although it was not plausible to well-informed people), whereas WTC 7 came down just as rapidly even though it was not hit by a plane. A couple of months after 9/11, *New York Times* writer James Glanz said that the collapse of this 47-story building was "a mystery" that, if the Twin Towers had not also come down, "would probably have captured the attention of the city and the world." As it was, there was little public discussion. But structural engineers were puzzled, said Glanz.

> [E]xperts said no building like it, a modern, steel-reinforced high-rise, had ever collapsed from an uncontrolled fire, [so] within the structural engineering community, [WTC 7] is considered to be much more important to understand [than the Twin Towers].[2]

It was more important because, given the agreement that the destruction of WTC 7 could not be explained by either airplane impact, or jet-fuel explosions, or a combination of these, there seemed to be no way to explain it—at least, no acceptable way: It was not acceptable for people or agencies within the government to suggest that the building was brought down by explosives and/or incendiaries, because that suggestion would mean that the collapse was caused by people other than al-Qaeda hijackers.

This difficulty of coming up with an acceptable hypothesis was illustrated by the 2002 FEMA report, mentioned in the previous chapter. Needing to find some explanation, FEMA provided an imaginative scenario, according to which burning debris from the collapse of the North Tower (WTC 1) ignited the "diesel fuel on the premises." This fuel, continued the scenario, "contained massive potential energy," which produced a raging inferno in WTC 7 that, after burning for seven hours, brought the building down. However, calling this their "best hypothesis," the authors of this report admitted that its scenario had "only a low probability of occurrence."[3] It was especially low, given the fact that, as videos and photos showed, there *was* no "raging inferno."

NIST'S ATTEMPT

Taking over for FEMA, NIST then had the task of providing a plausible account of WTC 7's collapse. That this task was not easy is shown by the fact that it took a very long time to come up with a report. At first, NIST was going to issue its report on WTC 7 at the same time as the reports on WTC 1 and 2, which came out in 2005. However, although NIST issued progress reports on WTC 7 in 2002 and 2003, an Interim Report in 2004, and a preliminary report in 2005, it kept delaying a draft of the Final Report on WTC 7 until 2008.

Although the authors of these reports over the years kept trying different theories, one element remained the same—the claim that "NIST has seen no evidence that the collapse of WTC 7 was caused by controlled demolition."[4] Because of this constant element, NIST had to resort to miracles.

The Basic Miracle

NIST's basic miracle is the one already discussed—that for the first time in the known universe, a steel-framed high-rise building was brought down by fire, without the aid of explosives or incendiaries. Recall Hume's discussion of how we identify laws of nature: through "a firm and unalterable experience." Many steel-frame buildings have come down, but not a single one of these has come down without the aid of explosives or incendiaries. Moreover, by understanding the principles of physics and structural engineering, we can understand why such buildings could not possibly come down without such aid.

Prior to NIST's Final Report in 2008, there were numerous attempts to try to make this claim seem not totally outrageous, especially a 2006 book published by *Popular Mechanics*, entitled *Debunking 9/11 Myths: Why Conspiracy Theories Can't Stand Up to the Facts*.[5] Citing NIST's "current working hypothesis," the *Popular Mechanics* book said that WTC 7's diesel fuel had probably fed the fires "for up to seven hours." Also, based on NIST's then-current thinking, *Popular Mechanics* claimed that "WTC 7 was far more compromised by falling debris than the report indicated."[6]

Accordingly, said *Popular Mechanics*, people should not reject NIST's theory on the grounds that it was the first steel-framed high-rise to fail "because of fire alone." Rather, it claimed, WTC 7's collapse was analogous to the collapses of the Twin Towers: "A combination of physical damage from falling debris [analogous to the damage caused by the airplane impacts] and prolonged exposure to the resulting [diesel-fuel-fed] fires [analogous to the jet-fuel-fed fires in the Twin Towers]."[7]

Matthew Rothschild used the analysis by *Popular Mechanics* to argue that there is no mystery about the collapse of WTC 7, for two reasons. First, "On about a third of the face to the center and to the bottom—approximately ten stories—about 25 percent of the depth of the building was scooped out." Second, "the fire in the building lasted for about eight hours, in part because there were fuel tanks in the basement and on some of the floors."[8]

However, NIST'S final report did not affirm either element in this twofold explanation. On the one hand, NIST said, "fuel oil fires did not play a role in the collapse of WTC 7."[9] On the other hand, NIST said: "Other than initiating the fires in WTC 7, the damage from the debris from WTC 1 [the North Tower] had little effect on initiating the collapse of WTC 7."[10] Accordingly, NIST admitted, the collapse of WTC 7 was "the first known instance of fire causing the total collapse of a tall building."[11] NIST did nothing, therefore, to undermine the fact that the collapse of WTC 7 had to be considered a miracle.

As far as I know, Rothschild never explained how, in light of NIST's denial of the two key claims in the explanation given by *Popular Mechanics*, there was still no mystery about the collapse of WTC 7.

In any case, the miraculous nature of this collapse was made even more obvious by the fact that the fires allegedly responsible for it were relatively unimpressive, in comparison with fires in some other steel-framed high-rises. In 1991, a huge fire in Philadelphia's One Meridian Plaza lasted for 18 hours and gutted eight of the building's 38 floors. In Caracas in 2004, a fire in a 50-story building raged for 17 hours, completely gutting the building's top 20 floors. In neither case, however, did the building, or even a single floor, collapse.[12]

In WTC 7, by contrast, NIST reported long-lasting fires on only six of the building's 47 floors, with "long-lasting" meaning merely that they were burning up to seven hours. In fact, NIST admitted, it had no evidence that any of the fires lasted for much over three hours.[13] NIST's conclusion that this steel-framed building was brought down without explosives, for the first time ever, constitutes a rather remarkable miracle-claim.

The Miraculous Imitation of an Explosives-Caused Implosion

More clearly miraculous was the *precise way* in which WTC 7 collapsed: symmetrically (straight down, with an almost perfectly horizontal roofline), into its own footprint. In order for this symmetrical collapse to occur, all the steel columns supporting the building had to fail simultaneously. There were 82 of these columns, so NIST was implying that fire caused 82 steel columns to fail at the same instant.

Such a symmetrical failure would have been virtually impossible even if the building had been entirely engulfed by fire, so that all the floors would have been evenly covered with fire. But as it was, there were fires on only a few floors, and these fires never covered an entire floor at the same time. The official account implies, therefore, that a very asymmetrical pattern of fires produced an entirely symmetrical collapse. If that would not be a genuine miracle, what would be?

Moreover, even if a symmetrical collapse could be caused by an asymmetrical pattern of fires, a fire theory could not explain the *sudden onset* of WTC 7's collapse. People wanting to support the official account sometimes say that, even if steel may not melt at 1,500 degrees Fahrenheit, it loses enough strength to cause the support columns and beams to fail. However, even if, *per impossibile*, the fire could have heated the steel up to this temperature in a few hours, the fire would have weakened the steel gradually, causing it to start sagging. Videos would, accordingly, show deformations in the building before it came down.

But they do not. One moment the building was perfectly immobile, and the next moment it was accelerating downward in free fall.[14] As Australian chemist Frank Legge observed: "There is no sign of the slow start that would be expected if collapse was caused by the gradual softening of the steel."[15]

The videos show the collapse of WTC 7 to be the type of controlled demolition known as "implosion," in which explosives and/or incendiaries are used to slice the building's steel support columns, so as to cause the building to collapse into its own footprint. Engineering an implosion, so as not to damage nearby buildings—explains a controlled demolition website—is "by far the trickiest type of explosive project," which "only a handful of blasting companies in the world" possess enough experience to perform.[16] Mark Loizeaux, the president of Controlled Demolition, Inc., has explained that the demolition must be "completely planned," using "the right explosive [and] the right pattern of laying the charges."[17]

Would it not be a miracle if a fire-induced collapse, based on scattered fires on a few of the 47 floors of WTC 7, had produced a collapse that perfectly imitated the kind of planned demolition that can be carried out by only a few companies in the world?

WTC 7's Descent in Absolute Free Fall

Critics of the official account of WTC 7's destruction had from the beginning pointed out that this building descended at virtually the same rate as a free-falling object. NIST, however, long denied this. As late as August 2008, when NIST issued its report on WTC 7 in the form of a Draft for Public Comment, it claimed that the time it took for the upper 17 floors—the only floors that were visible on the videos—to come down "was approximately 40 percent longer than the computed free fall time and was consistent with physical principles."[18] As this statement implied, any assertion that the building *did* come down in free fall (assuming a non-engineered collapse) would *not* be consistent with physical principles—meaning the basic laws of Newtonian physics.

The reason why free fall would not be consistent with these laws was explained in a briefing by NIST's lead investigator, Shyam Sunder. Free fall

only happens, he pointed out, to "an object that has no structural components below it." By contrast, he said, the time that it took those 17 floors to
disappear was roughly 40 percent longer than free fall. "And that is not at
all unusual," Sunder added,

> because there was structural resistance that was provided in this particu-
> lar case. And you had a sequence of structural failures that had to take
> place. Everything was not instantaneous.[19]

In saying this, Sunder was presupposing NIST's theory that the building
was brought down by fire, which—if it could have produced a collapse
of any type—could have produced only a gradual, *progressive* collapse,[20]
rather than an instantaneous one.

In response, physics and mathematics professor David Chandler, who
submitted a question at this briefing, challenged Sunder's denial of free
fall, stating that his "40 percent longer" claim contradicted "a publicly visible, easily measurable quantity."[21] Chandler then placed a video on the
Internet showing that, by measuring this publicly visible quantity, anyone
understanding elementary physics could see that "for about two and a half
seconds. . . , the acceleration of the building is indistinguishable from free-
fall."[22] (This is, of course, free fall through the air, not through a vacuum.)

In its final report on WTC 7, which came out in November 2008,
NIST changed what it had said in the August draft: NIST now admitted
free fall. Dividing the building's descent into three stages, NIST described
the second phase as "a freefall descent over approximately eight stories
at gravitational acceleration [free-fall] for approximately 2.25 seconds."[23]
NIST thereby accepted Chandler's case (except for maintaining that the
building was in absolute free fall for only 2.25, rather than 2.5, seconds).
NIST had thereby affirmed a violation of one or more laws of physics.

This would be a violation of physical laws, Chandler explained, because
"[f]ree fall can only be achieved if there is zero resistance to the motion."[24]
In other words, the upper portion of WTC 7 could have come down in
free fall only if something had suddenly removed all the steel and concrete
in the lower part of the building, which would have otherwise provided
resistance (to make a considerable understatement).

If everything had *not* been removed and yet the upper floors had come
down in free fall anyway, even if for only a fraction of a second, this would
have been a violation of physical principles—a miracle. Explaining one of
the principles involved, Chandler said:

> Anything at an elevated height has gravitational potential energy. If it
> falls, and none of the energy is used for other things along the way, all

of that energy is converted into kinetic energy—the energy of motion, and we call it "free fall." If any of the energy is used for other purposes, there will be less kinetic energy, so the fall will be slower. In the case of a falling building, the only way it can go into free fall is if an external force removes the supporting structure. None of the gravitational potential energy of the building is available for this purpose, or it would slow the fall of the building.[25]

Sunder himself had explained this the previous August, saying that free-fall happens only to "an object that has no structural components below it." But NIST then in November, while still defending the fire theory of WTC 7's collapse, agreed that, as an empirical fact, free fall *had* happened. For a period of 2.25 seconds, NIST admitted, the descent of WTC 7 was characterized by "gravitational acceleration (free fall)."[26]

Accordingly, Sunder himself had stated that a free-fall descent of WTC 7, without the aid of explosives or incendiaries, would be a miracle.

Besides pointing out that the free-fall descent of WTC 7 implied that the building had been professionally demolished, Chandler observed that this conclusion is reinforced by two features of the collapse mentioned above:

> [P]articularly striking is the suddenness of onset of free fall. Acceleration doesn't build up gradually. . . . The building went from full support to zero support, instantly. . . . One moment, the building is holding; the next moment it lets go and is in complete free fall.

Moreover, Chandler added, besides being sudden, the free fall "extended across the whole width of the building."

> The fact that the roof stayed level shows the building was in free fall across the entire width. The collapse we see cannot be due to a column failure, or a few column failures, or a sequence of column failures. All 24 interior columns and 58 perimeter columns had to have been removed . . . simultaneously, within a small fraction of a second.[27]

Significantly, knowing that it had affirmed a miracle, NIST no longer claimed that its analysis was consistent with the laws of physics. Back in its August draft, in which it was still claiming that the collapse occurred 40 percent slower than free fall, NIST claimed three times that its analysis was "consistent with physical principles."[28] In the final report, however, every instance of this phrase was removed. NIST thereby almost explicitly admitted that its report on WTC 7, by affirming absolute free fall while continuing to deny intentional demolition, is *not* consistent with basic principles of physics. NIST thereby admitted that it could not explain the collapse of WTC 7 without appealing to miracle.

Moreover, once scientists have appealed to a miracle, their entire theory is shown to be worthless. Sunder and his colleagues at NIST might just as well have said: "Allah did it!"

Metal-Melting Fires

In claiming that fires caused the total collapse of WTC 7, even though raging fires had never previously caused the collapse of a single floor of a steel-framed building, NIST implied that the WTC 7 fires had miraculous powers. This claim was even more obviously implied by the fact that these fires had to be capable of melting various kinds of metal. Evidence of metal-melting fires was, in fact, found in the rubble of all three WTC buildings, but this evidence is discussed here only in relation to WTC 7.

Melted Iron: A Deutsche Bank building close to WTC 7 was damaged on 9/11. But its insurance company declined to pay off, claiming that the damage to the building had not resulted from the destruction of WTC 7. In response, Deutsche Bank hired the RJ Lee Group, a scientific research organization, to show that the dust contaminating its building after 9/11 was not ordinary building dust, but resulted from the destruction of the World Trade Center.

The RJ Lee Group's reports showed that the dust in the bank's building shared the unique chemical signature of the WTC dust, part of which was "[s]pherical iron . . . particles."[29] Moreover, there were enormous amounts of these particles: Whereas iron particles constitute only 0.04 percent of normal building dust, they constituted (a whopping) 5.87 percent of the WTC dust.[30] The existence of these particles, the RJ Lee Group said, proved that iron had "melted during the WTC Event."[31]

The identification of iron spheres showed that the WTC fires had miraculous powers, because the melting point of iron is 2,800°F, whereas the WTC fires could not possibly have produced temperatures above 1,800°F.[32] Moreover, NIST reported that it showed that there were no core columns—and only three perimeter columns—that had "reached temperatures above 250°C [482°F]."[33] Fires that normally could have raised the temperature of steel columns only to about 250°C must have been given quite a boost by some unknown force in order to get steel or iron to melt.

Melted Molybdenum: Scientists at the US Geological Survey, in a study intended to aid the "identification of WTC dust components," discovered an even more miraculous effect of the fires. Besides finding the spherical iron-rich particles, these scientists found that molybdenum, the melting point of which is 4,753°F (2,623°C), had also melted. These USGS scientists, being employed by the US Government, understandably failed to mention this discovery in their published report.[34] But another group of scientists, having obtained the USGS team's data through an FOIA request, reported evidence showing that the USGS scientists had devoted serious study to "a molybdenum-rich spherule."[35] The melting of molybdenum would have required supernatural assistance even more clearly than the melting of iron.

Swiss-Cheese Steel: Within a few months after 9/11, three professors from Worcester Polytechnic Institute (WPI) issued a brief report about a piece of steel recovered from the WTC 7 debris. According to this report, this piece of steel had undergone "microstructural changes," including "intergranular melting."[36] A greatly expanded version of this report—which also contained a description of a similarly eroded piece of steel from one of the Twin Towers—was included as an appendix to the FEMA report on the destruction of the WTC issued in 2002.[37]

A *New York Times* story, noting that parts of these pieces of steel had "melted away," even though "no fire in any of the buildings was believed to be hot enough to melt steel outright," said that these discoveries constituted "[p]erhaps the deepest mystery uncovered in the investigation."[38] Describing these mysterious pieces of steel more fully, an article in WPI's magazine, entitled "The 'Deep Mystery' of Melted Steel," said:

> [S]teel—which has a melting point of 2,800 degrees Fahrenheit—may weaken and bend, but does not melt during an ordinary office fire. Yet . . . [a] one-inch column has been reduced to half inch thickness. Its edges—which are curled like a paper scroll—have been thinned to almost razor sharpness. Gaping holes—some larger than a silver dollar—let light shine through a formerly solid steel flange. This Swiss cheese appearance shocked all of the fire-wise professors, who expected to see distortion and bending—but not holes.[39]

One of the three WPI professors, Jonathan Barnett, was quoted by the *Times* as saying that the steel "appear[ed] to have been partly evaporated in extraordinarily high temperatures."[40]

That the steel had actually evaporated—not merely melted—was also reported in another *New York Times* story. Professor Abolhassan Astaneh-Asl of the University of California at Berkeley, speaking of a horizontal I-beam from WTC 7, reportedly said: "Parts of the flat top of the I, once five-eighths of an inch thick, had vaporized."[41]

Why do these phenomena involve miracles? Because the building fires could not possibly, even under the most ideal conditions (which did not occur), have been hotter than 1,800°F, whereas the melting point of steel is only slightly lower than the melting point of iron (2,800°F), and the boiling point of steel is 5,182°F.[42] So if one accepts the official account, according to which all the heat was produced by fires fueled only by building materials, then one must believe that these fires had miraculous powers.

NIST, having taken over from FEMA the task of writing the official reports on WTC 7, avoided this issue by simply not mentioning any of these pieces of steel. In fact, NIST—and this is one of the most amazing features of its reports about WTC 7—even explicitly claimed that no steel had been recovered from this building. In its final report on WTC 7, issued in 2008, NIST claimed that no recovered steel from WTC 7 could be identified, because the steel used in this building, unlike that used in the Twin Towers, "did not contain . . . identifying characteristics."[43]

This claim was obviously important to NIST, because it had made it repeatedly in previous reports. For example:

- "No steel from WTC 7 has been identified from the pieces of recovered WTC steel in NIST's possession" (June 2004).[44]

- "NIST recovered no steel from WTC 7" (2005).[45]

- "No metallography could be carried out because no steel was recovered from WTC 7" (2005).[46]

- "The lack of WTC 7 steel precludes tests on actual material from the structure" (2005).[47]

- "Because NIST recovered no steel from WTC 7, it is not possible to make any statements about its quality" (2005).[48]

This claim was especially amazing, because NIST itself had talked about steel recovered from WTC 7. In 2005, a NIST report referred to steel recovered from WTC 7—including the piece with the Swiss-cheese appearance discussed by the WPI professors.[49] Also, NIST's 2008 claim about not identifying any WTC 7 steel was made in August, *after* the airing in July of that year of a BBC program on WTC 7, in which one of those WPI professors, Jonathan Barnett, had discussed an "eroded and deformed" piece of steel from WTC 7, which he and his colleagues had studied in 2001. These professors knew "its pedigree," Barnett explained, because "this particular kind of steel" had been used only in WTC 7, not in either of the Twin Towers.[50] So much for the claim that the steel used to construct WTC 7 "did not contain . . . identifying characteristics."

So, although it called the collapse of WTC 7 "the first known instance of fire causing the total collapse of a tall building,"[51] NIST had demonstrated its awareness of at least one piece of steel recovered from this building that could not have been produced by fire—unless it was a previously unknown kind of fire.

Supernatural Sulfur

In the reports about the Swiss-cheese-appearing piece of steel that had been recovered from the WTC 7 rubble (as well as one from one of the Twin Towers), there was an element that deserves special consideration: The report of the three WPI professors said that the thinning of the steel had resulted from sulfidation, but there was no explanation for the source of the sulfur or the mechanism through which it could have entered into the steel.

According to a preliminary analysis reported by the professors, "sulfur released during the fires—no one knows from where—may have combined with atoms in the steel to form compounds that melt at lower temperatures."[52] This phenomenon was discussed more fully in the aforementioned WPI article, "The 'Deep Mystery' of Melted Steel." According to this article, the scientists attributed the holes and the thinning to "a eutectic reaction" that "occurred at the surface, causing intergranular melting capable of turning a solid steel girder into Swiss cheese."[53]

In summarizing their findings in the paper that was included in the FEMA report, the three professors wrote:

1. The thinning of the steel occurred by a high-temperature corrosion due to a combination of oxidation and sulfidation.

2. Heating of the steel into a hot corrosive environment approaching 1,000°C (1,832°F) results in the formation of a eutectic mixture of iron, oxygen, and sulfur that liquefied the steel.

3. The sulfidation attack of steel grain boundaries accelerated the corrosion and erosion of the steel.[54]

Then, having mentioned sulfidation in each of these three points, the professors added: "The severe corrosion and subsequent erosion of Samples 1 and 2 are a very unusual event. No clear explanation for the source of the sulfur has been identified. . . . A detailed study into the mechanisms of this phenomenon is needed."[55]

However, although Arden Bement, who was the director of NIST when it took over the WTC project from FEMA, said that NIST's report would address "all major recommendations contained in the [FEMA] report,"[56] NIST ignored this recommendation. Indeed, as we saw earlier, it did not even mention the Swiss-cheese-appearing steel.

Also, when NIST was later asked about the sulfidation, it tried to maintain that the source of the sulfur was not actually a mystery, saying that "sulfur is present in the gypsum wallboard that was prevalent in the interior partitions."[57] But there were serious problems with this explanation.

First, gypsum is calcium sulfate, so if all the sulfur discovered had been from gypsum wallboard, it would have been matched by about the same percentage of calcium. That, however, was not the case.[58]

Second, the WPI professors reported not merely that there was sulfur in the debris, but that the steel had been *sulfidized*. This means that sulfur had entered into the *intergranular structure* of the steel (which the *New York Times* article had indicated by saying that sulfur had "combined with atoms in the steel"). As chemist Kevin Ryan has pointed out, the question NIST would need to answer is: "[H]ow did sulfates, from wallboard, tunnel into the intergranular microstructure of the steel and then form sulfides within?"[59] Physicist Steven Jones added:

> [I]f NIST claims that sulfur is present in the steel from gypsum, they should do an (easy) experiment to heat steel to about 1000°C in the presence of gypsum and then test whether sulfur has entered the steel. . . . [T]hey will find that sulfur does *not* enter steel under such circumstances.[60]

Why it would not has been explained by Danish chemistry professor Niels Harrit: Although gypsum contains sulfur, this is not elemental sulfur, which can react, but sulfur in the form of calcium sulfate, which cannot.[61]

The official account of the destruction of the WTC 7, therefore, implies that the sulfidized steel had been produced by a twofold miracle: Besides the fact that the fires, as we saw earlier, could have melted steel only if they had possessed supernatural powers, such powers would also have been necessary for the wallboard sulfur to enter into the steel.

Once again, a non-miraculous explanation is available: We need only suppose that thermate, a well-known incendiary, had been employed. As Steven Jones has written: "The thermate reaction proceeds rapidly and is in general faster than basic thermite in cutting through steel due to the presence of sulfur. (Elemental sulfur forms a low-melting-temperature eutectic with iron.)"[62]

Besides providing an explanation for the eutectic reaction, thermate could also, Jones pointed out, explain the melting, oxidation, and sulfidation of the steel:

> When you put sulfur into thermite it makes the steel melt at a much lower temperature, so instead of melting at about 1,538°C [2,800°F] it melts at

approximately 988°C [1,820°F], and you get sulfidation and oxidation in the attacked steel.[63]

NIST, however, insisted that no incendiaries, such as thermate, were employed: WTC 7 was brought down by fire alone (while the Twin Towers were brought down by ordinary building fires combined with damage from the airplane impacts). Those who endorse the official account, therefore, are stuck with yet more miracles.

THE 12 MIRACLES OF LOWER MANHATTAN

There are many features of NIST's report on the collapse of WTC 7 that are almost certainly false. The present chapter, however, deals only with features that, contradicting principles of physics, must be classified as miracles. There are at least six of these miracles: (1) WTC 7 was destroyed without the use of explosives or incendiaries; (2) the collapse of WTC 7 perfectly imitated the kind of implosion that can ordinarily be caused only by a world-class demolition company; (3) the building came down in free-fall for over two seconds, which by physical principles could happen only if explosives and/ or incendiaries had simultaneously removed all 82 steel support columns; (4) the WTC 7 fires melted steel, iron, and even molybdenum, all of which have melting points far higher than ordinary building fires can reach; (5) Swiss-cheese-appearing steel from WTC 7 cannot be explained as resulting from an ordinary building fire, unless it had supernatural assistance; (6) this Swiss-cheese-appearing steel had been sulfidized—a process that could not have been produced by ordinary building fires.

By adding these six miracles to the six miracles discussed in the previous chapter, we get a total of 12 miracles that happened in lower Manhattan on 9/11—miracles that are entailed by NIST's account of the destruction of the World Trade Center.

At the end of the previous chapter, part of a letter to *Europhysics News* from former NIST employee Peter Ketcham was quoted. Immediately after his charge that "NIST had reached a predetermined conclusion by ignoring, dismissing, and denying the evidence," he added:

> Among the most egregious examples is the explanation for the collapse of WTC 7 as an elaborate sequence of unlikely events culminating in the almost symmetrical total collapse of a steel-frame building into its own footprint at free-fall acceleration.[64]

If journalists continue to endorse the official account of the destruction of the World Trade Center, they should begin their articles by saying: "I believe in miracles—lots of them."

14 • THE MIRACULOUS ATTACK ON THE PENTAGON

In addition to the 9/11 attacks on WTC 1, 2, and 7, there was an attack on the Pentagon. According to the official account of this attack, the Pentagon was struck by American Airlines Flight 77 (AA 77), which was a Boeing 757 airliner, piloted by al-Qaeda hijacker Hani Hanjour.

There were many features of this reported attack that raised questions about the truthfulness of the official account. One question was raised above in Chapter 11—namely, whether Vice President Cheney had issued a stand-down order to allow an aircraft approaching the Pentagon to strike it. Also, Norman Mineta's account of a conversation between Cheney and a young man, which could be interpreted as a stand-down order, contradicted the official account, according to which Cheney had not yet entered the PEOC at the time of this reported conversation. But another element especially important for the official account was a report by Theodore "Ted" Olson, who was the Solicitor General for the Bush-Cheney administration.

THE OLSON PHONE CALLS

Ted Olson reported that his wife, Barbara Olson, was on AA 77, which was a Boeing 757. He also reported that his wife had called him twice, telling him that her plane had been hijacked by terrorists with knives and box cutters.[1] These reports were important, because the FAA, having lost signals from AA 77's transponder, came to suspect that it had crashed. The reported calls from Barbara Olson, which came shortly before AA 77 allegedly hit the Pentagon, provided the only evidence that this flight, after having left Washington's Dulles Airport for Los Angeles, had headed back toward Washington. The Olson calls were also the only basis for the idea that any of the flights had hijackers with knives and box cutters. "I think the Olson calls were so important," quipped researcher Rowland Morgan, "that they had to happen."[2]

There has also been much discussion of whether Barbara Olson made those reported calls, partly because it was unclear how she could have done so. Ted Olson went back and forth on whether she had used her cell phone or an onboard phone.[3] Most of the first stories said she had used her cell phone, but it soon became known that the plane would have been too high for cell phone calls to the ground to be connected.[4] It seemed, therefore, that she must have used an onboard phone. But then researchers learned from American Airlines that its Boeing 757s did not have onboard phones.[5] It seemed, accordingly, that Barbara Olson's calls must have been miraculous.

In 2006, however, the FBI reported that the phone records from AA 77 indicated that Barbara Olson had attempted only one call, which was not connected, so it lasted "0 seconds."[6] This report thereby implied that Ted Olson's report about the two calls from his wife was not true, so the evidence that AA 77 had headed back towards Washington, along with evidence that any of the 9/11 flights had hijackers with knives and boxcutters, was undermined.

THE ATTACKING AIRCRAFT AND ITS PILOT

Another much-discussed question has been whether the aircraft that struck the Pentagon was actually AA 77, as maintained by the official account. There has even been debate as to whether the Pentagon was struck by a large airliner of any type. But 9/11 scholars agree on at least one point: *The Pentagon was not struck by AA 77 under the control of Hani Hanjour.*[7] One of the reasons this element in the official account has been so widely considered false is that the piloting of a Boeing airliner into the Pentagon by Hani Hanjour would have been a miracle. The remainder of this chapter discusses this issue.

The Attacking Aircraft's Amazing Trajectory

In describing the end of flight AA 77, *The 9/11 Commission Report* said:

> American 77 was then 5 miles west-southwest of the Pentagon and began a 330-degree turn. At the end of the turn, it was descending through 2,200 feet, pointed toward the Pentagon and downtown Washington. The hijacker pilot then advanced the throttles to maximum power and dove toward the Pentagon.

The Commission's report then identified the "hijacker pilot" as Hani Hanjour.[8]

However, in the first three days after the attack, Hani Hanjour was not named as the pilot; indeed, his name was not even on the list of hijackers released to the public on the afternoon of September 14.[9]

Prior to the time that Hanjour was identified as the pilot, the final minutes of Flight 77's trajectory had been described as one requiring great expertise. For example, a *Washington Post* story on September 12 said:

> [J]ust as the plane seemed to be on a suicide mission into the White House, the unidentified pilot executed a pivot so tight that it reminded observers of a fighter jet maneuver. The plane circled 270 degrees to the

right to approach the Pentagon from the west. . . . Aviation sources said the plane was flown with extraordinary skill, making it highly likely that a trained pilot was at the helm.[10]

On September 13, a story in the *Detroit News* said:

Whoever flew at least three of the death planes seemed very skilled. . . . Investigators are particularly impressed with the pilot who slammed into the Pentagon and, just before impact, performed a tightly banked 270-degree turn at low altitude with almost military precision.[11]

The fact that this maneuver required great skill was reinforced by subsequent reports. Barbara Walters interviewed Danielle O'Brien, an air traffic controller at Dulles International Airport who had been in the radar room on the morning of 9/11. Recounting how she had seen "an unidentified plane to the southwest of Dulles, moving at a very high rate of speed" towards the protected airspace over Washington, she said:

The speed, the maneuverability, the way that he turned, we all thought in the radar room, all of us experienced air traffic controllers, that that was a military plane.[12]

The 9/11 Commission also referred to President Bush, saying: "As a former pilot, the President was struck by the apparent sophistication of some of the piloting, especially Hanjour's high-speed dive into the Pentagon."[13]

The Amazing Incompetence of Hani Hanjour

Although the trajectory of the aircraft that struck the Pentagon suggested that the pilot had extraordinary ability, stories in the press made clear that Hani Hanjour did not. For example, a story in *Newsday* entitled "America's Ordeal: Tracing Trail of Hijackers," said:

At Freeway Airport in Bowie, Md., 20 miles west of Washington, flight instructor Sheri Baxter instantly recognized the name of alleged hijacker Hani Hanjour when the FBI released a list of 19 suspects in the four hijackings. Hanjour, the only suspect on Flight 77 the FBI listed as a pilot, had come to the airport one month earlier seeking to rent a small plane. However, when Baxter and fellow instructor Ben Conner took the slender, soft-spoken Hanjour on three test runs during the second week of August, they found he had trouble controlling and landing the single-engine Cessna 172. Even though Hanjour showed a federal pilot's license and a log book cataloging 600 hours of flying experience, chief flight instructor Marcel Bernard declined to rent him a plane without more lessons.[14]

The *Washington Post* then lifted up the problem even further in a story entitled "Hanjour: A Study in Paradox." Besides mentioning several incidents in which instructors had "questioned his competence," including the refusal of Freeway Airport to rent a plane to Hanjour, this story said: "How and where Hanjour obtained a commercial pilot's license remains a lingering question that FAA officials refuse to discuss."[15]

The following year, reports of Hanjour's incompetence received even greater national exposure. In May 2002, Jim Yardley, in a *New York Times* story entitled "A Trainee Noted for Incompetence," wrote:

> Hani Hanjour . . . was reported to the aviation agency in February 2001 after instructors at his flight school in Phoenix had found his piloting skills so shoddy and his grasp of English so inadequate that they questioned whether his pilot's license was genuine.[16]

Yardley's story ended with a quotation from a former employee of the flight school who was, he said, "amazed that [Hanjour] could have flown into the Pentagon," because he "could not fly at all."[17] A week later, CBS News put out a story entitled "FAA Was Alerted to Sept. 11 Hijacker," which said:

> [M]anagers at an Arizona flight school [called JetTech] reported [Hanjour] at least five times to the FAA . . . because his English and flying skills were so bad . . . they didn't think he should keep his pilot's license. "I couldn't believe he had a commercial license of any kind with the skills that he had," said Peggy Chevrette, the manager.[18]

On the first anniversary of 9/11, the contradiction between Hanjour's incompetence, on the one hand, and the skill that would have been required to fly American 77 into the Pentagon, on the other, was made explicit by the *Washington Post*. In an article entitled "Mysterious Trip to Flight 77 Cockpit," Steve Fainaru and Alia Ibrahim wrote: "[N]o one has been able to offer a definitive portrait of Hanjour, leaving unreconciled a number of seemingly contradictory facts about his life." For example:

> After the attacks, . . . aviation experts concluded that the final maneuvers of American Airlines Flight 77—a tight turn followed by a steep, accurate descent into the Pentagon—was the work of "a great talent . . . virtually a textbook turn and landing."

However, they continued, just months before the attacks, Hanjour had failed to earn a rating to fly an airliner. "His instructors became so alarmed by his crude skills and limited English they notified the FAA to determine whether his pilot's license was real."[19]

Attempts to Minimize the Contradiction

Both *The 9/11 Commission Report* and *Popular Mechanics* tried to minimize the contradiction between the abilities of Hani Hanjour and the reported skill of the pilot of the plane that struck the Pentagon.

The 9/11 Commission Report: On the one hand, the 9/11 Commission cited some of the stories reporting Hanjour's lack of flying ability. For example, the Commission reported an incident in the summer of 2001, just months before 9/11. After Hanjour, with an instructor on board, had flown the Hudson Corridor in a small plane owned by Air Fleet Training Systems in Teterboro, New Jersey, the Commission wrote: "[H]is instructor declined a second request because of what he considered Hanjour's poor piloting skills."[20] The Commission even admitted that a flight instructor in Arizona had described Hanjour as "a terrible pilot."[21]

On the other hand, the Commission made some comments suggesting that Hanjour was quite accomplished. In a note referring to KSM (Khalid Sheikh Mohammed), the alleged "mastermind" of the 9/11 attacks, the Commission said: "KSM claims to have assigned the Pentagon specifically to Hanjour, the operations' most experienced pilot."[22] But the Commission failed to ask how a "terrible pilot" could have been described as the operation's "most experienced pilot." The Commission, to be sure, could have reconciled these statements by saying that the other three pilots were even worse. But it did not suggest this solution. In any case, the Commission also wrote:

> Hanjour successfully conducted a challenging certification flight super-vised by an instructor at Congressional Air Charters of Gaithersburg, Maryland, landing at a small airport with a difficult approach. The in-structor thought Hanjour may have had training from a military pilot because he used a terrain recognition system for navigation.[23]

But the Commission did not explain how this instructor could have had such a radically different view of Hanjour's abilities from that of all the others, who said he was incompetent, right up through the second week of August 2001.

Besides making the statements contradicting what the press had re-ported, the 9/11 Commission did not quote the strongest statements about the pilot of the aircraft that struck the Pentagon, such as that the downward spiral would have required a pilot "with extraordinary skill," who could fly with "almost military precision."

Popular Mechanics: A similar approach was taken by the *Popular Mechanics* book, *Debunking 9/11 Myths*, which admitted Hanjour's failings while seeking to claim that they were not fatal. On the one hand, it admitted that "none of the hijacker pilots had ever flown a commercial-size airline jet" and that their "flying skills were indeed rudimentary."[24]

On the other hand, *Popular Mechanics* said, although the pilots "may not have been highly skilled," they did not need to be, because the planes were already in flight when they took over. "All they had to do was pretty much point and go." The hijackers probably had portable GPS (Global Positioning System) units, *Popular Mechanics* speculated, so they would have needed "only to punch the destination coordinates into the flight management system and steer the planes while looking at the navigation screen."[25]

However, while that could in principle have been true about the flights aimed at the Twin Towers, it was certainly not true of the trajectory reportedly taken by AA 77. How did the authors of the *Popular Mechanics* book deal with the downward spiral, after which the plane came in at virtually ground level to strike the Pentagon between its first and second floors? They *simply ignored it*. In their only statement about the final minutes of this flight, they wrote:

> The flight data recorder . . . of Flight 77 indicated that Hanjour input autopilot instructions to Reagan National Airport. . . . He steered the plane manually for only the final eight minutes of the flight.[26]

It was, however, precisely during those "final eight minutes" that the plane was reportedly "flown with extraordinary skill," with "almost military precision."

What did *Popular Mechanics* say about the downward spiral? *Nothing.* Referring to all the 9/11 planes, it acknowledged that they "made sharp turns of up to 330 degrees and at times dropped precipitously." But it did not point out that AA 77 supposedly executed a 330-degree turn in "the final eight minutes of the flight," during which "Hanjour . . . steered the plane manually."[27]

More than one airline pilot has stated that it would have been impossible for an incompetent amateur pilot such as Hanjour to fly those final minutes. For example, former Pan-American Airlines pilot Ted Muga, who had previously been a US Navy pilot, said: "The maneuver at the Pentagon was . . . a tight spiral coming down out of 7,000 feet." And while a commercial aircraft "can in fact structurally somewhat handle that maneuver," Muga added, it would be very, very, difficult. It "would take considerable training" and "some very, very talented pilots to do that. I just can't imagine an amateur even being able to come close to performing a maneuver of that nature."[28]

Accordingly, *Popular Mechanics*, like the 9/11 Commission, failed to face up to the question of how Hanjour, with his "rudimentary" flying skills, could have piloted AA 77 into the Pentagon. The contradiction remains. Therefore, the 9/11 Commission and *Popular Mechanics* failed to explain why the claim that Hani Hanjour hit the Pentagon should not be rejected as an impossible miracle story.

Could AA 77 Have Handled the Trajectory?

Some pilots have suggested that even the best pilots in the world could not have flown the reported trajectory in 757. For example, Ralph Kolstad, who was a US Navy pilot with "top gun" training before becoming a commercial airline pilot, said: "I have 6,000 hours of flight time in Boeing 757s and 767s and I could not have flown it the way the flight path was described."[29]

In line with Muga's statement that a 757 can "structurally somewhat handle that maneuver," some researchers have suggested "the possibility that the plane was hijacked by an on-board device, pre-programmed to take over the autopilot."[30] In the words of other researchers, "the plane may have been flown by some kind of automatic controls and/or guided by a homing beacon."[31]

However, these researchers nevertheless assert that the official account of Flight 77 is false, because Hani Hanjour could not possibly have flown the final eight minutes of the trajectory in order to strike the Pentagon.

Moreover, in addition to the fact that the Pentagon could not possibly have been struck by AA 77 under the guidance of Hani Hanjour, there are other reasons why, even if the al-Qaeda hijackers had had a much better pilot, they would not have tried to fly the official trajectory:

- The Pentagon's Wedge 1, which was struck, was the one section of the Pentagon that would have provided an obstacle for an attacking airplane.

- While an extremely difficult maneuver would have been needed to hit Wedge 1, even a mediocre pilot might have been able to strike the roof, which provided a much bigger target.

- Flying through the most restricted airspace in the United States, al-Qaeda hijackers should have feared that AA 77 would be shot down by fighter jets. Executing the downward spiral in order to hit Wedge 1, instead of simply flying into the roof, would have given fighter jets more time to shoot AA 77 down.

- It was well known that the offices of Secretary of Defense Donald Rumsfeld and the Pentagon's top brass, which al-Qaeda terrorists would presumably have wanted to strike, were on the opposite side of the Pentagon, safely away from Wedge 1.

- Wedge 1 had just been renovated with steel-reinforced concrete, blast-resistant windows, fire-resistant Kevlar cloth, and a new sprinkler system, so it was the part of the Pentagon that was least vulnerable to attack. A strike on Wedge 1 would have caused less damage than hitting almost any other part of the Pentagon.

- Wedge 1 was still sparsely occupied, so fewer people were killed there than would have been killed in virtually any other part of the Pentagon.[32]

Accordingly, even if hijackers had had the world's best pilot, they would not have aimed at Wedge 1. The main point, in any case, is that the only way a Boeing 757 could have possibly struck Wedge 1 would have been if the aircraft was being directed by an autopilot system.[33]

CONCLUSION

For Hani Hanjour to have flown AA 77 into the Pentagon would have been impossible. To endorse the official story of the Pentagon attack is to confess belief in two more 9/11 miracles: Barbara Olson's phone call(s) and Hani Hanjour's flight. These impossibilities bring our miracle count up to 14.

15 • THE MIRACULOUS TRANSFORMATION OF MOHAMED ATTA

Thus far, the examples of miracles in the official account of 9/11 have involved reported events that would have been physically impossible, except with the aid of supernatural intervention. But people also speak of miraculous transformations in people, as when a thieving scoundrel becomes honest, kindly, and generous. Although sometimes these transformations are attributed to divine influence, they are not miracles in the strict sense of being violations of the principles of physics and chemistry. It appears, however, that Mohamed Atta, called the ringleader of the hijackers, underwent a miraculous transformation in the fullest sense of that term.

THE 9/11 COMMISSION ON ATTA

The statements about Atta by the 9/11 Commission were radically different from the stories about him in the press. *The 9/11 Commission Report* said that the four 9/11 planes were hijacked by devout Muslims. With regard to Mohamed Atta himself, the Commission said that he had become very religious, even "fanatically so."[1] This image of Atta and the other alleged hijackers as devout Muslims contributed to the Commission's characterization of them as a "cadre of trained operatives willing to die."[2]

STORIES ABOUT SEX AND ALCOHOL IN THE PRESS

However, the stories about these men in the press gave a completely different picture. For example, the *Boston Herald* published an article entitled "Terrorists Partied with Hooker at Hub-Area Hotel," which said:

> A driver for a pair of local escort services told the *Herald* yesterday that he drove a call girl to the Park Inn in Chestnut Hill on Sept. 9 around 10:30 PM where she bedded down with one of the mass murderers. It was her second trip to the terrorist's room that day. . . . In Florida, several of the hijackers—including reputed ringleader Mohamed Atta—spent $200 to $300 each on lap dances in the Pink Pony strip club.[3]

The *South Florida Sun-Sentinel* brought out the contradiction implicit in such stories explicitly. In an article entitled "Suspects' Actions Don't Add Up," this newspaper said:

> Three guys cavorting with lap dancers at the Pink Pony Nude Theater. Two others knocking back glasses of Stolichnaya and rum and Coke at a fish joint in Hollywood the weekend before committing suicide and mass murder. That might describe the behavior of several men who are

suspects in Tuesday's terrorist attack, but it is not a picture of devout Muslims.

In particular, the story said, it is not a picture of religious zealots in their final days on Earth: "[A] devout Muslim [cannot] drink booze or party at a strip club and expect to reach heaven, said Mahmoud Mustafa Ayoub, a professor at Temple University in Philadelphia." Pointing out that "the most basic tenets of the religion forbid alcohol and any sex outside marriage," he added: "Something here does not add up.[4]

The reference to drinking Stolichnaya vodka was about Atta and two other men in a Miami bar four days before the 9/11 attacks. The story was told by many publications around the world, including *Newsweek*, which wrote:

> Last week Atta and two of his buddies seem to have gone out for a farewell bender at a seafood bar called Shuckums. Atta drank five Stoli-and-fruit-juices, while one of the others drank rum and Coke. For once, Atta and his friends became agitated, shouting curse words in Arabic, reportedly including a particularly blasphemous one that roughly translates as "F--k God."[5]

The version in *Time* magazine added that, according to the bartender, "They were wasted."[6]

THE 9/11 COMMISSION'S TREATMENT OF SUCH STORIES

People who have read only *The 9/11 Commission Report* do not know these stories about sex and alcohol, because the Commission ignored all of them. For example, the *San Francisco Chronicle*, in an article entitled "Agents of Terror Leave Their Mark on Sin City," said that five of these al-Qaeda hijackers, including Mohamed Atta, "engaged in some decidedly un-Islamic sampling of prohibited pleasures in America's reputed capital of moral corrosion." Investigators, added the article, found that the group had "made at least six trips here."[7] Even the *Wall Street Journal* wrote about the Las Vegas trips in an editorial entitled "Terrorist Stag Parties."[8]

However, *The 9/11 Commission Report* said: "Beyond Las Vegas's reputation for welcoming tourists, we have seen no credible evidence explaining why, on this occasion and others, the operatives flew to or met in Las Vegas."[9]

Atta's Cocaine and His Girlfriend

Immediately after 9/11, stories in newspapers in Venice, Florida, reported that Atta had lived there for several months. A couple of months after 9/11, investigative reporter Daniel Hopsicker went to Venice to interview people mentioned in the stories. He learned that Atta and a young woman named Amanda Keller took a trip to Key West with a few other people, during which they drank heavily and used cocaine (which Atta could obtain at the place where he was taking flying lessons). Having been kicked out of his apartment, Atta moved into her apartment, for which he paid the rent.[10] But Keller quickly learned to dislike him and, now earning a lot of money as a stripper, told him to move out. Shortly after leaving, he came back while she was not there and disemboweled her cat and dismembered its kittens.[11]

Needless to say, the 9/11 Commission did not report about this episode in Atta's life. Indeed, at the first hearing of the 9/11 Commission in March 2003, a member of the press asked Commissioner Richard Ben-Veniste: "If Atta belonged to the fundamentalist Muslim group, why was he snorting cocaine and frequenting strip bars?" Ben-Veniste replied: "You know, that's a heck of a question."[12] But it was a question that the 9/11 Commission, when it issued its report sixteen months later, did not address.

ATTA'S PERSONAL TRANSFORMATION

The account thus far is not about a miraculous transformation. Rather, comparing the press stories with *The 9/11 Commission Report* merely gives us a stark contradiction. The only suggestion of transformation is the Commission's statement that Atta had become very religious. When Atta arrived in Germany, said the Commission, he was not fanatically religious at first, but "[t]his would change."[13]

But in light of the press stories of Atta's behavior, the description of him as having recently become extremely religious is completely unbeliev-able. However, one might reconcile the radically different portraits of Atta by supposing that he had originally been very devout but then got seduced by sex, alcohol, and cocaine. But it would be hard to believe that the man Atta became had been very devout just a short time earlier. This would indeed be close to being a miracle—although one inspired not by God or Allah but by the Devil.

Is there any other way to explain the change? Yes, it could be explained if the man the world came to know as Mohamed Atta was not the original Mohamad Atta. There is good evidence, moreover, that this is the case.[14]

It is known that Atta had studied urban planning at the Technical University of Hamburg-Harburg. Professor Dittmar Machule, who was his thesis advisor, has been interviewed many times about his acquaintance with Atta. Machule knew this student, incidentally, as Mohamed el-Amir, although his full name was the same as that of his father: Mohamed el-Amir Atta. Machule said that this student was "very religious," prayed regularly, and never touched alcohol. "I would put my hand in the fire," said the professor, "that this Mohamed El-Amir I know will never taste or touch alcohol."[15]

Moreover, by contrast with the American Atta, who regularly paid for lap dances and prostitutes, the student he knew as Mohamed el-Amir Atta, said the professor, would not even shake hands with a woman on being introduced to her.

In addition, researcher Elias Davidson provided many quotations illustrating that, whereas all people who said anything about the American Atta described him as unpleasant, arrogant, and obnoxious, Mohamed el-Amir Atta of Hamburg was always described as reserved, introverted, polite, and very nice.[16]

Nevertheless, although it would be virtually beyond belief, one might still think that the Mohamed el-Emir Atta known by Professor Machule might have been transformed behaviorally into the man described by Daniel Hopsicker and the press. But what about his physical appearance?

ATTA'S PHYSICAL TRANSFORMATION

The American Atta was often described as having a hard, cruel face, and the standard FBI photo of him bears this out. A *Los Angeles Times* reporter wrote: "Atta, whose hard gaze has fumed from a billion television screens and newspaper pages, has become, for many, the face of evil incarnate." Another writer said that Atta's face "had the grim mouth and blank eyes we associate with cruelty." A writer for the *Observer* said, "it is not hard to see Atta, whose face gazes out from the passport photograph released by the FBI, as that of the mass murderer of Manhattan."[17] One could add that this Atta also looks like a man who could disembowel a cat and dismember its kittens.

By contrast, photographs taken of Mohamed Atta during his university years show a person who, while looking slightly like the American Atta, had a very soft and kind face.[18] Also, this young man was known to his father as a "gentle and tender boy," who was nicknamed "nightingale."[19]

Moreover, Professor Machule described his student as "very small," being "one meter sixty-two" in height, which means slightly under 5'4". But the American Atta has been described as 5'8" and sometimes as 5'10" tall.[20] In addition, Machule said, his former student was not a "bodyguard type" but "more a girl looking type."[21] No one looking at the American Atta's picture would describe him that way.

SUMMARY

The transformation from the Hamburg student named Mohamed el-Amir Atta to the man known in America as Mohamad Atta was as miraculous as the transformation of WTC 7 from the state in which it had fires on a few floors to the state of complete destruction. This is most obviously the case with his becoming several inches taller, because this would have been a full-fledged (physical) miracle. Adding this physical transformation means that, to accept the official account of 9/11, one must implicitly believe that 15 miracles happened on that day.

CONCLUSION

Most members of the US press and government ridicule any alternative account of 9/11 as absurd conspiracy theory. But what could be less credible than a theory that entails several miracles—defined as occurrences that contradict the basic laws of physics and chemistry—to explain events?

Along with philosophers, scientists, and other intellectuals, news reporters and media editors generally reject miracles, thus understood, as explanations of events. But reporters and editors have accepted—or at least refused to question or to reject publicly—the official account of 9/11 as presented by the Bush-Cheney administration and Zelikow's *9/11 Commission Report*. They have thereby publicly endorsed, regardless of what their private beliefs may be, an account based on at least 15 major miracles:

1   The Twin Towers and WTC 7 were the only steel-framed high-rise buildings ever to come down without explosives or incendiaries.

2   The Twin Towers, each of which had 287 steel columns, were brought down solely by a combination of airplane strikes and jet-fuel fires.

3   WTC 7 was not even hit by a plane, so it was the first steel-framed high-rise to be brought down solely by ordinary building fires.

4   These World Trade Center buildings also came down in free fall—the Twin Towers in virtual free fall, WTC 7 in *absolute* free fall—for over two seconds.

5   Although the collapses of the WTC buildings were not aided by explosives, the collapses imitated the kinds of implosions that can be induced only by demolition companies.

6   In the case of WTC 7, the structure came down symmetrically (straight down, with an almost perfectly horizontal roofline), which meant that all 82 of the steel support columns had to fail simultaneously, although the building's fires had a very *asymmetrical* pattern.

7   The South Tower's upper 30-floor block changed its angular momentum in midair.

8   This 30-floor block then disintegrated in midair.

9   With regard to the North Tower, some of its steel columns were ejected out horizontally for at least 500 feet.

10 The fires in the debris from the WTC buildings could not be extinguished for many months.

11 Although the WTC fires, based on ordinary building fires, could not have produced temperatures above 1,800°F, the fires inexplicably melted metals with much higher melting points, such as iron (2,800°F) and even molybdenum (4,753°F).

12 Some of the steel in the debris had been sulfidized, resulting in Swiss-cheese-appearing steel, even though ordinary building fires could not have resulted in the sulfidation.

13 As a passenger on AA Flight 77, Barbara Olson called her husband, telling him about hijackers on her plane, even though this plane had no onboard phones and its altitude was too high for a cell phone call to get through.

14 Hijacker pilot Hani Hanjour could not possibly have flown the trajectory of AA 77 to strike Wedge 1 of the Pentagon, and yet he did.

15 Besides going through an unbelievable personal transformation, ringleader Mohamed Atta also underwent an impossible physical transformation.

Still other miracles also could be recounted. For example:

- The claim that the passport of alleged hijacker Ziad Jarrah—said to be on United Airlines Flight 93, which crashed in Pennsylvania—was found on the ground at the crash site, even though nothing else at the site suggested that a giant airliner had crashed there. Nothing was visible because the plane, which descended at 580 miles per hour, buried itself deep in the ground. Nevertheless, the passport escaped at the last millisecond and fell to the ground.[1]

- The claim that the passport of alleged hijacker Satam al-Sugami was found at the site of the WTC's North Tower, meaning that the passport escaped intact after the plane perished in a giant fireball.[2]

Still more miracles have been discussed in an excellent movie, *Incontrovertible*, by British filmmaker Tony Rooke. A review by James McDowell, "Seeing Through the Miracles of 9/11," begins: "To believe the official 9/11 conspiracy theory, one must also believe that September 11, 2001, was a day of miracles." The title of the film emphasizes the fact that, because the official account is full of miracles, the falsity of that account is *incontrovertible*.[3]

Moreover, the official account includes many other claims, beyond those that are strictly miraculous, that are incredible.

THE INCREDIBLE OFFICIAL ACCOUNT OF 9/11

Numerous authors have provided summaries of the official story that bring out its fallacies or contradictions. One such summary is provided by John B. Cobb, Jr., one of America's leading theologians:

> The story [about 9/11] that was told us at the time, and that has been revised and amplified ever since, is, on the surface, both humiliating and implausible. The world's most powerful air force was not able to offer any defense against supposedly hijacked civilian planes. The world's finest radar system was not able to track one plane coming toward the Pentagon, and the world's best defended building was unable to offer any resistance at all. Our vast intelligence network provided no warning, as a small band of Saudis, with modest skills at best, planned, prepared for, and executed a truly amazing attack on an apparently helpless or totally incompetent United States.
>
> It seems remarkable that the American public dutifully vented its rage entirely on the supposed Muslim attackers and has not even demanded a serious investigation of those to whom we give hundreds of billions of dollars every year to plan and execute our defense...
>
> Apparently, we as a people have accepted the idea that all blame for the failure of our defenses goes to the bungling stupidity of the usually highly efficient Federal Aviation Administration. Yet despite the official account of gross dereliction of duty, no one in the FAA has even been demoted, much less fired...
>
> Also remarkable is that the public has accepted the extraordinary story that two planes caused fires that totally destroyed three buildings. Although fires had never previously caused the total collapse of a building of this sort, they brought down three on that day, all in just the way controlled demolition would have collapsed them. The many reports of explosions of the sort that accompany such demolitions were confiscated and concealed until their disclosure was demanded by the *New York Times*. The steel whose examination could easily have settled the question of what caused the collapse was quickly shipped away and melted down.[4]

WILL THE MEDIA EXAMINE THE EVIDENCE?

Of course, such treatments of the official account as unreliable will not convince some people, because they assume that all such problems have been explained by *The 9/11 Commission Report* or the more readable defense by *Popular Mechanics.* However, serious studies of these books can show, to those willing to study the evidence, that it is the official account that "can't stand up to the facts."[5]

However, it has been difficult for people in the media, especially in America, to study the evidence. Or if they do and conclude that the official story is false, they are reluctant to share this conclusion with others. A major reason is that to question the official account is to be branded a "conspiracy theorist." Why should one fear this label?

As Lance deHaven-Smith explained in his book *Conspiracy Theory in America,* the CIA started using "conspiracy theory" as a pejorative term in 1964 to ridicule the growing belief, contrary to the Warren Report, that President Kennedy was killed by people within the US government, including the CIA itself. Republican blogger Ron Unz added:

> [T]he CIA distributed a secret memo to all its field offices requesting that they enlist their media assets in efforts to ridicule and attack such critics as irrational supporters of "conspiracy theories." Soon afterward, there suddenly appeared statements in the media making those exact points, with some of the wording, arguments, and patterns of usage closely matching those CIA guidelines. The result was a huge spike in the pejorative use of the phrase, which spread throughout the American media, with the residual impact continuing right down to the present day.[6]

The term soon came to be used to ridicule other charges that the government has given false accounts of events, usually to cover up its own criminality. As deHaven-Smith said, this was "one of the most successful propaganda initiatives of all time."[7]

Because of the success of this propaganda, people who wish to remain respectable, to continue to be taken seriously, and perhaps even to keep their jobs, are strongly motivated not to confess that they find the official account of 9/11 implausible. They may even believe that they should not take the Truth Movement's claims seriously enough to look at its evidence for these claims.

However, it is irrational to ridicule people for believing in conspiracies, because "conspiracy" is one of the major types of crime. Of course, the term "conspiracy theory" is used pejoratively primarily for claims that the US government had carried out secret criminal activity. But there should not even be anything irrational about believing in such conspiracies.

It is well-known that the US government has been guilty of deadly conspiracies, such as the alleged Gulf of Tonkin attack and, more recently, the claims that Iraq was affiliated with al-Qaeda and possessed weapons of mass destruction that Iraq was not allowed to possess. But these are no longer derided as "conspiracy theories," because the evidence has shown that our leaders in the White House did conspire to convince the American people of these lies. If our media were to report that the same White House also lied about the 9/11 attacks, then a claim of the 9/11 Truth Movement—that our own government orchestrated the 9/11 attacks—would go from being a "conspiracy *theory*" to being described as simply one more government conspiracy.

One journalist who does not fear this label is Paul Craig Roberts, who was an associate editor for the *Wall Street Journal* and assistant secretary of the Treasury Department during the Reagan administration. He, in fact, cites with approval the writings of Lance deHaven-Smith on the CIA's successful effort to turn "conspiracy theorist" into an accusation.[8] He then, on the fifteenth anniversary of 9/11, gave a summary of the official story of 9/11 similar to that of John Cobb. Roberts wrote:

> According to the official story, on September 11, 2001, the vaunted National Security State of the World's Only Superpower was defeated by a few young Saudi Arabians armed only with box cutters. The American National Security State proved to be totally helpless and was dealt the greatest humiliation ever inflicted on any country claiming to be a power.
>
> That day no aspect of the National Security State worked. Everything failed.
>
> The US Air Force for the first time in its history could not get interceptor jet fighters into the air.
>
> The National Security Council failed.
>
> All sixteen US intelligence agencies failed, as did those of America's NATO and Israeli allies.
>
> Air Traffic Control failed.
>
> Airport Security failed four times at the same moment on the same day. The probability of such a failure is zero.
>
> If such a thing had actually happened, there would have been demands from the White House, from Congress, and from the media for an investigation. Officials would have been held accountable for their failures. Heads would have rolled.[9]

THE TRUMP CARD

Nevertheless, no matter how ridiculous the official account is, the defenders have a trump card, intended to put to rest any claim that 9/11 was an inside job: *The government would not have done such a heinous things and, besides that, they would not have been smart enough.*

The "not evil enough" part of David Corn's version of this claim was quoted in Chapter 11. Saying that the Bush administration would not have been evil enough to arrange the attacks, he said: "This is as foul as it gets—to kill thousands of Americans, including Pentagon employees."[10] The "not smart enough" part of his claim is even more amusing: "Such a plot—to execute the simultaneous destruction of the two towers, a piece of the Pentagon, and four airplanes and make it appear as if it all was done by another party—is far beyond the skill level of US intelligence." So Corn believed that the US government, with its 16 intelligence agencies and its Pentagon, with its three military branches, including its highly trained air force, could not have pulled off the operation, but al-Qaeda, with a bunch of untrained young men, with little if any pilot training and only knives and box cutters for weapons, could have easily done it.

The "not evil enough" and "not smart enough" claims were also given in Dave Gilson's argument, also quoted in Chapter 11: "George W. Bush and his neocon cronies were [not] either evil or, more important, smart enough to have orchestrated the terrorist attacks on the United States."[11] Evidently, Gilson as well as Corn failed to consider the fact that Cheney, who was essentially the president at the time, *was* both smart enough, having been the secretary of defense, and—as later demonstrated by his lying America into attacking Iraq—evil enough. So even if Corn in 2002 knew of no reason to suppose Cheney to be sufficiently evil, there would be no excuse for believing so now.

THE NEED TO EXAMINE THE EVIDENCE

Once it is seen that the "trump card" does not work, it becomes clear that the question of whether the Bush-Cheney White House and its Rumsfeld-led Pentagon engineered the 9/11 attacks should be answered, not by *a priori* arguments about the goodness of our leaders, but by looking at the empirical evidence. Of course, people have been made afraid to raise questions about the official story for fear of being called "conspiracy theorists."

Relevant to this problem is the second major purpose of Part One: to make clear how disastrous has been the neoconservative drive, led by Cheney, to create a global empire. Given the fact that the current trajectory has been destroying America's democracy, and that it could be headed toward a global holocaust—perhaps even human extinction—large numbers of opinion makers, who knew the official account to be a lie, should recognize that it is now necessary to speak out. If they had not already known this, they should take the time to study the evidence and then, if they find it convincing, speak out—pointing out that the neocon death-trajectory is based on the "big lie" told by the Bush-Cheney White House—the lie that Muslims attacked America on 9/11.

The term "big lie" is based on Adolf Hitler's statement that people "more readily fall victims to the big lie than the small lie." Why? "It would never come into their heads to fabricate colossal untruths, and they would not believe that others could have the impudence to distort the truth so infamously." With regard to 9/11, the big lie has worked on everyone who believes that the Bush-Cheney administration would not have been evil or smart enough to do it.

To call the official account of 9/11 false is to imply that 9/11 was a false-flag attack, in which an attack was organized to appear to be the work of another group. Although many people do not know about false-flag attacks, such attacks are far from uncommon.

- Many historians consider the beginning of World War II to have been the "Mukden Incident," in which the Japanese Army, wanting to make sure that it could continue to exploit Manchuria, destroyed its own railway track near the Chinese military base in Mukden and blamed the Chinese. This incident, which the Chinese call "9/18," was used as a pretext for taking control of Manchuria.[12]

- Shortly after the Nazis took power in 1933, they burned down the Berlin Reichstag and blamed the Communists. The Nazis then used this incident as a pretext to persecute Communists and Social Democrats, shut down left-wing newspapers, and annul civil rights.[13]

- Many US citizens might think that, although Japanese and Germans would do such things, American leaders would not. But that is disproved by Operation Gladio. After WW II, Western European countries wanted to dissuade their citizens from voting for Communists and other leftists. NATO—which is under US control—worked with right-wing organizations, the CIA, and the Pentagon to organize terrorist attacks, then plant evidence to implicate leftists. One example was a massive explosion in the railway station in Bologna, which killed 85 people and wounded another 200.[14]

- Near the end of his tenure, President Eisenhower asked the CIA to come up with a pretext to invade Cuba. The CIA formulated a plan to replace the Castro regime "in such a manner to avoid any appearance of US intervention."[15] Eisenhower approved it before he left office, but because of the Bay of Pigs fiasco, President Kennedy took the responsibility for Cuba away from the CIA and assigned it to the Joint Chiefs of Staff. Their plan, known as Operation Northwoods, described "pretexts which would provide justification for US military intervention in Cuba." One suggestion: "We could blow up a US ship in Guantánamo Bay and blame Cuba."[16]

The hope behind this book is that journalists, politicians, and other people, seeing that the neocon mania for empire has been leading America and the world in general to hell, will realize that concerns about reputation are trivial by comparison, so we may be emboldened to stop the madness by exposing the big lie for what it is.

Commentators such as Robert Parry marvel at the fact that neoconservative projects, especially those in Afghanistan, Iraq, Libya, and Syria, have been disasters, and yet the neocons remained influential, even continuing to drive US foreign policy.[17] It seems like neoconservative policies will not be challenged unless it is publicly revealed that the 9/11 attacks were planned by Cheney, Rumsfeld, and other neocons.

Those who orchestrated the 9/11 attacks are often described as unspeakably evil. For example, Jeffrey Goldberg in the *Atlantic* wrote:

> What we saw on the morning of September 11, 2001 was evil made manifest…The souls of men like Muhammad [sic] Atta and Khalid Sheikh Muhammad and Osama bin Laden are devoid of anything but hate, and murder is what erupted from these voids…With the murderous sociopaths of al Qaeda there is no compromise.[18]

If we, the American people, become aware that the "evil made manifest" on the morning of 9/11 was not that of al-Qaeda but that of Cheney, and his fellow neocons, we should from then on regard neocons with abhorrence.

If we as a people come to realize that the "murderous sociopaths" who organized the 9/11 attacks were American neocons, we should no longer pay any attention to them—except to get clear about what should be avoided.

If we collectively come to realize that the unspeakable evil of 9/11 was planned and carried out for the purpose of advancing the drive toward an all-inclusive empire, we may realize that that drive is inherently evil.

If we see that the goal of creating a global empire could not succeed without bringing about regime change in Russia, we may tell our leaders to give up that attempt, thereby avoiding the threat of nuclear holocaust.

If we realize that 9/11 was, as Goldberg says, a "murderous rampage committed by soulless men," we should commit ourselves to follow only leaders with souls.

Of course, this little sermon presupposes that the official account of 9/11 is false and that the true murderers were Cheney, Rumsfeld, other neocons, and leaders of the Pentagon (we do not know what role Bush played that day).

THE TYPES OF EVIDENCE

There are several types of evidence relevant to showing that the official story is false. In addition to the demonstration that this story involves miracles, here are three more types:

The 9/11 Attacks as Fulfilling Neocon Dreams: A remarkable feature of the 9/11 attacks is that it provided the Bush-Cheney administration the basis for fulfilling several long-held desires that would have otherwise been impossible. Unlike the argument about miracles, this evidence is not conclusive; but it is suggestive. Here is a recap of examples mentioned in Part One of this book to focus attention to this question: Is it plausible to think that all of these fulfillments of desire were just coincidental?

- PNAC's 2000 document, *Rebuilding America's Defenses,* discussed the desirability of a "revolution in military affairs," adding that the needed transformation to actualize it "is likely to be a long one, absent some catastrophic and catalyzing event—like a new Pearl Harbor."[19] "The attacks of 11 September 2001," wrote Australian journalist John Pilger, provided "the 'new Pearl Harbor.'"[20] (But Pilger did not ask, at least in print, whether this was simply a happy coincidence.)

- 9/11 allowed, more generally, the neocon agenda to be put into action. Stephen Sniegoski said that "it was only the traumatic effects of the 9/11 terrorism that enabled the agenda of the neocons to become the policy of the United States of America." According to Halper and Clarke, "it was 9/11 that provided the political context in which the thinking of neo-conservatives could be turned into operational policy"[21]

- The idea of preemptive-preventive war had been advocated by neocons long before 9/11, but afterwards, this doctrine became official policy. "The events of 9/11," observed Bacevich, "provided the tailor-made opportunity to break free of the fetters restricting the exercise of American power."[22]

- The Bush-Cheney administration, wanting the Taliban to create a "unity government" in Afghanistan so that a desired pipeline could be constructed, told the Taliban in July 2001 that if they did not do what the US government demanded, America would bury them "under a carpet of bombs," with the bombing beginning "before the snows started falling in Afghanistan, by the middle of October at the latest."[23] Given the timing of the attacks on New York and the Pentagon, the US was able to begin its invasion on October 7. In 2004, Paul Wolfowitz told the 9/11 Commission that if the Department of Defense had asked Congress for permission to invade Afghanistan prior to 9/11, this request would not have been taken seriously. Likewise, Donald Rumsfeld said that prior to 9/11, the president could not have convinced Congress that the United States needed to "invade Afghanistan and overthrow the Taliban."[24]

- Treasury Secretary Paul O'Neill reported that in the first meeting of the National Security Council, the topic was going after Saddam, with the only issue being "finding a way to do it." Neocon Kenneth Adelman said: "At the beginning of the administration people were talking about Iraq but it wasn't doable. . . . That changed with September 11."[25]

- 9/11 also granted the neocon wish to increase the nation's military power. On the evening of 9/11, Rumsfeld held a news briefing on the Pentagon attack, at which Senator Carl Levin, the chair of the Senate Armed Services Committee, was asked: "Senator Levin, you and other Democrats in Congress have voiced fear that you simply don't have enough money for the large increase in defense that the Pentagon is seeking. . . . Does this sort of thing convince you that an emergency exists in this country to increase defense spending?"[26] Congress immediately appropriated an additional $40 billion for the Pentagon and much more later.

- Although Bernard Lewis and others had, after the end of the Cold War, been leading the transference from Communism as the arch-enemy, said Deepa Kumar, it was felt that something more dramatic was needed to get the American public to support the neocon argument that major interventions were needed in the Muslim world. "What better way to promote this ideology," asked Kumar, "than to create an over-arching enemy, the Muslim 'evildoers' . . . against whom America, the great and the good, should make war?

September 11 provided the neocons with the enemy they needed to promote their vision."[27]

When a crime has been committed by an unknown person or group, the first question is usually: Who benefited? Who had a motive? The Bush-Cheney administration had motives in spades for engineering the 9/11 attacks and, as summarized above, it received large number of benefits. But thus far few journalists have pointed out this fact.

The Overwhelming Consensus of Experts: In most debated questions, people rely on the opinions of scientists and other experts. This is often not true with regard to ideologically-charged issues such as climate change and, of course, 9/11. But to remain rational requires rejecting prejudice in favor of expert opinion. And among independent (non-governmental) professionals who have studied the evidence, the overwhelming majority of them reject the official account as clearly false. These professionals, such as scientists, firefighters, architects, and engineers, have formed organizations. The largest of these organizations is Architects and Engineers for 9/11 Truth, which by mid-2017 had almost 2,900 members.

One might assume, of course, that these architects and engineers are not first-rate people in their fields, but gullible third-rate minds, easily persuaded by absurd conspiracy theories. Being "9/11 truthers," moreover, they may not even be capable of rational thought. For example, in his *Atlantic* essay, Jeffrey Goldberg said that the minds of 9/11 truthers "are warped in such a way as to render impossible the processing of observable reality."[28]

So it may be helpful to list some of the members of Architects and Engineers for 9/11 Truth. Here are some of the *architects:*

- Daniel B. Barnum, an award-winning Fellow of the American Institute of Architects (AIA) and a founder of the Houston AIA Residential Architecture Committee.

- David Paul Helpern, a Fellow of the AIA and the founder of Helpern Architects.

- David A. Johnson, an internationally known architect and city planner, who has chaired the planning departments at Syracuse and Ball State universities and also served as president of the Fulbright Association of the United States.

- Kevin A. Kelly, a fellow of AIA, who wrote *Problem Seeking: An Architectural Programming Primer*, a standard textbook.

- Dr. David Leifer, Coordinator of the Graduate Program in Facilities Management at the University of Sydney.

- Paul Stevenson Oles, a Fellow of the AIA, which in 1989 called him "the dean of architectural illustrators in America."

Here are a few of the *engineers*:

- Dr. John Edward Anderson, Professor Emeritus of Mechanical Engineering at the University of Minnesota, and former Professor of Aerospace and Mechanical Engineering at Boston University.

- Dr. Robert Bowman (deceased), former head of the Department of Aeronautical Engineering at the US Air Force Institute of Technology, and the Director of Advanced Space Programs Development ("Star Wars") under Presidents Ford and Carter.

- Dwain Deets, former Director for Research Engineering and Aerospace Projects at NASA Dryden Flight Research Center, where his work earned him the NASA Exceptional Service Award and inclusion in "Who's Who in Science and Engineering."

- Dr. Joel Hirschhorn, former Professor of Metallurgical Engineering at the University of Wisconsin, Madison, and a former member of the Congressional Office of Technology Assessment's staff.

- Dr. Jack Keller, Professor Emeritus of Engineering at Utah State University, who was named by *Scientific American* in 2004 as one the world's 50 leading contributors to science and technology benefiting society.

Cass Sunstein, rather than calling truthers "warped," much more kindly says that their problem is that they are "exposed only to skewed information."[29] Given that diagnosis, it might be of special interest to consider *Intelligence Officers for 9/11 Truth,* the membership list of which includes:

- Terrell E. Arnold, who served as an analyst in the US State Department's Office of Intelligence and Research, then became the Principal Deputy Director of the State Department's Office of Counterterrorism.

- William Christison (deceased), whose career with the CIA included being the National Intelligence Officer for South Asia, Southeast Asia, and Africa, followed by becoming the Director of the CIA's Office of Regional and Political Analysis.[30]

- Annie Machon, who served MI5 in the Counter-Subversion department, the Irish counter-terrorism section, and international counter-terrorism.[31]

- Captain Eric H. May, who as a US Army Intelligence Officer served as a Russian-fluent expert on the Soviet military and also served as a WMD inspector and interpreter for the Intermediate Nuclear Forces Treaty team.

- Ray McGovern, who as a CIA analyst prepared the *President's Daily Brief* for Presidents Nixon, Ford, and Reagan, and also conducted morning briefings for Vice President Bush.

- Major General Albert Stubblebine, former Commanding General of US Army Intelligence and Security Command. In his final command, he was responsible for all of the Army's strategic intelligence forces around the world, with responsibility for Signals, Photo-, Counter-, and Human-Intelligence.[32]

It appears to be Sunstein who is informationally deprived. In any case, of interest to the charges by Goldberg and Sunstein should be the membership list of *Scientists for 9/11 Truth,* which includes:

- Dr. Timothy E. Eastman, consultant in space physics and plasma sciences for Plasmas International, and Group Manager for Space Science Support at NASA's Goddard Space Flight Center.

- Dr. David L. Griscom, former Research Physicist at the Naval Research Laboratory; principal author of 100 papers in scientific journals; fellow of the American Association for the Advancement of Science; and fellow of the American Physical Society.

- Dr. Niels Harrit, Professor of Chemistry at the University of Copenhagen, with a specialty in nanochemistry.

- Dr. Herbert G. Lebherz, Professor Emeritus of Chemistry and Biochemistry at San Diego State University, where he was the co-founder of its Molecular Biology Institute.

- Dr. Lynn Margulis (deceased), professor of geosciences at the University of Massachusetts-Amherst, who was named a Distinguished University Professor and was given the National Medal of Science in 1999.[33]

Can one really believe that the journalists who write snide articles about "truthers" really believe that they know more about what happened on

9/11 than these architects, engineers, and physical scientists?[34]

The claims made by physical scientists have increasingly been accepted in mainline publications. For example, in 2016 *Europhysics News,* known as "the magazine of the European physics community," published a paper entitled "15 Years Later: On the Physics of High-Rise Building Collapses." The paper concluded: "[T]he evidence points overwhelmingly to the conclusion that all three buildings were destroyed by controlled demolition. In light of the far-reaching implications, it is morally imperative that this hypothesis be the subject of a truly scientific and impartial investigation by responsible authorities."[35]

The 9/11 Consensus Panel: In writing about skeptics regarding the official account of 9/11, newspapers have often not distinguished between 9/11 scholars and other skeptics, who may be uninformed and irrational. Ignoring this distinction has allowed the press to quote some silly statements by non-scholars and say, "This is what 9/11 Truthers believe." To try to reduce this problem, an organization called *Consensus 9/11: The 9/11 Best Evidence Panel,* was formed in 2011. This panel consists of 22 professional members from various fields—aerospace engineering, aviation, chemistry, civil engineering, journalism, law, physics, philosophy, and religion. Aimed at forming a list of well-documented points that contradict the official account of 9/11, the panel uses a well-known medical model for agreeing on consensus.[36] By examining the points included in Consensus 9/11, one can see a wide range of generally accepted "facts" about 9/11 that the panel has determined to be false. For example, the section labeled "Consensus Points about the Political and Military Commands on 9/11" shows that stories told by several top generals in the Pentagon about their actions on the morning of 9/11 were, like Cheney's story, false.

SAVING AMERICA AND THE WORLD

Accordingly, if in this case our society follows expert opinion, as it does on most issues, it will hold, as settled fact, that the official account, provided by Cheney and Zelikow, is entirely false.

On September 11, 2016, William Rivers Pitt, recalling that on 9/11 people in New York City were running for their lives, said:

> We are still running because September 11 never ended. To the contrary, it grew, expanded, metastasized and ultimately subsumed this nation. We are a wildly different place, and a wildly different people than we were fifteen years ago. . . . We accept [demeaning] things after a decade and

a half of taming and training. . . . September 11 gave us the horror and shame of Abu Ghraib as well as the disgrace of Guantánamo Bay. It gave us the concept of the Unitary Executive through which the president wields unlimited power in defiance of constitutional law. The PATRIOT Act exploded the surveillance dam and flooded the nation with watching eyes and ears. . . . Fifteen years later, the pall of poison smoke from that day still hangs low over us all. The great mission for the remainder of this century is plain: We must get out from under the control mechanism September 11 has become.[37]

The argument of this book is that we will not get out from under it unless the Big Lie of 9/11 is publicly exposed.

EPILOGUE

One of the many things that the neocons ruined was the presidency of Barack Obama. In an essay entitled "Barack Obama Was a Foreign-Policy Failure," Steven Walt said: "The 44th president of the United States promised to bring change but mostly drove the country deeper into a ditch." Although Obama won many important victories and would continue to be appreciated for his personal qualities, especially in comparison with his successor, his presidency's foreign policy was a tragedy.

> Obama had the opportunity to refashion America's role in the world, and at times he seemed to want to do just that. The crisis of 2008-2009 was the ideal moment to abandon the failed strategy of liberal hegemony that the United States had been pursuing since the end of the Cold War, but in the end Obama never broke with that familiar but failed approach. The result was a legacy of foreign-policy missteps that helped propel Donald Trump into the White House.[1]

In an essay entitled "Obama Bequeaths a More Dangerous World," Robert Parry gave an even more critical appraisal. Buying into the romantic notion of a "Team of Rivals," said Parry, Obama's choice of "hawkish Sen. Hillary Clinton to be his Secretary of State and Republican apparatchik Robert Gates to remain as Secretary of Defense—along with keeping Bush's high command, including neocon favorite Gen. David Petraeus—guaranteed that he would achieve little real foreign policy change."

Even after Clinton, Gates, and Petraeus were gone in Obama's second term, wrote Parry, "he continued to acquiesce to most of the demands of the neocons and liberal interventionists." Although Obama grumbled about some of the neocon/liberal-hawk policies, "he mostly went along, albeit half-heartedly at times." This approach led to disasters in both Libya and Syria. But perhaps "Obama's most dangerous legacy," opined Parry,

> is the New Cold War with Russia, which began in earnest when Washington's neocons struck back against Moscow for its cooperation with Obama in getting Syria to surrender its chemical weapons (which short-circuited neocon hopes to bomb the Syrian military) and in persuading Iran to accept tight limits on its nuclear program (another obstacle to a neocon bombing plan). The neocon-dominated US mainstream media, of course, portrayed the Ukrainian conflict as a simple case of 'Russian aggression,' and Obama fell in line with this propaganda narrative.

Indeed, "Obama chose to escalate the New Cold War in his final weeks in office by having US intelligence agencies leak unsubstantiated claims that

Putin interfered in the US presidential election."[2]

In a still more critical appraisal, Finian Cunningham wrote that Obama's "farewell to the nation" speech should have been billed as a "farewell to arms," made by "arguably one of the most belligerent presidents to ever have occupied the White House." Indeed, Cunningham said, "Obama's record in office is one of blood-soaked disgrace." For example, Cunningham wrote:

- "Obama expanded on his predecessor George W Bush's criminal foreign interventions. At least seven countries—Iraq, Afghanistan, Pakistan, Libya, Syria, Yemen and Somalia—have been routinely bombed under Obama's watch as the US Commander-in-Chief."

- "Last year [2016] alone, the US military reportedly dropped over 26,000 bombs around the world killing countless thousands of people."

- Drone assassinations "increased 10-fold under his command, killing thousands of innocent civilians as 'collateral damage.'"

- In Yemen, "it is reckoned that a child dies every 10 minutes from the American-supplied bombing campaign and blockade."

- "In Syria, just one of the countries to be afflicted by Obama's policy of covert collusion with jihadist terrorism for regime-change machinations, the death toll is estimated to be around 400,000, with millions more displaced by the US-led proxy war that began in March 2011."

- "In his final year in office, Obama has overseen a massive escalation in US military special operations around the world. These covert forces are now reported to be operating in 138 countries—70% of the world—a military deployment that represents a 130% increase on that under George W. Bush."

- "Relations between the US and Russia have sunk to new dangerous depths—never seen since the former Cold War—led largely by the Obama administration's demonizing of Moscow with a litany of fraudulent charges."

- Obama "tempted all-out war through reckless sanctions and expansion of NATO forces on Russia's borders."[3]

On top of all this, Pratap Chatterjee wrote that, in Obama's final days in office, he seemingly did everything possible to increase the Trump White

House's ability to wreak havoc around the world. Thanks in part to last-minute changes, said Chatterjee,

> When Trump moves in he'll find a formidable national security apparatus at his command, one that in its capabilities has left even the totalitarian regimes of the previous century in the shade. . . . [H]e's leaving a striking (and still expanding) series of oppressive and aggressive powers loaded and ready for action for the new president.[4]

As Stephen Walt said, the presidency of Barack Obama was a tragedy. He could have reversed the disastrous policies of the Bush-Cheney administration, preventing them from further ruining America and the world. Instead, Obama did not bring a single war to an end; he started a new cold war with Russia; he did nothing to reduce Islamophobia; he shredded the US Constitution far beyond what the Bush-Cheney administration had achieved; he allowed and even paid Israel to continue violating UN declarations; he used drone warfare to murder people in various countries; he ruined Libya and Syria. The failure of Obama's presidency was shown most dramatically by the fact that Russia, Syria, Turkey, and Iran did not invite him to the meetings to work out a peace settlement.

NOTES

Preface

1   Joseph Clifford said that after "Trump had been given about 2 billion dollars' worth of free coverage by media outlets," he suddenly "went from media darling, to the devil incarnate"—when he said he did not want a war with Russia but would instead move to "reset" US relations with Russia (Joseph Clifford, "Not Yet Inaugurated; Already a New War," OpEdNews, 14 January 2017).

Introduction

1   Vincent Warren, "The 9/11 Decade and the Decline of US Democracy," Center for Constitutional Rights, 9 September 2011.

2   Peter Van Buren, "How the US Wrecked the Middle East," TomDispatch, 22 October.

3   Tom Engelhardt, "14 Years After 911, the War on Terror Is Accomplishing Everything bin Laden Hoped It Would," *The Nation*, 8 September 2015.

4   Ahad Nil, "9/11 Used to Demonize Muslim World, Justify NSA Spying of US Citizens: Analyst," CNN, 28 February 2015.

5   Paul Craig Roberts, "9/11 after Thirteen Years: Continuous Warfare, Police State, Endless Falsehoods," 11 September 2014.

6   John W. Whitehead, "The Tyranny of 9/11: The Building Blocks of the American Police State from A-Z," Counterpunch, 8 September 2016.

7   Kevin Drum, "Since 9/11, We've Had 4 Wars in the Middle East. They've All Been Disasters," *Mother Jones*, 17 February 2015.

8   Karim Trabonylsi, "9/11 Hurt America, But It Destroyed the Middle East," The New Arab, 11 September 2015.

9   Zack Beauchamp, "Yes, Bush Helped Create ISIS — and Set up the Middle East for a Generation of Chaos," 2 June 2015.

10   Alex Emmons, "Fifteen Years After 9/11, Neverending War," Information Clearing House, 11 September 2016.

11   John Nichols, *Dick: The Man Who Is President* (New Press, 2004), 67.

12   Gary Tennis, "My Name is George, and I'm an Alcoholic," *Salon*, 26 July 2001.

13   Nichols, *Dick*, 166-67.

14   Ibid., 48-56.

15   Ibid., 60-71.

16   Ibid., 90-94.

17   Ibid., 97-100.

18   Ibid., 112-14; Lou Debose and Jack Bernstein, *Vice: Dick Cheney and the Hijacking of the American Presidency* (Random House, 2006), 100-01; see also Scott Peterson, "In War, Some Facts Less Factual," *Christian Science Monitor*, 7 September 2002.

19   Joshua Holland, "The First Iraq War Was also Sold to the Public Based on a Pack of Lies," Moyers and Company, 27 June 2014.

20   Charlie Savage, *Takeover: The Return of the Imperial Presidency and the Subversion of American Democracy* (Little, Brown, 2007), 2.

21   Nichols, *Dick*, 109-10.

22   Ibid., 128.

23   Ibid., 132, 142, 157-58.

24   Ibid., 168.

25   Ibid., 169-72.

26   Terry Gross, "'Angler' Takes Measure of Cheney's Influence," interview with Barton Gellman, NPR, 16 September 2008.

27   Barton Gellman, *Angler: The Cheney Vice Presidency* (Penguin Press, 2008), 23.

28   "Transcript of George W. Bush Remarks at Press Conference with Richard Cheney," Federal News Service, 25 July 2000.

29   Mike Allen, "Cheney's Vanishing Act Sparks Curiosity," *Washington Post*, 13 October 2001.

30   Nichols, *Dick*, 180.

31   Jean Edward Smith, *Bush* (Simon & Schuster, 2016), 174.

32   Nichols, *Dick*, 9.

Chapter 1: The Failure to Prevent 9/11

1   David Edwards, "Jeb Bush Gets Testy at CNN Debate about Brother's Record. 'There's One Thing I Know for Sure, He Kept Us Safe,'" Raw Story, 16 September 2015; Sophia Tesfaye, "Donald Trump Has No Qualms Blaming George W. Bush for 9/11: 'Say What You Want, the World Trade Center Came Down During His Time,'" *Salon*, 16 October 2015.

2   Tesfaye, "Donald Trump Has No Qualms."

3   Tai Kopan, et al., "Facing Backlash, Trump Dodges Questions on 9/11 Comments," CNN, 17 October 2015; Peter J. Ognibene, "No Jeb, President George W. Bush Did Not 'Keep Us Safe,'" Huffington Post, 19 October 2015; Robert Schlesinger, "Unsafe by any Definition: Donald Trump Is Right that George W. Bush Didn't Keep Us Safe, Regardless of Blame for 9/11," *US News & World Report*, 19 October 2015.

4   "Never Forget: The Bush Administration Failed to Prevent the September 11 Terrorist Attacks," Daily Kos, 25 April 2013.

5   "9/11 Chair: Attack Was Preventable," CBS, 17 December 2013.

6   Kurt Eichenwald, "The Deafness before the Storm," *New York Times*, 10 September 2012.

7   Peter Beinart, "Trump Is Right about 9/11," *Atlantic*, 19 October 2015.

8   Chris Whipple, "The Attacks Will Be Spectacular," Politico, 12 November 2015.

9   Ibid.

10   Ibid.

11   Conor Friedersdorf, "George W. Bush Didn't Keep Americans Safe before or after 9/11," *Atlantic,* 26 April 2013.

Chapter 2: The War on Terror and the Afghanistan War

1   "Remarks by the President in Photo Opportunity with the National Security Team," 12 September 2001.

2   "Responsibility to History Is Clear Says Bush," AustralianPolitics.com, 14 September 2001.

3   Manuel Perez-Rivas, "Bush Vows to Rid the World of 'Evil-Doers,'" CNN, 16 September 2001.

4   Jonathan Schell, *The Unconquerable World: Power, Nonviolence, and the Will of the People* (Metropolitan Books, 2003), 325.

5   Bob Woodward, *Bush at War* (Simon & Schuster, 2002), 49, 83-85.

6   Glenn Kessler, "US Decision on Iraq Has Puzzling Past," *Washington Post*, 12 January 2003.

7   "Transcript of President Bush's Address to a Joint Session of Congress on Thursday Night," 20 September 2001.

8   "White House Warns Taliban: 'We Will Defeat You,'" CNN, 21 September 2001; emphasis added.

9   Ibid.

10   David B. Ottaway and Joe Stephens, "Diplomats Met with Taliban on Bin Laden," *Washington Post*, 29 October 2001.

11   "Meet the Press," NBC, 23 September 2001; "Remarks by the President, Secretary of the Treasury O'Neill and Secretary of State Powell on Executive Order," White House, 24 September 2001.

12   Seymour M. Hersh, "What Went Wrong: The C.I.A. and the Failure of American Intelligence," *New Yorker*, 1 October 2001.

13   Office of the Prime Minister, "Responsibility for the Terrorist Atrocities in the United States," BBC News, 4 October 2001; "The Investigation and the Evidence," BBC News, 5 October 2001.

14   "The Vice President Appears on Meet the Press with Tim Russert," White House, 16 September 2001; emphasis added.

15   Tony Harnden, "Bin Laden Is Wanted: Dead or Alive, Says Bush," *Telegraph*, 18 September 2001.

16   "Bush Rejects Taliban Offer to Hand Bin Laden Over," *Guardian*, 14 October 2001.

17   The statements by Fleischer and Rice are quoted in Steve Shalom, "Obama Fudges History," *New Politics*, 2 December 2009.

18   President Barack Obama, "The Way Forward in Afghanistan and Pakistan " (remarks at the US Military Academy at West Point), 1 December 2009 .

19   "UN Security Council Resolution 1368 (2001)," US Department of State, 12 September 2001.

20   Sheryl Gay Stolberg, "Obama Defends Strategy in Afghanistan," *New York Times*, 18 August 2009.

21   "Declining Use of 'War on Terror,'" BBC News, 17 April 2007; Richard Norton-Taylor, "MI5 Former Chief Decries 'War on Terror,'" *Guardian*, 1 September 2011.

22   "Most Wanted Terrorists: Usama bin Laden," Federal Bureau of Investigation.

23   Ed Haas, "FBI says, 'No Hard Evidence Connecting Bin Laden to 9/11,'" Muckraker Report, 6 June 2006.

24   Bruce Lawrence is the editor of *Messages to the World: The Statements of Osama Bin Laden* (London and New York: Verso, 2005). He made these statements during a radio interview conducted by Kevin Barrett of the University of Wisconsin at Madison on 16 February 2007.

25   Ann Jones, "The Forgotten War: 12 Years in Afghanistan Down the Memory Hole," TomDispatch, 1 October 2013

26   Nika Knight, "In Historic First, ICC Preparing to Investigate US War Crimes in Afghanistan," Common Dreams, 1 November 2016.

27   Noam Chomsky, *Pirates and Emperors, Old and New: International Terrorism in the Real World*, revised ed. (South End Press, 2002), 2.

28   George Shultz, "Terrorism in the Modern World," State Department, 25 October 1984; discussed in Chomsky, *Pirates and Emperors*, 119. The idea that 9/11 began "the second age of terror" was also stated by Charles Hill in "A Herculean Task: The Myth and Reality of Arab Terrorism," in *The Age of Terror: America and the World after September 11,* ed. Strobe Talbott and Nayan Chanda (Basic Books, 2002), 81-112.

29   Rémi Brulin, "Israel's Decades-Long Effort to Turn the Word 'Terrorism' into an Ideological Weapon," *Mondoweiss*, 26 August 2014.

30   Mattia Toaldo, "The Reagan Administration and the Origins of the War on Terror: Lebanon and Libya as Case Studies," *New Middle Eastern Studies* 2 (2012).

31   Claire Sterling, *The Terror Network: The Secret War of International Terrorism* (Henry Holt, 1981); quoted by Chomsky, *Pirates and Emperors*, 120.

32   Norman Podhoretz, "Neoconservatism: A Eulogy," *Commentary* 101 (March, 1996).

33   Charles Krauthammer, "Universal Dominion: Toward a Unipolar World," *National Interest*, 18 (Winter 1989): 47-49.

34   Charles Krauthammer, "The Unipolar Moment," *Foreign Affairs* 70, Winter 1990.

35   Department of Defense, "Defense Planning Guidance," 18 February 1992.

36   Andrew J. Bacevich, *American Empire: The Realities and Consequences of US Diplomacy* (Harvard University Press, 2002), 44.

37   *Wall Street Journal*, 16 March 1992.

38   Quoted in Barton Gellman, "Aim of Defense Plan Supported by Bush," *Washington Post*, 12 March 1992.

39   Quoted in Barton Gellman, "Keeping the US First: Pentagon Would Preclude a Rival Superpower," *Washington Post*, 11 March 1992.

40   Gary Dorrien, *Imperial Designs: Neoconservatism and the New Pax Americana* (Routledge, 2004), 142.

41   Nicholas Lemann, "The Next World Order: The Bush Administration May Have a Brand-New Doctrine of Power," *New Yorker*, 1 April 2002.

42   David Armstrong, "Dick Cheney's Song of America," *Harper's*, October 2002.

43   Todd E. Pierce, "'We're All Cheneyites Now,'" *Consortium News*, 1 April 2014; Conor Friedersdorf, "Hillary Clinton Tempts Progressives to Embrace Cheneyism," *Atlantic*, 8 October 2015; Juan Cole, "How Bush-Cheneyism made Mideast in its Image: Wars, WOT, With us or Against Us," *Informed Comment*, 21 March 2016.

44   Bacevich, *American Empire*, 45.

45   Dorrien, *Imperial Designs*, 39.

46   Ibid., 42; "Defense Strategy of the 1990s," Department of Defense, 1992.

47   The fact that Cheney and Rumsfeld were major neoconservatives points to differences between first- and second-generation members of this movement. The first-generation neoconservatives, such as Irving Kristol and Norman Podhoretz, had moved to the right after having been on the left. Kristol, often called "the godfather of neoconservatism," famously defined neoconservatives as liberals who had been "mugged

by reality." No such move, however, has characterized most of the second-generation neocons, who came to dominate the movement in the 1990s. As Gary Dorrien has said, "the new neocons had never been progressives of any kind." Also, whereas this movement was started by Jews, such as Kristol and Podhoretz, more recently, pointed out Dorrien, "a significant number of prominent neocons were not Jews" (Dorrien, *Imperial Designs*, 15-16).

48   "Defense Strategy for the 1990s," Department of Defense, January 1993.

49   Andrew J. Bacevich, *The New American Militarism: How Americans Are Seduced by War* (Oxford University Press, 2005), 81.

50   Robert Kagan, "American Power: A Guide for the Perplexed," *Commentary*, April 1996.

51   "Statement of Principles," Project for the New American Century (PNAC), 3 June 1997.

52   *Rebuilding America's Defenses: Strategy, Forces and Resources for a New Century,* Project for the New American Century: September 2000, 4.

53   Bacevich, *The New American Militarism*, 133.

54   "Joint Vision 2010" (http://www.dtic.mil/jv2010/jvpub.htm).

55   General Howell M. Estes III, USAF, United States Space Command, "Vision for 2020," February 1997 (http://www.fas.org/spp/military/docops/usspac/visbook.pdf).

56   Ibid.

57   *Rebuilding America's Defenses*, 38, 54, 30.

58   Ibid., 51.

59   John Pilger, "Bush Terror Elite Wanted 9/11 to Happen," *New Statesman*, 12 December 2001.

60   *Washington Post*, 27 January 2002.

61   "Secretary Rumsfeld Interview with the New York Times," *New York Times*, 12 October 2001.

62   "Remarks by National Security Adviser Condoleezza Rice on Terrorism and Foreign Policy," 29 April 2002.

63   Lemann, "The Next World Order."

64   Quoted in Jonathan Freedland, "Is America the New Rome?" *Guardian*, 18 September 2002.

65   Robert Kaplan, "Supremacy by Stealth: Ten Rules for Managing the World," *Atlantic Monthly*, July/August 2003.

66   Claes Ryn, "The Ideology of American Empire," in D. L. O'Huallachain and J. Forrest Sharpe, eds., *Neoconned Again: Hypocrisy, Lawlessness, and the Rape of Iraq* (IHS Press, 2005), 63-79, at 65.

67   Stefan Halper and Jonathan Clarke, *America Alone: The Neo-Conservatives and the Global Order* (Cambridge University Press, 2004), 4. Identifying with the Reagan presidency, Halper and Clarke criticized the ideological agenda of the neocons from a "center-right" perspective (5-7).

68   Stephen J. Sniegoski, "Neoconservatives, Israel, and 9/11: The Origins of the US War on Iraq," in O'Huallachain and Sharpe, eds., *Neoconned Again,* 81-109, at 81-82.

69   See the two chapters entitled "The New Great Game" in Ahmed Rashid, *Taliban: Militant Islam, Oil and Fundamentalism in Central Asia* (Yale University Press, 2001), and Steve Coll, *Ghost Wars: The Secret History of the CIA, Afghanistan, and bin Laden, from the Soviet Invasion to September 10, 2001* (Penguin, 2004), 330.

70   Rashid, *Taliban,* 75-79, 163, 175.

71   Quoted in Jean-Charles Brisard and Guillaume Dasquié, *Forbidden Truth: US-Taliban Secret Oil Diplomacy and the Failed Hunt for Bin Laden* (Thunder's Mouth Press/Nation Books, 2002).

72   George Arney, "US 'Planned Attack on Taleban,'" BBC News, 18 September 2001 ("Taleban" is a spelling that has been preferred by British writers).

73   For these statements, see "Day One Transcript: 9/11 Commission Hearing," *Washington Post,* 23 March 2004.

74   *London Times,* 17 July 2002.

75   "President Bush Delivers the State of the Union ," White House, 28 January 2003.

76   Neta C. Crawford, "War-related Death, Injury, and Displacement in Afghanistan and Pakistan 2001-2014," Watson Institute for International Studies, Brown University, 22 May 2015.

77   Marc W. Herold, "The Pentagon's Fantasy Numbers on Afghan Civilian Deaths," Global Research, 18 April 2010; Herold, "US-NATO Killings of Civilians in Afghanistan," Global Research, 13 January 2011.

78   Dr. Gideon Polya, "US Afghanistan Invasion 10th Anniversary: 5.6 Million War-Related Deaths," *Countercurrents,* 10 October, 2011

79   David Jolly, "Afghanistan Had Record Civilian Casualties in 2015, UN Says," *New York Times,* 14 February 2016.

80   James A. Lucas, "America's Nation-Destroying Mission in Afghanistan," AntiWar.com, 6 March 2010; Tom Engelhardt, "We Destroyed Afghanistan: Americans Can't Remember, Afghans Will Never Forget," TomDispatch, 1 October 2013.

81   "Rights and Aspirations of the People of Afghanistan," White House, 8 July 2004.

82   Jones, "The Forgotten War."

83   Ibid.

84   Aunohita Mojumdar, "An Inflated Claim of Health Success in Afghanistan Exposed," *Christian Science Monitor,* 8 December 2008.

85   Jones, "The Forgotten War."

86   "Opium Production in Afghanistan," Wikipedia.

87   "Tomgram: Alfred McCoy, Washington's Twenty-First-Century Opium Wars," TomDispatch, 21 February 2016.

88   Ann Jones, "Afghanistan 'after' the American War: Once More Down the Rabbit Hole," TomDispatch, 5 November 2015.

89   Alfred W. McCoy, "How a Pink Flower Defeated a Superpower: The US Opium War in Afghanistan," TomDispatch, 23 February 2016.

90   Joseph Goldstein and Mujib Mashal, "Taliban Fighters Capture Kunduz City as Afghan Forces Retreat," *New York Times,* 28 September 2015.

91   Jones, "Afghanistan 'after' the American War."

92   Barack Obama, "My Plan for Iraq," *New York Times,* 14 July 2008; Don Gonyea, "Is Obama in an 'Afghan Box'?" NPR, 29 September 2009.

93   Ali Bharib, "Obama Pledged to Stop the Afghanistan War, but Its End Is Nowhere in Sight," *Guardian,* 15 October 2015.

94   Missy Ryan and Thomas Gibbons-Neff, "US Widens War in Afghanistan, Authorizes New Action against Taliban," *Washington Post,* 10 June 2016.

95   Lucas, "America's Nation-Destroying Mission in Afghanistan."

96   "80,000 Pakistanis Killed in US 'War on Terror': Report," *Express Tribune* (Pakistan), 29 March 2015.

97   Catherine Lutz and Neta C. Crawford, "Bad Things Happened: The AfPak War at 12," Huffington Post, 23 January 2014.

Chapter 3: Military Spending, Preemptive War, Regime Change

1   Norman Podhoretz, "The Reagan Road to Détente," *Foreign Affairs* 63 (1984), 452; "The Neo-Conservative Anguish over Reagan's Foreign Policy," *New York Times Magazine,* May 2, 1982; both quoted in Andrew J. Bacevich, *American Empire: The Realities and Consequences of US Diplomacy* (Harvard University Press, 2002), 74.

2   *Rebuilding America's Defenses: Strategy, Forces and Resources for a New Century,* Project for the New American Century: September 2000), 4.

3   Ibid., iv, 6, 50, 51, 59.

4   Dorrien, *Imperial Designs,* 45.

5   Ibid., 44-46; Bacevich, *The New American Militarism,* 152-64, 167-73.

6   "Andrew Marshall," *Source Watch*, Center for Media & Democracy.

7   Department of Defense News Briefing on Pentagon Attack, 11 September 2001.

8   Bacevich, *The New American Militarism*, 173.

9   Ibid., 173.

10   *The National Security Strategy of the United States of America*, September 2002: 29-30 (henceforth *NSS 2002*).

11   Ibid., 28.

12   In using this hyphenated term, I follow the precedent of Catherine Keller in "Omnipotence and Preemption," in David Ray Griffin, John B. Cobb, Jr., Richard Falk, and Catherine Keller, *The American Empire and the Commonwealth of God* (Louisville: Westminster John Knox Press, 2006).

13   Barton Gellman, "Keeping the US First: Pentagon Would Preclude a Rival Superpower," *Washington Post*, 11 March 1992.

14   Richard Perle et al., "A Clean Break: A New Strategy for Securing the Realm," Institute for Advanced Strategic and Political Studies, June 1996.

15   Bacevich, *American Empire*, 44.

16   "Statement of Principles," Project for the New American Century, 1997.

17   PNAC, Letter to President Clinton on Iraq, May 29, 1998.

18   Bacevich, *The New American Militarism*, 91.

19   "President Bush Delivers Graduation Speech at West Point," 1 June 2002.

20   *NSS 2002*, cover letter.

21   *NSS 2002*, 6, 15.

22   Ibid., 15.

23   Halper and Clarke, *America Alone*, 142.

24   Max Boot, "Think Again: Neocons," *Foreign Policy*, January/February 2004: 18.

25   James Mann, *Rise of the Vulcans: The History of Bush's War Cabinet* (New York: Viking, 2004), 316.

26   Ibid., 331.

27   "Statement of Principles," PNAC, 1997.

28   Roy Gutman and John Barry, "Beyond Baghdad: Expanding the Target List," *Newsweek*, 14 August 2002.

29   Wesley Clark reported this conversation in *Winning Modern Wars: Iraq, Terrorism, and the American Empire* (New York: Public Affairs, 2003), 120, 130. He then repeated it in his later book, *A Time to Lead: For Duty,*

Honor and Country (Palgrave Macmillan, 2007), 231. Although in this later book, he mentioned only Iraq, Syria, and Iran, he referred to the other countries during several interviews, including a Democracy Now! Interview on 2 March 2007, "Gen. Wesley Clark Weights Presidential Bid: 'I Think about It Everyday.'" For more details, see Joe Conason, "Seven Countries in Five Years," Salon, 12 October 2007.

30   See Gareth Porter, "Yes, the Pentagon Did Want to Hit Iran," *Asia Times*, 7 May 2008. As Porter reported, Rumsfeld's letter is discussed in Douglas J. Feith, *War and Decision: Inside the Pentagon at the Dawn of the War on Terrorism* (HarperCollins, 2008). Although this book blocked out the names of all the countries on this list except Iraq, Feith said, in response to Porter's question as to which of the other names on Clark's list were included in Rumsfeld's paper: "All of them."

31   Thomas E. Hicks, "Briefing Depicted Saudis as Enemies," *Washington Post*, 6 August 2002; Jack Shafer, "The Larouchie Defector who's Advising the Defense Establishment on Saudi Arabia," Slate, 7 August 2002.

32   Michael A. Ledeen, *The War Against the Terror Masters: Why It Happened. Where We Are Now. How We'll Win* (St. Martin's Griffin, 2003), 159.

Chapter 4: The Iraq War

1   James Mann, *Rise of the Vulcans: The Rise of Bush's War Cabinet* (Viking, 2004), 369.

2   Stephen Sniegoski, "Neoconservatives, Israel, and 9/11," 86-87, citing Arnold Beichman, "How the Divide over Iraq Strategies Began," *Washington Times*, 27 November 2002.

3   Albert Wohlstetter, "Help Iraqi Dissidents Oust Saddam," *Wall Street Journal*, 25 August 1992.

4   Albert Wohlstetter, "Meeting the Threat in the Persian Gulf," *Survey* 25 (Spring 1981): 128-88; discussed in Andrew J. Bacevich, *American Empire: The Realities and Consequences of US Diplomacy* (Harvard University Press, 2002), 191.

5   Arnaud de Borchgrave, "All in the Family," *Washington Times*, 13 September 2004.

6   Paul D. Wolfowitz and Zalmay M. Khalilzad, "Saddam Must Go," *Weekly Standard*, December 1997.

7   William Kristol and Robert Kagan, "Bombing Iraq Isn't Enough," *New York Times*, 30 January 1998; "Prepared Testimony of Paul D. Wolfowitz," House National Security Committee, US Congress, 16 September 1998; Paul Wolfowitz, "Iraqi Rebels with a Cause," *New Republic*, 7 December 1998.

8   "Letter to President Clinton on Iraq," Project for the New American Century [PNAC], 26 January 1998; "Letter to Gingrich and Lott on Iraq," PNAC, 29 May 1998.

9   *Rebuilding America's Defenses: Strategy, Forces and Resources For a New Century* (Project for the New American Century: September 2000), 14.

10   O'Neill is quoted to this effect in Ron Susskind, *The Price of Loyalty: George W. Bush, the White House, and the Education of Paul O'Neill* (Simon & Schuster, 2004). Susskind, whose book also draws on interviews with other officials, said that in its first weeks the Bush administration was discussing the occupation of Iraq and the question of how to divide up its oil; Richard Clarke, *Against All Enemies: Inside America's War on Terror* (Free Press, 2004), 264.

11   Adelman quoted in Elizabeth Drew, "The Neocons in Power," *New York Review of Books*, 50/10 (12 June 2003); Bob Woodward, *Bush at War* (Simon & Schuster, 2002), 83; John Mearsheimer and Stephen Walt, "The Israel Lobby," *London Review of Books*, 23 March 2006.

12   Rumsfeld note reported by CBS News, 4 September 2002; Woodward, *Bush at War*, 48-49.

13   Sniegoski, "Neoconservatives, Israel, and 9/11," 101.

14   Stefan Halper and Jonathan Clarke, *America Alone: The Neo-Conservatives and the Global Order* (Cambridge University Press, 2004), 230.

15   Sniegoski, "Neoconservatives, Israel, and 9/11," 108-09.

16   Ray McGovern, "Proof Bush Fixed the Facts," TomPaine.com, 4 May 2005.

17   Robert Dreyfuss, "A Memo and Two Catechisms," Tom Paine, 23 May 2005.

18   Halper and Clarke, *America Alono*, 203, 209, 210 (see also their seventh chapter, "The False Pretenses").

19   Charles Lewis and Mark Reading-Smith, "The War Card: False Pretenses," Center for Public Integrity, 23 January 2008; updated 30 June 2014.

20   "Vice President Speaks at VFW 103rd National Convention," White House, 26 August 2002; "Rumsfeld Comes Out Jabbing, Has No Regrets for Abu Ghraib, WMDs," Bloomberg News, 4 February 2011.

21   Colin Powell, "Remarks to the UN Security Council," 5 February 2003; Tyler Drumheller is quoted in "War Card: Key false statements," Center for Public Integrity, 23 January 2008; updated 26 June 2015; "Bush: 'All the World Can Rise to This Moment,'" CNN, 6 February 2003.

22   Martin Chulov and Helen Pidd, "Defector Admits to WMD Lies that Triggered Iraq War," *Guardian*, 15 February 2011.

23   John Walcott, "What Donald Rumsfeld Knew We Didn't Know About Iraq," Politico, 24 January 2016.

24   Ibid.

25   Powell, "Remarks to the UN Security Council."

26   Walcott, "What Donald Rumsfeld Knew We Didn't Know About Iraq"; this article discussed this and all the other statements quoted from "Iraq: Status of Iraq WMD."

27   Rumsfeld, press conference, Kuwait City, 11 June 2002; "Bush to UN: We Will Not Wait," CNN, 7 February 2003.

28   Powell, "Remarks to the UN Security Council."

29   "Radio Address by the President to the Nation," White House, 28 September 2002.

30   "Full Text of Tony Blair's Foreword to the Dossier on Iraq," *Guardian*, 24 September 2003.

31   Steve Rendall, "'Sexed Up' After All," Fair, 1 April 2008.

32   Even MasAskill et al., "Kelly's Chilling Words: 'I'll Be Found Dead in the Woods,'" *Guardian*, 23 August 2003; "How Was Dr. Kelly Silenced," The Insider, 21 August 2003; Dr. David Halpin and James Corbett, "Ten Years Ago: The Death of Dr. David Kelly: Murder on the Orders of Her Majesty's Government?" *Global Research*, 13 October 2011. One reason many people doubt the official explanation is that the two paramedics, who were among the first to see the body, said that they did not believe that it was suicide, because there was not nearly enough blood (Antony Barnett, "Kelly Death Paramedics Query Verdict," *Guardian*, 11 December 2004).

33   "Vice President Dick Cheney Speaks with Wolf Blitzer," CNN, 24 March 2002.

34   Thom Shanker, "Rumsfeld Says Iraq Has Chemical Arms Ready," *New York Times*, 11 June 2002.

35   Bush, "Remarks to the UN General Assembly," September 12, 2002.

36   "Remarks by the President on Iraq," White House, 7 October 2002.

37   *Meet the Press*, "Transcript for September 14, 2003: Guest: Dick Cheney, Vice President."

38   Michael R. Gordon and Judith Miller, "US Says Hussein Intensifies Quest for A-Bomb Parts," *New York Times*, 8 September 2002.

39   James Bamford, *A Pretext for War: 9/11, Iraq, and the Abuse of America's Intelligence Agencies* (Doubleday, 2004), 324.

40   Jonathan S. Landay, "CIA Report Reveals Analysts' Split over Extent of Iraqi Nuclear Threat," McClatchy, 4 October 2002.

41   "The 2003 State of the Union Address," White House, 28 January 2003.

42   Craig Unger "The War They Wanted, the Lies They Needed," *Vanity Fair*, 17 October 2006.

43 Bryan Burrough et al., "The Path to War," *Vanity Fair*, 19 December 2008.

44 Bamford, *A Pretext for War*; Seymour Hersh, "Who Lied to Whom?" *New Yorker*, 31 March 2003.

45 Jim VandeHei and Walter Pincus, "Role of Rove, Libby in CIA Leak Case Clearer," *Washington Post*, 2 October 2005.

46 Nick Wing, "Joe Wilson, Husband Of Valerie Plame: Dick Cheney Is A 'Traitor' (VIDEO)," Huffington Post, 25 May 2011.

47 Reported by CBS News, 4 September 2002.

48 "Iraq On the Record: The Bush Administration's Public Statements on Iraq," Prepared for Rep. Henry A. Waxman, United States House of Representatives, 16 March 2004.

49 "Bush: Don't Wait for Mushroom Cloud," CNN, 8 October 2002; *Meet the Press*, 14 September 2003; *Meet the Press*, 14 March 2003.

50 State of the Union Address, 28 January 2003.

51 Secretary of Defense Donald Rumsfeld, Speech to Council on Foreign Relations, 23 January 2003.

52 Murray Waas, "Bush Told No Iraq-9/11 Connection 10 Days after Attack," *National Journal*, 22 November 2005.

53 "The Vice President Appears on NBC's Meet the Press," White House, 9 December 2001.

54 Quoted in John Glasser, "9/11 and Iraq: The War's Greatest Lie," Antiwar.com Blog, 18 March 2013.

55 Bamford, *A Pretext for War*, 370.

56 Powell, "Remarks to the UN General Assembly."

57 Ray McGovern, "What's the Next Step to Stop Torture?" *Consortium News*, 11 December 2014.

58 Ibid.

59 Jonathan S. Landay, "Report: Abusive Tactics Used to Seek Iraq-al Qaida Link," McClatchy, 21 April 2009.

60 McGovern, "What's the Next Step to Stop Torture?"

61 Ron Suskind, *The Way of the World: A Story of Truth and Hope in an Age of Extremism* (Harper 2008), 371.

62 Bob Considine, "Author Claims Bush Knew Iraq Had No WMD," *Today*, 5 August 2008.

63 In a critique of Tenet's *At the Center of the* Storm, Sidney Blumenthal wrote that the book depicts Tenet "as feckless in defending [the men and women of the agency] from the intimidation of Cheney and the neoconservatives" (Blumenthal, "George Tenet, Spook for All Seasons," *Salon*, 3 May 2007).

64 Bryan Burrough et al., "The Path to War," *Vanity Fair*, 19 December 2008.

65 Melvin A. Goodman, "Dividing the CIA in Two," *Consortium News*, 23 December 2014.

66 Bamford, *A Pretext for War*, 379.

67 Walter Pincus and Dana Priest, "Some Iraq Analysts Felt Pressure from Cheney Visits," *Washington Post*, 5 June 2003.

68 Bamford, *A Pretext for War*, 333-34.

69 Quoted in David Swanson, "Pressuring the CIA to Lie, Calling Result an Accident," Let's Try Democracy, 31 December 2005.

70 Bamford, *A Pretext for War*, 384-85.

71 Sidney Blumenthal, "George Tenet, Spook for All Seasons."

72 "US Troops In Iraq: 72% Say End War in 2006," Zogby, 28 February 2006.

73 Halper and Clark, *America Alone*, 218.

74 Quoted in Gustave Gilbert, *Nuremberg Diary* (Farrar, Straus, & Co, 1947), 278. Gilbert was reporting a conversation he had with Hermann Göring on the evening of April 18, 1946, while the Nuremberg trials were going on.

75 Bamford, *A Pretext for War*, 377. (This is on the final page of the first [2004] edition; the 2005 edition has a new afterword.)

76 Ray McGovern, "The Phony 'Bad Intel' Defense on Iraq," *Consortium News*, 15 May 2015.

77 Paul Krugman, "Errors and Lies," *New York Times*, 18 May 2015.

78 Margaret Griffis, "Military Casualties in Iraq: The Human Cost of Occupation," AntiWar, 16 May 2015; Dan Froomkin, "How Many US Soldiers Were Wounded in Iraq? Guess Again," Huffington Post, 29 February 2012; "Iraq Troops' PTSD Rate as High as 35 Percent, Analysis Finds," Science Daily, 15 September 2009.

79 David M. Herszenhorn, *New York Times*, 19 March 2008; "Estimates of War Cost Were Not Close to Ballpark," *New York Times*, 19 March 2013; Daniel Trotta, "Iraq War Costs US More Than $2 Trillion: Study," *Reuters*, 14 March 2013; Hayes Brown, "US Wasted Billions Rebuilding Iraq," Think Progress, 6 March 2013.

80 Juan Cole, "What we Lost: Top Ten Ways the Iraq War Harmed the US," Informed Comment, 18 March 2013.

81 Lt. Gen. T. Michael Moseley, USAF, "Operation Iraqi Freedom—By The Numbers," 30 April 2003; Nafeez Mosaddeq Ahmed, "Western Wars Have Killed Four Million Muslims since 1990," *Voltaire Network*, 11 April 2015; Les Roberts et al., "Mortality before and after the 2003 Invasion of Iraq: Cluster Sample Survey," *The Lancet*, 11 October 2006;

Luke Baker, "Iraq Conflict Has Killed a Million Iraqis: Survey," Reuters, 30 January 2008; Dr. Gideon Polya, "12th Anniversary of Illegal Iraq Invasion—2.7 Million Iraqi Dead From Violence or War-imposed Deprivation," Countercurrents, 23 March 2015.

82   Nicolas J.S. Davies, "10 Years after the Invasion: America Destroyed Iraq but Our War Crimes Remain Unacknowledged and Unpunished," Alternet, 15 March 2013.

83   César Chelala, "Iraq: A Nation Destroyed by American Contempt," Common Dreams, 16 June 2015.

84   Davies, "10 Years after the Invasion."

85   "Consequences of the War and Occupation of Iraq," Global Policy Forum, 2015.

86   Dexter Filkins, "Did George W. Bush Create ISIS?" *New York Times*, 15 May 2015.

87   Juan Cole, "Top 10 Mistakes of Former Iraq PM Nouri al-Maliki (That Ruined His Country)," Informed Comment, 15 August 2014; "Elements of 'Civil War' in Iraq," BBC, 2 February 2007.

88   Jonathan Stein and Tim Dickinson, "Lie by Lie: A Timeline of How We Got Into Iraq," *Mother Jones*, September/October 2006; John Glasser, "9/11 and Iraq: The War's Greatest Lie," Antiwar.com Blog, 18 March 2013; Christopher Scheer et al., *The Five Biggest Lies Bush Told Us About Iraq* (Seven Stories Press, 2003).

89   Robert Scheer, "A Diplomat's Undiplomatic Truth: They Lied," *Salon*, 9 July 2003.

Chapter 5: Islamophobia

1   Peter Gottschalk and Gabriel Greenberg, *Islamophobia: Making Muslims the Enemy* (Rowman & Littlefield, 2008).

2   Andrew Shryock, "Introduction: Islam as an Object of Fear and Affection," in Andrew Shryock, ed., *Islamophobia/Islamophilia: Beyond the Politics of Enemy and Friend* (Indiana University Press, 2010), 9.

3   Stephen Sheehi, *Islamophobia: The Ideological Campaign against Muslims* (Clarity Press, 2011), 149.

4   "Salafi Movement," Wikipedia (accessed 5 July 2016); Bruce Livesey, "The Salafist Movement," Frontline, 5 January 2005; Shiraz Maher, *Salafi-Jihadism: The History of an Idea* (Oxford University Press, 2016)

5   *Islamophobia: A Challenge for Us All* (Commission on British Muslims and Islamophobia, 1997), 4.

6   Tomaž Mastnak, "Western Hostility toward Muslims: A History of the Present," in Shryock, ed., *Islamophobia/Islamophilia*, 33-34.

7   Ibid., 34-35.

8   Ibid., 35-36.

9   Ibid., 39-40.

10   Deepa Kumar, *Islamophobia and the Politics of Empire* (Haymaker Books, 2012), 179.

11   Zachary Lockman, *Contending Visions of the Middle East: The History and Politics of Orientalism* (Cambridge University Press, 2004), 31.

12   Kumar, *Islamophobia and the Politics of Empire*, 30.

13   Ibid., 32.

14   See Edward W. Said, *Orientalism* (Vintage, 1979).

15   Edward W. Said, *Covering Islam: How the Media and the Experts Determine How We See the Rest of the World* (Pantheon, 1980), 28.

16   Kumar, *Islamophobia*, 33.

17   John Feffer, "The Lies of Islamophobia," TomDispatch, 17 December 2010.

18   Sheehi, *Islamophobia*, 39.

19   Ibid., 67.

20   Ibid., 65.

21   Bernard Lewis, "The Roots of Muslim Rage," *Policy*, Summer 2001-2002, 17-26; originally published in 1990 in the *Atlantic Monthly*.

22   Sheehi, *Islamophobia*, 78.

23   Lewis, "The Roots of Muslim Rage," 19, 23.

24   Robert Kagan, "The Benevolent Empire," *Foreign Policy*, Summer 1998: 24-35; Charles Krauthammer, "The Bush Doctrine: ABM, Kyoto, and the New American Unilateralism," *Weekly Standard*, 4 June 2001.

25   Kumar, *Islamophobia and the Politics of Empire*, 177.

26   The Project for the New American Century, *Rebuilding America's Defenses: Strategy, Forces and Resources for a New Century*, September 2000, 51.

27   *Washington Post*, 27 January 2002.

28   Henry Kissinger, "Destroy the Network," *Washington Post*, 11 September 2001.

29   Robert Kagan, "We Must Fight This War," *Washington Post*, 12 September 2001.

30   Gottschalk and Greenberg, *Islamophobia*, 42.

31   Lance Morrow, "The Case for Rage and Retribution," *Time Magazine*, 12 September 2001.

32   Ann Coulter, "This is War," *National Review*, 13 September 2001.

33   Nicholas Lemann, "The Next World Order: The Bush Administration May Have a Brand-New Doctrine of Power," *New Yorker*, 1 April 2002.

34   Deepa Kumar, *Islamophobia and the Politics of Empire* (Haymaker Books, 2012), 135.

35   Ibid., 179.

36   Zbigniew Brzezinski, *The Grand Chessboard* (Basic Books, 1997), 210, 35.

37   Kumar, *Islamophobia*, 114.

38   Arundathi Roy, *An Ordinary Person's Guide to Empire* (South End Press, 2004), 34.

39   Greenberg and Gottschalk, *Islamophobia*, 41-42.

40   Mehdi Hasan, "Why I Miss George W. Bush," *New York Times*, 30 November 2015; Caitlin MacNeal, "Clinton: George W. Bush Was Right That 'We're Not At War With Islam,'" Talking Points Memo, CBS News, 14 November 2015.

41   Glenn Greenwald, "Let's Not Whitewash George W. Bush's Actual, Heinous Record on Muslims in the US," The Intercept, 30 November 2015.

42   John C. O'Day, "Bombs Speak Louder Than Words: The Liberal Reinvention of George W. Bush," 7 January 2016.

43   Sheehi, *Islamophobia*, 54, 79.

44   Ibid., 44-45.

45   Ibid., 69.

46   Sheehi, *Islamophobia*, 67; Michael Hirsh, "Bernard Lewis Revisited," *Washington Monthly*, November 2004.

47   Sheehi, *Islamophobia*, 134.

48   Steve Rose, "Since 9/11, Racism and Islamophobia Remain Intertwined," Huffington Post, 9 December 2013.

49   Ann Coulter, "This is War."

50   "Savage: Arabs Are 'Non-Humans' and 'Racist Fascist Bigots,'" *Media Matters*, 14 May 2004.

51   Ann Coulter, "Future Widows of America: Write Your Congressman," *Jewish World Review*, 28 September 2001.

52   Christopher Hitchens, *God Is Not Great: How Religion Poisons Everything* (Twelve, 2009); Christopher Hitchens, "Images in a Rearview Mirror," *The Nation*, 3 December 2001; Sam Harris, *The End of Faith: Religion, Terror, and the Future of Reason* 2nd ed. (Norton, 2004), 333.

53   Nathan Lean, *The Islamophobia Industry: How the Right Manufactures Fear of Muslims* (Pluto Press, 2012), 3; Christopher Smith, "Anti-Islamic Sentiment and Media Framing during the 9/11 Decade," *Journal of Religion and Society*, 2013.

54   Lean, *The Islamophobia Industry*, 3.

55   Smith, "Anti-Islamic Sentiment and Media Framing."

56   Charles Kurzman, "Anti-Muslim Sentiment Rising in the US: What Is Happening to Religious Tolerance?" *ISLAMiCommentary*, 13 February 2014.

57   Reza Aslan, *No God but God: The Origins, Evolution, and Future of Islam,* Preface to the Updated Edition (Random House, 2011).

58   Abdus Sattar Ghazali, "American Muslims 14 Years after 9/11," Al-Jazeera, CCUN, 14 September 2015.

59   Lean, *The Islamophobia Industry,* 13.

60   Ibid., 10.

61   Max Blumenthal, "Exposing Anti-Islam Author Ayaan Hirsi Ali's Latest Deception," AlterNet, 26 March 2015.

62   Ibid.

63   David Cohen, "Violence Is Inherent in Islam—It Is a Cult of Death"; "Islamic Faith Schools Must Close. Sharia Law Could Happen Here. Multiculturalism Has Failed. Islam Is the New Fascism" (interview of Ayaan Hirsi Ali), *Evening Standard,* 7 February 2007; Ayaan Hirsi Ali, *Infidel* (Simon & Schuster, 2007), 269.

64   Ed Brayton, "Shoebat Admits to Being a 'Proud Fascist,'" Dispatches from the Culture Wars, 8 December 2015.

65   Quoted in Ali et al., "Fear Inc.," 58, 31.

66   Chris Hedges, "Your Taxes Fund Anti-Muslim Hatred," Truthdig, 9 May 2011.

67   Drew Griffin and Kathleen Johnson, "'Ex-terrorist' Rakes in Homeland Security Bucks," CNN, 7 July 2011; Walid Shoebat, *Wikipedia* (accessed April 2016); Jorg Luyken, , "The Palestinian 'Terrorist' Turned Zionist," *Jerusalem Post,* 30 March 2008;

68   Alex Kane, "Anti-Muslim Bigot Walid Shoebat, Brought to You by US Taxpayers," Mondoweiss, 16 May 2011.

69   Ergun and Emir Caner, *Unveiling Islam: An Insider's Look at Muslim Life and Beliefs* (Kregel, 2002).

70   Lean, *The Islamophobia Industry,* 84-90.

71   Quoted in Oliver Willis, "Mark Williams Calls Allah a 'Monkey God': Is He Still Welcome on CNN's Air?" *Media Matters for America,* 18 May 2010.

72   Quoted in Matthew Duss et al., "Fear, Inc. 2.0: The Islamophobia Network's Efforts to Manufacture Hate in America."

73   Newt Gingrich, *Fox & Friends,* Fox News, 16 August 2010.

74   "Howard Dean: NYC Mosque a Real Affront,'" CBS News, 18 August 2010.

75   Sheehi, 31.

76   Robert Spencer, *Islam Unveiled: Disturbing Questions about the World's Fastest-Growing Faith* (Encounter, 2002).

77   Dean Obeidallah, "Muslim-Bashing Can Be Very Lucrative," Daily Beast, 8 May 2015; based on Duss et al. "Fear Inc. 2.0."

78   Scott Shane, "Killings in Norway Spotlight Anti-Muslim Thought in US," *New York Times,* 24 July 2011.

79   Glenn Greenwald, "The Omnipotence of Al Qaeda and Meaninglessness of 'Terrorism,'" *Salon,* 23 July 2011.

80   "Anders Behring Breivik Wants Acquittal or Death Penalty," BBC, 18 April 2012.

81   Robert Marquand, "Norway Attacks: Was Breivik a Christian Terrorist?" *Christian Science Monitor,* 1 August 2011.

82   Andrew Brown, "Anders Breivik is Not Christian but Anti-Islam," *Guardian,* 24 July 2011; "O'Reilly Shreds Media for Calling Norway Terrorist 'Christian,'" *Fox News,* 26 July 2011.

83   Terry Kreppel, "Sorry, O'Reilly: Anders Breivik Is a Christian," *Media Matters,* 27 July 2011; see also Alex Pareene, "Note to Conservatives: Anders Breivik Is a Christian," *Salon,* 26 July 2011.

84   Stephen Prothero, "My Take: Christians Should Denounce Norway's Christian Terrorist," CNN, 26 July 2011; Mark Juergensmeyer, "Is Norway's Suspected Murderer Anders Breivik a Christian Terrorist?" Religion Dispatches, 17 April 2012.

85   Julian Borger and Owen Bowcott, "Radovan Karadžić Sentenced to 40 Years for Srebrenica Genocide," *Guardian,* 24 March 2016; "Bosnian Genocide," History; Marcus Tanner, "Karadžić's 'Holy War,'" *Guardian,* 2 March 2010; Mitja Velikonja, *Religious Separation and Political Intolerance in Bosnia-Herzegovina* (Texas A&M University Press, 2003), 265.

86   See Jack Jenkins, "The Christian Terrorist Movement No One Wants to Talk About," Think Progress, 4 December 2014; Dean Obeidallah, "Yes, There Are Christian Terrorists," *Daily Beast,* 15 February 2015.

87   "The New York Times Presents Islam More Negatively than Cancer and Cocaine, Says New Study," Telesur English, 5 March 2016.

88   Owais Arshad et al., "Are Muslims Collectively Responsible? A Sentiment Analysis of the New York Times," 416LABS, 2015.

89   Efforts to describe Islam as a terrorist religion sometimes go to ridiculous lengths. In a volume by the Air Force Research Laboratory entitled *Countering Violent Extremism,* a self-described former Islamic extremist characterized wearing the hijab—the headscarves worn by Muslim women—as a form of "passive terrorism." The hijab, argued the

author, represents an implicit refusal to "speak against or actively resist terrorism." See Murtaza Hussain, "US Military White Paper Describes Wearing Hijab as 'Passive Terrorism,'" Intercept, 24 February 2016.

90   Jack Balkwill, "Have Millions of Deaths from America's 'War on Terror' Been Concealed?" Counterpunch, 30 June 2015. (The article gives the figure 7.5 million, but part of those deaths were from the sanctions imposed on Iraq in the 1990s.)

91   Scott McConnell, "Trump and the Riot of the Elites," *American Conservative*, 15 December, 2015; on Cruz's statement, see Simon Maloy, "Wait, Ted Cruz Wants to Nuke ISIS?" *Salon*, 11 December 2015.

92   McConnell, "Trump and the Riot."

93   Sofhia Tesfaye, "Thirty Percent of GOP Voters Support Bombing Any Arab-Sounding Nation—Even Fictional Lands," *Salon*, 18 December 2015.

94   Jeffrey L. Thomas, *Scapegoating Islam: Intolerance, Security, and the American Muslim* (Praeger, 2015), 93.

95   Charles Kurzman, "Anti-Muslim Sentiment Rising in the US: What Is Happening to Religious Tolerance?" *ISLAMiCommentary*, 13 February 2014; Libby Nelson, "Why Is Islamophobia Worse Now Than Just After 9/11? A Researcher Explains," Vox.com, 9 December 9, 2015.

96   Penny Edgell et al., "Atheists and Other Cultural Outsiders: Moral Boundaries and the Non-Religious in the United States," *Social Forces*, 17 August 2016.

97   Murtaza Hussain, "Huge Numbers of GOP Voters Favor Trump's Proposal to Ban Muslim Entry to US" Intercept, 2 March 2016.

98   Lydia Tomkiw, "Muslims Rank Lowest for Religious Rights Protection in US, Survey Finds," International Business Times, 30 December 2015.

99   Sheehi, *Islamophobia*, 141.

100   Ibid., 101.

101   Jack Jenkins, "Oklahoma Lawmaker Shares Article Arguing Islam Isn't a Religion, Calls for 'Final Solution,'" Think Progress, 21 June 2016.

102   Bruno Jantti, "Virulent Anti-Muslim Racism in the US Cultural Sphere," Telesur English, 3 May 2015.

103   Lindsay Gibbs, "Man Rips Off Woman's Hijab During Flight, Yells 'This Is America,'" ThinkProgress, 15 May 2016.

104   Linda Sarsour, "A Muslim Woman Was Set on Fire in New York. Now Just Going Out Requires Courage," *Guardian*, 14 September 2016.

105   Sheehi, 136; Kumar, *Islamophobia*, 143, 197.

106   Joshua Stanton, "The Destructive Nature of the Muslim 'Radicalization Hearings,'" *Journal of Inter-Religious Dialogue and Religious Freedom*, 20 February 2011.

107   Joanna Walters et al., "US Airports on Frontline as Donald Trump's Travel Ban Causes Chaos and Protests," *Guardian*, 28 January 2017.

Chapter 6: Global Chaos

1   Andrew Bacevich, *America's War for the Greater Middle East: A Military History* (Random House, 2016), xiv, xxii.

2   Ibid., 28.

3   Ibid., 6, 16.

4   Wesley Clark, *Winning Modern Wars: Iraq, Terrorism, and the American Empire* (New York: Public Affairs, 2003), 120, 130. In this book, Clark had the conversation with the three-star general occurring in 2002, but in his interview with Amy Goodman on Democracy Now! ("General Wesley Clark Tells 'Democracy Now' the Truth About Middle East and War On Iraq!" YouTube, 22 February 2012), he said this event occurred "ten days after 9/11."

5   Douglas J. Feith, *War and Decision: Inside the Pentagon at the Dawn of the War on Terrorism* (New York: HarperCollins, 2008). Although this book blocked out the names on this list except Iraq, Gareth Porter asked Feith which of the other names on Clark's list were included in Rumsfeld's letter to Bush, to which Feith said: "All of them." Gareth Porter, "Yes, the Pentagon Did Want to Hit Iran," *Asia Times*, 7 May 2008.

6   Bacevich, *America's War for the Greater Middle East*, 221.

7   Joe Conason, "Seven Countries in Five Years," *Salon*, 12 October 2007.

8   John Roberts, "Oil and the Iraq War of 2003," International Research Center for Energy and Economic Development," 2003: 19; quoted in Bacevich, *America's War for the Greater Middle East*, 243.

9   Glenn Greenwald, "Wes Clark and the Neocon Dream," *Salon*, 26 November 2011.

10   "'The Crazies Are Back': Bush Sr.'s CIA Briefer Recalls How the First Bush Administration Referred to Wolfowitz, Rumsfeld and Cheney," Democracy Now! 17 September 2003; Martin Bright, "Colin Powell in Four-Letter Neo-Con 'Crazies' Row," *Guardian*, 11 September 2004; Robert Freeman, "Is It Another Vietnam? It Is Already Lost," Common Dreams, 22 October 2006.

11   Karim Trabouylsi, "9/11 Hurt America, But It Destroyed the Middle East," The New Arab, 11 September 2015.

12   David Wurmser, "Coping with Crumbling States: A Western and Israeli Balance of Power Strategy for the Levant," 1996. (Fair Use Article, posted by Scott Horton, 27 January 2014.)

13   Graham Turner, "An American Odyssey," *Telegraph*, 25 April 2003.

14   William O. Beeman, "Who is Michael Ledeen?" Alternet, 7 May 2003.

15   Mahdi Darius Nazemroaya, "Plans for Redrawing the Middle East: The Project for a 'New Middle East,'" Global Research, 18 November 2006.

16   Elise Labott, "US to Restore Relations with Libya," CNN, 15 May 2006; Scott MacLeod, "Why Gaddafi's Now a Good Guy," *Time,* 16 May 2006.

17   Alan J. Kuperman, "Obama's Libya Debacle," *Foreign Affairs,* March/April 2015.

18   Jim Lobe, "US Neo-Cons Urge Libya Intervention," Al Jazeera, 27 February 2011.

19   Robert Parry, "The Neocons Regroup on Libyan War," *Consortium News,* 25 March 2011; "President Obama's Muddled Libya Policy," Editorial, *Washington Post,* 22 March 2011.

20   Robert Parry, "Yes, Hillary Clinton Is a Neocon," *Consortium News,* 16 April 2016; Gabby Morrongiello, "Rand Paul: 'Hillary Clinton Is a Neocon,'" *Washington Examiner,* 6 November 2015); Webster G. Tarpley wrote an article entitled "Hillary Clinton: The International Neocon Warmonger" (Voltaire Network, 13 April 2015); in "Hillary's Neocon Problem," Gerald Sussman called Clinton "a good neocon soldier for American exceptionalism" (Counterpunch, 15 April 2016).

21   Robert Parry, "What Neocons Want from Ukraine Crisis," *Consortium News,* 2 March 2014.

22   Parry, "Neocon Kagan Endorses Hillary Clinton," *Consortium News,* 25 February 2016; Jason Horowitz, "Events in Iraq Open Door for Interventionist Revival, Historian Says," *New York Times,* 15 June 2014.

23   Hillary Rodham Clinton, "Interview With Jake Tapper of ABC's This Week," 27 March 2011.

24   Kuperman, "Obama's Libya Debacle."

25   Charlie Savage, *Power* Wars: *Inside Obama's Post-9/11 Presidency* (Little, Brown, & Co., 2015), 640.

26   Kuperman, "Obama's Libya Debacle"; "Clinton on Qaddafi: 'We Came, We Saw, He Died,'" CBS News, 20 October 2011.

27   Robert Parry, "What Hillary Knew about Libya," *Consortium News,* 12 January 2016; Kuperman, "Obama's Libya Debacle."

28   Kuperman, "Obama's Libya Debacle."

29   Kelly Riddell and Jeffrey Scott Shapiro, "Hillary Clinton's 'WMD' Moment: US Intelligence Saw False Narrative in Libya," *Washington Times,* 29 January 2015; Gareth Porter, "US 'Regime Change' Madness in the Middle East," Middle East Eye, 4 January 2016.

30   Kelly Riddell and Jeffrey Scott Shapiro, "Secret Tapes Undermine Hillary Clinton on Libyan War," *Washington Times,* 28 January 2015.

31   Leon Panetta, *Worthy Fights: A Memoir of Leadership in War and Peace* (Penguin Press, 2014), *354.*

32   Damien McElroy, "CIA 'Running Arms Smuggling Team in Benghazi When Consulate Was Attacked," *Telegraph,* 2 August 2013; "Pulitzer-Prize Winning Reporter Sy Hersh: Benghazi Is a Huge Scandal . . . But Not for the Reason You Think," Washingtons Blog, 15 April 2014.

33   Alex Newman, "Gadhafi's Gold-Money Plan Would Have Devastated Dollar," New American, 11 November 2011; Brad Hoff, "Hillary Emails Reveal True Motive for Libya Intervention," *Foreign Policy Journal,* 6 January 2016.

34   Scott Shane and Joe Becker, "The Libya Gamble, Part 2: A New Libya, With 'Very Little Time Left,'" *New York Times*, 27 February 2016.

35   Ellen Brown, "Exposing the Libyan Agenda: A Closer Look at Hillary's Emails," 13 March 2016.

36   Ralph Nader, "Hillary Clinton Sugarcoating Her Disastrous Record," Huffington Post, 12 February 2015.

37   Robert Parry, "Hillary Clinton's Failed Libya 'Doctrine,'" *Consortium News*, 1 July 2015.

38   Jo Becker and Scott Shane, "Hillary Clinton, 'Smart Power' and a Dictator's Fall," *New York Times*, 27 February 2016.

39   Diana Johnstone, *Queen of Chaos* (CounterPunch Books, 2016), 123.

40   Paolo Sensini, *Sowing Chaos: Libya in the Wake of Humanitarian Intervention* (Clarity Press, 2016).

41   Helene Cooper and Steven Lee Myers, "US Tactics in Libya May be a Model for Other Efforts," *New York Times,* 28 August 2011.

42   Glenn Greenwald, "The US Intervention in Libya Was Such a Smashing Success That a Sequel Is Coming," The Intercept, 27 January 2016.

43   Kuperman, "Obama's Libya Debacle."

44   Dan Kovalik, "Clinton Emails on Libya Expose the Lie of 'Humanitarian Intervention,'" Huffington Post, 22 January 2016.

45   Kuperman, "Obama's Libya Debacle."

46   Greenwald, "The US Intervention in Libya Was Such a Smashing Success."

47   Andrea Germanos, "CIA Chief Just Confirmed 'War on Terror' Has Created a Lot More Terrorists," Common Dreams, 16 June 2016.

48   Ibid.; Kovalik, "Clinton Emails on Libya."

49   Kuperman, "Obama's Libya Debacle."

50   Nafeez Ahmed, "War Crime: NATO Deliberately Destroyed Libya's Water Infrastructure," *Ecologist*, 14 May 2015.

51   Shane and Becker, "The Libya Gamble, Part 2."

52   Kuperman, "Obama's Libya Debacle."

53   Jamie Merrill, "Obama Authorizes 30 Days of Air Strikes on Libya,"
      Middle East Eye, 4 August 2016.

54   Ben Norton, "U.K. Parliament Report Details How NATO's 2011
      War in Libya Was Based on Lies," Salon, 16 September 2016; "British
      Parliament Confirms Libya War Was Based On Lies … Turned
      Nation Into a 'Shit Show' … Spread Terrorism," WashingtonsBlog, 22
      September 2016.

55   Mnar Muhawesh, "Refugee Crisis & Syria War Fueled by Competing
      Gas Pipelines," MintPress News, 9 September 2015.

56   Lydia Depillis et al., "A Visual Guide to 75 Years of Major Refugee Crises
      around the World," *Washington Post*, 21 December 2015.

57   Tyler Durden, "A Short History: The Neocon 'Clean Break' Grand
      Design & the 'Regime Change' Disasters It Has Fostered," Zero Hedge, 1
      July 2015.

58   "Navigating through Turbulence: America and the Middle East in a
      New Century," *Washington Institute for Near East Policy*, 2001.

59   William Kristol, "Lead the World to Victory," Project for the New
      American Century, 20 September 2001.

60   Charles Glass, "Is Syria Next?" *London Review of Books*, 3 July 2003.

61   Robert Parry, "Risking Nuclear War for Al Qaeda?" *Consortium News,*
      18 February 2016.

62   Adrian Salbuchi, "Why the US, UK, EU & Israel Hate Syria," RT, 10
      September, 2013; William Blum, "Why Does the Government of the
      United States Hate Syrian President Bashar Al-Assad," Information
      Clearing House, 4 November 2015.

63   Andrew Cockburn, "The United States Teams Up With Al Qaeda …
      Again," *Harper's*, 18 December 2015.

64   Jonathan Marshall, "The US Hand in the Syrian Mess," *Consortium
      News*, 20 July 2015.

65   Robert Parry, "Democrats Are Now the Aggressive War Party,"
      Consortium News, 11 June 2016.

66   Marshall, "The US Hand in the Syrian Mess."

67   Seymour M. Hersh, "The Redirection," *New Yorker*, 5 March 2007.

68   Robert Naiman, "WikiLeaks Reveals How the US Aggressively Pursued
      Regime Change in Syria, Igniting a Bloodbath," *The WikiLeaks Files: The
      World According to US Empire* (Verso, 2015), Chapter 10.

69   Ibid.

70   Andrew Freedman, "The Worst Drought in 900 Years Helped Spark Syria's
      Civil War," Mashable, 2 March 2016; Elaisha Stokes, "The Drought That

Preceded Syria's Civil War Was Likely the Worst in 900 Years," Vice News, 3 March 2016; Francesco Femia and Caitlin Werrell, "Syria: Climate Change, Drought and Social Unrest," Think Progress, 3 March 2012.

71   James Fallows, "Your Labor Day Syria Reader, Part 2: William Polk," *Atlantic,* 2 September 2013.

72   Femia and Werrell, "Syria."

73   Ibid.; Jan Selby and Mike Hulme, "Is Climate Change Really to Blame for Syria's Civil War?" *Guardian,* 29 November 2015.

74   Femia and Werrell, "Syria."

75   Fallows, "Your Labor Day Syria Reader, Part 2: William Polk."

76   Jonathan Marshall, "Hidden Origins of Syria's Civil War," *Consortium News,* 20 July 2015.

77   Ibid.

78   Ibid.

79   Joshua Landis, "The Armed Gangs Controversy," Syria Comment, 3 August 2011.

80   Ibid.

81   F. William Engdahl, *The Lost Hegemon: Whom the Gods Would Destroy* (mine.Books, 2016).

82   Marshall, "Hidden Origins of Syria's Civil War."

83   Ibid.

84   Engdahl, *The Lost Hegemon,* 261.

85   Marshall, "Hidden Origins of Syria's Civil War."

86   Jim Lobe, "US Brief Talks with Syria Spur Speculation," Inter Press Service, 30 September 2008.

87   Fallows, "Your Labor Day Syria Reader, Part 2: William Polk.

88   Muhawesh, "Refugee Crisis & Syria War Fueled by Competing Gas Pipelines."

89   Robert Parry, "The NYT's Neocon 'Downward Spiral,'" *Consortium News,* 6 October 2016.

90   Muhawesh, "Refugee Crisis & Syria War Fueled by Competing Gas Pipelines."

91   "Guide to the Syrian Rebels," BBC News, 13 December 2013.

92   In June of [2014], wrote Steve MacMillan, "Assad won Syria's Presidential election with 88.7 percent of the vote. . . . A group of international observers emphasized that the election was a valid and democratic expression of the views of the Syrian people." Steve MacMillan, "Bashar al-Assad: The Democratically Elected President of Syria," *Near Eastern Outlook,* 20 December 2015.

93   Seymour M. Hersh, "The Red Line and the Rat Line," *London Review of Books*, April 2014; see also *Frederick Reese*, "Seymour Hersh: Benghazi Attack a Consequence of Weapons 'Rat-Line' to Syria," Mint Press News, 21 April 2014.

94   Ibid.; Aaron Klein, "CIA Ops Finally Revealed: What the US Ambassador in Benghazi was Really Doing," Global Research, 23 October 2015; Gareth Porter, "Why the US Owns the Rise of Islamic State and the Syria Disaster," TruthDig, 8 October 2015.

95   "Defense, State Department Documents Reveal Obama Administration Knew that al Qaeda Terrorists Had Planned Benghazi Attack 10 Days in Advance," Judicial Watch, 18 May 2015.

96   Alex Christoforou, "Julian Assange Says '1,700 Emails in Hillary Clinton's Collection' Proves She Sold Weapons to ISIS in Syria," The Duran/Democracy Now; James Barrett, "WikiLeaks: Hacked Emails Prove Hillary *Armed Jihadists* In Syria—Including ISIS," Daily Wire, 1 August 2016.

97   Eric Schmitt, "C.I.A. Said to Aid in Steering Arms to Syrian Opposition," *New York Times*, 21 June 2012; C.J. Chivers and Eric Schmitt," Arms Airlift to Syria Rebels Expands, With Aid from C.I.A.," *International New York Times,* 24 March 2013; Trevor Timm, "The US Decision to Send Weapons to Syria Repeats a Historical Mistake," *Guardian*, 19 September 2015; Adam Johnson, "Down the Memory Hole: NYT Erases CIA's Efforts to Overthrow Syria's Government," Common Dreams, 21 September 2015.

98   "Military to Military—Seymour M. Hersh on US Intelligence Sharing in the Syrian War," *London Review of Books,* January 2016.

99   Ben Reynolds, "There Are No Moderate Syrian Rebels," Counterpunch, 3 October 2014; Stephen Lendman, "No Moderate Syrian Rebels Exist," Global Research, 6 November 2015.

100   Quoted in Jonathan Marshall, "The US Hand in the Syrian Mess."

101   Ibid.; Parry, "Risking Nuclear War for Al Qaeda?"

102   Gareth Porter, "Obama's 'Moderate' Syrian Deception," *Consortium News*, 16 February 2016.

103   "Nusra Front's Rebranding: Story of Rats Trying to Pass for Fluffy White Rabbits" Sputnik International, 6 August 2016.

104   "Syrian Militants in Tumult after Israel Moves to Restructure Fatah Al-Sham Command in Quneitra," FARS News Agency, 28 September 2016; Alastair Crooke, "How the US Armed-Up Syrian Jihadists," *Consortium News,* September 29, 2016.

105   Mark Landler and Jonathan Weisman, "Obama Delays Syria Strike to Focus on a Russian Plan," *New York Times*, 10 September 2013; Juan Cole, "How Putin Saved Obama, Congress and the European Union

from Further Embarrassing Themselves on Syria," Informed Comment, 10 September 2013.

106   Mark Karlin, "Seymour Hersh on White House Lies about bin Laden's Death, Pakistan and the Syrian Civil War," Truthout, 14 August 2016.

107   Robert Parry, "Will We Miss President Obama?" *Consortium News*, 19 March 2016; Parry, "The Collapsing Syria-Sarin Case," *Consortium News*, 7 April 2014; Seymour M. Hersh, "The Red Line and the Rat Line," *London Review of Books*, April 2014.

108   Robert Parry, "Neocons Have Weathered the Storm," *Consortium News*, 15 March 2014.

109   Mark Landler, "51 US Diplomats Urge Strikes Against Assad in Syria," *New York Times,* 16 June 2015.

110   Veteran Intelligence Professionals for Sanity, "Intel Vets Call 'Dissent Memo' on Syria 'Reckless,'" *Consortium News,* 25 June 2016.

111   Center for Citizen Initiatives, "Seeking a Debate on 'Regime Change' Wars," *Consortium News,* 20 June 2016; Marjorie Cohn, "US Bombing Syrian Troops Would Be Illegal," *Consortium News,* 22 June 2016.

112   Parry, "Risking Nuclear War for Al Qaeda?"

113   Muhawesh, "Refugee Crisis & Syria War Fueled by Competing Gas Pipelines."

114   James Huang, "Who Exclusive: Gen. Wesley Clark on Oil, War and Activism," Who. What. Why., 24 September 2012.

115   Chris Floyd, "Seeing Ghosts: History's Nightmares Return in Syria," Empire Burlesque, 12 January 2016.

116   Dmitry Minin, "The Geopolitics of Gas and the Syrian Crisis," Strategic Cultural Foundation, 31 May 2013.

117   Pepe Escobar, *Empire of Chaos* (Nimble Pluribus, 2014).

118   F. William Engdahl, "The Syrian Pipeline War: How Russia Trumped USA Energy War in the Mideast," Russia Insider, 21 September 2016.

119   See David Ray Griffin, *Unprecedented: Can Civilization Survive the CO₂ Crisis?* (Clarity Press, 2015), 369-72.

120   F. William Engdahl, "Syria, Turkey, Israel and the Greater Middle East Energy War," Global Research, October 11, 2012

121   F. William Engdahl, "Silence of the Lambs-Refugees, EU and Syrian Energy Wars," NEO, 10 November 2016.

122   Pepe Escobar, "Syria: Ultimate Pipelineistan War," Strategic Culture, 7 December 2015.

123   Engdahl, "The Syrian Pipeline War."

124   Minin, "The Geopolitics of Gas and the Syrian Crisis."

125   Engdahl, "The Syrian Pipeline War.".

126   Escobar, "Syria: Ultimate Pipelineistan War."

127   Kathy Gilsinan, "The Pottery Barn Rule: Syria Edition," *Atlantic*, 30
        September 2015.

128   Franklin Lamb, "Don't Cry for Us Syria. . . . The Truth Is We Shall Never
        Leave You!" Counterpunch, 29 July 2016.

129   Parry, "Delusional US 'Group Think' on Syria, Ukraine."

130   Parry, "Democrats Are Now the Aggressive War Party."

131   Andre Damon, "The Media Disinformation Campaign on Russian
        Hacking and the US Debacle in Syria," Global Research, 9 January 2017.

132   Ben Hubbard and David E. Sanger, "Russia, Iran and Turkey Meet for
        Syria Talks, Excluding US," *New York Times*, 20 December 2016.

133   Judy Dempsey, "The Tide of Syrian Refugees Is Unraveling Europe,"
        Newsweek, 25 February 2016.

134   Karen Yourish et al., "Where ISIS Has Directed and Inspired Attacks
        around the World," *International New York Times*, 22 March 2016; "List
        of Terrorist Incidents Linked to ISIL," Wikipedia.

135   Terrence McCoy, "How the Islamic State Evolved in an American
        Prison," *Washington Post,* 4 November 2014.

136   Bobby Ghosh, "ISIS: A Short History," *Atlantic,* 14 August 2014; "Islamic
        State of Iraq and the Levant," *Wikipedia.*

137   Bill Palmer, "Why President Obama's Correct Usage of 'ISIL' vs 'ISIS'
        Drives Ignorant People Crazy," Daily News Bin, 20 December 2015;
        Kathya, "Why Obama Says 'ISIL' instead of 'ISIS' — Conspiracy Theory
        v. Logic," Liberal America, 11 December 2015.

138   Stephen Zunes, "The US and the Rise of ISIS," *National Catholic
        Reporter*, 10 December 2015.

139   Lauren Boyer, "Former US Military Official Says George W. Bush
        Created ISIS," *US News*, 1 December 2015.

140   Andrew Bacevich, "The George W. Bush Refugees," Politico, 18
        September 2015.

141   Andrew Kirell, "4 Most Noteworthy Moments from Obama's Interview
        with Vice News," 16 March 2015.

142   Savage, *Power Wars*, 684-86.

143   Pamela Engel, "The Air War against ISIS Is Costing the US about $11
        Million a Day," *Business Insider,* 19 January 2016.

144   David Swanson, "The US Wants the Islamic State Group to Win in
        Syria," TeleSUR, 29 March 2016.

145   Chris Floyd, "Seeing Ghosts: History's Nightmares Return in Syria,"
        Empire Burlesque, 12 January 2016.

146   Eric Margolis, "US Fight against 'Covert Western Asset' ISIS Is a 'Big
       Charade,'" Ron Paul Institute, 2 October 2015; "'US Has Always Been
       Main Sponsor of Islamic State'—Former CIA Contractor to RT," RT, 29
       September 2016.

147   Anne Barnard, "Audio Reveals What John Kerry Told Syrians Behind
       Closed Doors," *New York Times,* 30 September 2016.

148   Simon Tidsdall, "US Changes Its Tune on Syrian Regime Change as ISIS
       Threat Takes Top Priority," *Guardian,* 25 January 2015.

149   Mike Whitney, "Putin Ups the Ante: Ceasefire Sabotage Triggers Major
       Offensive in Aleppo," Smirking Chimp, 27 September 2016.

150   Vanessa Beeley, "White Helmets Campaign for War *Not* Peace—RLA &
       Nobel Peace Prize Nomination should be Retracted," 2 October 2016;
       Beeley, "The REAL Syria Civil Defence Exposes Fake 'White Helmets'
       as Terrorist-Linked Imposters," 21st Century Wire, 23 September 2016;
       Max Blumenthal, "How the 'White Helmets' Became Global Heroes
       While Pushing for US Military Intervention in Syria," Alternet, 4
       October, 2016; Tim Anderson, *The Dirty War On Syria: Washington,
       Regime Change and Resistance* (Global Research Publishers, 2016), 75.

151   "Syria's White Helmets Are Multi-million Funded, 'Can't Be
       Independent,'" RT, 7 October 2016.

152   "Syrian White Helmets a 'Terrorist Support Group & Western
       Propaganda Tool,'" RT, 25 October 2016.

153   Beeley, "White Helmets Campaign for War *Not* Peace."

154   "'We Don't Hide It': White Helmets Openly Admit Being Funded by
       Western Govts," RT, 19 October 2016.

155   Max Blumenthal, "Inside the Shadowy PR Firm That's Lobbying for
       Regime Change in Syria," Alternet, 3 October 2016.

156   "Syrian White Helmets a 'Terrorist Support Group'"; Sterling, "Seven
       Steps of Highly Effective Manipulators."

157   See "Journalist Eva Bartlett, 'I'm Back from Syria. The Media Is Lying
       to You!'" The Event Chronicle, 13 February 2016; "Liberty Report
       Talks to Vanessa Beeley: 'Everything the US Media Says about Aleppo
       Is Wrong,'" Liberty Report, 29 September 2016. She should not be
       described as an "Assad supporter," Beeley said, because she has various
       criticisms of him. She simply disagrees with the view that Syria should
       be destroyed in order to save it.

158   Stephen Kinzer, "The Media Are Misleading the Public on Syria," *Boston
       Globe,* 18 February 2016.

159   David W. Lesche and James Gelvin, "Assad Has Won in Syria. But Syria
       Hardly Exists," *New York Times,* 11 January 2017.

160 "Audio Evidence: John Kerry Privately Confirms Supporting and Arming Daesh," Voltaire Network, 13 January 2017; referring to "Absolutely Stunning—Leaked Audio of Secretary Kerry Reveals President Obama Intentionally Allowed Rise of ISIS," The Last Refuge (The Conservative Tree House), 1 January 2017.

161 "Why Is EU Struggling with Migrants and Asylum?" BBC, 3 March 2016.

162 Stefan Lehne, "How the Refugee Crisis Will Reshape the EU," Carnegie Europe, 4 February 2016.

163 Natalia Banulescu-Bogdan and Susan Fratzke, "Europe's Migration Crisis in Context: Why Now and What Next?" Migration Policy Institute, 24 September 2015.

164 Stefan Lehne, "How the Refugee Crisis Will Reshape the EU," Carnegie Europe, 4 February 2016.

165 "Mapping Mediterranean Migration," BBC, 15 September 2014; Barbara Tasch, "'The Only Difference': Gaddafi's Ghost Is Hovering over the European Refugee Crisis," Business Insider, 19 October 2015.

166 Esther Yu-Hsi Lee, "The Refugee Crisis Just Hit a New, Grim Milestone," ThinkProgress, 8 June 2016.

167 Banulescu-Bogdan and Fratzke, "Europe's Migration Crisis in Context."

168 Judy Dempsey, "The Tide of Syrian Refugees Is Unraveling Europe," *Newsweek*, 25 February 2016; Liz Alderman, "Aid and Attention Dwindling, Migrant Crisis Intensifies in Greece," *New York Times*, 13 August 2016.

169 Banulescu-Bogdan and Fratzke, "Europe's Migration Crisis in Context."

170 Lehne, "How the Refugee Crisis Will Reshape the EU"; Dempsey, "The Tide of Syrian Refugees Is Unraveling Europe."

171 Lehne, "How the Refugee Crisis Will Reshape the EU"; Dempsey, "The Tide of Syrian Refugees Is Unraveling Europe."

172 Robert Parry, "How Neocons Destabilized Europe," *Consortium News*, 8 September 2015.

173 Imogen Calderwood, "Merkel's Open Door Policy Has Brought 'Chaos' to Europe, Claims George Soros as German Leader is Blamed for Brexit Over Her Failure to Deal with Migrant Crisis," *Daily Mail*, 30 June 2016; Nick Squires, "More Countries Could Follow UK out of the EU, Says German Finance Ministry, as European Leaders Warn Radical Reform Is Needed," *Telegraph*, 25 June 2016.

174 Bill Van Auken, "Who Is Responsible for the Refugee Crisis in Europe?" World Socialist Web Site, 4 September 2015; referring to "A Refugee Crisis of Historic Scope," *Washington Post*, 29 August 2015; "Europe

Must Reform Its Deadly Asylum Policies," *New York Times*, 31 August 2015.

175   Philip Giraldi, "A Refugee Crisis Made in America," *American Conservative*, 9 September 2015.

176   Andrew Bacevich, "The George W. Bush Refugees," *Politico*, September 2015.

177   "The Nakba, 65 Years of Dispossession and Apartheid," Institute for Middle East Understanding, 8 May 2013; "Palestinian Refugees and the Right or Return," American Friends Service Committee.

178   Patrick Goodenough, "At UN, Israel Blamed for Spread of Terror Across the Region," CNSNews.com, 24 November 2015.

179   Edward Said, *The Progressive*, 30 May 1996.

180   If Americans Knew: What Every American Needs to Know about Israel/Palestine (website).

181   Francis A. Boyle, "The International Laws of Belligerent Occupation" (a segment of Boyle's *Palestine, Palestinians and International Law* [Clarity Press, 2011]).

182   Richard Falk, "December 2013 Report to UN Human Rights Council on Occupied Palestine."

183   John Mearsheimer and Stephen Walt, "The Israel Lobby," *London Review of Books*, 23 March 2006. A slightly revised version was later published as a book, *The Israel Lobby and US Foreign Policy* (Farrar, Straus and Giroux, 2007). As shown by the title of Mearsheimer and Walt's study, their major focus is on how the Israel Lobby has been effective in persuading the US government to give so much to Israel for so little in return.

184   Ibid.

185   Ibid., discussed more fully in Emad Mekay, "Iraq War Invaded 'to Protect Israel'—US Official," *Asia Times*, 31 March 2004.

186   "Although the Wikileaks transcript dates the email as December 31, 2000, this is an error on their part, as the contents of the email," explained the *New Observer* ("Hillary Clinton: Destroy Syria for Israel: 'The Best Way to Help Israel,'" 20 March 2016), "show that the email was in fact sent on December 31, 2012."

187   Jason Ditz, "Clinton Email Shows US Sought Syria Regime Change for Israel's Sake," AntiWar.com, 21 March 2016. At the end of his story, Ditz wrote: "Correction: A previous version of this story falsely attributed the authorship of the paper to then-Secretary Clinton, because the email was an attachment sent by her to a State Department employee. The original author, however, appears to be James Rubin, and Clinton was forwarding the attachment."

188   Ditz, "Clinton Email Shows US Sought Syria Regime Change for Israel's Sake."

189   Ibid.

190   Ibid.

191   Alison Weir, "US Ambassador: Support for Israel Drives All US Policies," *AntiWar.com*, 14 September 2011.

192   "Israel 'Deeply Appreciates' US Veto on UN Resolution Condemning Settlements," *Haaretz*, 19 February 2011.

193   Lara Friedman, "Israel's Unsung Protector: Obama," *New York Times*, 10 April 2016.

194   Boyle, "The International Laws of Belligerent Occupation."

195   Ibid.

196   Ben Ehrenreich, "How Israel Is Inciting Palestinian Violence," Politico, 14 June 2016.

197   If Americans Knew: What Every American Needs to Know about Israel/ Palestine: Statistics.

198   Jeremy Bender, "The 11 Most Powerful Militaries in the World," Business Insider, 23 April 2014; Military Equipment of Israel, Wikipedia.

199   Ann Talbot, "US Backs Ethiopia's Invasion of Somalia," World Socialist Web Site, 28 December 2006; Christian Albin-Lackey, "The US Role in Somalia's Calamity," Huffington Post, 29 December 2008; Julie Hollar, "Rediscovering Somalia," FAIR, 1 March 2008.

200   Bacevich, "The George W. Bush Refugees."

201   Juan Cole, "US-Iran War Averted by Agreement to Negotiate on Nuclear Enrichment," Informed Comment, 24 November 2013.

202   Ray McGovern, "Preempting Cheney," Tom Paine, 3 August 2005; Gareth Porter, "Yes, the Pentagon Did Want to Hit Iran," *Asia Times*, 7 May 2008; Seymour M. Hersh, "Preparing the Battlefield," *New Yorker*, 7 July 2008; Savage, *Power Wars*, 631.

203   Mark Mazzetti, "US Says Iran Ended Atomic Arms Work," *New York Times*, 3 December 2007.

204   H. A. Feiveson, "The Iran Deal Explained," Truthout, 13 August 2015; Ken Walsh, "Obama: Iran Deal Beats Another Mideast War," *US News & World Report*, 15 July 2015. William Boardman, "Dick Cheney Calls for War on Iran," Reader Supported News, 29 October 2013; "Dick Cheney's Biggest Regret: Not Invading Iraq and Iran at Once," *Salon*, 5 July 2014.

Chapter 7: Drone Warfare and International Law

1   *NSS 2002*, cover letter.

2   Stefan Halper and Jonathan Clarke, *America Alone: The Neo-Conservatives and the Global Order* (Cambridge University Press, 2005), 142.

3   Medea Benjamin, *Drone Warfare: Killing by Remote Control*, updated edition (Verso: 2013), 60-61, 16.

4   Chris Woods, "The Story of America's Very First Drone Strike," *Atlantic*, 30 May 2015.

5   Mark Mazzetti, *The Way of the Knife: The CIA, a Secret Army, and a War at the Ends of the* Earth (Penguin, 2014).

6   Benjamin, *Drone Warfare*, 128; "The Way of the Knife: NYT's Mark Mazzetti on the CIA's Post-9/11 Move from Spying to Assassinations," Democracy Now! 10 April 2013.

7   Seymour Hersh, "Point of No Return: Obama's Legacy in the Middle East," *Harper's Magazine*, 7 May 2016.

8   Quoted in Jeremy Scahill, "The Drone Papers: Article No. 4," 15 October 2015.

9   Peter Van Buren, "Film Review: *National Bird* Looks Deeply in the Drone War's Abyss," AntiWar.com, 6 May 2016.

10   Charlie Savage, *Power Wars: Inside Obama's Post-9/11 Presidency* (New York: Little, Brown, & Co.), 272.

11   Mark T. Harris, "Drones and the Imperial Mindset," 17 January 2016.

12   Jeremy Scahill, "The Assassination Complex," Drone Papers No. 1, 15 October 2015.

13   Medea Benjamin, *Drone Warfare*, 129 (citing Jane Mayer, "The Predator War," *New Yorker*, 26 February 2009).

14   Adam Levine, "Obama Admits to Pakistan Drone Strikes," *CNN*, 30 January 2012.

15   Margaret Sullivan, "'Targeted Killing,' 'Detainee' and 'Torture': Why Language Choice Matters," Public Editor, *New York Times*, 12 April 2013.

16   "Assassination," *The Free Dictionary*.

17   "Dozens Arrested in US Anti-Drone Protest," *Democracy Now!* 25 April 2011.

18   Eugene Robinson, "Do We Still Think Drones Are a Good Idea?" *Washington Post*, 23 April 2015.

19   Sullivan, "'Targeted Killing,' 'Detainee' and 'Torture.'"

20   Ann Wright, "Army Chaplain Resigns over Drone Wars," *Consortium News*, 12 May 2016.

21   Abraham D. Sofaer, "Responses to Terrorism/Targeted Killing Is a Necessary Option," *San Francisco Chronicle*, 26 March 2004.

22   Rebecca Gordon, "How Extrajudicial Executions Became 'War' Policy in Washington," TomDispatch, 18 July 2016.

23   Ibid.

24   "Murder Is Washington's Foreign Policy," Paul Craig Roberts (blog), 4 March 2016.

25   Gordon, "How Extrajudicial Executions Became 'War' Policy.'"

26   Harold Hongju Koh, "The Obama Administration and International Law," US Department of State, 25 March 2010.

27   Hunter Miller, "British-American Diplomacy: The Caroline Case," Yale Law School, Avalon Project, 2008.

28   Savage, *Power Wars*, 275.

29   Ibid., 237.

30   William Boardman, "A Country at War with an Illusion," Information Clearing House,   19 August 2013.

31   Savage, *Power Wars*, 685-87.

32   Ibid., 276-79; Glenn Greenwald, "Nobody Knows the Identity of the 150 People Killed by US in Somalia, but Most Are Certain They Deserved It," Intercept, 8 March 2016.

33   Charlie Savage et al., "Obama Expands War With Al Qaeda to Include Shabab in Somalia," *New York Times*, 27 November 2016.

34   Sarah Lazare, "Obama Has Relied on the Flimsiest Rationale for Launching Attacks on Countries Across the Planet," AlterNet, 3 August, 2016.

35   Bill Quigley, "Five Reasons Drone Assassinations Are Illegal," Counterpunch, 15 May 2012.

36   Mary Ellen O'Connell, "Flying Blind: US Combat Drones Operate Outside International Law," *America: The National Catholic Review*, 15 March 2010.

37   "US President George W. Bush Addresses the Corps of Cadets," The Citadel Newsroom, 12 December 2001.

38   Scott Shane, "US Said to Target Rescuers at Drone Strike Sites," *New York Times*, 5 February 2012.

39   Charlie Savage, "Top US Security Official Says 'Rigorous Standards' Are Used for Drone Strikes," *New York Times*, 30 April 2012.

40   Michael V. Hayden, "To Keep America Safe, Embrace Drone Warfare," *New York Times*, 19 February 2016.

41   Chris Woods, "Drone Campaign: Unsuspecting Victims of a 'Precise' Warfare," *Express Tribune* (Pakistan), 12 August 2015 (excerpted from *Sudden Justice: America's Secret Drone Wars* [Oxford University Press, 2015]).

42   Daniel Klaidman, "Drones: The Silent Killers," *Newsweek*, 28 May 2012 (an excerpt from *Kill or Capture: The War on Terror and the Soul of the Obama Presidency* [Houghton Mifflin Harcourt, 2012]).

43   Spencer Ackerman, "Obama's First Drone Strike: 'I am the Living Example of What Drones Are,'" *Guardian*, 23 January 2016.

44   Jack Serle, "More than 2,400 Dead as Obama's Drone Campaign Marks Five Years," Bureau of Investigative Journalism, 23 January 2014.

45   Klaidman, "Drones: The Silent Killers."

46   "Hillary Clinton Interview: Edward Snowden, ISIS, Drone Strikes & Women's Rights," *Guardian*, 4 July 2014.

47   Deirdre Fulton, "UN Condemns US Drone Strike in Afghanistan that Killed 15 Civilians," Common Dreams, 30 September.

48   Jo Becker and Scott Shane, "Secret 'Kill List' Proves a Test of Obama's Principles and Will," *New York Times*, 29 May 2012; "Kill List Exposed: Leaked Obama Memo Shows Assassination of US Citizens Has No Geographic Limit," *Democracy Now!* 5 February 2013. (Savage pointed out that the description of the kill list process provided by the media was somewhat oversimplified; *Power Wars*, 283).

49   Jeremy Scahill, "The Assassination Complex," Drone Papers No. 1, 15 October 2015.

50   Ibid.

51   Josh Begley, "A Visual Glossary: Decoding the Language of Covert Warfare," Article 2 of the Drone Papers, 15 October 2015; Becker and Shane, "Secret 'Kill List' Proves a Test of Obama's Principles and Will."

52   Benjamin Wallace-Wells, "The Drama of the Drone Papers," *New York Magazine*, 19 October 2015.

53   John Hanrahan, "Why NYT Dissed the 'Drone Papers,'" *Consortium News*, 4 November 2015.

54   "As Delivered: Obama's Speech on Terrorism," *Wall Street Journal*, 23 May 2013.

55   Spencer Ackerman, "Fewer Deaths from Drone Strikes in 2013 after Obama Policy Change," *Guardian*, 31 December 3013.

56   Jack Searle et al., "US Airstrikes in Afghanistan Killing Civilians at Greatest Rate for Seven Years, New Figures Show," Bureau of Investigative Journalism, 18 February 2016.

57   Tom Vanden Brook, "New Rules Allow More Civilian Casualties in Air War against ISIL," *USA Today*, 19 April 2016.

58   "Medea Benjamin: If Americans Can Sue Saudis Over 9/11, Drone Victims Should Be Able to Sue the US," Democracy Now, 30 September, 2016.

59   Danya Greenfield, "The Case against Drone Strikes on People Who Only 'Act' Like Terrorists," *Atlantic*, 19 August 2013.

60   Klaidman, "Drones: The Silent Killers."

61   Tabassum Zakaria and Mark Hosenball, "US Drone Guidelines Could Reduce 'Signature Strikes,'" *Reuters*, 24 May 2013.

62   "Turning a Wedding into a Funeral: US Drone Strike in Yemen Killed as Many as 12 Civilians," Democracy Now! 21 February 2014; Tom Engelhardt, "Bride and Boom! We're Number One . . . in Obliterating Wedding Parties," 20 December 2013.

63   Arianna Huffington, "'Signature Strikes' and the President's Empty Rhetoric on Drones," Huffpost Politics, 10 July 2013.

64   Dan de Luce and Paul McCleary, "Obama's Most Dangerous Drone Tactic Is Here to Stay," *Foreign Policy*, 5 April 2016.

65   Savage, *Power Wars*, 257.

66   Bill Van Auken, "Obama's Drone Order: Institutionalizing a State Murder Operation," World Socialist Web Site, 2 July 2016.

67   John O. Brennan, "Strengthening Our Security by Adhering to Our Values and Laws," White House, 16 September 2011.

68   "As Delivered: Obama's Speech on Terrorism."

69   "US Policy Standards and Procedures for the Use of Force in Counterterrorism Operations Outside the United States and Areas of Active Hostilities," White House, 23 May 2013.

70   Daniel Klaidman, *Kill or Capture: The War on Terror and the Soul of the Obama Presidency* (Houghton Mifflin Harcourt, 2012).

71   Micah Zenko, "Why Did the CIA Stop Torturing and Start Killing?" *Foreign Policy*, 7 April 2013.

72   Joshua Keating, "Obama Says He'd Rather Capture Terrorists Than Kill Them. Then Why Doesn't He Do That?" *Slate*, 15 April 2015.

73   Micah Zenko, "Kill/Capture," *Foreign Policy*, 14 April 2015.

74   John Brennan, "The Efficacy and Ethics of US Counterterrorism Strategy," Wilson Center, 30 April 2012.

75   Abigail Hauslohner, "In Yemen, Questions and Anger over US Drone Targets after Civilian Deaths," *Washington Post*, 8 February 2014.

76   Scahill, "The Assassination Complex."

77   "'Between a Drone and Al-Qaeda': The Civilian Cost of US Targeted Killings in Yemen," *Human Rights Watch*, 21 October 2013.

78   Jeremy Scahill, "The Assassination Complex."

79   Zenko, "Why Did the CIA Stop Torturing and Start Killing?"

80   "The Way of the Knife: NYT's Mark Mazzetti on the CIA's Post-9/11 Move."

81   Michael Isikoff, "Justice Department Memo Reveals Legal Case for Drone Strikes on Americans," *NBC News*, 4 February 2013; James

Downie, "Obama's Drone War Is a Shameful Part of His Legacy," *Washington Post*, 5 May 2016.

82   Jameel Jaffer, "The Justice Department's White Paper on Targeted Killing," ACLU, 4 February 2013; Conor Friedersdorf, "A Ray of Sunlight on Obama's Extrajudicial Killings," *Atlantic*, 24 June 2014;

83   William Saletan, "Editors for Predators," *Slate*, 8 February 2013 (the quotation is from Brennan, "Strengthening our Security by Adhering to our Values and Laws").

84   Savage, *Power Wars*, 246.

85   Gordon, "How Extrajudicial Executions Became 'War' Policy."

86   Marjorie Cohn, "Numbers in Obama's Drone Deaths Report Just Don't Add Up," TruthDig, 5 July 2016.

87   "'Counterproductive' US Drone Program "Terrorizes" Pakistan," Common Dreams, 25 September 2012.

88   "Pakistani Public Opinion Ever More Critical of US: 74% Call America an Enemy," Pew Research Center, 27 June 2012.

89   Avi Zenilman, "Jane Mayer on Predator Drones and Pakistan," *New Yorker*, 20 October 2009.

90   "Retired US General: Drones Cause More Damage than Good," *AlJazeera*, 16 July 2015.

91   Scahill, "The Assassination Complex."

92   Conor Friedersdorf, "'Every Person Is Afraid of the Drones': The Strikes' Effect on Life in Pakistan," *Atlantic*, 25 September 2012.

93   Vivian Salama, "Death from Above: How American Drone Strikes Are Devastating Yemen," *Rolling Stone*, 14 April 2014.

94   Ibid.

95   "'Counterproductive' US Drone Program 'Terrorizes' Pakistan," Common Dreams, 25 September 2012.

96   "Pakistan: US Drone Killed My Friend, Now 'I Simply Hate America'—Drone Victim," *Voice of America*, 28 April 2014.

97   Hinsa Shamsi, "Obama Apologized for the Drone Killings of Two Western Victims. What About Everyone Else?" ACLU, 13 May 2015.

98   David Kilcullen and Andrew McDonald Exum, "Death from Above, Outrage Down Below," *International New York Times*, 16 May 2009.

99   Tom Engelhardt, "The Superpower Conundrum: The Rise and Fall of Just About Everything," TomDispatch, 2 July 2015.

100   Mattea Kramer, "The Grief of Others and the Boasts of Candidates," TomDispatch, 3 March 2016; Harris, "Drones and the Imperial Mindset."

101   Pratap Chatterjee, "Inside the Devastation of America's Drone Wars," TomDispatch, 21 April 2016.

102   Heather Linebaugh, "I Worked on the US Drone Program. The Public Should Know What Really Goes On," *Guardian*, 29 December 2013.

103   Pratap Chatterjee, "Drone Pilots Quitting Due to PTSD," TomDispatch, 6 March 2015.

104   Jeremy Scahill, "US Has Become 'Nation of Assassins,'" Common Dreams, 30 April 2012.

105   Ken Dilanian and Emily Swanson, "AP Poll: Most Democrats and Republicans Support Drone Strikes against Terrorists Overseas," Associated Press, 1 May 2015.

106   Chris Floyd, "The NYT's Love Letter to Death Squads," Counterpunch, 29 May 2012.

107   Ann Wright, "Army Chaplain Resigns over Drone Wars," *Consortium News*, 12 May 2016.

108   James Downie, "Obama's Drone War Is a Shameful Part of His Legacy," *Washington Post*, 5 May 2016.

109   Charles Krauthammer, "In Defense of Obama's Drone War," *Washington Post*, 14 February 2013; Eugene Robinson, "President Obama's Immoral Drone War," *Washington Post*, 2 December 2013.

110   Charlie Savage and Scott Shane, "US Reveals Death Toll from Airstrikes Outside War Zones," *New York Times*, 1 July 2016.

111   Marjorie Cohn, "US Targeted Killing Rules Conflate Legality and Politics," Truthout, 15 August 2016.

112   Paul Craig Roberts, "Murder Is Washington's Foreign Policy," 4 March 2016.

113   Amy Goodman, "Jeremy Scahill and Glenn Greenwald Probe Secret US Drone Wars in New Book," 3 May 2016.

114   Bill Van Auken, "Obama's Drone Order: Institutionalizing a State Murder Operation," World Socialist Web Site, 2 July 2016; Patrick Martin, "Obama's Drone-Missile Machinery of Murder," World Socialist Web Site, 8 August 2016.

115   "UN Human Rights Expert Questions Targeted Killings and Use of Lethal Force," UN News Centre, 20 October 2011.

116   Dan Falcone and Saul Isaacson, "Noam Chomsky: Obama's Drone Wars Are the Worst Terror Campaigns on the Planet," CounterPunch, 4 June 2016.

117   Nick Turse, "US Military is Building a $100 Million Drone Base," Intercept, 29 September 2016.

Chapter 8: Shredding the Constitution

1   Paul Craig Roberts, "Does the United States Still Exist?" Paul Craig Roberts Website, 26 March 2016.

2   Peter Van Buren, "Shredding the Fourth Amendment in Post-Constitutional America," TomDispatch, 26 June 2014.

3   Jonathan Turley, "10 Reasons the US Is No Longer the Land of the Free," Jonathan Turley (Blog), 15 January 2012.

4   Vincent Warren, "How 9/11 Began the Decline in Our Democracy," CNN, 7 September 2012; Vincent Warren, "The 9/11 Decade and the Decline of US Democracy," Center for Constitutional Rights, 9 September 2011.

5   John V. Whitbeck, "'Terrorism': The Word Itself is Dangerous," *Daily Star* (Lebanon), 7 December 2001.

6   Paul Craig Roberts, "9/11 After Thirteen Years: Continuous Warfare, Police State, Endless Falsehoods," Paul Craig Roberts Website, 11 September 2014.

7   Louis Fisher, "Invoking Inherent Powers: A Primer," *Presidential Studies Quarterly*, March 2007.

8   "Inherent Powers," Lectric Law Dictionary.

9   Louis Fisher, "The Unitary Executive and Inherent Executive Power," *Journal of Constitutional Law*, February 2010.

10   Charlie Savage, "Hail to the Chief: Cheney's Quest to Expand Presidential Powers," *Boston Globe*, 26 November 2006.

11   Barton Gellman, *Angler: The Cheney Vice-Presidency* (Penguin, 2008), 135.

12   Ibid., 137.

13   Ibid., 136; Cass R. Sunstein, "The 9/11 Constitution" (review of John Yoo, *The Powers of War and Peace: The Constitution and Foreign Affairs After 9/11*), New Republic, 15 January 2006.

14   Fisher, "The Unitary Executive and Inherent Executive Power."

15   Bruce Fein and Louis Fisher, "Institutional Powers of Congress," Constitution Project, 3 November 2014.

16   Fisher, "The Unitary Executive and Inherent Executive Power."

17   "Nondelegation Doctrine," Wikipedia (accessed 8 July 2016).

18   Sean Wilentz, "Mr. Cheney's Minority Report," New York Times, 9 July 2007.

19   Savage, "Hail to the Chief."

20   John W. Dean, "How the War on Terrorism Is Shrinking Congressional Powers: Part One," 11 October 2002.

21   John Yoo, "The President's Constitutional Authority to Conduct Military Operations against Terrorist and Nations Supporting Them," 25 September 2001.

22   "Separation of Powers," Constitution USA with Peter Sagal, PBS.

23   Fisher, "Invoking Inherent Powers: A Primer."

24   Harold Hongju Koh, "Repairing Our Human Rights Reputation," *Yale Law School*, 1 January 2009.

25   Renee Dopplick, "ASIL Keynote Highlight: US Legal Adviser Harold Koh Asserts Drone Warfare Is Lawful Self-Defense under International Law," Inside Justice.com, 26 March 2006.

26   Louis Fisher, "Don't Act Unilaterally to Close Guantánamo," Law.com, 4 December 2015.

27   Charlie Savage, "Barack Obama's Q&A," *Boston Globe*, 20 December 2007.

28   Louis Fisher, "Military Operations in Libya: No War? No Hostilities?" *Presidential Studies Quarterly*, March 2012.

29   Ibid.

30   Ibid.

31   Louis Fisher, "Separation of Powers: Interpretation Outside the Courts," *Pepperdine Law Review*, 15 December 1990.

32   David Cole and James X. Dempsey, *Terrorism and the Constitution: Sacrificing Civil Liberties in the Name of National Security* (New Press, 2006), 165.

33   Ibid.

34   "A Call to Courage: Reclaiming Our Liberties Ten Years after 9/11," ACLU, September 2011.

35   Jeanne Theoharis, "US Citizen's Solitary Confinement Raises Serious Questions," *The Progressive*, 1 March 2010.

36   "Comment of Senator Patrick Leahy on Application Of Material Support Laws To Humanitarian Relief In Somalia," Press Release, 2 August 2011.

37   David Cole, "Criminalizing Speech: The Material Support Provision," in Stewart Baker and John Kavanagh, ed., *Patriot Debates: Experts Debate the USA Patriot Act* (American Bar Association, 2005), 145-46.

38   Adam Liptak, "Court Affirms Ban on Aiding Groups Tied to Terror," *New York Times*, 21 June 2010.

39   Committee Reports—107th Congress (2001-2002), House Report 107-236—Part I, Provide Appropriate Tools Required to Intercept and Obstruct Terrorism [PATRIOT] Act of 2001.

40   Dia Kayyali, "Congress Must Not Authorize More Chilling of the First Amendment with Material Support Laws," Electronic Frontier Foundation, 29 May 2015.

41   Gellman, *Angler*, 141.

42   Ibid., 142-43.

43   Ibid., 289-324.

44   "United States of Secrets," *Frontline*, 13 May 2014.

45   Ibid. The script had "about" before "terrorists," which was not in the original on PBS.

46   Ibid.

47   Ibid.

48   Ibid.

49   "Obama's Remarks on Health Care and Surveillance," *International New York Times*, 7 June 2013.

50   Barton Gellman, "Code Name 'Verax': Snowden, in Exchanges with Post Reporter, Made Clear he Knew Risks," 9 June 2013.

51   Peter Van Buren, "Shredding the Fourth Amendment in Post-Constitutional America: Four Ways It No Longer Applies," TomDispatch, 26 June 2014.

52   "Edward Snowden: 'Fourth Amendment No Longer Exists,'" CNET, 9 May 2014.

53   Andrew P. Napolitano, "A Worthless Piece of Paper: Without Fourth Amendment Protections, the Constitution Means Nothing," *Washington Times*, 11 February 2015.

54   Steven Nelson, "NSA Whistleblowers Oppose Freedom Act, Endorse Long-Shot Bill," *USA News*, 27 April 2015.

55   Shahid Buttar, "Dragnet NSA Spying Survives: 2015 in Review," Electronic Frontier Foundation, 25 December, 2015.

56   Kate Knibbs, "The US Just Voted to Stop the NSA's Bulk Data Collection," Gizmodo, 13 May 2015,

57   David Segal, "Demand Progress Decries Passage of USA Freedom Act," Demand Progress, 4 June 2015.

58   "N.C. Should Fight to Protect the Fourth Amendment," *Daily Tar Heel*, 18 February 2016.

59   Roberts, "Does the United States Still Exist?"

60   Glenn Greenwald, "Key Similarity between Snowden Lead and Panama Papers: Scandal Is What's Been Legalized," The Intercept, 4 April 2016.

61   Mark Joseph Stern, "Justice Sotomayor Slams US Police State in Scathing Dissent," *Slate*, 21 June 2016.

62 John W. Whitehead, "US Supreme Court Guts Fourth Amendment, Sanctions Police Fishing Expeditions, Giving Police More Leeway to Stop, Arrest and Search Citizens," Rutherford Institute, 21 June 2016.

63 John Nichols, "Sonia Sotomayor's Epic Dissent Explains What's at Stake when the Police Don't Follow the Law," *Nation,* 20 June 2016.

64 Whitehead, "US Supreme Court Guts Fourth Amendment."

65 Ibid.

66 Ibid.

67 Nichols, "Sonia Sotomayor's Epic Dissent."

68 Stern, "Justice Sotomayor Slams US Police State"; Nichols, "Sonia Sotomayor's Epic Dissent."

69 Stern, "Justice Sotomayor Slams US Police State."

70 Ibid.

71 Isaac Chotiner, "Is Donald Trump a Fascist? Yes and No," Slate, 10 February 2016; John McNeill, "How Fascist Is Donald Trump? There's Actually a Formula for That," *Washington Post,* 21 October 2016.

72 Becker and Shane, "Secret 'Kill List' Proves a Test of Obama's Principles and Will."

73 Ibid.

74 Glenn Greenwald, "How Extremism Is Normalized," *Salon,* 30 May 2012.

75 Charlie Savage, "Secret US Memo Made Legal Case to Kill a Citizen," *New York Times,* 8 October 2011.

76 Conor Friedersdorf, "This Lawyer Enabled the Extrajudicial Killing of an American," *Atlantic,* 7 May 2014.

77 Adam Server, "Colbert on Targeted Killing: 'Due Process Just Means There's A Process That You Do,'" *Mother Jones,* 7 March 2012.

78 "Due Process," Wex Legal Dictionary, Legal Information Institute, Cornell University Law School.

79 Tom Carter, "The Legal Implications of the Al-Awlaki Assassination," Worldwide Socialist Web Site, 10 October 2011.

80 Conor Friedersdorf, "How Team Obama Justifies the Killing of a 16-Year-Old American," *Atlantic,* 24 October 2012; Nasser al-Awlaki, "The Drone that Killed My Grandson," *International New York Times,* 17 July 2013. (Attorney General Eric Holder claimed that the boy was not "specifically targeted.")

81 Benjamin, *Drone Warfare,* 128.

82 "Transcript: Former Vice President Gore's Speech on Constitutional Issues," *Washington Post,* 16 January 2006.

83   Glenn Greenwald, "How Extremism Is Normalized," *Salon*, 30 May 2012.

84   Warren Richey, "Judge Dismisses Bid to Remove Anwar al-Awlaki from US 'Kill List,'" *Christian Science Monitor*, 7 December 2010.

85   "Judge Acknowledges ACLU and CCR Case Raises Important Questions about Legality of Obama Administration's Claimed Authority to Kill Americans Outside Combat Zones," ACLU, 7 December 2010.

86   *Al-Aulaqi v. Panetta—Constitutional Challenge to Killing of Three US Citizens*, ACLU 2012; *Court Dismisses Lawsuit Challenging US Drone Killings of Three Americans*, ACLU, 2014.

87   Savage, *Power Wars*, 290.

88   John Knefel, "Trump Is Inheriting Power to Assassinate Anyone, Including US Citizens, With No Oversight," Truthout, 9 December 2016.

89   Matt Ford, "Antonin Scalia's Case for Torture," *Atlantic*, 13 December, 2014.

90   Marjorie Cohn, "Under US Law Torture Is Always Illegal," *CounterPunch*, 6 May 2008.

91   Mark Mazzetti, "'03 US Memo Approved Harsh Interrogations," *New York Times*, 2 April 2008.

92   *60 Minutes II: Abuse at Abu Ghraib*, CBS News, 28 April 2004; Seymour M. Hersh, "Torture at Abu Ghraib," *New Yorker*, 30 April 2004.

93   Karen J. Greenberg, "The Road from Abu Ghraib: A Torture Story without a Hero or an Ending," TomDispatch, 27 April 2014.

94   Bob Fitrakis and Harvey Wasserman, *How the GOP Stole America's 2004 Election and Is Rigging 2008* (CICJ Books, 2005); Mark Crispin Miller, *Fooled Again: How the Right Stole the 2004 Election and Why They'll Steal the Next One Too* (Basic Books, 2005); Robert F. Kennedy Jr., "Was the 2004 Election Stolen?" *Rolling Stone*, 1 June 2006; Michael Parenti, "The Stolen Presidential Elections," Michael Parenti Website, May 2007.

95   Louis Jacobson, "Wide Agreement that Obama's Torture Ban Has Held," PolitiFact, 14 November 2011.

96   Glenn Greenwald, "US First Shields Its Torturers and War Criminals from Prosecution, Now Officially Honors Them," The Intercept, 5 December 2015.

97   Rupert Stone, "Has Obama Banned Torture? Yes and No," Al Jazeera, 1 December 2015.

98   *The Senate Intelligence Committee Report on Torture: Committee Study of the Central Intelligence Agency's Detention and Interrogation Program* (Melville House, 2014).

99   Jane Mayer, "The Real Torture Patriots," *New Yorker*, 15 December 2014.

100 Zachary Roth, "On Torture, Obama's Hands Aren't Entirely Clean," MSNBC, 10 December 2014.

101 Greenwald, "US First Shields Its Torturers and War Criminals from Prosecution."

102 Joy Yang, "Cheney Slams Senate Torture Report, Says Practices Were Effective," MSNBC, 10 December 2014.

103 Andy Borowitz, "Cheney Calls for International Ban on Torture Reports," *New Yorker*, 12 December 2014.

104 Matthew Weaver and Spencer Ackermann, "Trump Claims Torture Works but Experts Warn of Its 'Potentially Existential' Costs," *Guardian*, 26 January 2017.

105 John W. Whitehead, "The Tyranny of 9/11: The Building Blocks of the American Police State from A-Z," Counterpunch, 8 September 2016.

106 Warren, "The 9/11 Decade and the Decline of US Democracy."

107 James Zogby, "NYPD: Shredding the Constitution," Reader Supported News, 18 March 2012.

108 Ajamu Baraka, "Trump's Neo-Fascism Will Be Built on Neo-Fascism of Obama and Democrat Party," Black Agenda Report, 3 January 2017.

Chapter 9: Nuclear Holocaust

1 Eliot Cohen, "World War IV : Let's Call This Conflict What It Is," *Opinion Journal*, 20 November 2001; Jeffrey Lord, "So Begins World War IV?" *American Spectator*, 12 August 2014.

2 Paul Craig Roberts, "Why WWIII Is on the Horizon," Paul Craig Roberts Website, 28 December, 2015; John Pilger, "A World War Has Begun: Break the Silence," teleSUR, 25 March 2016.

3 Roberts, "Why WWIII Is on the Horizon."

4 Gregory Kulacki, "Obama Visits Hiroshima Amid Growing Risk of Nuclear War With China," Huffington Post, 24 May 2016.

5 Gregory Kulacki, "The Risk of Nuclear War with China: A Troubling Lack of Urgency," Union of Concerned Scientists, May 2016.

6 Amy Goodman, "Noam Chomsky: Climate Change & Nuclear Proliferation Pose the Worst Threat Ever Faced by Humans," Democracy Now! 16 May 2016.

7 Paul Craig Roberts, "Neoconservatives' Hegemonic Goal of Making Sovereign Countries Extinct Is Bringing the Extinction of Planet Earth," Paul Craig Roberts Website, 12 December 2015.

8 Nicholas Lemann, "The Next World Order: The Bush Administration May Have a Brand-New Doctrine of Power," *New Yorker*, 1 April 2002.

9 David Armstrong, "Dick Cheney's Song of America," *Harper's*, October 2002.

10   Robert M. Gates, *Duty: Memoirs of a Secretary at War* (Knopf, 2014), 97.

11   Ray McGovern, "Rebuilding the Obama-Putin Trust," *Consortium News*, 3 January 2015; Eric Zuesse, "How America Double-Crossed Russia and Shamed West," Strategic Culture Foundation, 9 October 2015.

12   Walter Isaacson & Evan Thomas, *The Wise Men: Six Friends and the World They Made* (Simon and Schuster, 1999); Strobe Talbott, *The Russia Hand: A Memoir of Presidential Diplomacy* (New York: Random House, 2003), 220.

13   "Vice President's Remarks at the Ambrosetti Forum," White House, Office of the Vice President, 6 September 2008.

14   John D. McKinnon, "Cheney Chides Russia in Speech to European Security Conference," *Wall Street Journal*, 7 September 2008.

15   Polina Devitt, "Lavrov Accuses West of Seeking 'Regime Change' in Russia," *Reuters*, 22 November 2014.

16   Robert Parry, "The Crazy US 'Group Think' on Russia," *Consortium News,* 18 December 2014.

17   Eric Zuesse, "US Elite Wants to Destroy Russia at Any Price," Strategic Culture Foundation, 6 January 2016.

18   Neil Clark, "Regime Change in Russia? Think Again, Neocons," RT, 25 July 2015.

19   Ibid.

20   Alastair Crooke, "US Game-Playing Means Hot Syrian Summer," *Consortium News*, 21 June 2016.

21   John Pilger, "A World War Has Begun: Break the Silence," teleSUR, 25 March 2016.

22   Philip Giraldi, "How the World Ends: Baiting Russia Is Not Good Policy," Unz Review, 24 May 2016.

23   Ryan Browne, "US Launches Long-Awaited European Missile Defense Shield," CNN, 12 May 2016; Andrew E. Kramer, "Russia Calls New US Missile Defense System a 'Direct Threat,'" *New York Times*, 12 May 2016.

24   Robin Emmott, "US to Switch on European Missile Shield Despite Russian Alarm," *Reuters*, 11 May 2016.

25   Ibid.

26   "Putin: 'We Know When US Will Get New Missile Threatening Russia's Nuclear Capability,'" RT, 18 June, 2016.

27   William J. Broad and David E. Sanger, "As US Modernizes Nuclear Weapons, 'Smaller' Leaves Some Uneasy," *New York Times*, 11 January 2016; Julian Borger, "America's New, More 'Usable', Nuclear Bomb in Europe," *Guardian,* 10 November 2015.

28   Ibid.

29   "Statement by President Barack Obama on the Release of Nuclear Posture Review," White House, 6 April 2010.

30   Broad and Sanger, "As US Modernizes Nuclear Weapons, 'Smaller' Leaves Some Uneasy."

31   Hans M. Kristensen, "General Confirms Enhanced Targeting Capabilities of B61-12 Nuclear Bomb," in NATO, Nuclear Weapons, United States, 23 January 2014.

32   Broad and Sanger, "As US Modernizes Nuclear Weapons."

33   "Russia Slams US Test of B61-12 Atomic Bomb as 'Provocative,'" Press TV, 13 July 2015.

34   Robert Parry, "What Neocons Want from Ukraine Crisis," *Consortium New*, 2 March 2014; Zuesse, "US Elite Wants to Destroy Russia at Any Price."

35   On Russian policy, see Alexey Arbatov, "The Hidden Side of the US-Russian Strategic Confrontation," Arms Control Association, September 2016.

36   Paul Sonne et al., "'No First Use' Nuclear Policy Proposal Assailed by US Cabinet Officials, Allies," *Wall Street Journal*, 12 August 2016.

37   Mahdi Darius Nazemroava, "From Energy War to Currency War: America's Attack on the Russian Ruble," Strategic Culture Foundation, 26 December 2014.

38   Neil Clark, "Putin Demonized for Thwarting Neocon Plan for Global Domination," Neil Clark Website, 8 November 2014.

39   Jonathan Marshall, "Risky Blowback from Russian Sanctions," *Consortium News*, 19 January 2015.

40   Devitt, "Lavrov Accuses West of Seeking 'Regime Change' in Russia."

41   David Jackson, "Obama Aides Say Sanctions Are Biting Russia's Economy," *USA Today*, 16 December 2014.

42   Nazemroava, "From Energy War to Currency War."

43   Carol Adl, "Ex-CIA Official Proposes Assassination of Putin," YourNewsWire.com, 28 August 2014.

44   Gregor Peter Schmitz, "US Loses Patience with Europe: Washington Wants Tough Russia Sanctions," Spiegel Online International, 22 July 2014.

45   John Mearsheimer, "Why the Ukraine Crisis Is the West's Fault," *Foreign Affairs*, September/October 2014.

46   Seumas Milne, "In Ukraine, Fascists, Oligarchs and Western Expansion Are at the Heart of the Crisis," *Guardian*, 29 January 2014.

47 "Washington Was Behind Ukraine Coup: Obama Admits that US 'Brokered a Deal' in Support of 'Regime Change,'" Global Research, 3 February 2015.

48 Parry, "The Whys Behind the Ukraine Crisis," Consortium News, 3 September 2014.

49 Ray McGovern, "Rebuilding the Obama-Putin Trust," Consortium News, 3 January 2015; "Ukraine Crisis: Transcript of Leaked Nuland-Pyatt Call," BBC News, 7 February 2014.

50 Eric Zuesse, "The Paet-Ashton Transcript," Fort Russ, 3 February 2015; Michael Bergman, "Breaking: Estonian Foreign Minister Urmas Paet and Catherine Ashton Discuss Ukraine over the Phone," YouTube, 5 March 2014.

51 Ray McGovern, "Rebuilding the Obama-Putin Trust," Consortium News, 3 January 2015.

52 Robert Parry, "Ukraine, Through the US Looking Glass," Consortium News, 16 April 2014;

53 Ivan Katchanovski, "The 'Snipers' Massacre' on the Maidan in Ukraine," Social Science Research Network, 5 September 2015.

54 Engdahl, The Lost Hegemon, 261.

55 "Vladimir Putin Not Responsible for Ukrainian Civil War, Expert Says," Truthdig, 21 March 2015

56 Robert Parry, "NYT Still Pretends No Coup in Ukraine," Consortium News, 6 January 2015; Andrew Higgins and Andrew E. Kramer, "Ukraine Leader Was Defeated Even Before He Was Ousted," New York Times, 3 January 2015.

57 Eric Zuesse, "Head of Stratfor, 'Private CIA,' Says Overthrow of Yanukovych Was 'The Most Blatant Coup in History,'" Global Research, 21 December 2014.

58 "Washington Was Behind Ukraine Coup."

59 Alan Yuhas, "Ukraine Crisis: An Essential Guide to Everything that's Happened So Far," Guardian, 13 April 2014.

60 Robert Parry, "NYT's One-Sided Ukraine Narrative," Consortium News, 26 May 2014.

61 Robert Parry, "NYT Discovers Ukraine's Neo-Nazis at War," Consortium News, 10 August 2014.

62 Andrew Higgins, "Mystery Surrounds Death of Fiery Ukrainian Activist," New York Times, 12 April 2014.

63 Tom Parfitt, "Ukraine Crisis: The Neo-Nazi Brigade Fighting Pro-Russian Separatists," Telegraph, 11 August 2014.

64 "Neo-Nazi Threat in New Ukraine: NEWSNIGHT," YouTube, 28 March 2014; see also Parry, "What Neocons Want from Ukraine Crisis."

65   Eric Zuesse, "G7 Boldly Displays Its Lies Regarding Anti-Russia Economic Sanctions," Global Research, 3 June 2016; "G7 Foreign Ministers' Meeting, 10-11 April 2016 in Japan: Extracts of the Joint Communiqué (12/04/2016)."

66   Robert Parry, "Who's Telling the 'Big Lie' on Ukraine?" *Consortium News*, 2 September 2014.

67   "Ukraine Preparing for 'Full-Scale War,' Says Former Envoy to Canada," *CBC News*, 21 February 2015."

68   Frank Coletta, "'MH17 Was Brought Down by Weapon Supplied by Russian Military': Report Claims 'Undeniable Evidence' that Missile Launcher Was Provided to Rebels in Ukraine," *Daily Mail,* 10 November 2014.

69   "US officials have not released evidence proving that Russia's military played a direct role in the downing of the jet or in training separatists to use the SA-11 missile system," Brian Bennett, "US Officials Believe Attack against Malaysian Plane Was Mistake," *Los Angeles Times*, 22 July 2004.

70   Robert Parry, "Blaming Russia as 'Flat Fact,'" *Consortium News*, 27 July 2014.

71   Dave Lindorff, "US Propaganda Campaign to Demonize Russia in Full Gear over One-Sided Dutch/Aussie Report on Flight 17 Downing," OpEdNews, 29 September 2016.

72   Samantha Power, *United Nations Address on the Downing of Malaysian Airlines Flight 17,* United Nations, American Rhetoric, 18 July 2014.

73   Peter Haisenko, "Revelations of German Pilot: Shocking Analysis of the 'Shooting Down' of Malaysian MH17. 'Aircraft Was Not Hit by a Missile,'" Global Research, 26 April 2016.

74   Alexander Kolyandr, "MH17 Pieces With Shrapnel-Like Holes, OSCE Says," *Wall Street Journal,* 24 July 2014.

75   Michel Chossudovsky, "Support MH17 Truth: Machine Gun-Like Holes Indicate Shelling from a Military Aircraft. No Evidence of a Surface-to-Air Missile Attack," Global Research, 8 March 2016; Robert Parry, "The Ever-Curiouser MH-17 Case," *Consortium News,* 16 March 2016; Eric Zuesse, "Western News-Suppression about the Downing of MH-17 Malaysian Jet," RINF, 5 November 2014.

76   Chossudovsky, "Support MH17 Truth"; "Deleted BBC Report. 'Ukrainian Fighter Jet Shot Down MH17,' Donetsk Eyewitnesses," Global Research News, 10 September 2014; "UKRAINE-Eyewitness-Confirm-Military-Jet-Flew-Besides-MH17 Airliner-BBC-Censors-Video," DailyMotion, 25 July 2014.

77   Robert Parry, "MH-17's Unnecessary Mystery," *Consortium News,* 14 June 2014.

78   Michel Chossudovsky, "Malaysian Airlines MH17 Brought Down by Ukrainian Military Aircraft. The BBC Refutes its Own Lies?" Global Research, 26 April 2016.

79   Eric Zuesse, "G7 Boldly Displays Its Lies Regarding Anti-Russia Economic Sanctions," Global Research, 3 June 2016.

80   Alex Gorka, "French MPs Visit Crimea: Suggesting Early End to Sanctions," Strategic Culture, 1 August 2016.

81   Roberts, "Neoconservatives' Hegemonic Goal of Making Sovereign Countries Extinct"; Parry, "What Neocons Want from Ukraine Crisis."

82   Philip Giraldi, "How the World Ends: Baiting Russia Is Not Good Policy," Unz Review, 24 May 2016.

83   Quoted in Ray McGovern, "Rebuilding the Obama-Putin Trust," *Consortium News*, 3 January 2015.

84   Giraldi, "How the World Ends."

85   Engdahl, *The Lost Hegemon*, 7.

86   Pilger, "A World War Has Begun."

87   Robert Parry, "Ukraine, Through the US Looking Glass," *Consortium News*, 16 April 2014.

88   Angela Borozna, "40 Million Russians Prepare for Nuclear War," The Duran, 4 October 2016.

89   Stephen Lendman, "Threatening Russia: Reckless US-NATO War Games in Poland," Global Research, 8 June 2016.

90   Deirdre Fulton, "Enormous, 'Seriously Destabilizing' NATO War Games Begin in Poland," 6 June 2016.

91   Robert Bridge, "With NATO Knocking, It's Time for Russian Military Games in Latin America," RT, 4 June 2016.

92   Paul Craig Roberts, "Are You Planning Your Retirement? Forget About It. You Won't Survive To Experience It," Paul Craig Roberts Website, 8 July 2015.

93   "MSNBC's Joe Scarborough: Trump Asked 'Three Times in an Hour Briefing, "Why Can't We Use Nuclear Weapons?"'" Media Matters, 3 August 2016.

94   James E. Cartwright and Bruce G Blair, "End the First-Use Policy for Nuclear Weapons," New York Times, 14 August 2016.

95   David E. Sanger and William J. Broad, "Obama Unlikely to Vow No First Use of Nuclear Weapons," *New York Times*, 5 September 2016.

96   Craig Whitlock, "US Begins Airstrikes Against Islamic State in Syria," *Washington Post*, 23 September 2014.

97   "Syria: US-Led Coalition Hits Deir Ezzur Again," FARS News Agency, 28 September 2016.

98 Ray McGovern, "Mike Morell's Kill-Russians Advice," *Consortium News*," 12 August 2016; "US Spox Threatens Russia with 'More Body Bags, Attacks on Russian Cities,'" Covert Politics, 29 September 2016.

99 John McCain, "Stop Assad Now—Or Expect Years of War," *Wall Street Journal,* 4 October 2016.

100 Danny Collins, "'We Will Destroy You,' US Army Chief Mark Milley Fires Terrifying Threat to Russia over Syria and Warns: 'We'll Beat You Anywhere,'" *The Sun*, 6 October 2016..

101 Lauren McCauley, "On Syria Policy, Critics Warn, Both Trump and Clinton Get It Very Wrong," Common Dreams, 10 October 2016; Justin Fishel, "Up to 30,000 Troops Needed for Syria Safe Zone, Kerry Says," ABC News, 24 February 2016.

102 Jaid Jilani, "In Secret Goldman Sachs Speech, Hillary Clinton Admitted No-Fly Zone Would 'Kill a Lot of Syrians,'" Intercept, 10 October 2016.

103 Bill Van Auken, "Syrian No-fly Zone Means War with Russia," The 4th Media, 25 September 2016.

104 "Russia to Take Down any Airplane or Missile Targeting Syrian Army," South Front, 7 October 2016.

105 Josh Rogin, "Obama Administration Considering Strikes on Assad, Again," *Washington Post*, 4 October 2016. Although the motivation was reportedly the desire to prevent more war crimes, arguably the real motive was given by a "senior administrative official" to a *Post* reporter: "The CIA and the Joint Staff have said that the fall of Aleppo would undermine America's counterterrorism goals in Syria," a senior administration official told the *Post*.

106 "Russia Will Protect Its Assets if US Strikes Syrian Bases: Lavrov," Press TV, 9 October 2016.

107 Jason Ditz, "Russia to Expand Syria Naval Base, Make It 'Permanent,'" Antiwar.com, 10 October 2016. Kerry's assistant said the US leverage is based on the notion that "Russia will eventually become weary"; Rogin, "Obama Administration Considering Strikes on Assad, Again."

108 Andrew Osborn, "Russia to Build Permanent Syrian Naval Base, Eyes Other Outposts," Reuters, 10 October 2016; "Russia in Talks with Egypt to Lease Military Base: Report," Press TV, 10 October 2016.

109 Ian Greenhalgh, "Russia to Upgrade Syrian Navy Base into 'Permanent' Facility," 10 October 2016; "Russia Expanding Military Presence in Middle East," South Front, 11 October 2016.

110 See Ron Suskind, *The One Percent Solution: Deep Inside America's Pursuit of Its Enemies since 9/11* (Simon & Schuster, 2006).

111 Parry, "What Neocons Want from Ukraine Crisis."

112   Robert Parry, "NYT's One-Sided Ukraine Narrative," *Consortium News*, 26 May 2014.

113   Dave Lindorff, "The Dumbed Down Times Columnist," *New York Times*, 29 August 2016.

114   Stephen Kinzer, "Could Trump Reform US Foreign Policy?" *Boston Globe*, 10 November 2016. |

115   Joseph Clifford, "Not Yet Inaugurated; Already a New War," OpEdNews, 14 January 2017.

116   Glenn Greenwald, "The Deep State Goes to War with President-Elect, Using Unverified Claims, as Democrats Cheer," The Intercept, 11 January 2017; The Saker, "The Neocon's Declaration of War against Trump," 13 January 2017.

117   Lisa Hagen, "Trump: NATO Is 'No Longer Obsolete,'" The Hill, 12 March 2017; "Donald Trump Says US Relations with Russia 'May Be at All-Time Low,' *Guardian*, 13 April 2017.

118   Leo Shane, "Trump: I'm Giving the Military 'Total Authorization,'" *Military Times*, 13 April 2017; The Saker, "Trump Has Lost Control Over the Pentagon," 17 April 2017.

119   "Donald Trump Is a Maverick, Unlike Hillary Clinton, Argues John Pilger," Telesur, 22 March 2016.

120   Ibid.

121   "5 Mind-Boggling Things about 'The Coming War on China': Pilger's Documentary Airs on RTD," RT, 10 December 2016.

122   "US Provoking China Into Nuclear War? John Pilger's Film Reveals US Provocations against China as Donald Trump Provokes Beijing," News Prepper, 8 December 2016.

123   *Day Of Deceit: The Truth about FDR and Pearl Harbor* (Free Press, 2001); Stephen J. Sniegoski, "The Case for Pearl Harbor Revisionism," *Occidental Quarterly*, 1:2 (Winter 2001).

124   "US Provoking China Into Nuclear War?"

125   John Pilger, "The Coming War on China," *Counterpunch*, 2 December, 2016.

126   "5 Mind-Boggling Things about 'The Coming War on China': Pilger's Documentary Airs on RTD," RT, 10 December 2016.

127   Simon Tisdall, "Barack Obama's 'Asian Pivot' Failed. China Is in the Ascendancy," *Guardian*, 25 September 2016; Nathan Gardels, "How the US Election Has Derailed Obama's 'Pivot' to Asia," WorldPost, 25 October 2016.

128   Pilger, "The Coming War on China."

Chapter 10: Ecological Holocaust

1   Robinson Meyer, "Human Extinction Isn't That Unlikely," *Atlantic*, 2 May 2016.

2   Amy Goodman, "Noam Chomsky: Climate Change & Nuclear Proliferation Pose the Worst Threat Ever Faced by Humans," Democracy Now! 16 May 2016.

3   Tom Engelhardt, "Emperor Weather Turning Up the Heat on History: Planet of the Imperial Apocalypse," TomDispatch, 6 December 2015.

4   "Ocean Acidification: Global Warming's Evil Twin," Skeptical Science, 2012.

5   Nichols, *Dick*, 109-10.

6   Ibid.; Douglas Jehl with Andrew C. Revkin, "Bush Reverses Vow to Curb Gas Tied to Global Warming," *New York Times*, 14 March 2001; Gellman, *Angler*, 84.

7   Memo to John Howard, White House Council on Environmental Quality, from ExxonMobil Lobbyist Arthur G. "Randy" Randol, 6 February 2001; Andrew Lawler, "Battle over IPCC Chair Renews Debate on US Climate Policy," *Science*, 12 April 2002.

8   Charles Clover, "US Climate Talks Chief 'Recommended by Oil Company,'" *Telegraph*, 15 May 2002.

9   Jehl and Revkin, "Bush Reverses Vow"; Global Climate Coalition, Source Watch.

10   Tim Dickinson, "Six Years of Deceit: Inside the Bush Administration's Secret Campaign to Deny Global Warming and Let Polluters Shape America's Climate Policy," 28 June 2007.

11   "Smoke, Mirrors & Hot Air: How ExxonMobil Uses Big Tobacco's Tactics to Manufacture Uncertainty on Climate Science," Union of Concerned Scientists, January 2007; citing Rick Piltz, "On Issues of Concern about the Governance and Direction of the Climate Change Science Program," memo to agency principals, 1 June 2005.

12   Henry Fountain, "Researchers Link Syrian Conflict to a Drought Made Worse by Climate Change," *New York Times*, 2 March 2015.

13   James Fallows, "Your Labor Day Syria Reader, Part 2: William Polk," *Atlantic*, 2 September 2013.

14   Stephan Lewandowsky, "Media Failure on Iraq War Repeated in Climate Change Coverage," *Guardian*, 6 December 2013.

15   Joe Romm, "Bush Will Go Down in History as Possibly a Person Who Has Doomed the Planet," Climate Progress, 13 December 2008.

16   NOAA National Weather Service, Office of Climate, Water, and Weather Services, 2012.

17   Joe Romm, "Mother Nature Is Just Getting Warmed Up: June 2011 Heat Records Crushing Cold Records by 13 to 1," Climate Progress, 11 June 2011.

18   "Global Warming: Future Temperatures Could Exceed Livable Limits, Researchers Find," ScienceDaily, 4 May 2010.

19   Joe Romm, "Royal Society Special Issue on Global Warming Details 'Hellish Vision' of 7°F (4°C) World—Which We May Face in the 2060s!" Climate Progress, 2 June 2011; World Bank, *Turn Down the Heat: Why a 4°C World Must Be Avoided,*" November 2012.

20   Damian Carrington, "Climate Change Scientists Warn of 4C Global Temperature Rise," *Guardian*, 28 November 2010; Mark New et al., "Four Degrees and Beyond: The Potential for a Global Temperature Increase of Four Degrees and Its Implications," *Philosophical Transactions of the Royal Society*, 369/1934 (November 2011).

21   Kevin Anderson, "Climate Change Beyond Dangerous—Brutal Numbers and Tenuous Hope," in Niclas Hällström, ed., *What Next? Volume III: Climate, Development and Equity*, September 2012 (online book), 16-40

22   "Tyndall Center: Global Warming Will Kill 90% of the Earth's Population," Real Science, 29 November 2009.

23   Orrin H. Pilkey and Rob Young, *The Rising Sea* (Shearwater, 2009).

24   Rob Young and Orrin Pilkey, "How High Will Seas Rise? Get Ready for Seven Feet," Environment 360, 14 January 2010; Brady Dennis and Chris Mooney, "Scientists Nearly Double Sea Level Rise Projections for 2100, because of Antarctica," *Washington Post*, 30 March 2016.

25   Lester Brown, "Could Food Shortages Bring Down Civilization?" *Scientific American*, 22 April 2009.

26   Lester R. Brown, *Full Planet, Empty Plates: The New Geopolitics of Food Scarcity* (New York: W.W. Norton, 2012), 122.

27   Max Frankel, "Intensifying Midwestern Drought Threatens Farmers, Water Supplies," Climate Progress, 6 July 2012; Jeff Wilson, "US Corn Growers Farming in Hell as Midwest Heat Spreads," Bloomberg, 9 July 2012.

28   "Annan: Climate Impacts Are Devastating World Food Supplies," Associated Press, 10 November 2011; Adam Gorlick, "At Stanford, Kofi Annan Warns of Worldwide Hunger, Political Unrest if Climate Change Persists," Stanford Report, 11 November 2011; "Climate Change vs. Food Security: A Bleak Future for the Poor," Oxfam International, 5 September 2012.

29   Nafeez Ahmed, "Peak Soil: Industrial Civilization Is on the Verge of Eating Itself," Earthsight Blog, *Guardian*, 7 June 2013; "Creating a

Sustainable Food Future I: The Great Balancing Act," World Resources Institute, 2013.

30   Kathleen McAuliffe, "Ocean Acidification: A Global Case of Osteoporosis," *Discover*, July 2008; Alex Morales, "Oceans Acidifying Fastest in 300 Million Years Due to Emissions," Bloomberg News, 2 March 2012.

31   "Ocean Acidification: Global Warming's Evil Twin," Skeptical Science, 2012; "Acid Oceans Warning," ARC Center of Excellence Coral Reef Studies, October 2007.

32   Seth Borenstein, "Plankton, Base of Ocean Food Web, in Big Decline," Associated Press, 28 July 2010; Steve Connor, "The Dead Sea: Global Warming Blamed for 40 Per Cent Decline in the Ocean's Phytoplankton," *Independent*, 29 July 2010. Daniel G. Boyce, Boris Worm, et al., "Global Phytoplankton Decline over the Past Century," *Nature*, 29 July 2010.

33   "Ocean Acidification: Global Warming's Evil Twin."

34   Julian Siddle, "Marine Life Faces 'Acid Threat,'" BBC News, 25 November 2008; "Acid Oceans Warning," ARC Center of Excellence Coral Reef Studies, October 2007.

35   "Save the Sea"; "Oceans, Rio+20: The Future We Want," United Nations.

36   "Acid Oceans Warning," ARC Center of Excellence Coral Reef Studies, October 2007.

37   Elizabeth Kolbert, *The Sixth Extinction: An Unnatural History* (New York: Henry Holt, 2014), 267-68.

38   Paul R. Ehrlich and Anne H. Ehrlich, "Can a Collapse of Global Civilization Be Avoided?" *Proceedings of the Royal Society B*, 9 January 2013.

39   Tom Engelhardt, "Is Climate Change a Crime against Humanity?" TomDispatch, 22 May 2014.

40   Stephanie Rogers, "Human Could Go Extinct within 100 Years, Says Renowned Scientist," Mother Nature Network, 25 June 2010; discussing Cheryl Jones, "Frank Fenner Sees No Hope for Humans," *The Australian*, 16 June 2010.

41   Gwynne Dyer, *Climate Wars: The Fight for Survival as the World Overheats* (Oxford: Oneworld, 2010).

42   Joe Romm, "Syria Today Is a Preview of Veterans Day, 2030," Climate Progress, 11 November 2013.

43   John Kerry, "Remarks With Swedish Prime Minister Fredrik Reinfeldt," US Department of State, 14 May 2013.

44   Bryan Bender, "Chief of US Pacific Forces Calls Climate Biggest Worry," *Boston Globe*, 9 March 2013.

45   Seth Borenstein, "UN Report: Global Warming Worsens Security Woes," Associated Press, 30 March 2014; Nafeez Ahmed, "UN—Climate 'Perfect Storm' Is Already Here. Time to Slay Zombie Big Oil," Earth Insight, *Guardian*, 3 April 2014.

46   Gwynne Dyer, *Climate Wars: The Fight for Survival as the World Overheats* (Oxford: Oneworld, 2010), xii, xi.

47   Gen. Anthony C. Zinni, USMC (ret.), "On Climate Change, Instability and Terrorism," *National Security and the Threat of Climate Change*, CNA Corporation, 2007.

48   Dyer, *Climate Wars*, 19-20.

49   Charles J. Krebs, *Ecology: The Experimental Analysis of Distribution and Abundance*, 6th ed. (San Francisco: Benjamin Cummings, 2009), 572.

50   Chris D. Thomas et al., "Extinction Risk from Climate Change," *Nature*, 8 January 2004; "Global Warming—Ecosystem Collapse—An Unnatural Disaster," *Anaspides*, 8 January 2004.

51   Paul Alois and Victoria Cheng, "Keystone Species Extinction Overview," Arlington Institute, July 2007.

52   Johan Rockström, "Planetary Boundaries: Exploring the Safe Operating Space for Humanity," *Ecology and Society* 14/2 (2009). The other six boundaries involve ocean acidification, stratospheric ozone, phosphorus inflow to the ocean, global freshwater use, chemical pollution, and atmospheric aerosol loading.

53   David P. Bell, "Earth on Brink of 'Irreversible' Collapse of Global Ecosystem, New SFU Study Warns," *Vancouver Observer*, 6 June 2012.

54   Anthony D. Barnosky et al., "Approaching a State Shift in Earth's Biosphere," *Nature*, 7 June 2012; "Environmental Collapse Now a Serious Threat: Scientists," *Agence France-Presse*, 6 June 2012; Brian Merchant, "Scientists Fear Global Ecological Collapse Once 50% of the Natural Landscape Is Gone," Treehugger, 6 June 2012.

55   Joe Romm, "Nature Bombshell: Climate Experts Warn Thawing Permafrost Could Cause 2.5 Times the Warming of Deforestation!" Climate Progress, 1 December 2011.

56   Alan Buis, "Is a Sleeping Climate Giant Stirring in the Arctic?" NASA, 10 June 2013.

57   Ibid.; Justin Gillis, "As Permafrost Thaws, Scientists Study the Risks," *New York Times*, 16 December 2011.

58   Dahr Jamail, "Mass Extinction: It's the End of the World as We Know It," Truthout, 14 July 2015.

59   Natalia Shakhova et al., "Extensive Methane Venting to the Atmosphere from Sediments of the East Siberian Arctic Shelf," *Science*, 5 March 2010; "Methane Releases from Arctic Shelf May Be Much Larger and

Faster than Anticipated," National Science Foundation, Press Release, 4 March 2010; Kevin Schaefer et al., "Amount and Time of Permafrost Carbon Release in Response to Climate Warming," Tellus B, 15 February 2011.

60   Brian Merchant, "If We Release a Small Fraction of Arctic Carbon, 'We're Fucked': Climatologist," Motherboard, 1 August 2014.

61   "Stable" Antarctic Permafrost Melting Faster than Expected, Researchers Say," Nature World News, 24 July 2013.

62   Andrew Glikson, "Methane and the Risk of Runaway Global Warming," The Conversation, 26 July 2013.

63   Dahr Jamail, "The Methane Monster Roars," Truthout, 13 January 2015.

64   Ibid.

65   Robert Hunziker, "What if Climate Change Is Worse than We Thought?" Counterpunch, 20 October 2014.

66   Quoted in "Tomgram: Dahr Jamail, The Climate Change Scorecard," Tom Dispatch, 17 December 2013.

67   Nafeez Ahmed, "Seven Facts You Need to Know about the Arctic Methane Timebomb," Guardian, 5 August 2013.

68   Robert Hunziker, "The Arctic Turns Ugly," Counterpunch, 29 February 2016.

69   Quoted in Dahr Jamail, "Are We Falling Off the Climate Precipice? Scientists Consider Extinction," Tom Dispatch, 17 December 2013.

70   Guy R. McPherson, "19 Ways Climate Change Is Now Feeding Itself," Transition Voice, 19 August 2013; Going Dark (Baltimore: PublishAmerica, 2013).

71   Guy McPherson, "Self-Reinforcing Feedback Loops," Monster Climate-Change Essay, Nature Bats Last, 24 June 2016.

72   Michael Welch, "Near-Term Human Extinction: A Conversation with Guy McPherson," Global Research, 18 March 2014.

73   See, for example, "Dorsi Diaz, "Climate Change and the Methane Crisis: An Interview with Dr. Guy McPherson," Examiner, 26 August 2014;

74   Jamail, "Mass Extinction: It's the End of the World as We Know It"; Jamail, "Are We Falling Off the Climate Precipice?"

75   Malcolm P.R. Light, "The Non-Disclosed Extreme Arctic Methane Threat," Runaway Global Warming, 22 December 2013.

76   Malcolm Light, "Focus on Methane," Arctic News, 14 July 2014.

77   Romm, "Bush Will Go Down in History as Possibly a Person Who Has Doomed the Planet."

78   Martin Luther King, "Beyond Vietnam: A Time to Break Silence," 4 April 1967.

79   Nafeez Ahmed, "Paris Attacks and Climate Change Push Us to Fix a World of Broken Systems," *Yes Magazine*, 19 November 2015.

80   "COP19: Lord Nicholas Stern on Why the Costs and Risks of Inaction Will Be Severe," Responding to Climate Change, 19 November 2013.

81   Joe Romm, "Climate Panel Stunner: Avoiding Climate Catastrophe Is Super Cheap—but Only If We Act Now," Climate Progress, 13 April 2014; Romm, "The $4 Trillion Mistake: Climate Action Delayed Is Climate Action Denied," Climate Progress, 14 May 2014, referring to *Energy Technology Perspectives 2014*, International Energy Agency, 13 May 2014.

82   "Climate Crisis Finance: Poor Countries Are Left in the Dark," Countercurrents, 11 November 2013.

83   Kimberly Amadeo, "US Military Budget: Components, Challenges, Growth," useconomy.about.com, 23 February 2016; "The United States More on Defense than the Next Seven Countries Combined," Peter G. Peterson Foundation, 18 April 2016.

84   Lawrence S. Wittner, "The Trillion Dollar Question the Media Have Neglected to Ask Presidential Candidates," History News Network, 14 March 2016.

85   Elizabeth Woodworth and David Ray Griffin, *Unprecedented Climate Mobilization: A Handbook for Citizens and their Governments* (Clarity Press, 2017).

86   Bill McKibben, "A World at War," *New Republic*, 15 August 2015.

87   Michael T. Klare, "Drowning the World in Oil: Trump's Carbon-Obsessed Energy Policy and the Planetary Nightmare to Come," TomDispatch, 15 December 2016.

88   Nika Knight, "China Leaves US in Dust With $361 Billion Renewable Energy Investment," Common Dreams, 5 January 2017.

Chapter 11: Why Bush and Cheney Should Not Be Trusted on 9/11

1   Paul Craig Roberts, *How America Was Lost: From 9/11 to the Police/Warfare State* (Clarity Press, 2014), 75.

2   See, for example, Jonathan Stein and Tim Dickinson, "Lie by Lie: A Timeline of How We Got Into Iraq," *Mother Jones*, September/October 2006; Simon Maloy, "Yes, Bush Lied about Iraq: Why Are We Still Arguing about This?" Salon, 10 February 2015.

3   Robert Scheer, "A Diplomat's Undiplomatic Truth: They Lied," *Salon*, 9 July 2003.

4   "Most Wanted Terrorists: Usama bin Laden," Federal Bureau of Investigation; Ed Haas, "FBI says, 'No Hard Evidence Connecting Bin Laden to 9/11,'" Muckraker Report, 6 June 2006.

5   David Ray Griffin, "Osama bin Laden as Responsible for the 9/11 Attacks: Is This Belief Based on Evidence?" Veterans Today, October 30, 2009.

6   "Could the Bin Laden Video Be a Fake?" BBC News, 14 December 2001; "'Feeble' to Claim Bin Laden Tape Fake: Bush," CBC, December 14, 2001.

7   "Could the Bin Laden Video Be a Fake?"

8   Jeff Stein, "CIA's Wacky Idea: Depict Saddam As Gay," Washington Post, 25 May 2010.

9   Statement made February 16, 2007, during a radio interview at the University of Wisconsin at Madison (http://www.radiodujour.com/people/lawrence_bruce).

10   For documentation and discussion, see David Ray Griffin, Osama bin Laden: Dead or Alive? (Interlink Books, 2009), 27-29.

11   "Dr. Sanjay Gupta: Bin Laden Would Need Help if on Dialysis," CNN, 21 January 2002; for the tape, see "Osama Bin Laden Tape Dezember [sic] 2001" (http://www.myvideo.de/watch/3760193/Osama_Bin_Laden_Tape_Dezember_2001).

12   "Report: Bin Laden Already Dead," Fox News, 26 December 2001; translation of Egyptian report (http://www.welfarestate.com/binladen/funeral); Amir Taheri, "The Death of bin Ladenism," New York Times, 11 July 2002.

13   "Bin Laden 'Confession' Video" (https://www.youtube.com/watch?v=KhctMpvszqQ); "Osama bin Laden Gets a Nose Job"; "Osama bin Laden—November 9th 2001" (http://www.youtube.com/watch?v=x0FVeqCX6z8).

14   Griffin, Osama bin Laden: Dead or Alive? 31-33.

15   See chapters 3 and 5 of Griffin, Osama bin Laden: Dead or Alive? (I had made an error about one video in Chapter 2, which I discussed in Griffin, "Did Osama bin Laden Confess to the 9/11 Attacks, and Did He Die, in 2001?" Global Research, 30 April 2010.)

16   Crofton Black & Abigail Fielding-Smith, "Pentagon Paid for Fake 'Al Qaeda' Videos," Bureau of Investigative Journalism, 1 October 2016.

17   See, for example, Paul Craig Roberts, "The Mysterious Death of Osama bin Laden: Creating Evidence Where There Is None," Global Research, 4 August 2011; "Ex-US Official Belies Claim Osama Was Killed in Abbottabad," News International, 9 November 2014 ; James Robertson, "The Deaths of Osama bin Laden, Crimes of Empire," 12 May 2015; Sean Adl-Tabatabai, "Pakistan TV, Exposes Osama bin Laden Killing Hoax (Video)," YourNewswire.com., 28 September 2015.

18   David Corn, "When 9/11 Conspiracy Theories Go Bad," AlterNet, 28 February 2002.

19	Dave Gilson, "Are Any 9/11 Conspiracy Films Plausible?" *Mother Jones*, September/October 2008.

20	"911—David Ray Griffin on Tucker Carlson's Aug. 9, 2006," MSNBC, 9 August 2005.

21	Frank Thomas Smith (Editor), "Debunking the 9/11 Conspiracy Theories," *Southern Cross Review*, 13 February 2002; Cinnamon Stillwater, "The Truth about 9/11 Conspiracy Theories," *Southern Cross Review*, 19 April 2006.

22	Sean Murphy, "The Worst People in America: Dick Cheney," *The Weeklings*, 1 July 2015.

23	Chris Adams, "Millions Went to War in Iraq, Afghanistan, Leaving Many with Lifelong Scars," McClatchy, 14 March 2013; Jack Balkwill, "Have Millions of Deaths from America's 'War on Terror' Been Concealed?" 30 June 2015.

24	"Bush asks Daschle to Limit Sept. 11 Probes," CNN, 29 January 2002.

25	See "Jersey Girls," Wikipedia. Their role is described in a documentary film, "9/11: Press for Truth."

26	David Corn, "Probing 9/11," *The Nation*, 7 July 2003: 14 18, at 15.

27	See, for example, David Ignatius, "Not a Job for Kissinger," *Washington Post*, 20 December 2002; Ken Guggenheim, "Kissinger to 9/11 Relatives: I'll Be Fair; Says Business Links No Concern, but Isn't Saying What They Are," *Chicago Sun Times*, 13 December, 2002.

28	"The Kissinger Commission," *New York Times*, 29 November 2002.

29	David Firestone, "Threats and Responses: The Investigation; Kissinger Pulls Out as Chief of Inquiry into 9/11 Attacks," *New York Times*, 14 December 2002.

30	Philip Shenon, *The Commission: The Uncensored History of the 9/11 Investigation* (Twelve, 2008), 175-76.

31	Ibid., 15, 19, 29.

32	Peter Dale Scott, *The Road to 9/11: Wealth, Empire, and the Future of America* (University of California Press, 2007), 101-07.

33	Shenon, *The Commission*, 33.

34	*The 9/11 Commission Report: Final Report of the National Commission on Terrorist Attacks upon the United States*, Authorized Edition (W. W. Norton, 2004), xv.

35	Clarke is quoted as saying, with regard to the warning issued to the incoming Bush administration about the al-Qaeda threat: "It was very explicit. Rice was briefed, and Hadley was briefed, and Zelikow sat in" (Philip Shenon, "Clinton Aides Plan to Tell Panel of Warning Bush Team on Qaeda," *New York Times*, 20 March 2004).

36   James Mann, *Rise of the Vulcans: The History of Bush's War Cabinet* (Viking, 2004), 316.

37   Stefan Halper and Jonathan Clarke, *America Alone: The Neo-Conservatives and the Global Order* (Cambridge University Press, 2004), 142. Technically, the new doctrine is a doctrine of *preventive* war. But most writers, as Halper and Clarke illustrate, use the term "preemptive."

38   Ashton Carter, John Deutch, and Philip Zelikow, "Catastrophic Terrorism: Tackling the New Danger," *Foreign Affairs*, November/December 1998: 80-94.

39   Joe Conason, "The Widows Are Watching," *Salon*, 2 April 2004.

40   Thomas H. Kean and Lee H. Hamilton (with Benjamin Rhodes), *Without Precedent: The Inside Story of the 9/11 Commission* (Alfred A. Knopf, 2006), 244.

41   Shenon, *The Commission*, 60.

42   Ibid., 244.

43   Ibid., 269-70.

44   Kean and Hamilton, *Without Precedent*, 116.

45   Ibid., 270.

46   Shenon, *The Commission*, 388-89.

47   Ibid., 389.

48   Shenon, *The Commission*, 69-70, 86.

49   Ibid., 167.

50   Ibid., 69, 83.

51   Ibid., 317.

52   Ibid., 277; emphasis added.

53   Ibid., 390.

54   Ibid., 321.

55   Ibid., 106-07.

56   Ibid., 107.

57   Ibid., 106-07.

58   Ibid., 171.

59   Ibid., 174.

60   *Time*, 26 March 2003.

61   "Independent Probes of Clinton Administration Cost Nearly $80 Million," CNN, 1 April 1999.

62   *Seattle Times*, 12 March 2003.

63   Philip Shenon, "9/11 Commission Could Subpoena Oval Office Files," *New York Times*, 26 October 2003.

64   Dan Eggen, "9/11 Panel Unlikely to Get Later Deadline," *Washington Post*, 19 January 2004.

65   "9/11: Press for Truth."

66   Joseph Murtagh, "9/11 Widows Keep on Asking the Tough Questions," Muckraker Report, 22 February 2007.

67   Alex Beam, "The 'Truthers' and 9/11," *Boston Globe*, 16 November 2015.

68   "9/11: Interviews by Peter Jennings," ABC News, 11 September 2002.

69   Philip H. Melanson, *Secret Service: The Hidden History of an Enigmatic Agency* (Carroll & Graf, 2002), as quoted in Susan Taylor Martin, "Of Fact, Fiction: Bush on 9/11," *St. Petersburg Times*, 4 July 2004.

70   Jennifer Barrs, "From a Whisper to a Tear," *Tampa Tribune*, 1 September 2002; Bill Sammon, *Fighting Back: The War on Terrorism: From Inside the Bush White House* (Regnery, 2002), 89-90.

71   Andrew Card, "What if You Had to Tell the President," *San Francisco Chronicle*, 11 September 2002; "9/11 Interview with Campbell Brown," *NBC News*, 11 September 2002.

72   Scot J. Paltrow, "Government Accounts of 9/11 Reveal Gaps, Inconsistencies," *Wall Street Journal*, 22 March 2004. See "5-Minute Video of George W. Bush on the Morning of 9/11," The Memory Hole, 26 June 2003.

73   Paltrow, "Government Accounts."

74   Martin, "Of Fact, Fiction: Bush on 9/11."

75   *The 9/11 Commission Report*, 40.

76   "9/11 Interview with Campbell Brown," NBC News, 11 September 2002.

77   Richard A. Clarke, *Against All Enemies: Inside America's War on Terror* (Free Press, 2004), 1-4.

78   "Sept. 11's Moments of Crisis: Part 2: Scramble," ABC News, 14 September 2002.

79   "The Vice President Appears on Meet the Press with Tim Russert," MSNBC, 16 September 2001. For more detail, see David Ray Griffin, "Tim Russert, Dick Cheney, and 9/11," Information Clearing House, 17 June 2008.

80   9/11 Commission Hearing, 23 May 2003. When Timothy Roemer, one of the 9/11 Commissioners, asked how long this conversation occurred after Mineta's 9:20 entry into the PEOC, Mineta said, "Probably about five or six minutes." That, as Roemer pointed out, would have been "about 9:25 or 9:26."

81   Evan Thomas, "The Day That Changed America," *Newsweek*, 30 December 2001.

82 These three interviews were reported by *The 9/11 Commission Report*, 464 n. 211.

83 Evan Thomas and Mark Hosenball, "Bush: 'We're at War,'" *Newsweek*, 24 September 2001.

84 *The 9/11 Commission Report*, 40.

85 "Interview: Norman Mineta: From Internment Camp to the Halls of Congress," Academy of Achievement, 3 June 2006.

86 "9/11 Seattle Truth Meets Norm Mineta," You Tube.

87 United States Secret Service, "Actions of TSD Related to Terrorist Incident," September 12, 2001. FOIA released to Aidan Monaghan on April 23, 2010, contained in Aidan Monaghan, *Declassifying 9/11: A Between the Lines and Behind the Scenes Look at the September 11 Attacks* (iUniverse, 2002).

88 "USSS Statement and Interview Reports," 9/11 Commission, July 28, 2003. The interviewees included SS agents Nelson Garabito, Carl Truscott, and Danny Spriggs. This declassified document is contained in ibid.

89 Sarah Moughty, "New Photos Show Bush Administration Reaction to 9/11 Attacks," *Frontline*, 24 July 2015.

90 "Graeme MacQueen, "Terror and the Patriot Act of 2001, Implemented in the Immediate Wake of 9/11," Global Research, 10 September 2014. (My discussion of the anthrax attacks is based almost entirely on the work of MacQueen, who is the world's expert on the relation of the anthrax attacks to the 9/11 attacks, as exemplified in his book, *The 2001 Anthrax Deception: The Case for a Domestic Conspiracy* [Clarity Press, 2014].)

91 Rick Weiss, "Bioterrorism: An Even More Devastating Threat," *Washington Post*, 17 September 2001.

92 "First Case of Bioterrorism-Related Inhalational Anthrax in the United States, Palm Beach County, Florida, 2001," *Emerging Infectious Diseases*, October 2002.

93 John Lancaster, "Senators Question an Anti-Terrorism Proposal," *Washington Post*, 26 September 2001.

94 James Dao, "Defense Secretary Warns of Unconventional Attacks," *New York Times*, 1 October 2001; Dana Milbank, "More Terrorism Likely, US Warns; Bush Wants National Airport Reopened," *Washington Post*, 1 October 2001.

95 Maureen Dowd, "From Botox to Botulism," *New York Times*, 26 September 2001; Tamar Lewin, "Anthrax Scare Prompts Run on an Antibiotic," 27 September, 2001.

96 Lancaster, "Senators Question an Anti-Terrorism Proposal."

97   Jesse J. Holland, "Senator Blocks Attempt to Block Bill," Associated Press, 10 October 2001.

98   MacQueen, *The 2001 Anthrax Deception*, 56.

99   "Second Alleged Senate Anthrax Letter Found," ABC News, 16 November 2001.

100   See MacQueen, *The Anthrax Deception*, Chapter 5.

101   MacQueen, "Terror and the Patriot Act of 2001."

102   Dan Eggen and Bob Woodward, "Terrorist Attacks Imminent, FBI Warns; Bush Declared Al Qaeda Is 'On the Run'; Assaults on US Called Possible in 'Next Several Days,'" *Washington Post*, 12 October 2001.

103   Sandra Sobieraj, "White House Mail Machine Has Anthrax," *Washington Post*, October 23, 2001.

104   "Feds Sued Over Anthrax Documents: Legal Group Wonders Why White House Took Cipro before Attacks," *WorldNetDaily*, June 7, 2002.

105   David Rose and Ed Vulliamy, "Iraq 'Behind US Anthrax Outbreaks,'" *The Observer*, 14 October 2001; "The Anthrax Source," *Wall Street Journal* 15 October 2001.

106   Patrick E. Tyler with John Tagliabue, "Czechs Confirm Iraqi Agent Met With Terror Ringleader," *New York Times*, 27 October 2001.

107   Press Briefing by Ari Fleisher, White House, 17 December 2001.

108   Macqueen, *The 2001 Anthrax Deception*, Chapter 5; Scott Shane, "Former F.B.I. Agent Sues, Claiming Retaliation Over Misgivings in Anthrax Case," *New York Times*, 8 April 2015.

109   For a much more extensive discussion of the problems with the official account of 9/11, see David Ray Griffin, *The New Pearl Harbor Revisited: 9/11, the Cover-Up, and the Exposé* (Northampton: Interlink Books, 2008. But for Building 7, see *The Mysterious Collapse of World Trade Center 7: Why the Final Official Report about 9/11 Is Unscientific and False* (Northampton: Interlink Books, 2009).

Chapter 12: The Miraculous Destruction of the Twin Towers

1   Matthew Rothschild, "Enough of the 9/11 Conspiracy Theories, Already," *The Progressive*, 18 September 2006.

2   James Glanz and Eric Lipton, *City in the Sky: The Rise and Fall of the World Trade Center* (New York: Times Books/Henry Holt, 2004), 330.

3   Bill Manning, "$elling Out the Investigation," *Fire Engineering*, January 2002.

4   See "Learning from 9/11: Understanding the Collapse of the World Trade Center," House of Representatives' Committee on Science Hearing, 6 March 2002, under "Background" (http://web.archive.org/

web/20021128021952/http://commdocs.house.gov/committees/science/hsy77747.000/hsy77747_0.htm).

5   Manning, "$elling Out the Investigation."

6   James Glanz, "Engineers Suspect Diesel Fuel in Collapse of 7 World Trade Center," *New York Times*, 29 November 2001.

7   FEMA, *World Trade Center Building Performance Study*, May 2002.

8   *The 9/11 Commission Report: Final Report of the National Commission on Terrorist Attacks upon the United States*, Authorized Edition (W. W. Norton, 2004), 541 n. 1.

9   Tom Harris, "How the World Trade Center Worked: The World Trade Center Tube," How Stuff Works.

10   Ibid., 308.

11   "9/11: Truth, Lies and Conspiracy: Interview: Lee Hamilton," CBC News, 21 August 2006.

12   See David Ray Griffin, *The New Pearl Harbor: Disturbing Questions about the Bush Administration and 9/11* (Olive Branch [Interlink Books], 2004), 12-13, citing Thomas Eagar, professor of materials engineering at MIT.

13   On some examples of prestigious members of these fields, see David Ray Griffin, *Cognitive Infiltration: An Obama Appointee's Plan to Undermine the 9/11 Conspiracy Theory* (Olive Branch: September 2010), 32-34.

14   Jennifer Rosenberg, "The Plane that Crashed into the Empire State Building," About.com.

15   *The 9/11 Commission Report*, 285.

16   Ibid. 302.

17   Ibid., 305.

18   "Fact Sheet: NIST's World Trade Center Investigation" (http://www.nist.gov/public_affairs/factsheet/nist_investigation_911.htm).

19   These points have been emphasized in Kevin Ryan, "What is 9/11 Truth? The First Steps," *Journal of 9/11 Studies*, Vol. 2/August 2006: 1-6 (http://www.journalof911studies.com).

20   Union of Concerned Scientists, "Restoring Scientific Integrity in Policymaking" (http://www.ucsusa.org/scientific_integrity/interference/scientists-signon-statement.html).

21   This former employee's written statement, dated October 1, 2007, is contained in "NIST Whistleblower" (http://georgewashington.blogspot.com/2007/10/former-nist-employee-blows-whistle.html). The perversion of NIST, this individual said, began in the mid-1990s but has "only grown stronger to the present." Although this former employee wanted to remain anonymous to prevent possible retaliation, the

authenticity of the self-representation has been confirmed by physicist Steven Jones (email from Jones, 3 December 2007).

22   See Dr. Crockett Grabbe and Lenny Charles, "Science in the Bush: When Politics Displaces Physics," Information Clearing House, September 8, 2007 (http://www.informationclearinghouse.info/article18344.htm).

23   Johnson's statement is at Patriots Question 9/11 (http://patriotsquestion911.com/engineers.html#Djohnson).

24   NIST, *Final Report on the Collapse of the World Trade Center Towers*, September 2005: 146.

25   NIST, "Answers to Frequently Asked Questions," 30 August 2006, Question 2.

26   NIST NCSTAR 1, *Final Report on the Collapse of the World Trade Center Towers*, 146.

27   Jim Hoffman, "A Reply to the National Institute for Standards and Technology's *Answers to Frequently Asked Questions*" (http://911research.wtc7.net/reviews/nist/WTC_FAQ_reply.html).

28   William Rice's statement is quoted at Patriots Question 9/11 (http://patriotsquestion911.com/engineers.html#Rice).

29   "World Trade Physics: Why Constant Acceleration Disproves Progressive Collapse," Architects and Engineers for 9/11 Truth, 2016.

30   Graeme MacQueen and Tony Szamboti, "The Missing Jolt: A Simple Refutation of the NIST-Bazant Collapse Hypothesis," *Journal of 9/11 Studies*, January 2009.

31   Gordon Ross, "Momentum Transfer Analysis of the Collapse of the Upper Storeys of WTC 1," *Journal of 9/11 Studies*, Vol. 1: June 2006: 32-39, at 37.

32   Don Paul and Jim Hoffman, *Waking Up from Our Nightmare: The 9/11/01 Crimes in New York City* (Irresistible/Revolutionary, 2004), 34.

33   Steven Jones, "Why Indeed Did the WTC Buildings Completely Collapse?" *Journal of 9/11 Studies*, Vol. 3 (September 2006), 1-47, at 28.

34   Quoted in Liz Else, "Baltimore Blasters" *New Scientist*, 24 July 2004.

35   NIST, "Answers to Frequently Asked Questions," 30 August 2006, Question 2.

36   Richard Gage, Steven Jones, et al., "Request for Correction Submitted to NIST," *Journal of 9/11 Studies*, Vol. 12: June 2007.

37   The statement by Deets is at Architects and Engineers for 9/11 Truth (http://www.ae911truth.org/profile.php?uid=998819).

38   For a video, see either "911 Eyewitness: Huge Steel Sections Ejected More than 600 Feet" or "9/11 Mysteries: Demolition."

39 NIST, *Final Report on the Collapse of the World Trade Center Towers*, brief version, September 2005: xxxvi.

40 NIST, *Final Report on the Collapse of the World Trade Center Towers*, long version, Vol. 1 (September 2005), 125.

41 NIST, *Final Report on the Collapse of the World Trade Center Towers*, September 2005: 16.

42 Ibid., 183, 184.

43 "[T]he presence of gravity does not affect the horizontal motion of the projectile. The force of gravity acts downward and is unable to alter the horizontal motion. There must be a horizontal force to cause a horizontal acceleration" ("Characteristics of a Projectile's Trajectory," The Physics Classroom).

44 Eric Lipton and Andrew C. Revkin, "The Firefighters: With Water and Sweat, Fighting the Most Stubborn Fire," *New York Times*, 19 November 2001; Jonathan Beard, "Ground Zero's Fires Still Burning," *New Scientist*, 3 December 2001.

45 Trudy Walsh, "Handheld APP Eased Recovery Tasks," Government Computer News, 21/27a: 11 September 2002.

46 Niels H. Harrit, Jeffrey Farrer, Steven E. Jones et al., "Active Thermitic Material Observed in Dust from the 9/11 World Trade Center Catastrophe," *Open Chemical Physics Journal*, 2 (2009), 7-31.

47 Kevin R. Ryan, James R. Gourley, and Steven E. Jones, "Environmental Anomalies at the World Trade Center: Evidence for Energetic Materials," *The Environmentalist*, 29 (2009), 56-63, at 58, 56.

48 Ibid.

49 Ibid.

50 "The Ultimate Con." Although Thompson began the report by saying "at 10:30," she was off by several minutes, because the North Tower collapsed at 10:28.

51 Ibid.

52 "Special Report: Terrorism in the US," *Guardian*, 12 September 2001.

53 Geraldine Baum and Maggie Farley, "Terrorists Attack New York, Pentagon," *Los Angeles Times*, 12 September 2001.

54 "The Ultimate Con."

55 *The 9/11 Commission Report*, 306.

56 NIST, *Final Report on the Collapse of the World Trade Center Towers*, September 2005, "Abstract."

57 NIST, *Final Report*, brief version, xxxviii: 146, 176.

58 "9/11: Truth, Lies and Conspiracy: Interview: Lee Hamilton," CBC News, 21 August 2006.

59   Graeme MacQueen, "118 Witnesses: The Firefighters' Testimony to Explosions in the Twin Towers," *Journal of 9/11 Studies*, Vol. 2/August 2006: 49-123. (The Fire Department of New York [FDNY] includes emergency medical workers as well as firefighters.) MacQueen has also published a later report, which deals with 156 eyewitness and also responds to the major objections to his conclusions: "Eyewitness Evidence of Explosions in the Twin Towers," in James Gourley, ed., *The 9/11 Toronto Report* (CreateSpace, 2012), 173-96.

60   9/11 Oral Histories, *New York Times* (http://graphics8.nytimes.com/packages/html/nyregion/20050812_WTC_GRAPHIC/met_WTC_histories_full_01.html), Oral History: Firefighter Richard Banaciski, 3.

61   Oral History: Chief Frank Cruthers, 4.

62   Oral History: Firefighter Kenneth Rogers, 3-4.

63   Although Tardio's testimony was not included in the FDNY oral histories that are provided at the NYT website, he was quoted in Dennis Smith, *Report from Ground Zero: The Story of the Rescue Efforts at the World Trade Center* (Penguin, 2002), 18.

64   Oral History: Captain Karin Deshore, 15-16.

65   Steven Jones, Robert Korol, Anthony Szamboti, and Ted Walter, "15 Years Later: On the Physics of High-rise Building Collapses," *Europhysics News*, July-August 2016: 22-26, at 26.

66   Peter Michael Ketcham, Letter to the Editor, *Europhysics News*, November 2016.

Chapter 13: The Miraculous Destruction of WTC 7

1   "9/11: Truth, Lies and Conspiracy: Interview: Lee Hamilton," CBC News, 21 August 2006.

2   James Glanz, "Engineers Suspect Diesel Fuel in Collapse of 7 World Trade Center," *New York Times*, 29 November 2001.

3   See FEMA, *World Trade Center Building Performance Study*, Ch. 5, Sect. 6.2, "Probable Collapse Sequence."

4   "WTC 7 Collapse," NIST, 5 April 2005: 6.

5   *The 9/11 Commission Report: Final Report of the National Commission on Terrorist Attacks Upon the United States* (W. W. Norton, 2004); David Dunbar and Brad Reagan, eds., *Debunking 9/11 Myths: Why Conspiracy Theories Can't Stand Up to the Facts* (Hearst Books, 2006).

6   Dunbar and Reagan, eds., *Debunking 9/11 Myths*, 53, 56.

7   Ibid., 53-54, 29. (For a critique of the book by *Popular Mechanics* [which was written by a new team, which had replaced the previous staff just before the work for this book began], see David Ray Griffin, *Debunking*

9/11 Debunking: An Answer to Popular Mechanics and Other Defenders of the Official Conspiracy Theory, Ch. 4.[Olive Branch, 2007]).

8   Matthew Rothschild, "Enough of the 9/11 Conspiracy Theories, Already," *The Progressive*, 18 September 2006.

9   *Final Report on the Collapse of World Trade Center Building 7* (brief version), National Institute of Standards and Technology, NIST NCSTAR 1A, November 2008: xxxvi.

10   Ibid., xxxvii.

11   "NIST WTC 7 Investigation Finds Building Fires Caused Collapse," NIST, 21 August 2008.

12   J. Gordon Routley, Charles Jennings, and Mark Chubb, "High-Rise Office Building Fire, One Meridian Plaza, Philadelphia, Pennsylvania," FEMA (Federal Emergency Management Agency), 1991; "Fire Practically Destroys Venezuela's Tallest Building," Venezuela News, Views, and Analysis, 18 October 2004.

13   Shyam Sunder, "Opening Statement," NIST Press Briefing, 21 August 2008; *Structural Fire Response and Probable Collapse Sequence of World Trade Center Building 7* (Final Report on WTC 7, long version), NIST NCSTAR 1-9: 244-45. For discussion, see David Ray Griffin, *The Mysterious Collapse of World Trade Center 7: Why the Final Official Report about 9/11 Is Unscientific and False* (Northampton: Olive Branch [Interlink Books], 2009), 170-77.

14   See "WTC7 Demolition on 9/11—Video Compilation," YouTube (http://www.youtube.com/watch?v=DlTBMcxx-78). For video and analysis, see "WTC7: This Is an Orange," YouTube, and David Chandler, "WTC7: NIST Finally Admits Freefall (Part III)," at 2:25-4:00.

15   See Frank Legge, "9/11: Acceleration Study Proves Explosive Demolition," *Journal of 9/11 Studies*, Vol. 5, November 2006.

16   "The Myth of Implosion" (http://www.implosionworld.com/dyk2.html).

17   Liz Else, "Baltimore Blasters," *New Scientist*, 24 July 2004: 48.

18   *Structural Fire Response and Probable Collapse Sequence of World Trade Center Building 7* (Final Report on WTC 7, long version), NIST NCSTAR 1-9, Draft for Public Comment, Vol. 2, August 2008: 596.

19   "WTC 7 Technical Briefing," NIST, 26 August 2008. Although NIST originally had a video and a transcript of this briefing at its website, it eventually removed both of them. However, Nate Flach has made the video available at Vimeo (http://vimeo.com/11941571), and the transcript, under the title "NIST Technical Briefing on Its Final Draft Report on WTC 7 for Public Comment," is available at David Chandler's website: http://911speakout.org/wp-content/uploads/NIST_Tech_Briefing_Transcript.pdf

20   "[WTC 7] fell because thermal expansion," said NIST, "caused a fire-induced progressive collapse"; Shyam Sunder, "Opening Statement," NIST Press Briefing, 21 August 2008. NIST defined "a progressive collapse" as "the spread of local damage, from an initiating event, from element to element, eventually resulting in the collapse of an entire structure" (NIST NCSTAR 1A: xxxvi).

21   Ibid.

22   David Chandler, "WTC7 in Freefall—No Longer Controversial," 4 September 2008, at 2:45.

23   NIST NCSTAR 1-9, Vol. 2: 607.

24   Chandler, "WTC7 in Freefall—No Longer Controversial," at 3:27.

25   Chandler, "WTC7: NIST Finally Admits Freefall (Part III)," 2 January 2009, at 1:19.

26   "Questions and Answers about the NIST WTC 7 Investigation," NIST, 21 August 2008, updated 21 April 2009. Whereas the original version of this document denied free fall, the updated version affirms it. Although both versions have been removed from NIST's website, Jim Hoffman's website has both the 2008 version (http://911research.wtc7.net/mirrors/nist/wtc_qa_082108.html) and the 2009 version (http://911research.wtc7.net/mirrors/nist/wtc_qa_042109.html).

27   Chandler, "WTC 7: NIST Finally Admits Freefall (Part III)," at 2:20, 3:15.

28   NIST NCSTAR 1-9, Draft for Public Comment, Vol. 2: 595-96, 596, 610.

29   RJ Lee Group, "WTC Dust Signature," Expert Report, May 2004: 11.

30   RJ Lee Group, "WTC Dust Signature Study: Composition and Morphology," December 2003: 24.

31   Ibid., 17.

32   WebElements: The Periodic Table on the Web: Iron.

33   *Final Report on the Collapse of the World Trade Center Towers*, NIST, September 2005 (http://wtc.nist.gov/NCSTAR1/PDF/NCSTAR%201.pdf), 88.

34   Heather A. Lowers and Gregory P. Meeker, US Geological Survey, US Department of the Interior, "Particle Atlas of World Trade Center Dust," 2005.

35   Steven E. Jones et al., "Extremely High Temperatures during the World Trade Center Destruction," *Journal of 9/11 Studies*, January 2008: 4.

36   Jonathan Barnett, Ronald R. Biederman, and Richard D. Sisson, Jr., "An Initial Microstructural Analysis of A36 Steel from WTC Building 7," *JOM* 53/12 (2001), 18.

37   Jonathan Barnett, Ronald R. Biederman, and R. D. Sisson, Jr., "Limited Metallurgical Examination," Appendix C of *World Trade Center Building Performance Study*, FEMA, 2002.

38   James Glanz and Eric Lipton, "A Search for Clues in Towers' Collapse," *New York Times*, 2 February 2002.

39   Joan Killough-Miller, "The 'Deep Mystery' of Melted Steel," *WPI Transformations*, Spring 2002.

40   James Glanz, "Engineers Suspect Diesel Fuel in Collapse of 7 World Trade Center," *New York Times*, 29 November 2001. I have here quoted Glanz's paraphrase of Barnett's statement.

41   See Kenneth Change, "Scarred Steel Holds Clues, and Remedies," *New York Times*, 2 October 2001.

42   WebElements: The Periodic Table on the Web: Iron (http://www. webelements.com/iron/physics.html).

43   "Questions and Answers about the NIST WTC 7 Investigation," 21 August 2008. This statement was repeated in a version of this document that was updated 21 April 2009 (http://911research.wtc7.net/mirrors/nist/wtc_qa_042109.html). Thanks are due to Jim Hoffman for preserving these documents at his website, after NIST had removed them from its own.

44   NCSTAR 1-3: xxxvii.

45   NCSTAR 1-3: 114.

46   NCSTAR 1-3: 115.

47   NCSTAR 1-3B: iii.

48   NCSTAR 1-3D: 273.

49   See NIST NCSTAR 1-3C, *Damage and Failure Modes of Structural Steel Components*, September 2005, in which the authors, Stephen W. Banovic and Timothy Foecke, referred to "the analysis of the steel from WTC 7 (Sample #1 from Appendix C, BPAT/FEMA study) where corrosion phases and morphologies were able to determine a possible temperature region" (233).

50   *The Conspiracy Files: 9/11—The Third Tower*, BBC, 6 July 2008; the statement by Barnett is at 48:00. (I am indebted to Chris Sarns for this discovery.)

51   "NIST WTC 7 Investigation Finds Building Fires Caused Collapse," NIST, 21 August 2008.

52   Glanz and Lipton, "A Search for Clues in Towers' Collapse."

53   Joan Killough-Miller, "The 'Deep Mystery' of Melted Steel," *WPI Transformations*, Spring 2002.

54   Barnett, Biederman, and Sisson, Jr., "Limited Metallurgical Examination," Appendix C.

55   Ibid., C-13.

56   Dr. Arden L. Bement, Jr., Testimony before the House Science Committee Hearing on "The Investigation of the World Trade Center Collapse," 1 May 2002. In the quoted statement, the name "FEMA" replaces "BPAT," which is the abbreviation for "Building Performance Assessment Team," the name of the ASCE team that prepared this report for FEMA.

57   "Answers to Frequently Asked Questions," NIST, Question 12.

58   Jones et al., "Extremely High Temperatures during the World Trade Center Destruction," 3.

59   Email letter from Kevin Ryan, 16 October 2008.

60   Email letter from Steven Jones, 17 October 2008.

61   Personal communication, 8 May 2009.

62   Steven E. Jones, "Revisiting 9/11/2001: Applying the Scientific Method," *Journal of 9/11 Studies*, Vol. 11: May 2007, 81.

63   Ibid., 75.

64   Peter Michael Ketcham, "Thoughts from a Former NIST Employee," letter to *Europhysics News*, November 2016.

Chapter 14: The Miraculous Attack on the Pentagon

1   Tim O'Brien, "Wife of Solicitor General Alerted Him of Hijacking from Plane," CNN, 11 September 2001.

2   Email to Elizabeth Woodworth, 6 April 2011.

3   See Chapter 8, "Did Ted Olson Receive Phone Calls from His Wife?" in David Ray Griffin, *9/11 Contradictions: An Open Letter to Congress and the Press* (Olive Branch Press, 2008).

4   Ibid.

5   Ibid.

6   See Ibid. and "Detailed Account of Phone Calls From September 11th Flights" (http://911research.wtc7.net/planes/evidence/calldetail.html#ref1).

7   See David Ray Griffin, "A Consensus Approach to the Pentagon," Chapter 7 of 9/11 *Ten Years Later: When State Crimes Against Democracy Succeed* (Olive Branch, 2011).

8   *The 9/11 Commission Report*, 9, 239.

9   "List of Names of 18 Suspected Hijackers," CNN, 14 September 2001; "FBI List of Individuals Identified As Suspected Hijackers," CNN, 14 September 2001, 2:00 PM.

10   Marc Fisher and Don Phillips, "On Flight 77: 'Our Plane Is Being Hijacked,'" *Washington Post*, 12 September 2001.

11   John Hanchette, "Clues to Attackers Lie in Wreckage, Computer Systems," *Detroit News*, 13 September 2001.

12   "'Get These Planes on the Ground': Air Traffic Controllers Recall Sept. 11," *20/20*, ABC News, 24 October 2001.

13   *The 9/11 Commission Report*, 334.

14   Thomas Frank, "America's Ordeal: Tracing Trail Of Hijackers," *Newsday*, 23 September 2001.

15   Amy Goldstein, Lena H. Sun, and George Lardner Jr., "Hanjour: A Study in Paradox," *Washington Post*, 15 October 2001.

16   Jim Yardley, "A Trainee Noted for Incompetence," *New York Times*, 4 May 2002.

17   Ibid.

18   "FAA Was Alerted To Sept. 11 Hijacker," CBS News, 10 May 2002.

19   Steve Fainaru and Alia Ibrahim, "Mysterious Trip to Flight 77 Cockpit: Suicide Pilot's Conversion to Radical Islam Remains Obscure," *Washington Post*, 10 September 2002.

20   *The 9/11 Commission Report*, 242.

21   Ibid., 520 n. 56.

22   Ibid., 530 n. 147.

23   Ibid., 531 n. 170.

24   David Dunbar and Brad Reagan, eds., *Debunking 9/11 Myths: Why Conspiracy Theories Can't Stand Up to the Facts* (Hearst Books, 2006), 5, 7.

25   Ibid., 6.

26   Ibid., 6.

27   Ibid., 7, 6.

28   "Pilots and Aviation Professionals Question the 9/11 Commission Report."

29   Alan Miller, "US Navy 'Top Gun' Pilot Questions 911 Pentagon Story," OpEdNews.com, 6 September 2007.

30   Frank Legge, "What Hit the Pentagon? Misinformation and its Effect on the Credibility of 9/11 Truth," *Journal of 9/11 Studies*, 15 February 2010.

31   "Joint Statement on the Pentagon: David Chandler and Jon Cole," 911Blogger, 7 January 2011.

32   Griffin, "A Consensus Approach to the Pentagon."

33   Aidan Monaghan, "Plausibility Of 9/11 Aircraft Attacks Generated By GPS-Guided Aircraft Autopilot Systems," *Journal of 9/11 Studies*, 3 October 2008.

Chapter 15: The Miraculous Transformation of Mohamed Atta

1   *The 9/11 Commission Report: Final Report of the National Commission on Terrorist Attacks upon the United States,* authorized edition (W. W. Norton, 2004), 160.

2   Ibid., 154.

3   David Wedge, "Terrorists Partied with Hooker at Hub-Area Hotel," *Boston Herald,* 10 October, 2001.

4   Jody A. Benjamin, "Suspects' Actions Don't Add Up," *South Florida Sun-Sentinel,* 16 September 2001.

5   Evan Thomas and Mark Hosenball, "Bush: 'We're at War,'" *Newsweek,* 24 September 2001.

6   Johanna McGeary and David Van Biema, "The New Breed of Terrorist," *Time,* 24 September 2001.

7   Kevin Fagan, "Agents of Terror Leave Their Mark on Sin City," *San Francisco Chronicle,* 4 October 2001.

8   "Terrorist Stag Parties," *Wall Street Journal,* 10 October 2001.

9   *The 9/11 Commission Report,* 248.

10 Daniel Hopsicker, *Welcome to Terrorland: Mohamed Atta and the 9-11 Cover-Up in Florida* (MadCow Press, 2004).

11 Daniel Hopsicker, "The Secret World of Mohamed Atta: An Interview With Atta's American Girlfriend," *InformationLiberation,* 20 August 2006.

12 Sander Hicks, "No Easy Answer: Heroin, Al Qaeda and the Florida Flight School," *Long Island Press,* 26 February 2004.

13 *The 9/11 Commission Report,* 160.

14 The remainder of this chapter is dependent on Elias Davidsson, "The Atta Mystery: Double Agent or Multiple Attas?" Aldeilis.net, 5 October 2011.

15 "Professor Dittmar Machule," Interviewed by Liz Jackson, A Mission to Die For, Four Corners, 18 October 2001.

16 Davidsson, "The Atta Mystery."

17 Terry McDermott, "A Perfect Soldier," *Los Angeles Times,* 27 January 2002; Donna Britt, "Terrorists' Faces Are All Over the Lot," *Washington Post,* 17 October 2001; John Hooper, "The Shy, Caring, Deadly Fanatic: Double Life of Suicide Pilot," *Observer,* 23 September 2001.

18 "Photographs Taken of Mohamed Atta during His University Years" (http://www.abc.net.au/4corners/atta/resources/photos/university.htm).

19 "Kate Connolly, "Father Insists Alleged Leader Is Still Alive," *Guardian,* 2 September 2002.

20   Elaine Allen-Emrich and Jann Baty, "Hunt for Terrorists Reaches North Port, *Charlotte Sun*, 14 September 2001.

21   "Professor Dittmar Machule."

Conclusion

1   David Ray Griffin, *The New Pearl Harbor Revisited: 9/11, the Cover-Up, and the Exposé* (Northampton: Olive Branch, 2008), 171.

2   Ibid., 170-71.

3   *Incontrovertible*, Killing Auntie Films (www.incontrovertible911evidence.co.uk/); James McDowell, "A Review of Incontrovertible, the New Documentary by Tony Rooke."

4   John B. Cobb, Jr., "Truth, 'Faith,' and 9/11," in Matthew Morgan, ed., *The Impact of 9/11 on Religion and Philosophy: The Day that Changed Everything?* (Palgrave Macmillan, September, 2009).

5   David Ray Griffin, *The 9/11 Commission Report: Omissions and Distortions* (Interlink Books, 2005); Griffin, *Debunking 9/11 Debunking: An Answer to Popular Mechanics and Other Defenders of the Official Conspiracy Theory* (Interlink Books), 2007).

6   Ron Unz, "How the CIA Invented 'Conspiracy Theories,'" American Pravda, 5 September, 2016.

7   Lance deHaven Smith, *Conspiracy Theory in America* (University of Texas Press, 2013), 25. The book contains the secret memo to which Unz referred, CIA Dispatch #1035-960, obtained recently through an FOIA request.

8   Paul Craig Roberts "Are You a Mind-Controlled CIA Stooge?" Paul Craig Roberts website, 31 August 2016.

9   Paul Craig Roberts, "9/11 After Thirteen Years: Continuous Warfare, Police State, Endless Falsehoods," Paul Craig Roberts website, 11 September 2014. (Roberts' article, written in paragraphs, was here converted, for the sake of clarity, into a series of points.)

10   David Corn, "When 9/11 Conspiracy Theories Go Bad," AlterNet, 28 February 2002.

11   Dave Gilson, "Are Any 9/11 Conspiracy Films Plausible?" *Mother Jones*, September/October 2008.

12   "Mukden Incident," *Wikipedia*; Walter LaFeber, *The Clash: US-Japanese Relations throughout History* (New York: Norton, 1997), 164-66.

13   William Shircr, *The Rise and Fall of the Third Reich* (New York: Simon and Schuster, 1990), 191–93; Alexander Bahar and Wilfried Kugel, *Der Reichstagbrand: Wie Geschichte Gemacht Wird* (Berlin, Edition Q, 2001), summarized in Wilhelm Klein, "The Reichstag Fire, 68 Years On," World Socialist Website, 5 July 2001.

14   Daniele Ganser, *NATO's Secret Armies: Operation Gladio and Terrorism in Western Europe* (Routledge, 2004).

15   "A Program of Covert Operations Against the Castro Regime," April 16, 1961 (declassified CIA document).

16   Ibid.

17   Robert Parry, "A Media Unmoored from Facts," *Consortium News*, 7 April 2016; Parry, "Are Neocons an Existential Threat?" *Consortium News*, 15 September 2015.

18   Jeffrey Goldberg, "The Real Meaning of 9/11," *The Atlantic*, 29 August 2011.

19   *Rebuilding America's Defenses: Strategy, Forces and Resources for a New Century*, Project for the New American Century (September 2000), 51.

20   John Pilger, "Bush Terror Elite Wanted 9/11 to Happen," *New Statesman*, 12 December 2001.

21   Stephen J. Sniegoski, "Neoconservatives, Israel, and 9/11: The Origins of the US War on Iraq," in ibid., 81-109, at 81-82; Stefan Halper and Jonathan Clarke, *America Alone: The Neo-Conservatives and the Global Order* (Cambridge University Press, 2004), 230.

22   Bacevich, *The New American Militarism*, 91.

23   Jean-Charles Brisard and Guillaume Dasquié, *Forbidden Truth: US-Taliban Secret Oil Diplomacy and the Failed Hunt for Bin Laden* (Thunder's Mouth Press/Nation Books, 2002); George Arney, "US 'Planned Attack on Taleban,'" BBC News, 18 September 2001.

24   For these statements, see "Day One Transcript: 9/11 Commission Hearing," *Washington Post*, 23 March 2004.

25   Ron Susskind, *The Price of Loyalty: George W. Bush, the White House, and the Education of Paul O'Neill* (Simon & Schuster, 2004); Elizabeth Drew, "The Neocons in Power," *New York Review of Books*, 50/10 (12 June 2003).

26   Department of Defense News Briefing on Pentagon Attack, 11 September 2001.

27   Deepa Kumar, *Islamophobia and the Politics of Empire* (Haymaker Books, 2012), 177.

28   Goldberg, "The Real Meaning of 9/11."

29   Cass R. Sunstein and Adrian Vermeule, "Conspiracy Theories: Causes and Cures," *Journal of Political Philosophy*, June 2009: 202-27, at 210.

30   In 2006, Christison published an essay entitled "Stop Belittling the Theories About September 11," www.dissidentvoice.org, August 14, 2006. In a letter to friends explaining why he wrote it, he said: "I spent the first four and a half years since September 11 utterly unwilling to consider seriously the conspiracy theories surrounding the attacks of

that day. . . . [I]n the last half year and after considerable agony, I've changed my mind" ("Letter from Bill Christison to Friends," e-mail letter sent August 14, 2006).

31   Annie Machon, *Spies, Lies and Whistleblowers: MI5, MI6, and the Shayler Affair* (London: Book Guild Publishing, 2005).

32   Intelligence Officers for 9/11 Truth (http://IO911Truth.org).

33   Scientists for 9/11 Truth (http://sci911truth.org).

34   For still more "for 9/11 truth" organizations, see my *Cognitive Infiltration: An Obama Appointee's Plan to Undermine the 9/11 Conspiracy Theory* (Interlink Books, 2010), Chap. 4.

35   Steven Jones, Robert Korol, Anthony Szamboti, and Ted Walter, "15 Years Later: On the Physics of High-Rise Building Collapses," *Europhysics News*, July-August 2016: 21-26. For an excellent commentary on this paper, see Darius Shahtahmasebi, "Physicists Say Twin Towers Destroyed by Controlled Demolition on 9/11," AntiMedia, 11 September 2016.

36   The panel uses a "best evidence" Delphi Method to evaluate proposed Points. Remaining blind to each other, the panelists add a proposed Point to the consensus only if it, after three rounds, receives a positive vote of at least 85%. See the section on "Methodology" on the Consensus 9/11 website (www.consensus911.org).

37   William Rivers Pitt, "9/11 at 15: The Falling Dominoes of September," Truthout, 11 September 2016.

Epilogue

1   Stephen Walt, "Barack Obama Was a Foreign-Policy Failure," *Foreign Policy,* 19 January 2017.

2   Robert Parry, "Obama Bequeaths a More Dangerous World," *Consortium News,* 24 January 2017.

3   Finian Cunningham, "Obama's 'Farewell To Arms' As War Presidency Ends," Strategic Culture, 12 January 2017.

4   "Tomgram: Pratap Chatterjee, Obama's Last Chance," TomDispatch, 4 December 2016.

INDEX

ACKNOWLEDGMENTS

For putting this book out, I am once again grateful to Michel Moushabeck and his team at Interlink Books.

In writing this book, I received much valuable help from Daniel Athearn, Timothy Eastman, Graeme MacQueen, John Whitbeck, and Elizabeth Woodworth.

I am also grateful to all of the very busy people who took time to write blurbs for this book.

Most of all, I am grateful to my wife, Ann Jaqua, who has done so many things, such as keeping me alive.